Putting Children First

Putting Children First

Visions for a Brighter Future
for Young Children and Their Families

edited by

Elizabeth J. Erwin, Ed.D.

Queens College of the City University of New York

·P A U L·H·
BROOKES
PUBLISHING CO.

Baltimore • London • Toronto • Sydney

Paul H. Brookes Publishing Co.
Post Office Box 10624
Baltimore, Maryland 21285-0624

Typeset by Signature Typesetting & Design, Baltimore, Maryland.
Manufactured in the United States of America by
Vail-Ballou Press, Binghamton, New York.

Library of Congress Cataloging-in-Publication Data

Putting children first : visions for a brighter future for young children and their families /
    edited by Elizabeth J. Erwin.
       p. cm.
    Includes bibliographical references and index.
    ISBN 1-55766-244-4
    1. Child welfare—United States.   2. Children—United States—Social conditions.
3. Children—Services for—United States.   4. Family policy—United States.
I. Erwin, Elizabeth J.
HV741.P87   1996
362.7—dc20

                                         96-11846
                                             CIP

British Library Cataloguing-in-Publication data are available from the British Library.

Contents

About the Editor

Elizabeth J. Erwin, Ed.D., Assistant Professor, School of Education, Department of Educational and Community Programs, Queens College of the City University of New York, Flushing, New York 11367

Elizabeth J. Erwin prepares graduate students to work in various early childhood settings. Since 1980, she has been a teacher and an advocate for young children with disabilities and their families. She has received funding for and consulted on several research and technical assistance grants that promote the inclusion of all children in community-based environments. She has published several articles on topics such as families, natural environments and supports, and social participation. She is Chair of the Early Childhood Committee for The Association for Persons with Severe Handicaps.

About the Contributors

Nancy Balaban, Ed.D., Director, Infant and Parent Development Program, Bank Street Graduate School of Education, 610 West 112 Street, New York, New York 10025

Nancy Balaban directs the Infant and Parent Development Program at Bank Street, teaches courses, and supervises graduate students in field work. She is the author of *Starting School: From Separation to Independence* and numerous articles. Each summer, she co-directs the Bank Street Infancy Institute.

Ralph Beach, Teacher, Family Development Center, South Block Mezzanine, Boston City Hospital, 818 Harrison Avenue, Boston, Massachusetts 02118

Ralph Beach has been an early childhood teacher since 1985. Since 1992, he has worked at the Family Development Center at Boston City Hospital with children whose lives have been affected by violence. In addition to being a teacher, he is the father of two children and is a professional artist. He serves as Vice President of the Boston Afro-American Artist Association.

Julie Blackman, Ph.D., 49th Floor, 1251 Avenue of the Americas, New York, New York 10020

Julie Blackman, forensic social psychologist, expert witness on family violence, and trial strategy consultant, is self-employed and is affiliated with the intellectual property law firm Fish & Neave. She has studied the results of severe family violence for more than 15 years. She is the author of *Intimate Violence: A Study of Injustices,* and she contributed a chapter, "At the Frontier: In Pursuit of Justice for Women," to *Psychology in Litigation and Legislation.*

Ann Collins, M.P.A., Senior Program Associate, National Center for Children in Poverty, School of Public Health, Columbia University, 154 Haven Avenue, New York, New York 10032

Ann Collins is responsible for the National Center for Children in Poverty's work related to early childhood care and education. Previously, she was the program coordinator of the Child Care Action Campaign, where she managed a research and advocacy project on the implementation of child care subsidy programs.

Jerlean Daniel, Ph.D., Assistant Professor, Program in Child Development and Child Care, School of Social Work, University of Pittsburgh, 1717 Cathedral of Learning, Pittsburgh, Pennsylvania 15260

Jerlean Daniel is President of the National Association for the Education of Young Children. She was a child care center administrator for 18 years. Her research interests include infant and toddler child care, financing of child care, and the developmental basis for high-quality early childhood environments. She serves on numerous community and professional boards, including the Board of Directors of Beginning with Books and the Advisory Board of Wheelock College Center for Career Development in Early Care and Education. She is Chair of the Allegheny County Policy Council for Youth and Workforce Development Early Childhood Task Force and Co-Chair of the United Way of Allegheny County Early Childhood Initiative Coordinating Committee.

Dana Friedman, Ed.D., Co-Founder and Co-President, Families and Work Institute, 330 Seventh Avenue, 14th Floor, New York, New York 10001

Dana Friedman designs national research studies, employee needs assessments, human resources strategic plans, and management training programs at the Families and Work Institute. Previously, she worked at the Carnegie Corporation of New York and spent 6 years in Washington, D.C., as a lobbyist for the Day Care Council of America and the Coalition for Children and Youth. She is the author of several publications, including *Child Care and Employees' Kids, Liberty, Equality, Maternity!* and *The Productivity Effects of Family Problems and Programs.* She has served as a consultant to the U.S. Department of Labor, the National Governors' Association, and President Reagan's Task Force on Private Sector Initiatives. She is a member of the boards of the Child Care Action Campaign and Women on the Job.

Ellen Galinsky, M.S., Co-Founder and Co-President, Families and Work Institute, 330 Seventh Avenue, 14th Floor, New York, New York 10001

Ellen Galinsky directs a nationally representative longitudinal study of the U.S. workforce, EQUIP (the Early Education Quality Improvement Project), as well as studies of family leave, child care and education, and family involvement in children's education. She was on the faculty of Bank Street College of Education and is a past president of the National Association for the Education of Young Children. She served in various capacities on numerous committees, including the Board of the Child Care Action Campaign, and served as Chair of New York State's Task Force on Early Childhood Services. She has published more than 75 articles in academic journals and magazines and authored 18 books and reports, including *The New Extended Family: Day Care that Works, The Six Stages of Parenthood,* and *The Preschool Years.* She has appeared extensively on television programs, including *Today* and *The MacNeil/Lehrer News Hour.*

James J. Gallagher, Ph.D., Kenan Professor of Education, Senior Investigator, Frank Porter Graham Child Development Center, University of North Carolina at Chapel Hill, 137 East Franklin Street, Chapel Hill, North Carolina 27514

James J. Gallagher has been involved since 1980 in studies of public policy, including the implementation of the Infant and Toddler Component of the Individuals with

Disabilities Education Act. He is a past director of the Bureau of Education for the Handicapped in the U.S. Office of Education and a past president of the Council for Exceptional Children. He is the coauthor of the seventh edition of *Educating Exceptional Children* and has authored or edited several books and numerous articles relevant to early childhood.

Betsy McAlister Groves, M.S.W., Director, Child Witness to Violence Project, Maternity 5, Boston City Hospital, 818 Harrison Avenue, Boston, Massachusetts 02118

Betsy McAlister Groves directs a counseling program for young children and families who witness violence, a project that also provides training and consultation to professionals working with children. Her experience includes working with young children and families in mental health settings and directing an adolescent parenting project in Boston. She is Assistant Clinical Professor of Pediatrics at Boston University School of Medicine and has served on the faculties of Wheelock College and Suffolk University. She serves on advisory boards for the Massachusetts Department of Social Services, Department of Public Health, Trial Court Administration, and Attorney General's Office to assist in establishing policies and protocols that better detect and serve children who witness violence. She has published articles in medical and educational journals and has lectured extensively on the topic of children and violence.

Tracy Hardy is a home child care provider. She has five children: Jeremy, age 16; Adam, age 11; Wesley, age 5; Michelle, age 4; and Michael, age 12, who is a foster child.

Beverly Roberson Jackson, Ed.D., Director of Public Policy and Public Education, ZERO TO THREE/National Center for Clinical Infant Programs, 734 Fifteen Street, NW, Suite 1000, Washington, D.C. 20005

Beverly Roberson Jackson is the author of *Coping with Family Crises, Shaping Public Policy for Children and Families,* and *If They Need Special Care.* She has served as a consultant for the National Cancer Institute, the National Institute for Drug Abuse, the Office of Substance Abuse Programs, the U.S. Department of Education, and the U.S. Department of Agriculture.

Susan Janko, Ph.D., Assistant Professor, College of Education, University of Washington, Miller Hall, Box 353600, Seattle, Washington 98195

Susan Janko, a past associate director of the University of Washington UAP, has worked with infants and young children with disabilities and their families for more than 20 years. She conducts ethnographic and policy research on the inclusion of children who are at risk for developing or who have disabilities and their families in school and community settings. She has an ongoing interest in education and social policies related to children and families experiencing difficult life circumstances.

Margot Kaplan-Sanoff, Ed.D., Associate Clinical Professor of Pediatrics, Boston University School of Medicine, Maternity 5, Boston City Hospital, 818 Harrison Avenue, Boston, Massachusetts 02118

Margot Kaplan-Sanoff is Clinical Director of Pediatric Pathways to Success, an expanded two-generational model of pediatric care at Boston City Hospital. She also is Co-Director of the Healthy Steps Initiative at Boston University School of Medicine, an ambitious project to provide child development and family support services within the context of pediatric well-child care at 15 sites throughout the United States. She was Co-Director of Women and Infants Clinic, a model of one-stop shopping for mothers in recovery from cocaine addiction and for their infants.

Karen Kochanski, PA-C, Physician Assistant, Post Office Box 60, Buffalo, New York 14223

Karen Kochanski, a physician assistant, has worked with Doris J. Rapp, M.D., in private practice specializing in environmental medicine. She has worked in pediatrics for 10 years and is an adjunct faculty member in the Physician Assistant Program at D'Youville College in Buffalo.

Janet M. Krumm, *The New Hampshire Challenge,* Post Office Box 579, Dover, New Hampshire 03821

Janet M. Krumm founded and is Editor of *The New Hampshire Challenge,* a statewide newspaper for families who have members with disabilities. She is married and is the mother of three children, the youngest of whom has a disability. Her advocacy for her son has led to her involvement with various advisory groups, boards of directors, and parent support efforts, including the Special Education Advisory Subcommittee of the Dover School District; Family Support Group for Community Developmental Services Agency, Inc.; Board of Directors of Special Families United; and Editorial Board of the National Association for People with Mental Retardation (NAPMR) quarterly journal, as well as her participation in Leadership New Hampshire. She also is a graduate of the Family Leadership Services of the Institute on Disability, University of New Hampshire UAP.

Mary Larner, Ph.D., Policy Analyst and Editor, Center for the Future of Children, The David and Lucile Packard Foundation, 300 Second Street, Suite 102, Los Altos, California 94022

Mary Larner develops and edits the Center for the Future of Children's journal, *The Future of Children,* which summarizes knowledge relating to the well-being of children for policy makers. Previously, at the National Center for Children in Poverty and at the High/Scope Educational Research Foundation, she studied child care issues facing low-income families, home visiting programs for new parents, and the long-term effects of preschool programs. She began her career working in child care and family support programs and has coauthored two books and several reports and articles.

Joan Lombardi, Ph.D., Early Childhood Policy Specialist, care of Ellen Galinsky, Families and Work Institute, 330 Seventh Avenue, 14th Floor, New York, New York 10001

Joan Lombardi has served as an early childhood policy advisor to a variety of national organizations and state agencies. She served as a senior policy advisor to several national organizations, including The National Association of State Boards of Education, The National Head Start Association, and the Families and Work Institute. She is the author of numerous publications, including *Creating a 21st Century Head Start,* the landmark report of the Secretary's Advisory Committee on Head Start Quality and Expansion, and coauthor of *Caring Communities* and *Right from the*

Start. She is the first associate commissioner of the Child Care Bureau within the U.S. Department of Health and Human Services. Her contributions to this book were made before her appointment and do not necessarily represent the views of the Department of Health and Human Services.

Bruce L. Mallory, Ph.D., Professor, University of New Hampshire, Department of Education, College of Liberal Arts, Morrill Hall, Durham, New Hampshire 03824

Before his appointment to the University of New Hampshire in 1979, Bruce L. Mallory was a classroom teacher, a VISTA volunteer, a Head Start director, a legislative researcher, and a research associate at the Center for the Study of Families and Children at Vanderbilt University. He established the Graduate Program in Early Childhood Special Needs at the University of New Hampshire and has worked continuously with community agencies and public schools to implement preschool and early intervention services. His research and writing have focused on the impact of social policies on young children with disabilities and their families as well as the need to reconceptualize theory and practice to create inclusive and effective early childhood special education services. His recent work has included cross-cultural analyses of childhood disability in developing societies, the role of social constructivist theory in inclusive early education programs, and applications of Scandinavian study circle models to address contested values on public education within local communities.

Rebecca S. New, Ed.D., Associate Professor and Coordinator, Graduate Program in Early Education, University of New Hampshire, Department of Education, College of Liberal Arts, Morrill Hall, Durham, New Hampshire 03824

Rebecca S. New joined the early education field in the late 1960s as an elementary school teacher in the Florida public school system, where she developed interests in emergent curricula and home–school relations. Her research interests in sociocultural bases of parenting resulted in a long-term study of Italian child care and development, which, in turn, led to her collaborative affiliation with Reggio Emilia educators. Her scholarly interests remain focused on the theoretical and cultural bases of early education and development, with particular interest in the relations among cultural values, adult ideologies, and child care policies and practices. A commitment to cultural diversity and the promotion of inclusive early childhood practices is reflected in her recent work, such as *Diversity and Developmentally Appropriate Practices: Challenges for Early Childhood Education,* a volume she coedited with Bruce L. Mallory.

Charles A. Peck, Ph.D., Professor, Department of Teaching and Learning, Washington State University, Vancouver, 1812 East McLoughlin Boulevard, Vancouver, Washington 98663

Charles A. Peck's research focuses on the ecological analysis of factors affecting the implementation of educational innovations, issues related to inclusive schools, and early childhood education. He has served as Associate Editor for the *Journal of Early Intervention* and for the *Journal of The Association for Persons with Severe Handicaps.* He has also coedited two volumes summarizing research and development work in severe disabilities and early intervention.

Beverly Rainforth, Ph.D., P.T., Associate Professor, School of Education and Human Development, State University of New York at Binghamton, Post Office Box 6000, Binghamton, New York 13902

Beverly Rainforth, a physical therapist and special educator, is experienced in working with infants, children, and adults with developmental disabilities. She co-directs the Consortium on Inclusive Schooling Practices, a project that assists state and local education agencies in building capacity to educate all children in general education settings. She has written extensively on collaboration among educators and related services providers. She also is Chair of The Association for Persons with Severe Handicaps Critical Issues Subcommittee on Related Services.

Doris J. Rapp, M.D., F.A.E.M., F.A.A.A., F.A.A.P., 8157 East Del Cuarzo, Scottsdale, Arizona 85258

Doris J. Rapp is board certified in pediatrics, pediatric allergy, and environmental medicine. She has been in clinical practice and has conducted research in both allergy and diagnostic medicine for 40 years. She has written more than 30 medical articles, seven chapters in medical texts, eight books (including the bestseller, *Discovering and Treating Unrecognized Food Allergies: Is This Your Child?*), and three booklets about allergy. She has also produced educational videotapes and audiotapes for parents, educators, and physicians through the Practical Allergy Research Foundation.

Anne Raymer, M.A., 15827 Haynes Road, Laurel, Maryland 20707

Anne Raymer is a full-time homemaker. She holds a master's degree in speech and language pathology and works part time in the suburbs surrounding Washington, D.C.

Garrett and Betsy Silveira, 3 Sylvia Street, Newburgh, New York 12550

Garrett Silveira is an attorney specializing in educational law in the Mid-Hudson Valley region of New York. Betsy Silveira is a fabric designer temporarily on hiatus while she raises their three children, the oldest of whom has a visual impairment. Betsy is President of the Mid-Hudson Valley Association of Parents of the Visually Impaired and a member of the Hudson Valley Lighthouse Advisory Board and the New York Commission for the Blind and Visually Impaired Regional and State Advisory Boards.

Walter Thies, M.S.Ed., Sinergia, Inc., 15 West 65th Street, New York, New York 10023

Walter Thies is the coordinator of a habilitation service. He became active in New York City schools first as a parent, then as a professional, in hope of enhancing the educational career of his son, Keith, whom he adopted in 1991. In 1995, Walter Thies earned his master's degree from Hunter College, where he also received the Barbara Sherry Memorial Award for outstanding graduate work in special education.

Emma Tolbert, A.B.A., Budget Analyst, Action for Boston Community Development, Inc., Head Start (ABCD), 178 Tremont Street, Eighth Floor, Boston, Massachusetts 02111

Emma Tolbert has been a staff member at Action for Boston Community Development, Inc., since 1982. She is a community activist who serves on the Board of Parents United for Child Care and is a member of the Executive Committee of the Board of the Massachusetts Human Services Coalition.

Valora Washington, Ph.D., Vice President of Programs, W.K. Kellogg Foundation, One Michigan Avenue East, Battle Creek, Michigan 49017

Valora Washington is the author of six books and more than 40 journal articles. She serves on the boards of several organizations, including the President's Advisory Board of Historically Black Colleges and Universities; Michigan's Children, a statewide advocacy organization of which she was founding Co-Chairperson; the National Council of Jewish Women's Center for the Child; and the ERIC Clearinghouse on Higher Education. She is a past secretary of the National Association for the Education of Young Children and a past board member of the National Advisory Committee on Head Start Quality and Expansion, the Governor's Michigan 2000 Committee, and the Michigan Department of Education Early Childhood Ad Hoc Advisory Committee.

Marilyn R. Wessels, Training Coordinator, Capital District Office, Parent Network of New York State, 500 Balltown Road, Schenectady, New York 12304

Marilyn R. Wessels, the mother of a young adult with developmental disabilities, has worked on behalf of individuals with disabilities for more than 25 years in various capacities. She is the founder, a past president, and a current co-chair of Schools Are For Everyone, Inc. (SAFE), a national coalition for the inclusion of all students with disabilities in the United States through supported education. In the past, she was a strong advocate for the passage of early childhood legislation as Director of the New York State Senate Select Committee on the Disabled. She serves on various statewide committees, such as the New York State Education Department's Preschool Special Education Advisory Council.

Rita A. Wilder is the pseudonym for a mother of two children. She is recovering from a 29-year addiction to alcohol and heroin, which she abused as a way of coping with traumatic childhood events. She is in a treatment program, learning to heal one day at a time.

Preface

It is hoped that there will be no need for this book or others like it in the next millennium. This text initially was conceived in an effort to document and analyze critical issues that are faced by young children and their families. The intent is to challenge early childhood professionals, advocates, and families to rethink some of the basic assumptions that are embedded into the social fabric and political structure of the United States. The role of values in guiding attitudes, policy, and practice is a consistent theme throughout the book.

In her essay, Valora Washington refers to the widely known African proverb "It takes a whole village to raise a child" and then adds, "It takes all of us working together to make a village." This insight captures the true essence of why this project came to be. Building community, establishing partnerships, and strengthening support networks all are key elements that have guided the development and subsequent progression of this publication. There is a compelling need to work collectively to break down the walls of isolation and fragmentation. More energy must be spent on creating more meaningful outcomes and connections for and among young children as well as their families.

THE CONCEPTUALIZATION AND EVOLUTION OF THIS TEXT

This edited text is designed to provide a unique platform for reviewing, critiquing, and confronting critical issues that affect the lives of young children and their families. Two driving forces have guided the evolution of the project. One is the need for closer examination of national problems and challenges that touch the lives of far too many young children and demand immediate action. Numerous social problems continue to plague the United States (e.g., poverty, violence, substance abuse, health care issues). These challenges can affect young children and families regardless of age, gender, ethnicity, or cultural background. In addition, the enduring and ever-growing need for affordable, accessible, high-quality early care and education remains among the greatest embarrassments of the United States. How can a country so rich in resources be so neglectful in providing a secure and healthy future for children—one of its most important treasures? This irony is shocking.

The second influence behind the birth of the text involves emerging legislative trends (e.g., PL 101-476, the Individuals with Disabilities Education Act [IDEA] of 1990; PL 101-336, the Americans with Disabilities Act [ADA] of 1990) as well as a current shift in recommended practices in early childhood. There have been steady discussion and movement in early care and education toward addressing the commonalities, as well as the diversity (i.e., developmental, cultural, economic), among all children in ways that promote unity rather than isolation. The opportunity for young children to learn from and grow with one another regardless of ability, race, ethnicity, or socioeconomic standing is a value that has challenged early childhood communities to rethink assumptions in early care and education in the United States.

This text is one of the first to integrate literature from a variety of knowledge bases (e.g., early childhood education, early childhood special education, public policy, medicine) into a publication designed specifically to confront contemporary early childhood challenges. Although concerns affecting typically developing children often are the very same issues germane to children with disabilities, these issues are not necessarily addressed from a unified platform or disseminated widely. This book addresses an unmet need in the field by creating an integrated forum for examining critical issues that affect young children with and without disabilities. Thus, the intent of this text is to generate healthy discussion and debate regarding all young children and their families, which, it is hoped, eventually will translate into improvement of early childhood policies and practices. This text is grounded in a vision of a better future for all children and families.

ORGANIZATION OF THIS TEXT

One of the most distinctive features of this edited volume is the diverse list of exceptional contributing authors, who include parents, professionals, and scholars. The text contains nine chapters that are arranged into three sections: **Social Problems and Challenges Affecting the Lives of Young Children and Their Families, Care and Education Issues in Early Childhood,** and **A Model for the 21st Century.** Chapters in the first two sections are accompanied by insightful essays written by parents. Parents have written intimate and provocative essays about their experiences with and perspectives on specific issues that are identified throughout the book. Each parent essay frames thoughtfully its corresponding chapter by providing powerful, firsthand insight about the remarkable challenges that the author's family endured. Instead of writing a book *about* young children and their families, the intent of this project was to write a book *with* families in a way that values their contributions.

Additional essays are found in each of the three sections. These essays, written by leading advocates and distinguished experts, address the basic question, "What would an ideal world look like for young children and their families in the 21st century?" The authors contemplate many of the critical issues confronted throughout the text and offer some fundamental and pragmatic recommendations for the approaching millennium.

The chapters are written by nationally respected individuals who are well known for their work in the early childhood field. The following three main themes are consistent across each of the nine chapters: 1) the vital role of social values in understanding challenges and solutions; 2) the firm belief that families are a constant and paramount influence in the lives of young children; and 3) the recognition that meaningful resources and support to young children and families must reflect a menu of options and be flexible, coordinated, and individualized.

In the introduction, Janko and Peck articulate eloquently a future for young children and their families that is firmly embedded in and guided by a clear set of values. The introduction sets the stage for examining critically the numerous issues and recommendations explored throughout the text. Chapter 1 provides a historical perspective to give the reader a fuller understanding of this examination.

In the first section, **Social Problems and Challenges Affecting the Lives of Young Children and Their Families,** the issues of community and family violence, poverty, substance abuse, and environmental causes of health and education problems are explored. These intriguing chapters provide the reader with a comprehensive understanding of how and why these problems continue to exist and of the profound impact they have on young children. Each chapter offers excellent recommendations for addressing these multifaceted problems in ways that confront the root causes in contemporary society.

The second section, **Care and Education Issues in Early Childhood,** begins with an excellent chapter about the paradox of developmental and cultural diversity that serves as a solid foundation for conceptualizing many of the complex issues raised throughout the entire text. As the chapter authors suggest, diversity in American culture "is both cause for celebration and basis for discrimination." Two chapters that deal with programs and services provide a thorough examination of the historical, social, and political perspectives that have guided societal attitudes toward practices in early care and education. The last chapter in this section examines critically the idea of building healthier partnerships in early childhood by crossing disciplinary and interagency boundaries as well as by strengthening collaborative efforts between professionals and families.

The third section, **A Model for the 21st Century,** contains two powerful essays that provide a framework for envisioning a more promising future for young children and their families. Both essays articulate the need for stronger community responsibility and linkages to promote high standards in early care and education.

By addressing some of the attitudinal and political sources of problems that affect young children and their families, the text has evolved into a call for social justice in the United States. Marian Wright Edelman (1992) best reflected the spirit in which the book is grounded, when she wrote, "It would be rather absurd to work passionately and unrelentingly for integrated schools and not be concerned about the survival of a world in which to be integrated" (p. 43).

The survival of children and that of the world depend on building strong alliances and vocal advocates for the future. It is, therefore, no coincidence that the primary audience for this publication is graduate and doctoral-level students pursuing degrees in early childhood education and/or early childhood special education. Because the design of this project creates a unique framework for combining knowledge bases, this text may appeal to a diverse audience, including educators, administrators, policy makers, related services personnel, and university professors, that is interested in receiving a timely and global analysis of early childhood challenges and solutions. In addition, it is hoped that this book will attract families who are concerned with the present status and future direction of programs and services for all children.

REFERENCES

Americans with Disabilities Act (ADA) of 1990, PL 101-336. (July 26, 1990). Title 42, U.S.C. 12101 et seq: *U.S. Statutes at Large, 104,* 327–378.

Edelman, M.W. (1992). *The measure of our success.* New York: HarperCollins.

Individuals with Disabilities Education Act (IDEA) of 1990, PL 101-476. (October 30, 1990). Title 20, U.S.C. 1400 et seq: *U.S. Statutes at Large, 104,* 1103–1151.

Acknowledgments

A project such as this is not possible without the unwavering support and guidance of a close-knit network of family, friends, and colleagues. The members of the Erwin family, Jules, Harriet, and especially Bill, are deserving of special recognition, for without them, the lessons of survival, endurance, and family strength might never have been learned. Caroline Bakerson also has remained a steadfast source of inspiration—the wonderful legacy of family tradition could not have been possible without her. Although her life came to an end before the publication of this book, her determination, vitality, and courage reflected her belief that life is really a celebration. A sense of humor and love are always in abundance from Mark Blackman, my husband and friend. Mere words cannot express my deep gratitude to him. Dependable friendships and other family ties, too many to name, have clearly provided a strong sense of direction and balance in moving this project successfully to completion.

Sincere appreciation is also extended to Dr. Julie Blackman, Dr. Leonard Blackman, Dr. Fredda Brown, Mrs. Harriet Erwin, and Dr. Leslie Soodak, all of whom provided invaluable guidance and editorial feedback during the early stages of this project. Positive encouragement and generous support were provided by the faculty, staff, and graduate students of the School of Education at Queens College of the City University of New York. The family at Paul H. Brookes Publishing Company largely was responsible for realizing the unmet need for a text such as this, and they offered generously their expertise in transforming this vision into reality. The accessibility and skillful direction of Theresa L. Donnelly, Editorial Director, Melissa A. Behm, Vice President, and Melissa M. Furrer, Production Editor, were invaluable in creating a highly positive experience that was both exhilarating and affirming. Perhaps the most significant influence for this project has been learning from and along with the many parents who struggle to make the world more humane for all children. This book is a tribute to them.

To Alyssa Beatrice Blackman,
who recently entered this world,

and to Barbara Sherry,
who recently departed this world,

both of whom help keep me grounded
by reminding me about the joy and the magic of life

REENVISIONING THE 21ST CENTURY FOR CHILDREN AND FAMILIES

The Struggle for Access, Participation, and Belonging

Susan Janko and Charles A. Peck

Prophesying what life will be like—or what we would like life to be like—for young children and families during the 21st century is a challenging task. Characterizing what life *is* like for young children and families in America is equally difficult. Although the United States is more affluent than its citizens might ever imagine it being, it leads most other developed nations in rates of teen pregnancy, single parenthood, divorce, poverty, and infant mortality (Hobbs & Lippman, 1990). American affluence comprises the country's space, as well as its natural, monetary, and personnel resources, but many U.S. citizens feel disconnected from the ideals of neighborhood and community, which once guided codes of social behavior and offered a sense of belonging (Drucker, 1994).

The United States is a nation of extremes. As academicians and researchers in an institute that studies inclusive early childhood programs, we have occasion to observe exemplary inclusive education practices for young children with and without disabilities in a renovated school that is situated in an affluent urban area. The school schedule is flexible to accommodate the schedules of working parents. Parents drive their children to school in cars that are expensive—not to mention safe and operable. The children are clean, healthy, well nourished, appropriately dressed, and alert. They know and are known by staff. Each child has personal space at the school and can leave belongings in an individual cupboard, which is spacious and full of treasures. The children can count on finding their belongings the next day; nothing will have been stolen or destroyed.

A second school the authors have visited is in a suburban area where the residences are indistinguishable apartment buildings and mobile home parks; block after block of these buildings is tucked behind the miles of strip malls that line a busy highway. There is a remarkable absence of centrally located markets, libraries, parks, and like structures or spaces where people may gather communally. One is struck by a sense that although there are many people who live near each other, there are no towns or connections among the citizens who live there. In this area's elementary school, the attrition rate for children enrolled in the school is approximately 98% each year. *For every 100 children enrolled in the school each autumn, only two children finish the entire school year in the same community.* Children are likely to arrive at school on buses or on foot feeling hungry, tired, sad, or afraid—hardly ready to learn. Not only are families and teachers unlikely to know each other, but the children themselves can form only the most tenuous of attachments to other children and adults, for it is almost certain that every other person will leave at some point before the school year has ended.

Since the publication of *Nation at Risk: The Full Account* (National Commission on Excellence in Education, 1984), a report on America's education system, national attention has focused on the adequacy with which public educational institutions are meeting one of their primary functions—to teach children elementary knowledge and skills. From the viewpoint of many educators, the improvement of educational outcomes for children is related to two issues: 1) the quality of the public education system's personnel and curricula and 2) the relationship between home and school (Bowman, 1994). From the viewpoint of many citizens not directly involved in the education system, the improvement of educational outcomes for children is a problem related to the functions of the country's education system. In the words of social philosopher Peter Drucker:

> One of the major reasons for the steady decline in the capacity of the schools to do their job—that is to teach children elementary knowledge skills—is surely that since the 1950s the United States has increasingly made the schools the carriers of all kinds of social policies: the elimination of racial discrimination, of discrimination against all other kinds of minorities, including the handicapped, and so on. Whether we have actually made any progress in assuaging social ills is highly debatable; so far the schools have not proved particularly effective as tools for social reform. But making the school the organ of social policies has, without any doubt, severely impaired its capacity to do its own job. (1994, p. 78)

A similar sentiment is expressed in an excerpt from an interview one of the authors conducted with a school district administrator. During a school district meeting about education services for non–English-speaking children and children with disabilities, the administrator said,

> One community member posed the question, "Can't we just say the room is full? Because we don't want them in it." The question is out there. But I believe those children and their families are part of the community as much as any of us....And it is our charge to serve them.

From the authors' perspective, and in contrast to those who believe that education should function separate from the contexts of families, communities, and society, all of the issues these examples convey are important to the future of children and families during the 21st century. As Bronfenbrenner (1979) stated convincingly in his description of an ecological model of human development, social conditions that inhibit or promote the abilities of families to provide environments that nurture the growth and development of children are important. Likewise, conditions in social institutions that inhibit or promote educators' abilities to provide environments that nurture the growth and development of children are important. Furthermore, conditions in schools and classroom that inhibit or promote the educational outcomes of all children are important. And, of particular importance, in the authors' view, are the relationships among each of those conditions, or social contexts, and educational outcomes in the daily lives and futures of all children.

VALUED OUTCOMES

The authors are critical of the prevailing ideology surrounding the term *outcomes* as it is used in education and related fields. The current conceptualization of outcomes for children and families should be broadened so that it draws attention to the ways in which children and families participate in society (Lave & Wenger, 1991). Specifically, the outcomes the authors envision are related to changes in the access children and families have to participate in valued roles, activities, and settings within the culture. For all children, but especially children who are vulnerable to the oppressions of race, class, gender, and ability grouping, this vision entails improved access to high status roles in the classroom and other contexts of daily life—roles such as leading, helping others, and being responsible for work on which others depend. These roles not only require competence, but also instill feelings of confidence and shared responsibility. The authors' vision implies changes in children's access to participation in valued activities, such as increasing girls' participation in advanced science and mathematics courses, supporting the participation of a third-grader with Down syndrome on a community soccer team, or involving a classroom of preschool-age children and their families in planting and tending a community garden. Changes in access to participation in valued settings require increasing the opportunities children with disabilities have to be educated in general classrooms. All of these outcomes require substantial change in the forms of social practice that characterize classrooms, schools, communities, and social policies.

CHANGES IN SCHOOLS AND CLASSROOMS

The authors envision the boundaries between schools and communities becoming more permeable. This means that closer relationships among children, teachers, and other members of the community would be promoted and nurtured. Children would spend more time in community contexts and would participate in the activities of the community, learning about the "real world" of their culture. At the early childhood level, this might mean that small groups of children regularly visit settings in which adults carry out their work; the children might even participate in some limited aspects of the adults' work. Adult members of the community would also have more visible and regular roles within the school, working actively to assist children to understand and represent their experiences through language and art (Edwards, Gandini, & Forman, 1993). At the secondary school level, these linkages between school and community would be forged through regular internships, apprenticeships, and service-learning activities.

The authors also envision changes in the kinds of activities that take place in classrooms. Viewing access to participation in valued roles, activities, and settings as the most fundamental outcome for children implies that what occurs inside classrooms should have more direct relevance to the forms of social practice that occur outside of the classrooms. This means that curricula and instructional practices would less often emphasize the direct instruction of basic skills outside of realistic social contexts; instead, more emphasis would be placed on activity-based (Bricker & Cripe, 1992) and project-oriented (Chard & Katz, 1989) curriculum strategies. At the early childhood level, this would mean that children learn and practice new skills in the context of doing the real work of creating things together, communicating with important people in their lives, and solving problems of conflict and cooperation that arise during school life. At the elementary level, this might mean that children share their emerging ideas and experiences with science projects via an electronically mediated "virtual" science fair or that they take increasingly active responsibility for classroom and school governance. At the university level, this might mean that students learn educational research methods by participating with the instructor in asking meaningful questions about the teaching and learning process and in collecting and analyzing data that address those processes of change.

CHANGES IN COMMUNITY AND INSTITUTIONAL CONTEXTS

Achieving the outcomes the authors envision also implies substantial change in forms of social and institutional practice that influence what occurs in classrooms and schools. Education practices intended to increase the confidence, competence, and sense of shared responsibility among children and families through participation in valued activities are unlikely to be realized unless two other conditions exist to support those practices. First, educators must model desired behaviors—confidence, competence and shared responsibility with children and families. Second, educators and families must participate in relationships that are founded on mutual accommodation and trust and that include an ongoing exchange of information and communication related to the development and well-being of individual children (Bronfenbrenner & Neville, 1994).

Both of these conditions require specific action by schools and political institutions. Boundaries between families and schools, like boundaries between schools and communities, must become more permeable. Strong relationships between schools and families are unlikely to be established and grow when schools are temporally, geographically, logistically, or socially inaccessible to families. Families must be invited and permitted to co-own their community schools. Co-ownership can occur only when families, like children, participate in valued activities and when families have opportunities to engage with educators and administrators in joint planning, decision making, and evaluating important aspects of their children's education. Family involvement must go far beyond a yearly conference about a child, rubber stamp approval of school curriculum, or volunteerism in the classroom. School staff must find ways to engage all families in creating community schools, especially families whose voices are likely to be missed because they do not speak the language of the dominant culture or do not understand the professional language of schools as well as families who seem disinterested because they do not know how to participate in ways that are meaningful to them. The confidence and competence that children experience through participation in meaningful activities must be echoed by the confidence and competence educators and families experience as they invest in the creation of schools and educational experiences that reflect their personal values and aspirations and fit with their daily lives within family, work, and community settings.

Educators and administrators who are co-creating schools without boundaries also must be supported with professional development activities that increase their confidence and competence in new skill areas, such as communication and collaboration. Educators also must be supported through organizational restructuring that allocates time and space for joint planning, decision making, creating, and evaluating with families. Values and assumptions about the need for co-ownership and increased family and community participation in education are the foundation for systemic change in the country's education system, but they cannot be realized without a commitment of human, temporal, physical, and monetary resources by the greater society.

FUTURE DIRECTIONS

It is clear from the discussion in this introduction that the authors envision change and development as a co-evolutionary process at both individual and cultural levels (Vygotsky, 1978). The sociopolitical changes that have occurred in the 1990s, such as increased poverty, domestic and community violence, and single-parent families and concomitantly decreased personal, social, and financial resources for certain subgroups of citizens, have further clarified that the direction of this co-evolutionary process must be shaped by values, rather than a political struggle between individuals and groups with competing values and disparate resources. The authors' vision of a desirable future for children and families in the 21st century is grounded in a set of values that is an issue in American and world politics. Perhaps the most easily forecast aspect of the future for children, families, and those who advocate for them is that of an ongoing and intensifying struggle for voice, power, and resources.

REFERENCES

Bowman, B. (1994). Home and school: The unresolved relationship. In S.L. Kagan & B. Weissbourd (Eds.), *Putting families first: America's family support movement and the challenge of change* (pp. 51–72). San Francisco: Jossey-Bass.

Bricker, D., & Cripe, J.W. (1992). *An activity-based approach to early intervention.* Baltimore: Paul H. Brookes Publishing Co.

Bronfenbrenner, U. (1979). *The ecology of human development: Experiments by nature and design.* Cambridge, MA: Harvard University Press.

Bronfenbrenner, U., & Neville, P.R. (1994). America's children and families. In S.L. Kagan & B. Weissbourd (Eds.), *Putting families first: America's family support movement and the challenge of change* (pp. 3–27). San Francisco: Jossey-Bass.

Chard, S., & Katz, L. (1989). *Engaging children's minds: The project approach.* Norwood, NJ: Ablex.

Drucker, P. (1994, November). The age of social transformation. *The Atlantic Monthly,* pp. 53–80.

Edwards, C., Gandini, L., & Forman, G. (1993). *The hundred languages of children: The Reggio Emilia approach to early childhood education.* Norwood, NJ: Ablex.

Hobbs, F., & Lippman, L. (1990). *Children's well-being: An international comparison.* Washington, DC: U.S. Bureau of the Census.

Lave, J., & Wenger, E. (1991). *Situated learning and legitimate peripheral participation.* New York: Cambridge University Press.

National Commission on Excellence in Education. (1984). *Nation at risk: The full account.* Portland, OR: USA Research.

Vygotsky, L. (1978). *Mind in society.* Cambridge, MA: Harvard University Press.

1

History of
the Development of Social Policies
Affecting Young Children

Beverly Roberson Jackson

It is important to understand the historical evolution of social policy affecting children and families in the United States to understand the changes taking place in the 1990s. In the 1990s, social policy is in the process of evolving from the old European adage "a man's home is his castle" to the African proverb "it takes a whole village to raise a child." These statements reflect social policies that have shaped laws and attitudes toward children and families throughout the history of the United States.

The concept "a man's home is his castle" implies that whatever happens in the home is within the province of the owner of that home and under the auspices of the family rather than the state. This belief is illustrated by the fact that most U.S. child welfare and health policies were not enacted until 100 years after the birth of the United States. Ensuring the health, safety, early care, and education of young children prior to school age was considered the responsibility of each individual family and not a matter of U.S. policy (Kadushin & Martin, 1988). The belief that "a man's home is his castle" and its influence on the development of early social policy in the United States was a reaction to centuries of European feudal ownership of and responsibility for children.

The African proverb "it takes a whole village to raise a child" conveys a different social policy message: Child rearing should involve the entire community not just the family. This concept contradicts traditional U.S. values concerning family policy; it could, however, precipitate the evolution of U.S. social policy into the 21st century. Policies related to helping families build strengths have become an accepted part of the social policy debate in the late 20th century (Bremner, 1970).

Children have not always been protected by U.S. social policy. During the colonial period and post–Revolutionary War era, children in the United States often were poor, indentured, enslaved, or otherwise tied to the U.S. agricultural economic base. Later, children accounted for much of the labor force in the early years of the Industrial Revolution.

HISTORY OF THE DEVELOPMENT OF POLICIES
AFFECTING CHILDREN AND FAMILIES IN THE UNITED STATES

Since the mid-19th century, the United States has been moving toward social policies that create a sheltered period of time in childhood for education and protection. Historically, however, the U.S. government has been reluctant to create policies that affect children and families, as Steiner (1975) noted

> When politicians consider legislation affecting children generally, they do so hesitantly and reluctantly knowing that the American social system presumes that barring economic disaster or health crisis, a family should and will care for its children without public intervention. (p.1)

Changes in the U.S. economy and the evolving role of women have been major factors challenging this reluctance. Economic pressure and the need for the participation of women and children in the labor force at various times in history have forced policy makers to legislate family policy. The following U.S. economic milestones have signaled changes in child and family policy:

1. The Industrial Revolution in the United States
2. The early 20th century movement from a primarily agricultural society to an industrial society (including the women's suffrage movement)
3. The movement toward a postindustrial or service/communication society

Each of these economic upheavals has signaled changes in social policies affecting children and families in the United States. These upheavals also have affected decisions made by parents, such as family size.

In an agricultural society, the number of children available to work on a family's farm affected the earnings of that family. Large families were prized, because children added to family wealth. Furthermore, children who were orphans or whose families could not care for them were sent to live on farms to help with the work. With the advent of the Industrial Revolution, entire families went to work in factories; children as young as 6 or 7 years old contributed to a family's income. Somewhat smaller families began to be valued. Then, in the 1890s, mandatory school attendance and child labor laws were first enacted in some states. As a result, children were not able to contribute to family income, and the popularity of large families declined further; families shrunk from an average of 5–10 children per family in the 19th century to an average of 2.3 children per family in the second half of the 20th century.

Much as the three periods of economic upheaval affected policy-making decisions, three major periods of policy upheaval united and later divided the early education and child care fields. The following three events signaled policy upheaval:

1. The first White House Conference on the Care of Dependent Children in 1909
2. The Depression and World War II

3. The rebirth of feminism in the United States and the War on Poverty of the 1960s

The White House Conference on the Care of Dependent Children

No vehicle for social policy development and implementation has yet to rival the 1909 White House Conference on the Care of Dependent Children convened by President Theodore Roosevelt at the behest of educators, social workers, and social reformers. (Table 1.1 shows the evolution of subsequent White House Conferences on Children.) One major accomplishment of this conference was the establishment of the Children's Bureau, a single U.S. government agency committed to addressing the needs of children and their families. (The Children's Bureau is discussed in greater detail later in this chapter.) The White House Conference also established that children younger than school age were best served when they were cared for by their mothers; this belief resulted in the creation of the first mother's allowance program to provide income for mothers raising children without the aid of fathers.

For more than 6 decades, most women who received the mother's allowance were widows. This mother's allowance exists in the 1990s as Aid to Families with Dependent Children (AFDC). The mother's allowance originally was developed to enable children to remain at home until they reached school age and to enable mothers to provide this early care and nurture without the risk of living in poverty. During the early- to mid-1900s, the U.S. public did not accept the widespread use of child care and early childhood education programs; exceptions were reserved for situations in which such child care services were needed desperately. In contrast, in the 1990s, given the increased pressure for women to enter the paid labor force and the recognition of the value of early childhood education and child care for young children, a primary goal of AFDC is to move mothers into jobs or training programs and children into child care programs.

Table 1.1. Highlights of the White House Conferences on Children

- In 1919, the Second White Conference on Children focused on child welfare standards. President Woodrow Wilson asked for the development of minimum standards for the protection of the health, education, and welfare of children.
- In 1930, the Third White House Conference on Children produced the Children's Charter, which advocated rights for all children without regard to race, creed, color, or citizenship status.
- In 1940, the Fourth White House Conference focused on children in a democracy and the need for equality of opportunity.
- In 1950, a White House Conference reviewed past Conferences, examined the need for equality of opportunity, and championed the needs of children.
- In 1960, the groups that had met 10 years earlier came together again and further explored equality of opportunity.
- In 1970, a White House Conference for Children (birth to 13 years of age) was held, and, in 1971, a White House Conference for Youth (14–18 years of age) was held.
- In 1980, the White House Conference was redesigned. The purpose of the new design was to provide the conference with a broader focus—that of strengthening and supporting families. It was renamed the White House Conference on Families, and it was the last of the child/family-focused White House Conferences held in the 20th century. In the mid-1990s, the American Orthopsychiatric Society began a movement to call for the reestablishment of the White House Conferences.

The Depression and World War II

Child care and early childhood education programs were viewed positively during the Depression, when the U.S. government established emergency nursery schools and preschools under the auspices of the Works Progress Administration and the Federal Emergency Relief Administration. Nursery school and preschool programs were developed in part to provide jobs for public school teachers, custodians, cafeteria employees, and other workers, who had been displaced because communities were unable to provide financial support to the public school system. From 1933 until the end of World War II, nursery school and preschool programs were socially popular endeavors.

During World War II, women were encouraged to work in factories, because so many men were serving as soldiers or participating in other areas of the war effort that there was a critical shortage of workers. Child care was provided so that mothers of young children could work. Almost as soon as the war was over, however, women were removed from their factory jobs to make room for the men returning from war, and out-of-home child care lost the public support it had gained. Federal funds for all early care and education programs in the United States (e.g., child care, preschool) were revoked.

Rebirth of U.S. Feminism and the War on Poverty

In the 1960s, two unrelated movements, the feminist movement and the War on Poverty, converged and left a lasting impression on the early child care and early childhood education fields. The feminist movement gained political and social acceptance and heightened the debate about child care outside of the home. The movement focused on gaining rights, especially economic rights, and equal pay for women. At the same time, U.S. society was enjoying such economic optimism that it declared war on poverty. With this declaration to end poverty came a promise to develop supportive programs for low-income families with children. One major outcome of the War on Poverty was the birth of Head Start, which remains one of the most successful and long-lasting government-sponsored early care and education programs. Head Start provides primarily poor children with half- or full-day child care and education, health services, and social services and offers parenting programs for families.

For the remainder of the 1960s, other early care and education programs won acceptance because of the popularity of Head Start. In 1971, as the U.S. economy faced the first of a series of downturns that would last into the 1990s, the first murmurs that the U.S. government should not provide financial support for out-of-home child care were heard. Between 1971 and 1995, however, the funds appropriated for child care rose to more than $4 billion. The issues of the costs associated with and monitoring required for quality child care service delivery systems, however, continued to affect policy decisions. Nonetheless, well into the 1980s, public opinion polls found genuine acceptance for and popularity of early care and education programs.

Other Events Causing Policy Upheaval

In addition to the three major events that signaled policy upheaval, several other events affected the early child care and education fields. In the mid-1970s, some recommendations of the 1970 White House Conference on Dependent Children resulted in a call to examine the effect of child and family policies on the families themselves. The result of this recommendation was the founding of the Family Impact Seminar, initially funded by the Ford Foundation and developed by Drs. Sheila Kammerman and Alfred Kahn. Originally, only select researchers were privy to the discussions and findings of the Family Impact Seminar. Over time, however, the seminar became less exclusive, and, although the focus remained on policy makers, advocates were permitted to participate in the proceedings.

The 1970s were a difficult time: People awaited gains in the War on Poverty, family issues received coverage in the popular press, and family policy was debated openly. Many child advocates believed that the focus on children was lost in the family orientation of the 1970s. The value placed on the family was seen in situations such as the following: To maintain acceptance among churches and communities, the National Council of Churches had to change the name of its Children's Justice Project to The Child and Family Justice Project.

In 1979, the White House Conference on Children was postponed until December 1981. In 1980, the issues to have been addressed in the 1979 conference were incorporated into a White House Conference on Families. Although a national White House Conference on Families was never convened, regional White House Conferences on Families were held in Baltimore, Maryland; Minneapolis, Minnesota; and Los Angeles, California. During the 1980s, child and family policy faced a major setback. Various political pressures placed U.S. families, which always had been diverse in structure, custom, and tradition, under close scrutiny. Advocates and policy makers were divided over the issues of divorce, abortion, family planning, and family economics. As a result of this in-fighting, family policy issues lost public support. The White House Conferences on Children ceased, and no White House Conferences on Families were convened after 1980 (see Table 1.1).

In 1980, to provide a new forum to collect data on children and families and to promote policies to benefit families, the U.S. House of Representatives created the House Select Committee on Children, Youth, and Families. The House Select Committee on Children, Youth, and Families was abolished in 1992, when the House abolished all select committees. The loss of the Select Committee on Children, Youth, and Families, coupled with the fact that the decennial White House Conferences on Children had ceased, meant that no single governmental body was focusing on advocacy for children.

This void was quickly filled by child advocacy organizations. Foundations began to fund organizational collaboratives on behalf of young children. The Mailman Foundation Annual Meeting on Research and Child Advocacy gained new importance. The Children's Defense Fund, which had launched major public awareness campaigns in the late 1980s to educate U.S. society about the plight of poor children, gained new prominence. The Family Research Council began presenting its analyses of child and family issues in a broader context to a much broader audience.

HISTORY OF ADVOCACY IN THE UNITED STATES

Two types of child advocacy exist: case advocacy and class advocacy. *Case advocacy* champions the cause of one child or one family to ensure access to opportunities for success. Case advocacy, for example, may involve helping a child who has a visual impairment acquire braille textbooks so that he or she can participate in a general classroom. Such advocacy also may entail locating a qualified vision teacher to teach a child with a visual impairment how to read braille or locating a computer and scanner to translate reading materials into braille.

Class advocacy is more complex, costly, and time consuming than is case advocacy. Class advocacy focuses on an entire group of people. For example, concern for one child who has a visual impairment may prompt a class advocate to ensure that all children with disabilities have access to adaptive supports or age-appropriate, **natural** environments (see Chapter 8). The first step for the class advocate is to ensure that the community uses to the fullest extent possible all of the resources guaranteed by PL 101-476, the Individuals with Disabilities Education Act (IDEA) of 1990. IDEA, which entitles each child with disabilities to an education in the least restrictive environment, is a reauthorization of PL 94-142, the Education for All Handicapped Children Act of 1975.

This section describes the genesis and evolution of class advocacy in the United States. Social indicators that express the status of children help to illustrate the breadth of the problems that attracted advocates.

Role of Educators as Advocates

Educators have served as advocates for educational opportunities for very young children since the birth of the United States. Most of these education advocates focused first on religious education then on community socialization. The first community education laws were passed in the 1600s (Nakosteen, 1965). Although most education advocacy focused on school-age children, preschool education is discussed at length in this section.

Advocates for education in the 19th century, particularly those who fought for Sabbath or Sunday schools for children who worked in factories, found support within the labor movement. The two groups worked together to bring about the introduction of public education and the passage of child labor laws.

The early education and child care movements arose from a similar partnership between education advocates and child welfare advocates (social workers). Educators viewed early educational activities as an opportunity to enhance learning; social workers viewed child care as a way to provide a safe, nurturing environment for the children of factory workers and day laborers.

Beginning with the Industrial Revolution, education for preschool-age children in the United States had these two major aims: 1) the general nurture, moral development, and education of poor children and 2) the early development and intellectual stimulation of affluent children. These two aims complemented each other at times, but often they were at odds with each other.

In the late 19th and early 20th centuries, John Dewey and Horace Mann incorporated many of the theories of Swiss educator and child development advocate Johann Pestolozzi and Friedrich Froebel, the father of kindergarten, in the forerunners of contemporary kindergarten and prekindergarten programs. While the kindergarten movement was growing in Europe, a similar early education movement was taking hold in the United States, primarily in urban areas on the East Coast. Infant schools, developed for preschool-age children, began to appear. Cahan reported on this movement

> Will you not remember...those poor little ones who have no nursery and no mother deserving of the name? And will you not...come forward and afford your aid to their cause and not rest till every section of the city has its Infant School. (1989, p. 10)

Kindergartens took hold slowly in the United States. Although, in 1996, kindergarten programs still were not available in all parts of every state, in the 1980s, many states finally adopted legislation to fund kindergarten programs and incorporate them into the public school system (Hymes, 1990). Kindergarten and prekindergarten programs have, however, effected significant changes in early education since the 1960s: Most notably, these programs have resulted in the lowering of the minimum age at which children enter educational programs; this change is important because early intervention or stimulation has been shown to enhance the educational success of children in elementary school (Boyer, 1991; Shepard, 1992).

Whereas educators advocated for kindergarten and infant school programs, social workers advocated for early child care programs. In the early part of the 20th century, women's clubs, churches, and philanthropic and educational groups began to develop programs to meet the care and educational needs of young children. In the African American community, in particular, this time period brought growth in women's clubs and leagues and the birth of the college sorority movement. These organizations championed child care for young African American children. Close allies and convenient sites for care were found in the numerous churches in African American communities.

In factory-dominated cities on the East Coast, women's political philanthropic groups (e.g., the suffrage-oriented National Association of Women) also began to develop nursery school programs. Over time, a two-tiered process of early care and education service delivery was developed: Child care was provided for children from low-income families, and nursery school programs were provided for children from more affluent families. In many cases, the services offered and the training received by the providers were the same; one system was championed by social workers, however, and the other was championed by educators.

Professional Development

Educators served as advocates for themselves and for children by securing professional training and recognition for those who provide early care and education to children younger than 6 years of age. Toward the end of the 19th century, nursery school teachers began to organize into associations for professional development and support. The oldest of these associations is the Association for Childhood Education International, founded in the 1890s. The largest professional association in the United States is the National Association for the Education of Young Children (founded as the National Association of Nursery Educators in 1926), which helped to move the early childhood education profession into the social policy arena and helped to create strong professional development and program accreditation mandates. These organizations, which were composed mainly of women, grew with the women's suffrage movement and later supported aspects of the feminist movement of the 1960s.

Early childhood education advocates influenced U.S. policy development by directing attention to providing high-quality environments for children and compensation for workers. For example, the Child Care Employee Project, which later became the National Center for the Early Childhood Workforce, collected research data and organized grass roots efforts to focus the attention of policy makers on the economic and professional development needs of providers of early child care and education. In addition, since the 1950s, major advocacy organizations from both the education and social work fields have made a conscious attempt to unite and resolve the differences that have divided the two groups over the years. These differences, especially those concerning whether the purpose of out-of-home child care for preschool children should focus on education or custodial care, have shaped legislative decisions affecting the early care and education of children.

Role of Social Workers as Advocates

The role of social workers (and others who work on the behalf of children toward the common good) as advocates dates back to the birth of the United States. Little distinction can be made between professional social workers and individuals working for the common good as members of religious groups or private organizations in the 1600s and 1700s, because it is difficult to differentiate between religious and secular governance of programs during those centuries.

Social workers' advocacy for high-quality early care and education programs is discussed in the previous section. The role of social workers as child advocates is, perhaps, best illustrated by their attention to the issue of child abuse. For much of the history of the United States, mothers or other relatives were widely believed to be capable of assuming total responsibility for preschool-age children. One of the earliest problems to capture the attention of social workers, however, was the frequency and intensity of child abuse in the home.

The child abuse prevention movement grew out of the animal protection movement, a fact that epitomizes the reluctance of social policy makers to address the needs of children. The Humane Society was established in 1866 for the protection of animals; it did not establish its children's division until 1875, when a young girl, Mary Ellen, was represented as an animal to receive protection from abuse. In 1965, 90 years later, the first federal laws against child battering were passed, although essentially these were reporting laws. Not until 1974, approximately 100 years after child abuse was first recognized as a problem, was legislation enacted to ensure reporting of, fund treatment for, and provide legal remedy for child abuse (Kadushin & Martin, 1988). This legislation, originally passed as PL 93-247, the Child Abuse Prevention and Treatment Act of 1974, was recommended for repeal by the U.S. House of Representatives in 1995, but it was rescued by the U.S. Senate and, as of 1996, remains a law.

The passage of the child abuse and neglect laws is a clear example of the power of social workers as advocates who generate public acceptance and, thereby, policy change to address the needs of children. Like all other areas of advocacy, the creation of child abuse prevention policy required cooperation among advocates. In this case, social workers coordinated with physicians.

The introduction of more accurate and less harmful X-ray examination techniques enabled physicians to better diagnose repeated trauma and fractures presented by children. Beginning in the 1960s, U.S. social workers and physicians united to lobby the states and the federal government to pass battered baby laws. In 1963, California enacted the first child abuse reporting law, and, by 1967, all 50 states had laws requiring health care providers and others to report suspected abuse. In the early 1970s, the U.S. government unified the various laws in a national statute that included mandatory reporting requirements.

Once the reporting laws were passed, social workers shifted their focus to improving the lives of children despite the abuse and introduced amendments to the child welfare sections of PL 74-271 (Title IV), the Social Security Act of 1935, to strengthen foster care and adoption services. The amendments, PL 93-247, focused on treatment, rehabilitation, and child protection.

In the early 1980s, social workers began to encourage parents to become advocates/partners in the child welfare area. Parents and social workers recognized that families are not static units; family roles and behaviors can be changed and adapted. The social worker–parent partnerships proved successful, and the family resource and support movement began. At the same time, social policy in the United States began to move away from a strong interventionist policy on behalf of children toward a policy that was more inclusive of parents. PL 96-272, the Adoption Assistance and Child Welfare Act of 1980, is a prime example of how the family resource and support movement and the policy shift joined forces. PL 96-272 required child protection agencies to develop family treatment plans that protected children from abuse and provided rehabilitation for parents. PL 96-272 also set aside funding to subsidize the adoption of children whose families could not be rehabilitated; these improved child protection laws were affected by the fallout of the major societal upheaval of the 1980s.

Beginning in the mid-1980s, and continuing in the 1990s, the U.S. economy faltered; families experienced widespread unemployment and economic dislocation, which, in turn, resulted in a wave of criminal activity and substance abuse. Children were the principal casualties of this upheaval, and child protection agencies were overwhelmed by dramatic increases in abuse and neglect cases. In 1993, the Family Preservation and Support Services Act, subpart 2 of Title IV-B of the Social Security Act created by the Omnibus Budget Reconciliation Act of 1993, PL 103-66, provided additional funding to address the situation of families weakened by the societal disruption. This federal legislation was build on preexisting programs run by state governments. The primary model was Washington State's Homebuilders program; established in 1974, the program focused on family support, crisis prevention, and family preservation services. Social workers, child advocates, and parents promoted this legislation, which was based on the findings of almost 20 years of experience in recommended practices in child welfare.

Role of Public Health Workers as Advocates

In the late 1800s, advocates to improve the health and welfare of very young children included socially minded church congregations that provided space for health care and well-baby services and neighborhood cleanup and sanitation programs developed to prevent the spread of disease. The prevention movement took hold at this point in U.S. history as a result of medical discoveries leading to the prevention of insect-borne diseases, such as yellow fever and malaria, and increased knowledge and tools for better sanitation practices.

Local government and religious institutions in the United States joined the crusade for child health and safety before governmental policies were established on the state and national levels. For example, in 1907, New York City was the first locality to establish a child health division in its public health department. Dr. S. Josephine Baker, the first director, commented on the parallels between the movement to conquer tropical diseases and the beginning of the movement to prevent diseases affecting children:

> People were speaking of Colonel Gorgas' work in cleaning tropical disease out of the Canal Zone as if he had been a medieval archangel performing miracles with a flaming sword instead of a brilliant apostle of common sense and sound information in combating epidemics...If a person fell ill with a contagious disease, you quarantined him; if he committed a nuisance, you made him stop doing it or made him pay the penalty. It was all after-the-fact effort. (U.S. Department of Health, Education, and Welfare, 1976, p. 64)

Dr. Baker put her views into action, and, during World War I, she applied disease prevention methods in the New York City public school system; as a result, few children and teachers in New York City were infected with the influenza that killed thousands of people elsewhere in the United States. Unfortunately, public health and hygiene laws did not affect nursery schools in New York City or anywhere in the United States.

During the 1930s, the U.S. Public Health Service began to examine the causes of death in children, and a campaign was initiated to pasteurize milk, teach disease prevention, improve sanitation, and prevent over-crowded slums. As disease treatments and vaccines became available, health advocates promoted disease prevention activities targeting young children. Prevention efforts increased in the 1970s. Vaccines became more widely available and immunization against childhood diseases before school entry became mandatory; as a result, immunization levels rose. This trend ended with the measles epidemic of 1989, which struck more than 45,000 Americans and caused more than 100 deaths (National Vaccine Advisory Committee, 1992). The problem had been growing during the 1980s as a result of a steep rise in the cost of vaccines, the fact that 9.8 million children had no health insurance coverage, and the fact that, of those children who did have health insurance coverage, only approximately half were covered by insurance that paid for immunizations (Maternal and Child Health Information Resource Center, 1992). In 1991, an analysis of the epidemic by the Centers for Disease Control and Prevention revealed that many of the children who had been affected by the measles epidemic were younger than 5 years of age at the time (Children's Defense Fund, 1991).

Children younger than 6 years of age remained vulnerable to infectious diseases because of the prohibitive cost of vaccines, lack of reimbursement for physicians who immunized children from low-income families, and parental ignorance of vaccine schedules for preschool-age children. Children, particularly infants and toddlers, in child care settings were the most vulnerable. No single immunization plan existed for young children in out-of-home care; instead, the states devised their own laws. State immunization regulations affecting children in out-of-home care settings varied from no regulation to immunization being required for all unrelated children in groups of five or more being cared for outside of their homes.

Public health policy affecting children was influenced by the establishment of the aforementioned Children's Bureau on April 9, 1912. This federal agency drafted much of the legislation that was developed to better the health and social welfare of children. Many of the programs initiated by the Children's Bureau were delegated to other federal agencies as the U.S. government grew. As a result of the Children's Bureau's focus on the needs of children, maternal and child health programs (e.g., the recording of births) were created to prevent infant mortality. Infant mortality rates dropped steadily from the 1950s into the 1960s. In 1988, however, for only the second time since 1965, the U.S. infant mortality rate failed to show a decline. This is in stark contrast with the trend in the 1970s, when rates fell by an average of 4.7% annually, and the United States surpassed other developed nations in improving conditions for infants. During the late 1970s, the United States began to fall below other developing nations in preventing infant death and, by the 1990s, had slipped to twentieth place, below some underdeveloped nations (Children's Defense Fund, 1991). As mentioned earlier, in the 1960s, public health workers joined social workers in advocating for child abuse prevention and reporting laws; these two groups joined forces again in the 1990s to advocate for accurate death records for infants and toddlers to address the issue of the troubling infant mortality rate in the United States.

Role of Parents as Advocates

Throughout the history of the United States, many parents who needed social services and supports for their children viewed themselves as powerless because of their socioeconomic class, ethnicity, education level, immigrant status, or other disenfranchisement. These parents rarely assumed roles as advocates, with the exception of parents who were members of ethnic groups and parents of children with disabilities.

Multicultural Parents as Advocates

At the time of the first U.S. Census, in 1790, 750,000 African Americans lived in the United States; the number increased an average of 2% per year until the end of the Civil War in 1865 (U.S. Department of Commerce, Bureau of the Census, 1979). The late 1800s and early 1900s found the African American community in the United States facing a dearth of educational prospects, poor health status, and stagnant income levels as a result of the legacy of slavery and inequities in employment and education. In the late 1800s, parents and church groups in the African American community, led by Dr. Nannie Helen Burroughs, advocated for educational opportunities for their children. Organizations such as the National Association for the Advancement of Colored People focused primarily on educational opportunity. African American churches, the largest of which was the Baptist Church, began creating school programs and organizing self-help groups composed of women in the churches. In the secular community, Negro Women's Clubs emerged; these groups also emphasized self-help, family stability, and economic development.

In addition, various philanthropic families, both Caucasian (e.g., the Rockefellers) and African American (e.g., Ida Wells Barnett, Madame C.J. Walker, members of the very small African American middle and upper classes), were involved in increasing African American access to education. Because the African American population largely resided in rural areas, U.S. Department of Agriculture programs that improved agricultural proficiency, family development, and nutrition played a major role in small communities and, toward the end of the Agricultural era and beginning of the Industrial era, in college programs throughout the United States. These converging forces moved parents and educators to address the needs of children. The early work of African American sororities and fraternities, the common purpose of women's clubs, and, later, the development of the National Council of Negro Women all focused on creating better health, home environments, and access to education for children.

During the War on Poverty, parent and professional advocacy organizations proliferated; of these, the most enduring has been the National Black Child Development Institute, founded in 1970, which focuses on educational opportunity and safeguards toward developmentally appropriate practice in early care and education for children who were members of ethnic groups. In addition, a number of Hispanic women's organizations composed of mothers and professionals brought attention to the strengths found in multicultural families. Although Cuban American, Mexican American, and Puerto Rican parents all have their own advocacy organizations, they also have united to form an effective coalition of Hispanic social service and mental health organizations (known as the Coalition of Hispanic Social Service and Mental Health Organizations [COSSMHO]).

Parents of Children with Disabilities

In the 1950s, advances in technology and in physician training in obstetrics and newborn care ensured survival for increasing numbers of children with disabilities. As a result of their swelling numbers, parents of children with disabilities emerged as a powerful new group of advocates. Parent advocates worked for improved opportunities for children with disabilities; they advocated for better access to educational and vocational opportunities and better conditions in institutions. Later, these parents would advocate for deinstitutionalization.

Perhaps the most widely known parent advocacy organization for children with disabilities is The Arc (formerly the Association for Retarded Citizens and the National Association for Retarded Children). The Arc combined many parent groups operating on the local and state levels into a large force to lobby for improved conditions for children with disabilities in institutions and increased opportunities for treatment and education. In 1957, as a result of The Arc's efforts, $1 million was added to the Children's Bureau budget for this purpose.

Parents, in cooperation with physicians and special educators, have shaped much of the policy affecting children with disabilities. Policies have been developed to enable parents to provide in-home care for children with disabilities, to establish health care reimbursement practices, and to improve access to education. Two major policy decisions influenced by parent advocates are IDEA and the extension of Supplemental Security Income (SSI) benefits to children with disabilities (Moynihan, 1987).

The above-mentioned policies were the result of hard-fought battles on behalf of children with disabilities. Advocates credited the earlier passages of PL 89-110, the Voting Rights Act of 1965, and PL 88-352, the Civil Rights Act of 1964, with encouraging them to persevere. IDEA guarantees improved educational opportunities for children with disabilities. Two sections of IDEA focus on preschool-age children. Part H focuses on early diagnosis and intervention for infants and toddlers with disabilities beginning at birth and continuing until 3 years of age. Part B addresses the needs of children with disabilities between the ages of 3 and 5 years. IDEA also has ensured the meaningful inclusion of parents in the planning and decision-making processes for their children.

The provision of SSI benefits to families of children with disabilities did not come without some difficulty. When policy makers established Social Security benefits for veterans and other adults with disabilities, they wanted those benefits to extend to children with disabilities as well (Moynihan, 1987). Children were not fully included, however; instead, they were added when disability categories expanded in the 1980s. Not until 1990 were these benefits expanded through a court order to include more children with chronic illnesses and/or disabilities (*Sullivan v. Zebly*, 1990). In 1995, however, Congress began to protest that too many children received these benefits and proposed that only those children with recognized categorical disabilities should receive benefits.

Since the 1950s, the United States has made positive strides in national policies affecting children. Time and again, parents and professionals have joined forces to educate and persuade lawmakers to consider the needs of children. As a result of increased lobbying on behalf of parents and professionals, the federal budget for children with disabilities increased to more than $2 billion by 1995.

Advocacy on Behalf of Infants and Toddlers

All of the aforementioned groups have, to varying degrees, been advocates for infant and toddler care. Although issues surrounding the mental and physical health needs and child care needs of families with infants and toddlers arose during the White House Conference on Dependent Children in 1970, very little official follow-up occurred. Infant and toddler specialists in the fields of psychology, medicine, and family advocacy continued to address issues with the Joint Commission on Mental Health of Children, chaired by Dr. Reginald Lourie.

In 1977, Lourie and several infant and toddler clinicians in the disciplines of medicine, psychology, and sociology founded the National Center for Clinical Infant Programs (later renamed ZERO TO THREE/National Center for Clinical Infant Programs), which advocates for the needs of infants, toddlers, and their families; serves as a repository for and disseminator of research on infant development and recommended practices in infant and toddler care; and provides support and resources to families of infants and toddlers. ZERO TO THREE/National Center for Clinical Infant Programs produces materials for clinicians and the general public on early childhood. A bimonthly bulletin, *ZERO TO THREE*, addresses critical issues, such as early learning, early intervention for children with disabilities, and guaranteeing access to comprehensive health services and immunization for all infants and toddlers.

LESSONS LEARNED

Advocates and policy makers have learned important lessons in the process of advocating changes in U.S. policies affecting children and families. Chief among these lessons is that policies that affect children cannot and should not be separated from those that address the needs of families; this interrelationship is evidenced in the statement that there is no such thing as a baby—only a baby and someone (Winnicott, 1987). Other lessons learned are specific to particular age groups or conditions; these are discussed below.

Children Birth to 3 Years Old

Advocates for the needs of children from birth to 3 years of age have learned the importance of continually transmitting to the U.S. public new research about how very young children grow and gain skills and knowledge. The Carnegie Corporation's 1994 report on infants and toddlers urged policy makers and advocates to apply scientific knowledge about the critical nature of infancy and toddlerhood in child growth, development, and learning to early education practices to enrich learning environments for young children and to ensure good health and nutrition.

One example of translating research into policy and practice was presented in the ZERO TO THREE/National Center for Clinical Infant Programs 1991 report, which described program models that researchers found to be beneficial to infants and toddlers. Children who received special services as infants and toddlers were studied to see whether they differed from their peers at various stages of development (Gross & Hayes, 1991).

Another well-documented study traced the long-term consequences of an extensive program that offered child care and family support to low-income families in Syracuse, New York, during the first 5 years of their children's lives (Lally & Honig, 1977). A follow-up study 10 years later compared children who had participated in the program with children from similar backgrounds who had not (Lally & Mangione, 1988). The girls who had participated in the study were doing far better in school, the boys who had participated were committing fewer and less severe criminal offenses, and all participants were more likely to remain in school than were their peers who had not participated in the study.

A third study, conducted in Connecticut, followed two groups of low-income families with infants and toddlers (Provence & Naylor, 1983). One group received a coordinated set of health and social services; the other did not. At the 10-year follow-up, children in the first group were less likely to require special education, were likely to have better school attendance, and were more well liked by their teachers than were children in the second group. In addition, more of the mothers in the first group had achieved self-sufficiency, had completed more schooling, and had given birth to fewer subsequent children than had the mothers in the second group. Per family, families in the second group received, on average, almost $3,000 more per year in welfare and special education services than did those in the first group.

In the 1990s, both the Carnegie Corporation and ZERO TO THREE/National Center for Clinical Infant Programs began campaigns to inform the U.S. public about what helps and what hinders early development by publicizing the results of studies such as those described above. Such campaigns are costly, but, unless policy makers and the public are made to understand, in clear and concise terms, the benefits of specific programs and services, important programs will not receive the attention, support, and funding they require.

Child Care and Preschool Education

The most critical lesson learned by advocates for child care and preschool education is that educators and social workers must reach an agreement on principles that help all children (see Chapter 9). Divisions between social workers, who advocate developmentally appropriate, high-quality child care programs for poor children, and educators, who advocate developmentally appropriate early educational intervention for all children, have created an artificial dichotomy. Both of these needs can be and often are realized in practice.

A more enduring division will surround the issue of out-of-home care. Because advocates have been unable to reach a consensus, children in the United States have been provided a wide array of programs. These mismatched programs must be stitched together to create a seamless system to provide all parents with the option of high-quality, out-of-home early education and child care programs (see Chapter 7).

In 1994, some positive developments signaled that the lesson of unity had been learned. Dozens of early care and education organizations united under a common set of principles to advocate in a coordinated manner for developmentally appropriate, high-quality early care and education services for all children. The U.S. Department of Health and Human Services convened a conference of child advocates and state health, education, and social services administrators to address the goal of providing comprehensive services for children and families.

Elementary School–Age Children

For the lessons learned by early childhood advocates to make a real difference in the lives of young children, the care and nurture of young children must continue when they enter school. Elementary school educators have learned that continuity is critical. Schools must extend the developmentally appropriate practices children experience in early child care and education settings. Meeting the IDEA requirement to educate children with disabilities in the least restrictive environment must be accomplished through the use of a collaborative process that includes parents, educators, health care providers, and social workers to ensure that the gains made by all children in early childhood continue throughout life (see Chapter 8).

Children with Disabilities

Both parents and professional advocates have learned the importance of finding collaborative partners to meet the needs of families of children with disabilities. IDEA legislation was expanded by several collaborative efforts in the mid-1990s. Funding was shared among programs serving children considered at risk through the educational system (PL 89-10, the Elementary and Secondary Education Act of 1965, which was reauthorized as PL 100-297 in 1988), and PL 101-501, the Head Start Transition Project Act of 1990, and performance standards mandated cooperation with IDEA when providing services to children with special needs.

Many communities have already discovered and attempted to address the need for broad-based collaboration to fully serve children with disabilities. What remains, according to View and Amos (1994), is the need for increased commitment from state and federal authorities to support the collaborative process. Advocates for children with disabilities in the United States face the difficult task of bringing together local and national collaborations at the state level.

There also is a growing demand for more collaboration between early childhood special education and general education programs (see Chapter 9). Given the climate in the mid-1990s, it is imperative that early childhood programs, policies, and personnel preparation efforts support the education and care of young children with disabilities in natural, community-based settings (see Chapter 8). Without federal, state, and local support, these collaborative efforts cannot be sustained.

Children and Poverty

The impact of poverty on children cannot be ignored: More than 5 million children younger than 5 years of age were living in poverty during the 1980s and 1990s. The lesson learned from poverty is that it is not an acceptable living condition. (See Chapter 3 for a detailed discussion about the problem of poverty in the lives of young children and their families.)

The War on Poverty temporarily stabilized the poverty rate among children younger than 6 years of age at 17% until the mid-1970s. In 1980, however, the poverty rate among children younger than 6 years of age began a steady rise, reaching 25% in 1983 and then stabilizing at 20% in 1987. All told, the number of poor children younger than 6 years of age rose from 3.4 million in 1972 to 6 million in 1992 (Aber, 1995). In the 1980s, an average of 2.1 million Caucasian children, 1.6 million African American children, 1 million Hispanic children, and 250,000 other children lived in households in which income, including income from subsidies such as AFDC and food stamps, was below the U.S. poverty level. One fourth of the children in the United States spent part or all of their earliest, developmentally critical years living in poverty.

In response to the appalling poverty rates affecting children, almost every agency of the U.S. government includes at least one program devoted to helping low-income children. The U.S. Department of Health and Human Services houses AFDC, Child Care Subsidy Programs, and Head Start; it also oversees the U.S. Public Health Service, which provides the Maternal and Child Health Block Grant with funds for immunization, Healthy Start pre- and perinatal care, and statewide health initiatives. The U.S. Department of Education operates Education for the Disadvantaged, Even Start (family literacy), and Education for the Homeless programs. The U.S. Justice Department's Office of Juvenile Justice and Delinquency Prevention funds various programs through Title V Block Grants to states; these grants, the names of which vary among states, include after-school programs, programs for children making the transition from foster care, programs for families in high-risk environments, and so forth. The U.S. Department of Agriculture funds the Food Stamp program, Cooperative Extension Service (family education about food and nutrition), Child Care Food Program, and School Lunch Program.

FUTURE DIRECTIONS

Throughout this chapter, the barriers to adequate resources for children and families are described. The idea that all families can and will handle all of the needs of their children without assistance is being replaced by the notion that each child in each family in the United States deserves and needs the concern of government agencies, community groups, and individuals. History has proven, however, that governmental policies often serve more to cause arguments among advocates than to establish lasting, adequate policies affecting children. The general public often rejected policies that might have improved the lives of children for perceived economic or philosophical reasons.

At the outset, this chapter describes a model of policy evolution in which social policies affecting children and families move toward shared responsibilities and accountability among families, communities, and service providers. It is important to note, however, that this model is endangered by the political and economic climate in which it is developing, just as high-quality early child care and education programming faced setbacks at the end of World War II. In the 1990s, the United States faced an equally as volatile world with the end of the Cold War and the advent of a new communication age.

One positive development is the option of less costly professional training in early child care and education through the use of video conferencing and distance learning. The Children's Television Workshop, for example, has developed the Sesame Street Preschool Educational Program (PEP) for family child care providers. The PEP program teaches family child care providers to help children acquire the skills introduced on *Sesame Street*. In the future, family support and resource networks could create new virtual neighborhoods on the basis of access to communication media rather than actual geographic proximity.

Advances in science and technology are inevitable in the new millennium. Advocates for children and families must devote themselves to ensuring that these developments are used to support and improve the lives of children. By applying the lessons of history and using the most advanced technology available, professionals and parents will be able to influence policy-making decisions that will affect young children and families in the 21st century and beyond.

With these lessons in mind, the chapters that follow address the issues that affect young children and families in the 1990s, including domestic and community violence; poverty; parental substance abuse; environmental illness; and the lack of appropriate, accessible, high-quality child care, and propose changes needed to provide the care and education that children deserve, that is, diverse child care environments; community-based, natural settings; and collaboration. Essays by parents discuss the impact that the above-mentioned issues have had on their families; and essays by professionals look to the future, envisioning the ideal system for children and making suggestions for approximating that model.

REFERENCES

Aber, L. (1995). Number of poor children under six increased from 5–6 million 1987–1992. *National Center for Children in Poverty Report, 5*(1).

Adoption Assistance and Child Welfare Act of 1980, PL 96-272. (June 16, 1980). Title 42, U.S.C. 670 et seq: *U.S. Statutes at Large, 94*, 501–535.

Boyer, E.L. (1991). *Ready to learn: A mandate for the nation.* Princeton, NJ: The Carnegie Foundation for the Advancement of Teaching.

Bremner, R.H. (Ed.). (1970). *Children and youth in America* (Vol. 1). Cambridge, MA: Harvard University Press.

Cahan, E. (1989). *Past caring: A history of U.S. preschool care and education for the poor 1820–1965.* New York: National Center for Children in Poverty, Columbia University School of Public Health.

Carnegie Task Force on Meeting the Needs of Our Youngest Children. (1994). *Starting points: Meeting the needs of our youngest children.* New York: Carnegie Corporation.

Child Abuse Prevention and Treatment Act of 1974, PL 93-247. (January 31, 1974). Title 42, U.S.C. 5101 et seq: *U.S. Statutes at Large, 88,* 1-8.

Children's Defense Fund. (1991). *Annual report: The state of America's children.* Washington, DC: Author.

Civil Rights Act of 1964, PL 88-352. (July 2, 1964). Title 42, U.S.C. 241 et seq: *U.S. Statutes at Large, 78.*

Education for All Handicapped Children Act of 1975, PL 94-142. (August 23, 1977). Title 20, U.S.C. 1401 et seq: *U.S. Statutes at Large, 89,* 773–796.

Elementary and Secondary Education Act of 1965, PL 89-10. (April 11, 1965). Title 20, U.S.C. 239 et seq: *U.S. Statutes at Large, 79,* 27–58.

Elementary and Secondary Education Act of 1988, PL 100-297. (April 28, 1988). Title 20, U.S.C. 2701 et seq: *U.S. Statutes at Large, 102,* 140–184.

Gross, R.T., & Hayes, C. (1991). Implementing a multi-site, multidisciplinary clinical trial: The infant health and gevelopment program. *ZERO TO THREE, XI,* 4.

Head Start Transition Project Act of 1990, PL 101-501. (November 3, 1990). Title 42, U.S.C. 1238 et seq: *U.S. Statutes at Large, 104.*

Hymes, J.L. (1990). *Early childhood education: Twenty years in review, 1971–1990.* Washington, DC: National Association for the Education of Young Children.

Individuals with Disabilities Education Act (IDEA) of 1990, PL 101-476. (October 30, 1990). Title 20, U.S.C. 1400 et seq: *U.S. Statutes at Large, 104,* 1103–1151.

Kadushin, A., & Martin, J. (1988). *Child welfare services* (4th ed.). New York: Macmillan.

Lally, J.R. & Honig, A.S. (1977). *The family development research program: A program for prenatal, infant and early childhood enrichment (final report).* Syracuse, NY: Syracuse University.

Lally, J.R., & Mangione, P. (1988). More pride, less delinquency: Findings from the ten-year follow-up study of the Syracuse University family development research program. *ZERO TO THREE, 4,* 13–18.

Maternal and Child Health Information Resource Center. (1992). *Child health USA 92.* Washington, DC: U.S. Department of Health and Human Services.

Moynihan, D.P. (1987). *Family and nation.* San Diego, CA: Harcourt Brace Jovanovich.

Nakosteen, M. (1965). *The history and philosophy of education.* New York: Ronald Press.

National Center for Children in Poverty. (1990). *Five million children: A statistical profile of our poorest young citizens.* New York: Columbia University School of Public Health.

National Vaccine Advisory Committee. (1992). *Access to childhood immunizations: Recommendations and strategies for action.* Washington, DC: U.S. Department of Health and Human Services.

Omnibus Reconciliation Act of 1993, PL 103-66. (August 10, 1993). Title 42, U.S.C. 629 et seq: *U.S. Statutes at Large, 107,* 649–658.

Provence, S., & Naylor, A. (1983). *Working with disadvantaged parents and children: Scientific issues and practice.* New Haven, CT: Yale University Press.

Shepard, L. (1992). *Flunking grades: Research and policies on retention.* London: Falmer Press.

Social Security Act of 1935, PL 74-271. (August 14, 1935). Title 42, U.S.C. 301 et seq: *U.S. Statutes at Large, 15,* 687–1774.

Steiner, G. (1975). *The children's cause.* Washington, DC: The Bookings Institution.

Sullivan v. Zebly, 88 U.S. 1377. (1990, February 20). 20 C.R.F. 422.406.(b)(1).

U.S. Department of Commerce, Bureau of the Census. (1979). *The social and economic status of the Black population in the United States: A historical view, 1790–1978. Current population report.* Washington, DC: Author.

U.S. Department of Health, Education, and Welfare. (1976). *Two hundred years of children*. Washington, DC: Author.

View, V., & Amos, K. (1994). *Living and testing the collaborative process: A case study of community-based services integration*. Arlington, VA: ZERO TO THREE/National Center for Clinical Infant Programs.

Voting Rights Act of 1965, PL 89-110. (August 6, 1965). Title 42, U.S.C. 437 et seq: *U.S. Statutes at Large, 79*.

Winnicott, D.W. (1987). *The child, the family and the outside world*. Reading, MA: Addison-Wesley.

I

SOCIAL PROBLEMS AND CHALLENGES AFFECTING THE LIVES OF YOUNG CHILDREN AND THEIR FAMILIES

Our Children Are Getting the Wrong Message

Ralph Beach

I believe the most damaging violence to children is the subliminal violence they are bombarded with daily. At home, I closely monitored the commercials specifically targeted at my children (I have a son, age 9, and a daughter, age 3). Of the toys marketed primarily for boys, a considerable majority are violent toys, reinforcing the concept that the bigger the gun, the more powerful the individual. One toy manufacturer created the Ricochet, a remote control car that does not focus on hand–eye coordination. The pitch for selling it is "Drive it like you don't care." Another children's toy is the seemingly harmless car crusher that children use to make cars and then crush them. Mortal Kombat, one of the bloodiest and cruelest video games I have ever seen, allows children to choose the method of their opponent's bloody death. What messages are these toys giving our children? If we agree that play is a child's building block for learning, then, by playing with toys of this nature, our children are building violent foundations for learning. I think this is wrong.

Another concern I have about the issue of violence is how men, in particular African American men, are portrayed in U.S. society. As an African American man raising a son, I believe that I have a responsibility to be a good role model to my son and to dispel many of the negative stereotypes that are attached to all men but particularly to African American men. Television suggests that men are either beer-drinking sportsmen, boring intellectuals, or brutes who use violence to solve conflicts. The media stereotype African American men even further: They are portrayed as super athletes, individuals who are addicted to alcohol and/or other drugs, or criminals. They are rarely seen as caring, sensitive, responsible people. I constantly remind children that I am big *and* I am gentle, that when I am angry I do not hit, and that I have feelings and I respect other people's feelings. Our children are getting the wrong message. U.S. society glorifies violence, sexism, and racism. We must give our children the right messages about loving and caring.

2

GROWING UP IN A VIOLENT WORLD

The Impact of Family and Community Violence on Young Children and Their Families

Betsy McAlister Groves

Violence has become a hallmark of American culture and society. The international image of the United States includes reports of tourists being murdered randomly in Florida, a young mother who killed her two young children, a society whose heroes include Arnold Schwarzenegger and Sylvester Stallone, and a society whose children know how and where to get guns. The crisis of violence in the United States has left few families untouched. Violence comes into living rooms via television. Increasingly, children are witnessing real-life violence, either in their homes or on the streets. This epidemic constitutes both a public health crisis (Groves, Zuckerman, Marans, & Cohen, 1993; Koop, 1992) and a moral/philosophical crisis (Edelman, 1992; Emde, 1993).

The United States has the highest homicide rate in the world (Fingerhut & Kleinman, 1990). The homicide rate for young men is 73 times greater than the rate in similar industrialized nations (Prothrow-Stith & Weissman, 1991). The proliferation of guns and other lethal weapons is linked directly to the increased homicide rates among children as well as to the numbers of violent incidents that children may witness (Garbarino, Dubrow, Kostelny, & Pardo, 1992). Each day in the United States, 9 children are murdered, 30 children are wounded by guns, and 307 children are arrested for violent crimes (Children's Defense Fund, 1993).

As the impact of violence on families and young children is discussed in this chapter, it is important to consider the culture in which these families and individuals are embedded. The social history of the United States emphasizes traditions of individual rights and individualism over the collective good. This philosophical stance underlies the tolerance of violence against women and corporal punishment in families. Historically, these individual rights dictated that a man was the ruler of his household and that matters of family discipline were not the business of government or the courts. Before the late 1800s, children had few rights separate from the family. In fact, agencies were established to protect the rights of animals before agencies were established to protect the rights of children. Not until the 1960s were state agencies created with specific legal mandates to protect children from familial abuse and neglect. This historical tradition of the supremacy of individual rights also contributes to the inability of the United States to regulate gun ownership and possession. It is within this culture that families raise children.

DEFINITION OF TERMS

The term *violence* encompasses a broad spectrum of behaviors and events, some of which are beyond the scope of this chapter. This chapter focuses on family and community violence. It also includes a perspective on violence in the media. Family violence must, by definition, include child maltreatment and spousal abuse. Community violence includes assaults, shootings, and drug- and gang-related violence. Of particular interest to the author is the impact that being bystanders to violence has on children. Children who witness violence may not carry the physical scars associated with being direct victims of violence; instead, the children who witness violence are silent victims whose psychological scars often remain hidden. These children are the special focus of this chapter.

PREVALENCE OF CHILDREN'S EXPOSURE TO VIOLENCE

Media violence is the most ubiquitous source of violence encountered by the majority of children. Approximately 99% of U.S. households have at least one television; 66% have more than one television (Comstock & Strasburger, 1990). The average child sees 12,000 acts of violence on television each year (Dietz & Strasburger 1991).

Family violence touches the lives of many families. In the United States, an estimated 1.6 million children are seriously injured or impaired each year as a result of abuse or neglect; 1,100 children die as a result of child abuse each year. One third of all victims of child abuse are younger than 1 year of age (Children's Defense Fund, 1993). An additional 3.3 million children witness domestic violence between adults in the home (Jaffe, Wolfe, & Wilson, 1990). Twenty percent of adult women have been abused at least once by a male partner (Stark & Flitcraft, 1991). Nearly one half of the men who abuse their female partners also abuse their children (Walker, 1984). Domestic violence is an equal opportunity phenomenon and occurs in rural and urban areas without regard to class or ethnicity.

Community violence is a particular threat for families who live in areas where there are high concentrations of families with few economic, psychological, or personal resources. Although random violence occurs in all areas of U.S. society, community violence is associated primarily with urban areas. A study of elementary school children in New Orleans, Louisiana, revealed that more than 90% of the children had witnessed violence; more than 50% had been the victims of some form of violence; and 40% had seen a dead body (Osofsky, Wewers, Hann, & Fick, 1993). In Los Angeles, California, it is estimated that 10%–20% of all homicides are witnessed by children (Pynoos & Nader, 1990). Interviews with parents of children ages 6 years and younger at Boston City Hospital, Boston, Massachusetts, showed that 1 in 10 children had witnessed a stabbing or shooting by 6 years of age (Taylor, Zuckerman, Harik, & Groves, 1994).

MYTHS ABOUT CHILDREN'S EXPOSURE TO VIOLENCE

Several myths about violence in the lives of children and families bear careful consideration. The first myth is that young children, by virtue of age and developmental stage, may be less affected than older children by exposure to violence. With regard to children who witness violent events, clinical experience suggests that young children are deeply affected by witnessing violence, particularly when the perpetrator or victim of violence is a family member (Groves, 1994). Young children demonstrate a remarkable capacity for memory of traumatic events (Sugar, 1992; Terr, 1988). Children's vivid accounts of violent events stand in contrast to parents' reports that their children did not see the violence or were unaware of it. It is not uncommon for a parent to report that his or her child did not see or hear a violent episode in the home. Separate interviews with the child reveal the opposite: The child gives vivid details about the violent incident (Zuckerman, Augustyn, Groves, & Parker, 1995). Denial and minimization also occur with professionals who work with young children. At some level, such denial is understandable. Adults wish that children did not see violence; it is a reminder to them of their failure to provide adequate protection for children. Adults also hope that if the violence is not talked about, the children's memories of the violence will disappear.

A second myth is that violence is solely an urban problem. Violence has touched the lives of families and children across the United States in rural areas, in suburbs, and in inner cities. Domestic violence can occur anywhere. Child abuse and community violence occur with more frequency in areas where there are high concentrations of people with inadequate housing and income and high rates of drug abuse. This correlation speaks to the need to address the issues of poverty and inequity in the United States as one strategy for reducing violence.

A third myth is that violence is a racial problem that exists primarily in ethnic communities. Research suggests that violence is a function of poverty, not race. When people at the same income level are compared, few differences among races are found (American Psychological Association, 1993). This finding suggests that the context of poverty, not race, is the main risk factor for violence.

RESEARCH ON VIOLENCE AND YOUNG CHILDREN

A great deal of research has addressed the effects of television violence on children, the impact of maltreatment on children, and the scope of violence among adolescents. There has, however, been less systematic research on the effects that witnessing violence has on young children. Research projects underway in the 1990s in New Orleans, Louisiana, and Washington, D.C., sought to gain a better understanding of children who witness violence (Osofsky et al., 1993; Richters & Martinez, 1993). Harvard School of Public Health has begun a 10-year prospective study to learn more from young children about the precursors to violent behavior (Buka & Earls, 1993).

There are descriptions in the literature of children who have witnessed domestic violence (Hughes, 1988; Jaffe, Wolfe, & Wilson, 1990;

Silvern & Kaersvang, 1989). Methodological problems, however, exist with these studies. Most of these studies examined groups of children who were in domestic violence shelters, thereby making it difficult to determine whether behavior was the result of witnessing violence or was exacerbated by the stress of shelter living. Sample sizes were small; few data were available about young children.

Perhaps the most useful research about the effects of exposure to violence has been conducted by clinicians who were interested in learning more about the effects of trauma on children. Notable contributions in this area have come from Robert Pynoos and Lenore Terr. Both researchers have provided in-depth looks at the effects of single disasters on children ranging in age from 5 to 12 years (Pynoos et al., 1987; Pynoos & Nader, 1989; Terr, 1979, 1981, 1983). Their findings have added greatly to the clinical understanding of posttraumatic stress disorder (PTSD) (discussed later in this chapter). The effects of chronic exposure to community violence have been less well studied. James Garbarino and others have described eloquently the difficulties of growing up in environments of chronic danger (Dubrow & Garbarino, 1989; Garbarino et al., 1992; Kotlowitz, 1991). There is, however, a lack of systematic research that assesses the impact of growing up with this kind of violence.

IMPACT OF EXPOSURE TO VIOLENCE ON CHILDREN

Exposure to Media Violence

The development and proliferation of television has revolutionized U.S. society in a relatively short period of time. In the 1950s, only a small percentage of households could afford televisions. These televisions had small screens and produced black and white pictures. Networks were able to broadcast programs for only 2 or 3 hours in the evening. Now, the average preschooler watches 3.5–4 hours of television daily (Singer, 1989). This preschooler is likely to watch these programs on a large color screen using a remote control device to choose from dozens of channels.

Television has profoundly changed the way young children receive messages about the outside world. Before the advent of television, parents had much more control over when and how children learned about the larger culture. Parents could decide what to tell children and when to tell them; they could monitor what was read to a child or who a child saw. However, with the advent of television, parents' abilities to control these influences from the larger culture were greatly diminished. Some social scientists contend that television has destroyed the boundaries between adult knowledge and child knowledge (Myerowitz, 1985). Because parents cannot anticipate what will appear next on television, they are not able to protect children adequately from inappropriate information.

Perhaps no aspect of television has received more intensive study than has the relationship of violence on television to aggressive behavior in children. More than 3,000 studies have examined the correlation of television violence and violent behavior in children. These studies make a compelling case for the extent to which children are affected by media violence (Sege & Dietz, 1994).

Since the 1950s, the amount of violence in the United States has increased exponentially. Researchers note the parallels between this increase in violence and the proliferation of televisions. In 1951, the U.S. population was 150 million people. That year, 6,280 homicides were reported. In 1980, 30 years later, the population had increased to 220 million, a 47% increase; homicides had increased to 23,000, a 400% increase (Barry, 1993). This rise in violent crime is the result of a complex of social factors; it would be simplistic to attribute this rise solely to television's influence. It is, however, clear that violence on television has played a part in this dramatic rise.

Where Is the Violence?

In 1991, researchers tabulated violence on television during a typical 18-hour broadcast period in Washington, D.C. (Barry, 1993). They studied network, cable, and public broadcast television stations. Their analysis showed that the majority of violent acts occurred in children's television programming. (This included cartoon violence and toy commercials with violent content.) Cable television stations aired more violence than did either network or public broadcasting television stations. The most violent periods of the day were 6 A.M.–9 A.M. and 2 P.M.–5 P.M., the times when most children watch television.

How Does Violence on Television Affect Children?

Many studies have demonstrated the link between violence on television and aggressive behavior in children (Comstock & Strasburger, 1990; Dietz & Strasburger, 1991; Huesmann, 1986). Children imitate what they see on television. One need only talk to preschool teachers to learn the extent to which children imitate television violence in their play. The specifics of the imitation parallel current popular programming. In the early 1990s, preschoolers were karate chopping and fighting in the manner of the Teenage Mutant Ninja Turtles. When this book went to press in the mid-1990s, children were kicking and fighting in imitation of the Power Rangers (see Levin, 1994, for a discussion of the impact of television in preschool).

The tendency for children to learn behavior through imitation has been well studied. Researchers have shown children videotape clips of aggressive behavior and then asked them to imitate the behavior. Children's recall of the specifics of the behavior is impressive. Evidence also suggests that children recall with greater accuracy when they see that the aggressive behavior is rewarded (Bandura, Ross, & Ross, 1963).

Another study that has added to the knowledge of children and television violence is a longitudinal study conducted in Canada in the 1970s (Williams, 1986). In this study, researchers had the unique opportunity to conduct a prospective study of children before they were exposed to television. This study compared children from a town that had no access to television with those from a nearby town that had access to television. Baseline data were gathered on a cohort of 45 first- and second-grade students, using teacher and parent reports about their play. Television was then introduced to the first town. Data on children's play were collected 2 years after the introduction of television. The first measurements showed significantly less aggressive play among the children who did not have access to television. The follow-up data indicated no difference in the aggressive play between the two groups. After 2 years of exposure to television, the children who had not had access to television before the study engaged in as much aggressive play as did those in the control group. This study gives persuasive evidence about how television changes children's play.

Exposure to television violence also increases the viewer's apathy toward or desensitization to aggression. Children who see violence on television may be less empathic toward real-life violence. They see violence as a norm and are less likely to intervene to stop aggression. This desensitization has been demonstrated in experimental situations (Drabman & Thomas, 1974).

Finally, for children who have been exposed to real-life violence, television violence may represent a terrifying and realistic reenactment of their trauma. For these children, television violence precipitates acute anxiety and fear. It seems that exposure to real-life violence increases vulnerability to the effects of television violence. Family and community violence and television violence, therefore, may have a synergistic effect on children.

It is important to note that the research and descriptions cited above pertain only to violence on television. There is, perhaps, a far greater risk to children who view violent or frightening movies on videotapes. Many children may be exposed to horror films or slasher movies, either without their parents' knowledge or because their parents do not fully understand the impact of such movies on young children. These films are particularly troubling because of the vivid graphic depictions of violence. Many children have reacted with symptoms of extreme stress and anxiety after viewing these movies.

In general, it is agreed that young children are the most vulnerable to the effects of violent television programming. They have neither the cognitive nor emotional structures to understand the context of the violence. They do not understand the motives for the violence, nor do they grasp the consequences of the behavior. They are more likely to imitate the violence. Young children also are less able to distinguish reality from fantasy. This is particularly evident in the way young children respond to scary programs. They do not understand that the story is pretend, partially because it appears so real on television.

How Is Violence Portrayed on Television?

Violence on television often is disconnected from real consequences. Television violence is clean (i.e., lack of blood, minimal suffering, invincible cartoon characters). The use of violence on television is rewarded frequently. On television, there is a clear delineation between the good guy and the bad guy, unlike real life, in which there often are indistinct boundaries between good and bad. On television, the good guy gets recognition, material reward, and increased status; the bad guy suffers and is made to look weak or stupid. The heroes may have good values, and the message may be prosocial, but it is conveyed in ways that make violence seem justified. Violence on television also may be humorous. The movie *Home Alone*, which has been shown on network television, is an example of violence that is portrayed as humor. Again, the message is that if violence is funny, it is acceptable.

Finally, children who see violence on television begin to see the world as a dangerous place. Nowhere is the distorted view of the world more evident than in local newscasts. If children were to form their opinions about the world solely from television newscasts, they would believe that murders, rapes, and robberies occur everywhere and that it is only a matter of time before they fall victim to some act of aggression. This worldview is a troubling message to give to young children and may discourage the kind of curiosity and exploration that leads to knowledge, self-confidence, and mastery. Ralph Beach's essay presents concerns about the depiction of violence in the media from a parent's perspective.

CHILDREN WHO LIVE WITH VIOLENCE

For too many children in the United States, the violence they see is not confined to the television screen. Children may be direct victims of violence or helpless bystanders to violence. In either case, there is lasting psychological damage. The mechanisms by which children react to violence are perhaps best understood by considering how children respond to emotional trauma and by examining the psychological processes children use to adapt to the trauma.

Childhood trauma is defined as "the mental result of one blow or a series of blows, rendering the young person temporarily helpless and breaking past ordinary coping and defensive operations" (Terr, 1991, p. 11). For children, trauma may include witnessing or being victims of natural disasters (e.g., earthquakes, hurricanes), human disasters (e.g., automobile accidents, fires), or physical abuse or assaults. There is no age at which individuals are immune to the effects of trauma; both adults and children respond to trauma in certain predictable ways.

Historically, research on the effects of trauma has been confined to studies of soldiers of war. For centuries, there have been references to a set of symptoms associated most frequently with combat veterans. Terms such as *shell shock*, *combat neurosis*, and *battle fatigue* all referred to a mental state observed in soldiers after battle. After the Vietnam War, however, researchers initiated a more systematic look at the effects of trauma on returning soldiers. The work of van der Kolk (1984) greatly expanded the understanding of how external events of overwhelming terror or threat can produce enduring internal emotional changes in individuals. He found that the trauma of war evoked a constellation of symptoms and reactions that were remarkably consistent and similar in each soldier. This constellation of symptoms is known as PTSD.

There was, however, disagreement among child researchers about the extent to which children could experience the effects of PTSD. It was thought that children's reactions to trauma were more transient than were adults' reactions, and, therefore, the diagnosis of PTSD was inappropriate for children (Udwin, 1993).

In the early 1980s, Pynoos and Terr undertook separate studies of children who experienced trauma. Pynoos studied the effects on children of a fatal shooting in a schoolyard; Terr studied a group of children who were kidnapped in California (the Chowchilla kidnapping). Both researchers wanted to understand more about how a single, unforeseen, out-of-the-ordinary, terrifying event would affect children. They wanted to learn how children's responses to disaster may differ from adults' responses. They were interested in seeing whether age, gender, social class, or ethnicity affected children's responses. They also examined whether proximity to violence or previous exposure to violence affected the response. Both researchers found an enduring pattern of response in children that was very similar to the set of symptoms associated with PTSD in adults (Pynoos et al., 1987; Pynoos & Nader, 1989; Terr, 1979, 1981, 1983). This research laid to rest the controversy over whether children could, in fact, experience PTSD. In the 1990s, PTSD has become an acceptable diagnosis for children and frequently is used to classify children who experience violence or abuse.

Symptoms of PTSD may vary in intensity, depending on the specifics of the exposure to the trauma, including a child's proximity to the event, the victim's relationship to the child, and the presence of a parent or caregiver to mediate the intensity of the event. PTSD symptoms that may emerge in children include 1) diminished ability to concentrate in school because of intrusive thoughts and images; 2) persistent sleep disturbances; 3) disordered attachment behaviors with significant caregivers; and 4) nihilistic, fatalistic orientation to the future, which leads to increased risk-taking behaviors (Lyons, 1987). Witnessing violence adversely affects children's development in many areas, including the ability to function in school, emotional stability, and the ability to establish peer relationships (Dyson, 1989; Gardner, 1971; Terr, 1983). Clinical experience with these children suggests that they later engage in aggressive behavior and/or substance abuse as adolescents and adults.

The major research projects that have studied the effects of traumatic exposure to violence on children have focused on elementary school–age children and adolescents. Preliminary evidence suggests, however, that preschoolers also are vulnerable to the effects of traumatic exposure to violence. (Eth, Silverstein, & Pynoos, 1985). There are clinical reports of children as young as 18 months who remember traumatic events and are later affected by these memories (Sugar, 1992). Because young children's psychological and biological resources are easily overwhelmed, they may be particularly vulnerable to the trauma associated with witnessing violence (Famularo, Fenton, & Kinscherff, 1993). Young children lack the cognitive and physical ability to fully anticipate trauma or to protect themselves. Their sense of time is undeveloped. Young children live in the present and are unable to anticipate the future. They are both the most defenseless and the least able to communicate their fears.

One of the more sobering findings of the research studies conducted by Pynoos, Terr, and subsequent researchers, is the extent to which exposure to trauma in children changes the way they view the world. Terr (1983) found that, even after 4 years had elapsed since the kidnapping, the children carried with them a pervasive pessimism about the future. It seems that exposure to trauma produces a fundamental change in how children feel about the world and their place in it. This change in outlook has important implications for children's behavior, ambition, and wishes for the future.

Research has suggested that a full 50% of the children exposed to trauma before the age of 10 years develop psychiatric problems later in life (Davidson & Smith, 1990). Children who are victims of violence and those who are witnesses to violence are vulnerable to this symptomatology. The following sections describe two types of children who live with violence: children who are abused and children who witness violence.

Child Maltreatment

The first category of children who live with violence is those who experience maltreatment. Child maltreatment covers a spectrum of parental behaviors toward children that includes yelling, intimidating or shaming the child, neglecting the child, and physically abusing the child. Most researchers divide the broad topic of child maltreatment into two parts: parental acts of omission (neglect) and parental acts of commission (emotional and physical abuse). In fact, the majority of children who are abused experience more than one form of maltreatment. In one study of families in which children were mistreated, in 50%–60% of the families, children experienced both abuse and neglect; in 15% of the families, children experienced abuse only; and in 20% of the families, children experienced neglect only; in the remaining 5%–15% of families, children experienced "marginal maltreatment" (Crittenton, 1989). As stated above, young children, in particular, are at risk for child abuse. In 1990, almost 90% of those children who died from abuse or neglect were younger than 5 years of age; 53% were younger than 1 year of age (Daro & McCurdy, 1990).

Child maltreatment is the result of a complex set of interacting conditions, stresses, and other factors that affect families. Historically, the causes for child abuse and neglect were thought to rest within the family: The parents were emotionally unstable, had histories of abuse and neglect themselves, or lacked adequate knowledge about parenting. Some studies looked at factors associated with the children. Children who were abused were more likely to be highly active, to have been born prematurely, or to have a difficult temperament. Since the 1980s, sociologists and child development specialists have come to appreciate the influence of the community and larger culture in terms of how these levels of society may contribute to child maltreatment (Belsky, 1980; Pelton, 1985). Garbarino and Sherman (1980) demonstrated that there are higher rates of child abuse in areas of poverty and inadequate housing. These communities, which have fewer resources and a more fragile infrastructure, were less able to offer support to families, thereby demonstrating that child abuse not only is a product of parental inexperience or previous trauma, but also is a product of stressful and unsupportive environments. This understanding of the ecological context of child abuse has important implications for treatment and prevention. It is inadequate to address the problem of child abuse solely through parent counseling, because this approach assumes that the problem is entirely psychological. The ecological view of child abuse would target intervention to the environmental stressors of poverty, isolation, and inadequate services as a major component of treatment.

The United States has been reluctant to come to terms with child maltreatment. Few laws govern how parents may discipline their children. In many states, it is a felony to assault one's wife but not to abuse one's children. In a survey of attitudes across the United States about corporal punishment for children, 85% of the respondents believed that children could benefit from "a good spanking" occasionally (Gelles, 1994). Regulation of family discipline is thought to be outside of the scope of government intervention.

Effects of Abuse and Neglect on Children

Short of malnutrition and disease, there is probably no risk factor for children that has greater consequences for their development than maltreatment by their parents (Erickson, Egeland, & Pianta, 1989). Children who are maltreated are at risk in the domains discussed below.

1. *Development of secure attachment relationships*   The basic foundation for a child's sense of self and capacity to form caring relationships lies in the establishment of a secure, trusting relationship with a primary caregiver in the first year of life. Secure relationships are not only necessary for children to learn to trust; they also allow children to know that they are inherently lovable and worthwhile people. Many maltreated children come to see themselves as unlovable. They mistrust others, they are anxious, and they develop insecure attachments. This insecurity has implications for children's adjustment to preschool (Cichetti, Toth, & Hennessey, 1989). These children may be extremely wary of forming relationships with adults; they may have great difficulty with separations from caregivers.

2. *Development of peer relationships*   Because of their experiences at home, maltreated children may expect the same treatment from others. They engage in aggressive behavior because that is to what they are accustomed. They may misread social cues from their peers because they have learned to expect aggression from others. They have trouble making friends, which confirms their inadequacies and feelings of failure.

3. *Cognitive and language development*   Numerous studies have documented links between maltreatment and cognitive delays (Vadasy, 1989). Children who have experienced chronic neglect are at particular risk for delays. Maltreated infants begin to show cognitive delay in the first year of life. There also is evidence that these children experience language delay. Parents who are neglectful do not use language with their children as frequently as do those who are not neglectful. A child care center for maltreated children at Boston City Hospital, Boston, Massachusetts, reports moderate language delays for all of the children at the center. These children go to school without a basic grasp of language as a tool that can achieve desired results. They do not see language as facilitative, nurturing, or rewarding.

Children who have been physically abused may show symptoms associated with PTSD. Severe and chronic abuse may lead to more serious and intractable psychological states, including dissociative states and multiple personality disorders (Terr, 1990).

Children Who Witness Violence

The second category of children who live with violence is those who witness violence. As with maltreated children, there are fluid boundaries between the categories of children who are victims of violence and children who are witnesses to violence. Children who grow up in high-risk neighborhoods or families may be both victims and bystanders at points in their childhood. Little has been written about children who witness violence. This section describes one project that has targeted this group of children; the emphasis is on what has been learned from the children.

The Child Witness to Violence Project at Boston City Hospital, Boston, Massachusetts, was founded in 1992. This project grew out of concern from pediatric health care providers about the children they saw. Increasingly, providers heard stories from children about shootings on the street or about violence in the home. Their response to this problem was to establish a program specifically for young children who were witnesses to violence. This program offers counseling to children and support for families in a way that considers the particular developmental capacities of young children.

In the 2 years of the project's existence, staff have evaluated approximately 80 young children who have been exposed to violence. A great deal has been learned from these children about how violence affects their worldviews. A discussion of the findings from this project follows.

Types of Violence Witnessed

The Child Witness to Violence Project was conceptualized initially to help children cope with the phenomenal rise in drug-related assaults, street crime, and gang activity. The founders of the project were responding, in part, to the media attention to community violence. However, an analysis of the types of violence witnessed by children referred to the project reveals that domestic violence may be a far greater risk for young children than street violence. Approximately two thirds of the children referred to the Child Witness to Violence Project had witnessed domestic violence. It seems, therefore, that the earliest lessons a child learns about violence are learned in the home and are taught by caregivers.

Findings also show that even the youngest children referred to this project exhibit symptomatology associated with PTSD. Young children do not fully understand what they witness; they show clear evidence, however, of being frightened, confused, and anxious. Young children may exhibit sleep disturbances and increased anxiety at separations from caregivers. Their behavior may change dramatically: They either become highly anxious, active, and distractible or they withdraw and become emotionally passive and distant. Children show increased distress at anything that reminds them of the traumatic event. They also suffer from intrusive recollections of the event, which are the childhood equivalent of flashbacks in adults.

The following case example illustrates some of these symptoms in a very young child: Karen, age 2 years, 5 months, was referred for an assessment after she had been found by police in her home with her mother, who had been fatally shot. Apparently, she had been with her mother during the assault, which occurred several hours before police were summoned. In the beginning of the first assessment session, Karen immediately announced that her mother had been shot and was lying on the floor. She became overwhelmed and began to run around the room. For each of the next four sessions, she played out sequences in which she would call the police on the telephone, tell them about her mother, and describe how she was lying on the floor. Her grandmother, with whom she now lived, reported that Karen had difficulty falling asleep at night, verbalizing before bedtime her intense wishes to see her mother. She had nightmares, some of which seemed to involve themes of shooting and crawling on the floor. Her grandmother described what appeared to be traumatic reminders of the event, such as her becoming anxious when she saw police because of her association of them with her mother's death. Her grandmother also reported that her demeanor and personality seemed to have changed since the shooting. She was subdued, passive, and preoccupied and did not play with spontaneity or pleasure. Her grandmother contrasted this behavior with her previous cheerfulness and energy. Karen shows a range of symptomatology that is consistent of PTSD symptoms in older children and adults.

One of the more impressive findings from the children seen in the Child Witness to Violence Project is the clarity with which they may recall the violent events. It is not unusual for a child to tell about the event or to draw a picture of it that includes detailed information about the environment or the events immediately preceding the traumatic experience. For example, an 8-year-old girl drew a picture of a shooting on the street in front of her house in which her younger sister was injured. In the picture, her family members were located exactly in the positions where they had been during the event. She remembered the color of the cars on the street. As she drew, she talked about how the sun was shining at an angle across the buildings. She recalled that her sister had lost a slipper just before the shots rang out. She began to replay the events immediately preceding the shooting, perhaps in an effort to achieve another outcome to the tragedy. It was as though the event were recorded in her memory with the clarity of a camera. All of the details were there for her recall.

Children's memories of events are greatly shaped by their cognitive appraisals of those events. Children may use all of their senses in remembering an event. Their views of the event may be distorted and idiosyncratic. For example, a 3-year-old boy was sitting in the front seat of a car when his adult caregiver, seated next to him, was shot. There was no forewarning of the event. His perspective of the event focused on his tactile memory of feeling the blood and his auditory memory of hearing the gun: "The gun went POW," he said. He had no other perspective of the event.

Implications for Child Development

These responses in young children have several implications for their development. First, children are forced to learn early lessons about loss, death, and body injury. These lessons present themselves before the child has cognitive apparatus to understand. How does a 3-year-old understand murder? What explanation does a 5-year-old create to understand why his father has just beaten and kicked his mother? Children who witness violence also learn at an early age that the world is a dangerous and unpredictable place. Their natural curiosity about exploring and moving out into the world is affected. An 8-year-old boy who witnessed the shooting of his younger sister told his therapist that he did not think he would ever again feel safe going outside. This message about the world is exactly the opposite of what we want for young children. We know that young children begin to explore the larger world by cautiously moving out and sampling new experiences and sights. However, when children feel unsafe in this exploration, their curiosity is thwarted and their desire to learn by exploring is affected.

Second, children come to see the adults in their lives as unable to protect them. They believe they must take the responsibility on themselves, a prospect that causes great anxiety in children. A 5-year-old girl drew a picture of her mother, who is a victim of chronic domestic violence, lying on the floor beside her bed. The girl then told a story about how she and her little brother were playing alone in the next room. She began to worry that something might happen to her brother and that her mother would be unable to help her.

Third, children who witness violence experience overwhelming helplessness in the face of the trauma. This helplessness leads to feelings of incompetence and worthlessness. A 9-year-old boy who was shot in the leg on a playground managed to leave the playground during the melee. He did not tell his parents about the injury until they discovered blood several hours later. When asked about this astounding secrecy, he replied that he just wanted to be invisible because he feared he might be shot again.

Finally, children who feel so helpless and terrified sometimes turn to aggression and hostility as a means of coping with and transforming such vulnerability. It is safer to be aggressive than to be a helpless bystander. In the Child Witness to Violence Project, children who witnessed violence drew pictures of playground fights being settled with guns or pictures of themselves armed with weapons. It is possible that the 4-year-old bystander to violence becomes the 14-year-old perpetrator of violence because of his or her early experiences with violence.

Impact on Families

Parents often mirror the same helplessness in the face of violence that children exhibit. Parents speak of guilt at their failure to protect their children from witnessing violence. In the Child Witness to Violence Project, it has been found that there are significant differences between how parents cope with domestic violence and community violence. Although some of these differences are self-evident, they bear scrutiny in terms of the impact on children. Families that are torn apart because of domestic violence are less able to psychologically support children in times of crisis than are families that face trauma from an outside source. In the former family, the child may have no one to turn to for protection or reassurance. When one parent is the terrified victim and the other the perpetrator of violence, what choice does that child have? Mothers who are victims of domestic violence are worried about basic issues of survival and may be unaware of the extent of their children's terror. For women who do not leave their partners, constant tension and fear exist about the next violent explosion. Children are hypervigilant and anxious. Their mothers may be equally anxious and may focus most of their psychic energy on making sure there is not another violent episode.

When mothers and their children are forced to leave their homes and go into shelters, children face the additional trauma of loss of familiar space and belongings. They lose the support of their school or child care network. They are forced to live in shelters with other families who are equally traumatized. The daily routines of shelters are necessarily regimented and strict to accommodate the needs of groups and to ensure the safety of the women. However, these rules and practices may not be the best for children. Shelters often are stressful and chaotic for children.

Families who have witnessed community violence, but who do not live with domestic violence, respond to the violence differently. A violent event may throw a family into turmoil, temporarily rendering the parents unable to perform some basic parenting tasks. When the violence occurs outside the home, however, parents may be better able to offer emotional support and protection to children than may parents who are directly involved with violence. For example, one family with three children ranging in age from 8 to 17 years experienced the traumatic loss of a family friend as a result of a drive-by shooting. The shooting occurred on the family's front porch; the adolescent friend died in the front hall of their house. All of the children witnessed this incident. Immediately after the trauma, the parents reported that they were preoccupied with the incident, they experienced intense guilt; they felt they should have been able to save the adolescent's life. They described themselves as emotionally paralyzed. With intervention, however, these symptoms abated; the parents were able to help each child cope with the aftermath of this tragedy by encouraging the children to talk about it and plan a memorial to this young friend. The fact that both parents were emotionally available to the children made a crucial difference in the children's ability to accept this traumatic event.

The burden for parents who live in chronically dangerous environments becomes more complicated. Parents are forced to adapt their parenting styles to the realities of the environment. This adaptation may mean not letting children play outside, invoking strict curfews and other limits, and teaching children to be vigilant. Conflicts may arise between the children's need for autonomy and the parents' worries about safety. Children may end up spending a great deal of their nonschool hours in the house, perhaps watching television or playing video games. These pastimes do not promote peer relationships or a sense of accomplishment and purpose in children.

IMPLICATIONS FOR PRACTICE

A great deal has been reported on the impact of violence on children and families. The findings are grim; many professionals may be tempted to feel helpless and hopeless, mirroring the emotions parents feel. Research and clinical intervention efforts are, however, yielding valuable information about how to help children and families who are affected by violence. In general, caring professionals can help children and families who are affected by violence in several ways.

1. *Communicate a willingness to talk about the violence and to be a nonjudgmental listener.* Children need to know that it is permissible to talk about violence. Sometimes caregivers may subtly discourage children from talking about violence in their lives. It may be very upsetting to hear; caregivers may feel they do not have the answers, or they may believe that it will be less upsetting for the child if he or she does not talk about it. On the contrary, children often feel relieved and unburdened by sharing this information with trusted adults. It also may be useful therapeutically for children to review events, clarify misunderstandings, and air their fears by telling the story about the violent event. Although it is inadvisable to coerce children to tell their stories, reassurance or validation for children once they have brought it up is very helpful.

2. *Support families by helping them stabilize the environment for their children.* Women who are in domestic violence situations need help finding safety and/or making safety plans. These women may be unable (both financially and emotionally) to leave the situation. Helping them think about a safety plan is important. A discussion about help and support for the children also is important. Women who have left their abusive partners need assistance with planning and with securing concrete services. It also is important to help these mothers think about how to talk to their children about the decision to leave the abusive situation. Usually, the circumstances around a woman's departure from her home are chaotic and possibly dangerous. Children may be very frightened and confused and often do not understand what is happening. Helping the mothers to be sensitive to their children's perspectives is important.

3. *Remind parents that they are the most important emotional protectors for their children.* Parents can do a much better job of psychologically reassuring their children than professionals can. Research on children in World War II documented the importance of the parents' role in helping children feel safe, even in the face of war and other trauma (Freud & Burlingham, 1943). Parents can help their children talk about their fears, reassure children that they (parents) will do whatever is possible to protect their children, and allow children to stay close by after frightening events. These interventions will be very helpful for children.

PERSONNEL TRAINING AND STAFF SUPPORT

The fact that many children live with violence both in and out of the home has implications for schools, child care centers, and community-based programs. It is no longer unusual in many urban areas for children to use circle time to talk about a violent incident in their neighborhood. Service providers express their discomfort with such revelations and their uncertainty about how much to let children talk and how to help these children. In general, teachers have been trained inadequately to meet the challenges of working with young children who have been exposed to violence.

Practitioners need training in the following areas:

1. *Understanding the effects of violence on children.* Teachers need information about how to recognize children who are showing symptoms associated with exposure to violence.

2. *Effective intervention with these children.* Teachers need information about how to use the classroom setting to intervene effectively with children. Teachers need to talk to children either individually or in groups about violence. Teachers need guidelines for when to refer children for special help.

3. *Principles for establishing a nurturing classroom and teaching conflict resolution skills.* When children feel safe and nurtured in school, they are able to cope more effectively with stress and to learn better (Garbarino et al., 1992). It also is important to teach children alternatives to violence as a means of problem solving. A burgeoning number of programs and curricula teach conflict-resolution skills to children (Levin, 1994). These programs encourage children to be aware of conflict and to develop positive methods of solving conflict.

4. *Increased skills at recognizing and supporting resilience in children.* A great deal has been written about the importance of recognizing and supporting resiliency in children (Garmezy, 1987; Rutter, 1979; Werner & Smith, 1982). These strategies to support children's healthy adaptation and efforts to cope with adversity are important in working with children who are affected by violence.

In addition to training, teachers need ongoing support and supervision in their work. It is ironic that, in many instances, the schools with the highest numbers of children who are environmentally or psychologically at risk also are the schools with the fewest resources and the least amount of structured support for teachers. Working with children who are exposed to violence can be overwhelming for teachers. They may wish to avoid and deny the realities of some of their students' lives. Some of the issues children face may resonate with teachers' personal experiences. Teachers, then, begin to mirror the same hopelessness and helplessness seen in the children. This perceived hopelessness leads to emotional numbing and burnout in teachers. To avoid this reaction, teachers must have regular support and supervision designed to help them think about intervention with specific children and to give them a place to talk about how this work affects them personally and reflect on the many intense feelings that may be stirred up when working with populations at high risk.

In addition, all children need schools that are safe and nurturing. Schools can be a critical refuge for children who live with violence. Schools can provide training in conflict resolution skills and communicate clear values about the importance of nonviolence. School administrators must set a tone within schools that emphasizes respect, nurturing, and tolerance for all students.

FUTURE DIRECTIONS FOR RESEARCH

Several areas for research in the area of violence and children are important. These areas include a focus both on prevention and intervention. Evidence shows that aggression in young children is a strong predictor of
aggressive behavior in adults and that aggressive patterns of behavior
become more stable over time (Huesmann, Eron, Lefkowitz, & Walder,
1984). Prevention efforts in early childhood must, therefore, focus on how
children learn aggressive behavior and how best to intervene to change
these patterns of interaction before they become entrenched. A burgeoning
number of violence prevention curricula exist for children, and there are
ongoing efforts to evaluate these programs. Do these programs work? Are
they more effective for certain ages than others? Are certain approaches
better to use than others? Which ones are developmentally appropriate for
younger children? Additional research is needed in this important area of
prevention.

Another area of research in prevention is family support programs.
Many professionals are deeply committed to the notion of enhanced social
supports to all families as a way to eliminate some of the stresses that lead
to family violence. These supports include parent education resources,
universal supportive intervention after the birth of a child, access to high-
quality child care and after-school care for children, and access to a range of
community support services. The belief is that these programs relieve
stress in families, decrease isolation, and give specific information about
child rearing. Such interventions improve the quality of life within families and reduce violence in the family. Research is needed to determine
which models of family support are most effective (Schorr, 1988).

Yet another area of research lies in the exploration of the factors that
help children cope with exposure to violence. It is widely known that not
all children who grow up in violent environments have poor outcomes.
Some children survive great adversity and grow up to lead productive and
nonviolent lives. What are the protective factors that enable children to
cope with adverse environments? A greater understanding of the factors
that promote resilience in children would give valuable direction for treatment and prevention.

The final area in which research is needed is the analysis and evaluation of various treatment approaches for children who have been exposed
to violence. No studies exist of the efficacy of treatment for young children
who have witnessed violence. There are clinical and anecdotal descriptions of successful treatment of children (Malmquist, 1986; Pruett, 1979;
Schetky, 1978), but there are no controlled studies of intervention.

RECOMMENDATIONS

Any effort to address the problems of violence and its effects on young children and families must involve comprehensive and multidimensional
strategies. A single-focused intervention will fall short of its goals. Between
1993 and 1995, several commissions and professional organizations have
produced detailed recommendations for addressing the issues of violence in

U.S. society (American Psychological Association, 1993; Carnegie Task Force on Meeting the Needs of our Youngest Children, 1994; National Association for the Education of Young Children, 1993; Violence Study Group, ZERO TO THREE/National Center for Clinical Infant Programs, 1993). These reports share common elements. All of the reports include recommendations for communitywide collaborative approaches to dealing with violence. No single institution can take on the task alone. Schools must unite with health, mental health, and law enforcement agencies to provide services and support to families. Social institutions, such as churches and civic groups, must join the effort as well. Across the United States, for example, there are new collaborations among child development and law enforcement professionals and coalitions of ministers to address the issue of violence.

These recommendations also call for family-centered approaches to intervention. These approaches affirm that parents often are the most important helpers for children and that parents need help in coping with violence; they need information about what to tell children. They need universal support and education in child rearing to improve parenting skills and to learn about nonviolent ways of conflict resolution. When possible, parents should have access to this information *before* they have children so that this philosophy is woven into the context of parenting from the beginning.

It also is important to recognize the impact of poverty and racism on the epidemic of violence in the United States. Living in poverty increases the likelihood of experiencing child abuse in families and of experiencing violence in the community. Any effort to reduce violence must address these root causes. In Boston, Massachusetts, a community-based child abuse prevention program conducted a community survey to find out from families what services they needed the most. The responses included requests for basic services: a food pantry and adult literacy and English classes (Shay, 1995). When families have access to more concrete services, stress is reduced and the likelihood of violence is likewise reduced. Comprehensive violence prevention programs must first address basic family needs.

In the arena of public policy, five recommendations are put forward:

1. *The issue of media violence must be addressed.* The Federal Communications Commission should review, as a condition of license renewal, the efforts of television stations to decrease the amount of violence on television and to increase the amount of positive, prosocial programming. Individual citizens should make their voices heard in protest against violence in the media. Families and schools should sensitize children to the negative effects of television violence and teach children critical viewing skills.

2. *Efforts to support legislation to regulate gun ownership and licensing are critical.* Such efforts have been difficult to achieve because of the powerful lobbying efforts of organizations such as the National Rifle Association. However, it is imperative that the United States enact legislation that reduces the proliferation of guns and limits access to weapons.

3. *A campaign to decrease institutional violence, particularly the use of corporal punishment in schools, must be initiated.* As of 1993, corporal punishment still was legal in many states. If schools are to be a refuge for children, they must be models of nonviolence.
4. *Legislative efforts to address the social causes of violence—poverty and racism—must be initiated.* An alarming number of children are growing up with persistent poverty; the majority of these children are from ethnic groups (see Chapter 3, which addresses the impact of poverty on young children and families). Poverty is directly linked to family and community violence. Any efforts to reduce violence must, therefore, address this problem.
5. *Programs that provide intervention when children are young are critical in the efforts to reduce violent behavior.* This intervention may include family support, parent education, and specific violence prevention programs. Legislators seem reluctant, however, to allocate funding to programs that intervene early in children's lives. The 1995 debate in the United States on the federal crime bill provides a case in point. The debate is whether to put money into building more jails and hiring more police or to put money into programs for children that would reduce delinquent behavior. It seems shortsighted to treat the results of violence without addressing the causes. If intervention were to occur early in children's lives to provide adequate support for parents so that they could raise children in a healthy, safe, and nurturing way, then the need for jails would be decreased by reducing the number of criminals.

Noted psychiatrist and author, Judith Herman, writes: "When traumatic events are of human design, those who bear witness are caught in the conflict between victim and perpetrator. It is morally impossible to remain neutral in this conflict. The bystander is forced to take sides" (1992, p. 7). The caregivers of young children, therefore, must not be passive bystanders to the violence with which young children live. Those who care for children must raise their voices in protest at the ballot box, in the media, and in their work with families to make the world a safer place for children.

REFERENCES

American Psychological Association (1993). *Report of the American Psychological Association on violence and youth* (Vol. 1). Washington, DC: Author.

Bandura, A., Ross, D., & Ross, S.A. (1963). Imitation of film mediated aggressive models. *Journal of Abnormal Social Psychology, 66*, 3–11.

Barry, D.S. (1993). Growing up violent: Decades of research link screen mayhem with increase in aggressive behavior. *Media and Values, 62*, 8–11.

Belsky, J. (1980). Child maltreatment: An ecological integration. *American Psychologist, 35*, 320–335.

Buka, S., & Earls, F. (1993, Winter). Early determinants of delinquency and violence. *Health Affairs*, 46–64.

Carnegie Task Force on Meeting the Needs of Our Youngest Children. (1994). *Starting points: Meeting the needs of our youngest children.* New York: Carnegie Corporation.

Children's Defense Fund. (1993). *Annual report: The state of America's children.* Washington, DC: Author.

Cicchetti, D., Toth, S., & Hennessey, K. (1989). Research on the consequences of child maltreatment and its application to educational settings. *Topics in Early Childhood Special Education, 9*, 33–55.

Comstock, G., & Strasburger, V.C. (1990). Deceptive appearances: Television violence and aggressive behavior. *Journal of Adolescent Health Care, 11*, 31–44.

Crittenton, P. (1989). Teaching maltreated children in the preschool. *Topics in Early Childhood Special Education, 9*, 16–32.

Daro, D., & McCurdy, K. (1990). *Current trends in child abuse reporting and fatalities: The results of the 1990 annual fifty state survey.* Chicago: National Committee for the Prevention of Child Abuse.

Davidson, J., & Smith, R. (1990). Traumatic experiences in psychiatric outpatients. *Journal of Traumatic Stress Studies, 3*, 459–475.

Dietz, W.H., & Strasburger, V.C. (1991). Children, adolescents, and television. *Current Problems in Pediatrics, 21*, 8–31.

Drabman, R.S., & Thomas, M.H. (1974). Does media violence increase children's tolerance of real life aggression? *Developmental Psychology, 10*, 418–421.

Dubrow, N., & Garbarino, J. (1989). Living in the war zone: Mothers and young children in a public housing development. *Child Welfare, 68*, 3–21.

Dyson, J. (1989). Family violence and its effects on academic underachievement and behavior problems in school. *Journal of the National Medical Association, 82*, 17–22.

Edelman, M.W. (1992). *The measure of our success.* Boston: Beacon Press.

Emde, R. (1993). The horror! The horror! Reflections on our culture of violence and its implications for early development and morality. *Psychiatry, 56*, 119–123.

Erickson, M.F., Egeland, B., & Pianta, R. (1989). The effects of maltreatment on the development of young children. In D. Cicchetti & V. Carlson (Eds.), *Child maltreatment: Theory and research* (pp. 647–685). New York: University Press.

Eth, S., Silverstein, S., & Pynoos, R. (1985). Mental health consultation to a preschool following the murder of a mother and child. *Hospital and Community Psychiatry, 36*, 73–76.

Famularo, R., Fenton, T., & Kinscherff, R. (1993). Child maltreatment and the development of posttraumatic stress disorder. *American Journal of Diseases of Children, 147*, 755–760.

Fingerhut, L.A., & Kleinman, J.C. (1990). International and interstate comparisons of homicide among young males. *Journal of the American Medical Association, 265*, 3292–3295.

Freud, A., & Burlingham, J.C. (1943). *War and children.* New York: Medical War Books, Ernest Willard.

Garbarino, J., Dubrow, N., Kostelny, K., & Pardo, C. (1992). *Children in danger: Coping with the consequences of community violence.* San Francisco: Jossey-Bass.

Garbarino, J., & Sherman, D. (1980). High-risk neighborhoods and high-risk families: The human ecology of child maltreatment. *Child Development, 51*, 188–198.

Gardner, G.E. (1971). Aggression and violence: The enemies of precision learning in children. *American Journal of Psychiatry, 128*, 77–82.

Garmezy, N. (1987). Stress, competence and development: Continuities in the studies of schizophrenic adults and children vulnerable to psychopathology and the search for stress resilient children. *American Journal of Orthopsychiatry, 57*, 159–174.

Gelles, R. (1994). *Corporal punishment: Current trends.* Lecture given at the Conference on Supporting Families and Children, Marlborough, MA.

Groves, B. (1994). The Child Witness to Violence Project. *Discharge Planning Update, 14*, 14–18.

Groves, B., Zuckerman, B., Marans, S., & Cohen, D. (1993). Silent victims: Children who witness violence. *Journal of the American Medical Association, 269*, 262–264.

Herman, J.L. (1992). *Trauma and recovery.* New York: Basic Books.

Huesmann, L.R. (1986). Psychological process promoting the relation between exposure to media violence and aggressive behavior by the viewer. *Social Issues, 42,* 125–139.

Huesmann, L., Eron, L., Lefkowitz, M., & Walder, L. (1984). Stability of aggression over time and generations. *Developmental Psychology, 20,* 1120–1134.

Hughes, H.H. (1988). Psychological and behavioral correlates of family violence in child witnesses and victims. *American Journal of Orthopsychiatry, 58,* 77–90.

Jaffe, P.G., Wolfe, D.A., & Wilson, S.K. (1990). *Children of battered women.* Thousand Oaks, CA: Sage Publications.

Koop, C.E. (1992). Violence in America: Time to bite the bullet back. *Journal of the American Medical Association, 267,* 3075–3076.

Kotlowitz, A. (1991). *There are no children here.* New York: Doubleday.

Levin, D. (1994). *Teaching young children in violent times: Building a peaceable classroom.* Cambridge, MA: Educators for Social Responsibility.

Lyons, J.A. (1987). Post traumatic stress disorder in children and adolescents: A review of the literature. In S. Chess & A. Thomas (Eds.), *Annual progress in child psychiatry and development* (pp. 451–467). New York: Brunner/Mazel.

Malmquist, C. (1986). Children who witness parental murder: Posttraumatic and legal issues. *Journal of the American Academy of Child and Adolescent Psychiatry, 25,* 320–325.

Myerowitz, J. (1985). *No sense of place: The impact of electronic media on social behavior.* New York: Oxford University Press.

National Association for the Education of Young Children. (1993). NAEYC position statement on violence in the lives of young children. *Young Children, 48,* 80–84.

Osofsky, J.D., Wewers, S., Hann, D.M., & Fick, A. (1993). Chronic community violence: What is happening to our children? *Psychiatry, 56,* 36–45.

Pelton, L.H. (1985). *The social context of child abuse.* New York: Human Sciences Press.

Prothrow-Stith, D., & Weissman, M. (1991). *Deadly consequences.* New York: HarperCollins.

Pruett, K. (1979). Home-based treatment for two infants who witnessed their mother's murder. *Journal of the American Academy of Child Psychiatry, 18,* 647–659.

Pynoos, R.S., Frederick, C., Nader, K., Arroyo, W., Steinbergh, A., Eth, S., Nunez, F., & Fairbanks, L. (1987). Life threat and posttraumatic stress in school-age children. *Archives of General Psychiatry, 44,* 1057–1063.

Pynoos, R.S., & Nader, K. (1989). Case study: Children's memory and proximity to violence. *Journal of the American Academy of Child and Adolescent Psychiatry, 28,* 236–241.

Pynoos, R.S., & Nader, K. (1990). Children traumatized by witnessing acts of personal violence, homicide, suicide or rape behavior. In S. Eth & R. Pynoos (Eds.), *Post-traumatic stress disorder in children* (pp. 19–43). Washington, DC: American Psychiatric Press.

Richters, J., & Martinez, P. (1993). The NIMH community violence project. I. Children as victims of and witnesses to violence. *Psychiatry, 56,* 7–22.

Rutter, M. (1979). Protective factors to children's responses to stress and disadvantage. In M. Kent & J. Rolf (Eds.), *Primary prevention of psychopathology: Promoting social competence and coping in children* (Vol. III, pp. 49–74). Hanover, NJ: University Press of New England.

Schetky, D. (1978). Preschoolers' responses to murder of their mothers by their fathers: A study of four cases. *Bulletin of the American Academy of Psychiatry and Law, 6,* 45–53.

Schorr, L. (1988). *Within our reach: Breaking the cycle of disadvantage.* New York: Doubleday.

Sege, R., & Dietz, W. (1994). Television viewing and violence in children: The pediatrician as agent for change. *Pediatrics, 94,* 600–607.

Shay, S. (1995). *Building the twenty first century ark: Final report of Dorchester Cares.* (Grant No. 90-CA-1417). Washington, DC: National Center for Child Abuse and Neglect, U.S. Department of Health and Human Services.

Silvern, L., & Kaersvang, L. (1989). The traumatized children of violent marriages. *Child Welfare, 68,* 421–436.

Singer, D. (1989). Caution: Television may be hazardous to a child's health. *Developmental and Behavioral Pediatrics, 10,* 259–261.

Stark, E., & Flitcraft, A.H. (1991). Spouse abuse. In M.L. Rosenberg & M.A. Fenley (Eds.), *Violence in America* (pp. 123–157). New York: Oxford.

Sugar, M. (1992). Toddler's traumatic memories. *Infant Mental Health Journal, 13,* 245–251.

Taylor, L., Zuckerman, B., Harik, V., & Groves, B. (1994). Witnessing violence by young children and their mothers. *Journal of Developmental & Behavioral Pediatrics, 15,* 120–123.

Terr, L.C. (1979). Children of Chowchilla: A study of psychic trauma. *Psychoanalytical Study of the Child, 34,* 552–623.

Terr, L.C. (1981). Forbidden games: Post-traumatic child's play. *Journal of American Academy of Child Psychiatry, 20,* 741–760.

Terr, L.C. (1983). Chowchilla revisited: The effects of psychic trauma four years after a school bus kidnapping. *American Journal of Psychiatry, 140,* 1543–1550.

Terr, L.C. (1988). What happens to early memory of trauma? A study of twenty children under age five at the time of documented traumatic events. *Journal of the American Academy of Child and Adolescent Psychiatry, 27,* 96–104.

Terr, L.C. (1990). *Too scared to cry: Psychic trauma in childhood.* New York: Harper & Row.

Terr, L.C. (1991). Childhood traumas: An outline and overview. *American Journal of Psychiatry, 148,* 10–20.

Udwin, O. (1993). Annotation: Children's reactions to traumatic events. *Journal of Child Psychology and Psychiatry, 34,* 115–127.

Vadasy, P.F. (1989). Child maltreatment and the early childhood special educator. *Topics in Early Childhood Special Education, 9,* 56–73.

van der Kolk, B. (1984). *Post traumatic stress disorder: Psychological and biological sequelae.* Washington, DC: American Psychiatric Press.

Violence Study Group, ZERO TO THREE/National Center for Clinical Infant Programs. (1994). Call for violence prevention and intervention on behalf of very young children. In J. Osofsky & E. Fenichel (Eds.), *Hurt, healing, hope: Caring for infants and toddlers in violent environments* (pp. 38–41). Arlington, VA: Author.

Walker, L.D. (1984). *The battered women's syndrome.* New York: Springer-Verlag.

Werner, E., & Smith, R. (1982). *Vulnerable but invincible: A longitudinal study of resilient children and youth.* New York: McGraw–Hill.

Williams, T.M. (Ed.). (1986). *The impact of television: A natural experiment in three communities.* New York: Academic Press.

Zuckerman, B., Augustyn, M., Groves, B., & Parker, S. (1995). Silent victims revisited: The special case of domestic violence. *Pediatrics, 96*(3), 511–513.

Because I Love My Children

Tracy Hardy

In November 1990, I quit a good state job and went on welfare for the first time in my life. No one in my family had ever been on welfare. It was something that I did not want to do but was forced to do. I was divorced, 30 years old, and pregnant with my fourth child; the child care costs for my two youngest children were more than I could afford. I stayed on welfare only until my caseworker informed me that my child care costs would be paid if I found a job. I started working for the state again in February 1993, and, before my 1-year anniversary, I received a letter informing me that the 1-year limit on child care assistance was nearing, and I would no longer be receiving any support for child care. I was again faced with choosing to work and attempting to pay a $600 monthly child care bill or staying home to care for my children. I could not believe this was happening to me again. This time, however, I had accomplished too much to surrender without a fight.

I applied for a higher paying state job, and I started working nights and weekends at a restaurant to earn extra money to pay the child care bill. After 2 months of working 60-hour weeks and still $300 shy of covering the child care bill, I quit both jobs and went back on welfare. The challenge of supporting my family without assistance became more than I could bear—financially, emotionally, and physically. I was devastated that all of my efforts to improve the quality of life for my children and to eventually become totally self-sufficient had been swept away.

I rallied a group of mothers who were struggling with the same dilemma, and we lobbied at our state capitol building several times. I could not believe that many of the senators and representatives with whom we spoke believed that to provide hard-working mothers with child care assistance was not an important issue. They told us that it would cost more to pay our child care costs than to keep us on welfare. Did they not realize that children eventually go to school, so there would not be a need for long-term child care, but that people often stay on welfare for many, many years? Despite our efforts, the 1-year time limit on child care assistance was never extended to 2 years. I stayed on welfare for exactly 30 days. I found a different job that paid a lot less than my previous job had paid and was told that my child care costs would be paid for 1 year.

During that spring and summer, my children suffered greatly. They noticed the times when there was not much food in the refrigerator. They saw that I, who had always made them laugh many times a day, seldom even smiled. They were surrounded by an atmosphere of frustration and stress that made everyone unhappy. My 3-year-old daughter, Michelle, who was toilet trained, began wetting her pants. My 15-year-old son, Jeremy, was exhausted from babysitting nights and weekends so that I could work a second job. Jeremy and Adam, my 10-year-old son, often came to me in tears, expressing fears of losing our home. I talked with them openly concerning those fears. We hugged a lot. The turmoil caused a lot of grief and anxiety, but it made us stronger as a unit and closer in our love. I believe it taught them something they will cherish forever. You must keep faith in your heart and have hope, and you *can* rise above.

I learned so much about how our legislative system works; some things, I would have preferred not to know at all. When I testified at a house committee hearing, I wished that I had learned more in school about the legislative process. I did meet many caring and hard-working lobbyists who encouraged and directed us, which we needed desperately. I did not, however, understand how politicians, who made laws and ultimately decided our fate, who had never lived a day on welfare, and who had never had their self-esteem drop to nothing, could really know how to fix a system that everyone agrees is broken and useless.

I have always believed that everything in life happens for a reason. Today, I operate a home child care center and we take care of a foster child named Michael. Like all people, I know that I have made some wrong decisions in life, but my children have always been my top priority. Society views those who have been on welfare with a sour glance. Through my experiences, I have met and talked with countless mothers who truly love their children so much that they will do whatever is necessary to hold their lives together. Much too often, unfortunately, the fathers are either not willing to help or not capable of sharing the load. When I look at my happy, content, and loving children, I know that, when they see that life is not always easy, they will work even harder toward their goals and will never give up..

3

POVERTY IN THE LIVES OF YOUNG CHILDREN

Multifaceted Problem, Single-Focus Policies

Mary Larner and Ann Collins

Child poverty is in the public eye in 1996—capturing the attention of opinion makers, policy makers, the media, and researchers, as it has off and on since the 1960s. In the mid-1960s, the fact that poverty rates were high in the proud and economically strong United States was newsworthy. In the 1990s, however, few are shocked to learn that 20%–25% of American children are poor. Debates focus primarily on the causes of child poverty and the shortcomings of the policies that federal and state governments have implemented to address the increasingly familiar problem.

Why, after 3 decades of antipoverty legislation and programs designed to provide the poor with at least meager financial assistance, housing, food, education, job training, and political power, do so many families with children remain poor? Some accuse the weakened economy, which offers fewer and fewer jobs for low-skilled workers; others point to the increased acceptance of extramarital childbearing, which creates families headed by single women; still others find fault with the designs of the antipoverty programs themselves (Bianchi, 1993; Congressional Research Service, 1995). Public opinion polls suggest that Americans remain compassionate and willing to help children who find themselves in poverty through no fault of their own, but most are unsure what type of help is needed and whether government programs and policies will do any good.

Although debates over child poverty often are driven by partisan politics and ideological differences, they also can be informed by a rapid expansion in research-based understanding of how poverty influences the lives of young children. Before the mid-1980s, statistics on poverty did not even include breakdowns by children's ages but included all children under 18 years of age. In the 1990s, technology gives researchers direct access to census data that they can use to study problems and trends that affect specific groups of children. For instance, the National Center for Children in Poverty (1990) reanalyzed census data to report on the prevalence and characteristics of poverty among children younger than 6 years of age, and the U.S. General Accounting Office (1994c) published a report summarizing the poverty experiences of children younger than 3 years of age. Census data provide a valuable snapshot of child or family well-being at one point in time, but they do not show how that snapshot fits into a child's life and influences its course. Fortunately, in the mid-1990s, several longitudinal data sets that contain survey information gathered at regular intervals from the same households, such as the National Longitudinal Survey of Youth (Chase Lansdale, Brooks-Gunn, Mott, & Phillips, 1991) and the Panel Study of Income Dynamics (Duncan, 1984), have become available. Social scientists also have probed the information gathered from participants in programs designed to reduce poverty or deflect its damaging effects to gain provocative glimpses of the interrelations among poverty, parenting, interventions, and children's development (Campbell & Ramey, 1994; Duncan, Brooks-Gunn, & Klebanov, 1994; Larner, Halpern, & Harkavy, 1992; Musick, 1993; Siegel & Loman, 1991). Examples of these types of applied research into child poverty have been collected in several volumes (Huston, 1991; Huston, McLoyd, & Garcia Coll, 1994; Sherman, 1994).

New understanding about how poverty affects the lives of young children, in turn, provides a crucial foundation for the development of policies and programs designed to help those children and their families (Chafel, 1993; Hernandez, 1993; Powell, 1994). This chapter conveys some of the key facts that have been learned about poverty among young children—its scope and distribution among children, the situations in which poor children live, and the mechanisms through which poverty harms children's development. This chapter then examines closely two governmental responses to the needs of poor children and families. One is adult oriented and focuses on economics: Welfare reform and child care subsidies are offered to reduce the reliance of poor families on welfare payments and to increase their participation in the labor force. The second is child oriented and focuses on education: The expansion of Head Start reflects the belief that providing comprehensive services to preschool-age children from poor families will prepare them to escape poverty. The contrast between these policy initiatives illustrates how a piecemeal approach to policy development can create as many problems for families and children as it solves (see Chapter 7).

A key theme of this chapter is that children themselves are not wealthy or poor—they are members of families that vary in their abilities to gain access to economic and social resources. In the United States, the financial status of parents determines the material wealth or deprivation that both children and adults experience. Many other industrialized nations, such as France and Sweden, provide financial assistance to families with children to ensure an equitable living standard. In contrast, the cash assistance provided to America's poor families through Aid to Families with Dependent Children (AFDC) and related programs leaves recipient households well below the poverty line (U.S. General Accounting Office, 1995c). Only through the wages and wealth of their family members do children in the United States secure a decent standard of living. Because the economic well-being of children in the United States is yoked to that of their parents, one cannot improve the lot of children significantly without assisting their parents nor can one punish parents without imposing hardships on their children as well.

The intertwining of the lives and futures of children and their parents goes beyond their shared financial resources. Research has shown that poverty affects children primarily through its influence on the behavior of their parents. Parents decide how the family's available income will be used—will the shopping list include oranges or potato chips?—and parents choose a coping strategy to deal with poverty—will they attempt to work more, reduce spending, seek public assistance, or send a child to live with relatives? Perhaps most important, parents struggling with poverty may not have time to spend with their children; they may be depressed and withdrawn, angry and punitive, or anxious and erratic. Tracy Hardy's essay addresses the emotional toll of this stress on her children.

Although politicians and policy makers pay lip service to the importance of the family as the most powerful force in the lives of children, as this chapter illustrates, the programs created to assist the poor typically are designed for either adults or children. They seldom work well for both generations, and they forfeit effectiveness by that narrowness of purpose.

POVERTY EXPERIENCES OF YOUNG CHILDREN

A single statistical creation underlies most discussions of poverty in the United States—the poverty line. This is a threshold, or marker, established by the federal government to identify households that lack sufficient income to meet basic needs. A national estimate is made of the income required to provide essentials for a family. It is computed by tripling the cost of a minimal diet defined by the U.S. Department of Agriculture in the 1960s, when families made more of their meals from scratch. This estimate becomes the poverty line. It is then scaled according to the number of members in the family, and it is adjusted yearly to reflect changes in inflation. In calculating poverty status, the family's income includes gross wages or salary and cash payments received from such government programs as AFDC and Social Security, but it does not include assets, such as savings or property, or the value of in-kind public assistance, such as food stamps or Medicaid. In 1992, a family of two with an income under $9,137 was considered poor; for a family of three, the cutoff was $11,186; and, for a family of four, it was $14,335 (National Center for Children in Poverty, 1995).

Establishing a single threshold to define poverty for the entire United States makes it feasible to develop national calculations concerning poverty and to set uniform eligibility standards. It also means, however, that significant regional variations in the actual cost of living are overlooked. A mother with one child who tries to live on $761 per month (the poverty line for a family of two) will find it much more difficult to get by in New York City or Washington, D.C., than in a rural county in Alabama. In addition, setting a single threshold implies that poverty is a condition that one either has or does not have, whereas, in reality, the economic means available to families make up a continuum. Families earning $100 per year more than the poverty line are scarcely better off than are those earning $100 less than the poverty line (especially if the former families are ineligible for subsidized services or other benefits). Families with incomes that are below 50% of the poverty line find themselves in dramatically worse circumstances than do those with incomes that are just below the federal line. The contrast is not theoretical—in the United States in 1992, approximately one half of the poor children under 6 years of age lived in families with incomes below 50% of the federal poverty level (National Center for Children in Poverty, 1995). Despite these shortcomings, the federal poverty line is built into both research (the statistics gathered and reported by the Census Bureau) and practice (in eligibility criteria for many public programs and in formulas guiding state–federal financial partnerships), and it is used to organize the discussion in this chapter.

The percentage of people living in families with incomes below the federal poverty line is called the *poverty rate.* Figure 3.1 uses data from the Census Bureau to show how the poverty rates have changed between 1972 and 1992 for three groups: children under 6 years of age, children ages 6–17 years, and adults (including older adults). The graph shows that fully 26% of the youngest children in the United States were poor in 1992—a 20-year high that represents 6 million children. The graph also shows that the gap between the very young and other groups in their exposure to poverty has widened over the years. By 1992, children younger than 6 years of age were twice as likely as adults to live in poor households.

Which Children Are Poor?

Poverty is not distributed uniformly within the population of young children. Various characteristics of children, their families, and the communities in which they live make children more or less likely to experience poverty. Table 3.1 shows how the population of children under 6 years of

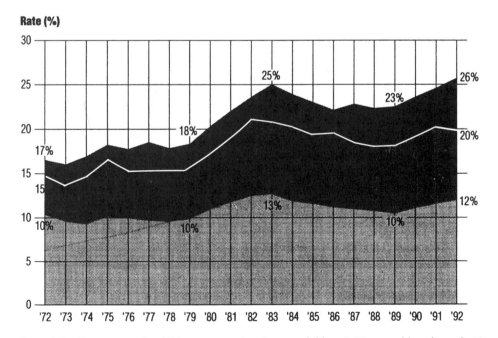

Rate (%)

Figure 3.1.   Poverty rates for children younger than 6 years, children 6–17 years old, and people 18 years and older between 1972 and 1992 (■ = children younger than 6 years; ■ = children 6–17 years old; ▨ = people 18 years and older). (From National Center for Children in Poverty. [1995]. *Young children in poverty: A statistical update.* New York: Author; reprinted by permission.)

Table 3.1. Likelihood of child poverty, determined by family characteristics

Family characteristic	Number of children (in millions)	Poverty rate for children (%)
Family residence		
Urban (central city)	7.1	35
Suburban	11.1	19
Rural	6.1	28
Race/ethnicity (of child)		
Caucasian	15.8	15
African American	3.8	54
Hispanic	3.0	44
Family type		
Single parent	5.6	58
Married couple	16.7	13
Parents' educational level (of best-educated parent)		
Less than high school	3.4	66
High school diploma	7.1	34
Postsecondary	12.7	10

Source: National Center for Children in Poverty (1995).

age is divided into categories on the basis of residence, race or ethnicity, family structure, and the educational level of the best-educated parent in the household. The total number of children in each category is shown, as is the percentage of those children who were poor in 1992—the poverty rate for that category.

The comparison of residences shows that poverty was most prevalent among children who lived in central cities (35% were poor), but almost one fifth of suburban children also were poor. African American or Hispanic children were especially likely to live in poverty (54% and 44%, respectively), compared with 15% of Caucasian children. Similar differences separated children in single-parent households (58% of whom were poor) from those living in families headed by married couples (13% of whom were poor). A less familiar but even more dramatic difference emerges when children's families are grouped by the education attained by the best-educated parent. Fully 66% of those children whose best-educated parent did not complete high school were poor, compared with only 10% of the children whose parents had some postsecondary education.

By listing these family characteristics individually, however, Table 3.1 obscures another fundamental fact about the distribution of poverty in the U.S. population—the piling up of poverty risks among certain groups. Because the various factors that predict poverty often overlap, risks accumulate disproportionately in some households and are absent from others. One study predicted the likelihood that a child in elementary school (between 7 and 12 years of age) would be poor from three simple pieces of information recorded at the time of birth: whether the mother had failed to finish high school, whether she was unmarried, and whether she was younger than 20 years of age (Zill & Nord, 1994). The results of this study are presented in Table 3.2. Only 8% of the children born facing none of the

Table 3.2. Accumulation of risk factors for poverty

Birth characteristics	Poverty 10 years later
Born with no risk factors	8%
Born with one risk factor	26%
Born with two risk factors	48%
Born with three risk factors	79%

Adapted from Zill & Nord (1994).

Note: Risk factors include mother had not completed high school at time of child's birth, mother was unmarried at time of child's birth, and mother was younger than age 20 years at time of child's birth.

three risk factors lived in poverty, compared with 26% of the children facing one risk and 48% of those facing two risks. A shocking 79% of the children confronted by all three risk factors lived in poverty. Furthermore, the accumulation of all three risks is not uncommon. The researchers estimate that 11% of children in the United States are born to mothers who lack high school degrees, are unmarried, and are teenagers at the time of the birth. These are the young women who become parents before they have secured the skills and supports needed by an independent head of household—the common image of the welfare mother.

Although the challenges facing unmarried, teenager-formed families are steep, theirs is only one of many profiles of poverty. Other poor children live with well-educated single mothers, who were married when they gave birth, but who are reeling from divorces that sharply cut the families' incomes and who lack experience working outside the home. One third of poor children live in two-parent families—some with parents who cannot find full-time work at good wages, others with immigrant parents who are closed out of most jobs and cannot apply for public assistance, and still others with at least one parent who has a disability or chronic health problems. For instance, this story is recounted in a report by Sherman:

> Sandy Wells told a *Time* magazine reporter in 1990 about how her family of five survives on her husband's $5.68 an hour making respirators in a local factory. Almost half his take-home pay is spent renting the trailer they live in and the lot at the trailer park. With the help of food stamps, they have meals. But they do without the extras—like the 50-cents-a-meeting fee they couldn't pay to keep her daughter in the Brownies, the $20 a month they could not afford for a telephone, and the $1.50 they can't afford for skate rental to send the children on class skating trips. (1994, p. 5)

It is clear that poverty comes to America's children in many different forms.

Most Poor Children Have Working Parents

The diversity of family situations in which poor children live contradicts the stereotypes that creep into media reports, policy debates, and the minds of taxpayers. For instance, many believe that the typical poor child is a member of an ethnic group whose mother is unmarried, lives in an inner-city neighborhood, and is fully dependent on public assistance payments. An objective look at the data shows a different picture, however. The majority of poor children (57% in 1992) live with a parent who works. Figure 3.2 shows that 18% of poor children under the age of 6 years in 1992

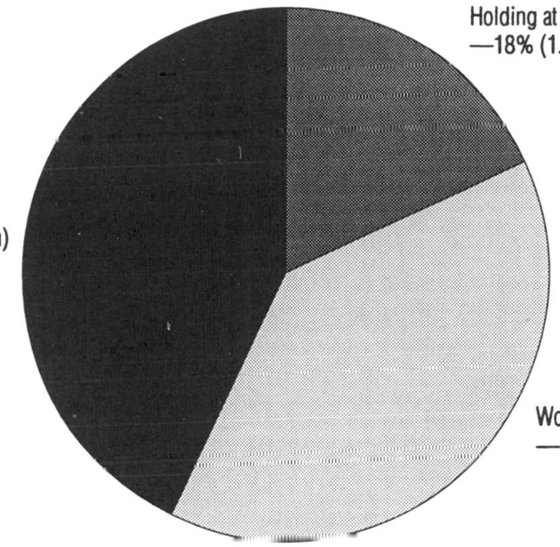

Figure 3.2. Percent distribution and number of poor children younger than 6 years based on parental employment status in 1992. (From National Center for Children in Poverty. [1995]. *Young Children in poverty: A statistical update.* New York: Author; reprinted by permission.) Numbers do not add up to 6.0 million people, because 0.3 million of these poor children did not live with parents.

lived in families in which the parent or parents worked the equivalent of full-time (one parent held a full-time job or each parent worked at least half time). Another 39% lived in families in which one parent worked part time or for part of the year. Only 43% had no parent involved in the labor force. Table 3.3 shows the proportions of poor families who rely on their earnings and on cash assistance for support. That work effort deserves more attention and support than it typically receives. When poor parents with a child under 6 years of age are employed, significant portions of their modest incomes are required to pay for child care, as Tracy Hardy explains in her essay (although a small number may receive the child care subsidies described later in this chapter).

The fact that parents in so many poor families work is surprising for two reasons. First, it contradicts the image of the poor family as a young mother watching television as she waits for her welfare check. Second, it challenges the expectation that a worker's wages should be enough to keep a family out of poverty. Since the 1970s, the average earnings of young workers, especially those with limited skills, have stagnated and then fallen. Duncan (1991) notes that, in 1970, a male worker, 20–24 years old, with a full-time, year-round job had median wages of $17.50 per hour, whereas,

Table 3.3.   Source of income in poor families with young children

Family income sources	Number of children (in millions)	Percentage of poor families
Earnings, no cash public assistance	2.3	38
Earnings and cash public assistance	1.2	20
Cash public assistance, no earnings	1.9	32
All other sources of income	0.6	10

Source: National Center for Children in Poverty (1995).

in 1986, after correcting for inflation, the same type of worker earned only $14.20 per hour. Strawn (1992) found that, in 1990, nearly one half (48%) of the women ages 18–34 years who worked full time did not earn enough to bring a family of four above the poverty line. Between the ages of 18 and 34 are the prime years for childbearing and child rearing and the time when many women are responsible for supporting families on their own (Strawn, 1992).

Hardships for young families also reflect the fact that, at the same time as wages for young workers were falling, public assistance payments were being cut (Bianchi, 1993). A more detailed discussion of trends in public assistance payments comes later in this chapter. Falling wage rates and benefit levels, combined with rising rates of divorce and extramarital childbearing, present poor mothers with young children with difficult choices. What balance can they strike between the effort to support their families through earnings and the security of relying on public assistance? One study by the Institute for Women's Policy Research found that 43% of mothers who receive welfare benefits spend substantial time at work, but

> their jobs pay an average of $4.29 per hour and their employers provide health insurance coverage less than one-third of the time they work....The most common jobs held by welfare mothers are maids, cashiers, nursing aides, child care workers, and waitresses. The top employers of welfare mothers are restaurants, nursing homes, private households, hotels and motels, department stores, and hospitals. (1995, p. 2)

One parent who worked full time, year round at $4.25 per hour (the 1992 minimum wage) would earn no more than $8,840. That income is more than $1,000 below the 1992 poverty line of $9,941 for a family with only a mother and one child, and it does not reflect any of the expenses or stresses associated with employment. Perhaps it should not be surprising that many mothers of young children, who lack skills that are valued or well compensated in the labor market, prefer to remain with their children during the earliest years of their childhoods. Meager public assistance paid for by taxpayers is their other alternative, but it is an option that will be more and more restricted if welfare reform plans like those under consideration in 1995 should take effect.

Children's Poverty Experiences

In the 1990s, there is far less optimism that poverty in the United States can be eliminated than there was a generation earlier. The key challenge in the 1990s seems to be to better understand how poverty affects children so as to develop policies that can at least diminish its force and soften its harsh impact. As noted earlier in this chapter, the study of poverty in the lives of children has been enriched by the availability of longitudinal studies that follow individual families over time, showing how their incomes fluctuate in relation to changes in family composition and employment and indicating how the well-being of various family members seems to be affected by spells of poverty versus economic comfort.

Persistence of Poverty

The pioneering longitudinal studies of family income revealed that some families are exposed only briefly to poverty, whereas others are trapped in long-lasting or persistent poverty. By using data from the Panel Study of Income Dynamics, which regularly surveys all of the members of an original, nationally representative sample of households drawn in 1968, Duncan (1984, 1991) tracked the household incomes of families with children over a 15-year period. Fully one third of those children, born in the late 1960s, lived below the poverty line during at least 1 of the 15 years. Exposure to long-term poverty, however, was much less common—only 1 in 20 children was poor during 10 or more of the 15 years studied.

The inequities in U.S. society are revealed in a closer analysis of the persistently poor. Whereas Caucasian children spent an average of approximately 1 year in poverty over the 15-year span, African American children spent an average of nearly 5 years in poverty. Moreover, these patterns have changed little from the 1960s to the 1980s. Duncan replicated his analysis with a second group of children born between 1977 and 1980, tracking their families' incomes over a 6-year period. The results of this study, presented in Table 3.4, show that Caucasian children were twice as likely as African American children to escape poverty altogether (74% versus 34% were never poor). In contrast, African American children were six times as likely as their Caucasian peers to be poor for most of the time (39% versus 6%). This finding highlights the unequal distribution of opportunity and pain to members of different ethnic and racial groups in the United States. This finding is made even more poignant by research indicating that it is the persistent experience of poverty that is especially harmful to children (Garrett, Ng'andu, & Ferron, 1994).

Effects of Poverty on Families and Children

It is not difficult to imagine how family poverty affects young children, although research that confirms what common sense suggests has only begun to accumulate (Klebanov, Brooks-Gunn, & Duncan, 1994). A report released by the Children's Defense Fund (Sherman, 1994) argues that money matters and describes succinctly the many pathways through which the lack of family income alters children's lives. For instance, money buys good food; it buys safe and decent shelter; it buys opportunities to learn; it reduces family stress and conflict; it buys a home in a safe neighborhood; it buys health care, health supplies, and safety devices,

Table 3.4. Persistence of poverty among young children

Groups of children	Duration of poverty[a] (in years)		
	0 (%)	1–4 (%)	5–6 (%)
Caucasian[b]	74	20	6
African American[c]	34	27	39

Adapted from Duncan, Brooks-Gunn, & Klebanov (1994).

[a]This study focused on the 6-year period between 1977 and 1983. Participating families had at least one child age 3 years or younger in 1980.

[b]This category includes all children not identified as African American; $n = 796$.

[c]$n = 568$.

such as smoke detectors and car seats; it buys healthy recreation; and it buys transportation (a family car), communication (telephone, television, and computers), and economic opportunities. All of these material resources and comforts directly shape the experiences children have in their homes and neighborhoods, and they influence the emotional tone of relationships among parents, children, and their peers.

The lack of good food, decent shelter, and access to health care all are seen in the higher exposure to serious health problems among children who are poor (Klerman, 1991). During infancy, these problems include higher rates of low birth weight and prematurity, vulnerability to neonatal respiratory distress, and increased risk of sudden infant death syndrome. Poor children are more likely to be hospitalized because of infectious diseases (in part because of lower immunization rates); to have chronic health problems, such as asthma, anemia, and lead poisoning; and to experience accidents and injuries (including abuse). Many of these health problems exert their influence throughout a child's life, limiting activity, hampering learning, and contributing to social and emotional difficulties.

In addition to these long-term consequences of poor health, poverty often limits a child's access to safe, varied environments that permit exploration and stimulate learning; and it takes away opportunities for warm, responsive interactions with adults. As a result, its effects show up in cognitive impairments. A study of eight hundred ninety-five 5-year-olds in eight sites, all of whom were born at low birth weights, found that poverty reduced children's IQ scores by 5 points, even when a host of other factors were held constant (Duncan et al., 1994). Moreover, children who were persistently poor evidenced IQ reductions twice as great as did those who experienced transitory poverty, confirming that the impacts of poverty on development accumulate and intensify the longer it lasts.

Another key way in which poverty harms children is by depleting the confidence and emotional strength on which parents draw when they try to cope with life and provide a warm, welcoming home for their children. The psychological effects of poverty on parents are especially severe in single-parent households. Single mothers are more prone than are married women to experience anxiety, depression, and health problems, and they bear the burdens of child rearing alone. Research has shown that poor single parents are likely to be more punitive, inconsistent, and unresponsive when they interact with their children than are other parents. A study by the Greater Minneapolis Day Care Association quotes a parent as follows:

> I go to bed...every night nervous or crying with frustration wondering if the money left will make it to my next paycheck. I'm finding myself short with the kids more and then stop myself and say, "Think. It's not fair. They are only kids...." So I give them hugs and say I'm sorry. (1995, p. 10)

Both harsh parenting and indifference can have devastating effects on children who, in turn, are more prone to psychological problems and behavioral disturbances (McLoyd & Wilson, 1991). Again, the accumulation of problems and pain brought on by chronic poverty intensifies the damage it does. The stress of poverty depletes the emotional reserves and undermines the coping abilities of parents whose best gift to their children might be a loving, reassuring home. Too often, poverty's effects show in the emotional climate in the home as surely as they show in the empty toybox and refrigerator.

Because the fates of parents and children are intertwined, it is essential to design policies with the needs of both groups in mind—a goal that is seldom reflected in practice, as the second half of this chapter shows. Too often, policies focus narrowly on achieving one or two goals: increasing employment among parents who receive welfare, for instance, or giving children from poor homes the preparation they need to succeed in school. Few policies aim at both objectives simultaneously. Although many factors contribute to the success or failure of any policy initiative, the analysis of two types of government investment in early childhood programs that follows shows how critical it is that policies designed for families with young children work for both children and parents.

U.S. POLICY RESPONSES TO CHILD POVERTY

In contrast with many Western European and other countries that create broad-based social insurance programs for families with children, the U.S. government tries to meet the needs of low-income children and their families through a range of focused, discrete, categorical programs (Kamerman & Kahn, 1987). Funding and support for early childhood services are provided through a jumble of federal programs that all target children of similar ages in similar types of families. In 1992, 31 federally funded early childhood programs supported education and child development for young children, and 27 provided referrals to child care, health, and social services that might benefit the entire family (U.S. General Accounting Office, 1994b). Rather than analyze more than 30 early childhood programs, this chapter examines two leading approaches used in the 1980s and 1990s to help poor young children—child care subsidies for families who depend on welfare and for working poor families and the expansion of the national Head Start program. One focuses on parents; the other focuses on children.

Although child care subsidy programs and Head Start have different goals and philosophies, they serve overlapping target populations and have both enjoyed popularity throughout the late 1980s and early 1990s. Significant federal funding was allocated to expand Head Start during both the Bush and the Clinton administrations, and federal child care subsidy programs were created by the Congress in 1990. Child care subsidies were developed in the context of welfare reform efforts to help poor parents achieve financial stability or self-sufficiency, whereas compensatory early childhood programs, such as Head Start, were created to benefit poor children directly by providing environments and experiences that would promote their development. Each of these approaches has strengths, and each has limitations. The contrast between them is especially instructive as an example of the importance of keeping both parents' and children's needs in mind when designing policies that affect entire families.

One Response to Poverty: The Federal Welfare System

Early childhood programs for poor children fit within a larger context of a range of federal policy responses to poverty. In general, such responses fit into two broad categories: 1) *social insurance programs* designed to prevent individuals from becoming poor, such as Social Security and unemployment insurance; and 2) *means-tested programs* intended to ensure that individuals in poverty will receive a basic level of goods and services, including AFDC, food stamps, Medicaid, and hundreds of targeted programs. The social insurance programs predominantly serve older Americans, whereas means-tested programs tend to serve families with children (Bianchi, 1993), and history has shown that the social insurance programs have been more effective at moving individuals out of poverty than have the means-tested programs. In 1992, federal programs reduced the poverty rate for individuals older than 65 years of age by 45%, but they reduced the poverty rate among families with children by less than 6% (Committee on Ways and Means, U.S. House of Representatives, 1994).

The major means-tested program that has attracted public attention is AFDC, most commonly known as welfare. Created in 1935, AFDC has been a controversial program and the focus of major reform efforts since the 1960s (Berrick, 1991; Congressional Research Service, 1995). The AFDC program provides cash assistance to poor children, and eligibility is determined by the state. Two thirds of AFDC recipients are children, most of whom live in single-parent families (Committee on Ways and Means, U.S. House of Representatives, 1994). Although only 60% of poor children receive AFDC at any one point in time (Strawn, 1992), a much larger number of children benefit from AFDC at some point in their lives. One estimate is that 22% of U.S. children born in the early 1970s received welfare for at least 1 year before reaching their 15th birthday (Zill, Moore, Smith, Stief, & Coiro, 1991).

Much of the attention focused on AFDC is rooted in dissatisfaction with a program that fulfills few of the policy objectives that it was designed to achieve. At the most basic level, AFDC is ineffective at providing families with sufficient income to bring them close to the federal poverty level. In 1993, the monetary value of AFDC and food stamps for a family of three in a median state was only 69% of the federal poverty level, or $5,508 per year. Not many people can manage a household on that amount of money. Moreover AFDC benefit levels vary widely among the states. The 1994 payment for a family of three was $164 in Alabama and $923 in Alaska. Those differences far exceed the differences between the costs of living in those states.

Another source of discontent with the AFDC program concerns the sharp distinction it draws between those who are eligible for benefits and those who are ineligible. Given low income cutoffs and restrictive rules, some 40% of children living below the poverty line are not eligible for AFDC. As a result, the program creates a troubling dichotomy between families receiving AFDC benefits and other poor families, who do not receive cash assistance or access to in-kind benefits. A Congressional Research Service report (1995) notes that "Indignation has risen about long-term support of able-bodied welfare mothers, especially since many blue-collar families, whose taxes help finance AFDC, are worried about job security and medical bills and a decline in real wages" (p. 2). The degree to which AFDC recipients actually participate in the labor force (and receive reduced benefits) is seldom recognized. In 1993, 38% of AFDC recipients reported some employment during the year (U.S. General Accounting Office, 1995c). Nonetheless, many policy makers believe that the benefits offered to the nonworking by the AFDC program are unfair to the working poor, and they argue that the sharp distinctions between the support provided by AFDC and the harsh conditions faced by other poor families discourage recipients from leaving the program, through marriage or through work.

Concerns about the costs, inequities, and long-term consequences of the AFDC program have led to a plethora of welfare reform proposals at the state and federal levels, which are designed to move parents from dependence on AFDC and into the work force. In 1988, a new federal approach to welfare policy was adopted in PL 100-485, the Family Support Act. The legislation built on state welfare-to-work experiments (Gueron & Pauley, 1991) to design the Job Opportunity and Basic Skills (JOBS) program to transform welfare offices from a source of monthly checks to a resource network providing parents with training to enable them to enter the work force. To receive federal funding, states were required to enroll increasing percentages of adult able-bodied AFDC recipients into education and training programs, addressing the underlying problems that prevent many poor parents from finding and keeping jobs that could support their families.

Welfare-Related Child Care Subsidies

Children—who are present in all AFDC families—enter into the policy debate about welfare reform because, when they are young, their presence can be a barrier to parents' employment. Parents with young children need child care if they are to work. PL 100-485, therefore, also guarantees child care subsidies that cover the costs of child care to families receiving AFDC, provided that the subsidies are needed for the parents to work or participate in a state-approved education or training program. To help parents who become employed keep their jobs during the difficult transition off welfare, the legislation also created the Transitional Child Care Program, which guarantees 1 year of additional child care subsidies to parents who leave welfare for work.

Recognizing that assistance in paying for child care is also needed by working parents with limited incomes, in 1990 Congress established two additional child care programs: the Child Care and Development Block Grant and the At-Risk Child Care Program. These programs provide child care subsidies primarily to the working poor, not to AFDC families. Together with the welfare-related child care funds, these programs have enabled significant numbers of low-income parents to work or, in the case of JOBS participants, to enroll in education and training. Estimates from the Administration for Children, Youth, and Families indicate that, in 1991, nearly 1.4 million children benefited from the child care payments provided by the federal subsidy programs (U.S. General Accounting Office, 1995b).

Nonetheless, two significant weaknesses limit the effectiveness of the federal subsidy programs in meeting even the adult-oriented goal that justified their creation—helping families become and remain employed. First, the categorical nature of the subsidy programs does not match the reality of families' lives (U.S. General Accounting Office, 1994a). The five major federal subsidy programs target discrete groups of families: AFDC recipients in education and training programs (JOBS Child Care), AFDC recipients who have begun working (AFDC Child Care Disregard), the working poor who have recently left AFDC (Transitional Child Care), the working poor who do not receive AFDC but are in danger of doing so if they do not receive child care assistance (At-Risk Child Care), and the working poor in general (Child Care and Development Block Grant). Despite the logic in these gradations, families make the transition from dependency to self-sufficiency only gradually and with considerable backsliding (Meyers, 1993; Siegel & Loman, 1991). Families who have newly entered the labor force often move among employment, unemployment, and welfare dependence a number of times before leaving the welfare system for good. Each move may change the family's child care eligibility status, often disrupting arrangements that were created painstakingly and that are emotionally important to the child.

Although child care subsidies have made a significant difference in the ability of poor parents to work, many who are eligible still do not receive needed assistance. Although solid information is lacking, state program administrators report that they can serve only a small proportion of those who are eligible—particularly among the working poor. Waiting lists for subsidies stretch to include thousands of names or are abandoned altogether (U.S. General Accounting Office, 1994a). Few options exist for parents who do not receive subsidies but who cannot afford to pay for child care. A national study showed that low-income families who pay for child care spend approximately 23% of their incomes to cover that one expense (Hofferth, Brayfield, Deich, & Holcomb, 1991). Such a financial burden causes parents to make painful choices concerning their work and family lives. In one survey of families on the child care waiting list in Minneapolis, Minnesota, 71% of parents reported that they had fallen into significant debt, and 24% had become dependent on AFDC. In addition, 33% of the parents had increased work hours to earn more to cover child care costs, 16% had reduced work hours to reduce child care expenses, and 14% had quit working because of child care problems (Greater Minneapolis Day Care Association, 1995). Decisions such as these can negate all of the gains the family had achieved when the parent or parents secured employment in the first place.

Child Care Subsidies: At What Price to Children?

Child care subsidy programs are only payment mechanisms, but they can influence the quality of care that children in low-income families receive, which, otherwise, often is so poor that it jeopardizes children's development. Studies of child care centers and family child care homes indicate that only 1 in 10 children of all income levels receives high-quality care, 6 in 10 receive care that is adequate or custodial, and 3 in 10 receive care that may be harmful (Galinsky, Howes, Kontos, & Shinn, 1994; Phillips, Voran, Kisker, Howes, & Whitebook, 1994). Excellent child care exists in the United States, but often it is expensive. Too seldom do the poor children with the greatest needs receive the best child care.

The payment rates built into subsidy systems are the largest problem for many families. The government officials who structure subsidy programs have finite resources, and they are forced to make trade-offs between the number of children to serve and the level of funding allocated for each child. Because the principal goal of welfare-related child care programs is to enable parents to work, states are pressured to set child care payment rates at a low level to allow the maximum number of parents to purchase care of adequate quality. It is difficult politically for officials to set high payment rates that would cover the costs of high-quality care but would assist fewer families.

Child care subsidy systems also can undermine the continuity of care that is so important to children. The subsidies that are linked directly to the JOBS program are provided only for care that is reasonably related to the hours in which the parent participates in work or training. The training provided in JOBS programs typically comes in a series of part-time components, each lasting from 3 weeks to several months. In most states, no child care subsidies are available to parents during the breaks between training components. Because parents who depend on the welfare system seldom can afford to pay for child care themselves, their children are moved in and out of child care arrangements according to the parents' schedules, without regard for the children's need for stable, continuous relationships with caregivers.

These problems with subsidy programs are not the only factors that conspire to leave poor children in child care that is of uncertain quality. Many low-income mothers lack educational credentials and are consigned to pink-collar jobs in service industries in which wages are low, benefits are lacking, and work hours often extend beyond the traditional workday, when formal child care programs are open. One study of working mothers who had been on welfare found that close to 30% of those with preschool-age children needed child care before 6 A.M., after 7 P.M., or on weekends (Sonenstein & Wolf, 1991). Moreover, many of these families live in poor, deteriorated neighborhoods that are underserved by public transportation and that lack high-quality child care facilities. Low-income parents are aware that their children often do not receive the quality of care they deserve and need; when interviewed, they complain of unsupervised playgrounds, broken toys, too much television viewing, and caregivers who spend little time with the children (Porter, 1991; Zinnser, 1991). The values and aspirations of low-income parents do not differ from those of more advantaged parents, but they face many more obstacles in attempting to find satisfactory child care.

As important as child care subsidies have been to families, they are not designed or funded in a manner that supports parents' efforts to give their children the best opportunity to thrive and develop. One study by Porter quotes a mother who received welfare and who had high hopes for her children's care: "I want them to get into an environment now where they can excel, where they can get the most social skills and all the things it takes to be a functioning human being, to get a better start" (1991, p. 13). To many low-income parents and professionals, that sentence describes a child-oriented, developmental program like Head Start, not a low-cost child care arrangement; but, even Head Start poses challenges to the poor families and children for whom it is designed.

A Second Response to Child Poverty: The Expansion of Head Start

Head Start is an example of a radically different approach to providing services to the poor—the compensatory education approach that focuses on children. The most popular of the War on Poverty programs, Head Start is a part-day, part-year preschool program designed to support child development. Head Start was created in the 1960s, when many believed that by providing enriched, stimulating environments, early interventions could greatly improve developmental outcomes for poor children. As Dr. Edward Zigler (Zigler & Styfco), one of the program's founders, recalls

> The nation had declared a War on Poverty, fully expecting to conquer this enemy by arming its victims with education and self-help opportunities. Although most antipoverty programs developed under the Equal Opportunity Act of 1964 targeted poor adults, Head Start was designed to enhance school readiness among their children....The planning document embraced a "whole child" philosophy that called for comprehensive programming: Head Start's goals would be to improve physical health, enhance "mental processes" (particularly conceptual and verbal skills), and foster social and emotional development, self-confidence, relationships with family and others, social responsibility, and a sense of dignity and self-worth for both the child and the family. (1994a, pp. 127–128)

Head Start programs enroll preschool children whose families live below the federal poverty line (although children with special needs whose families have higher incomes can comprise 10% of each program's enrollment), and they offer comprehensive services in the areas of education, health and nutrition, social services, and parent involvement. Because the Head Start founders viewed parents as pivotal partners in efforts to promote child development, parents have always played a major role in Head Start activities, serving as volunteers in the classroom and as decision makers on Parent Policy Councils.

The enthusiastic and vocal support that parents and community leaders have shown for Head Start throughout its 30-year history contributed significantly to the program's survival when many other War on Poverty programs were discontinued. This grass roots support was strengthened by research findings showing that poor children who participated in preschool programs such as Head Start went on to greater success in school and in life (Zigler & Styfco, 1994b). Research and public support have combined to translate into dramatic funding increases designed to make Head Start services available to all eligible children. From 1989 to 1994, federal investments in Head Start rose from $1.2 billion to $3.3 billion, and enrollment rose from 450,970 children to 740,300 children (U.S. General Accounting Office, 1995b). Despite this increase in funding, only 17% of eligible 3-year-olds and 41% of eligible 4-year-olds were served in 1993.

Grants to operate Head Start programs are awarded directly to approximately 1,400 local agencies that deliver the program's comprehensive services to eligible children in accordance with detailed federal performance standards. The federal guidelines, oversight, and funding levels work together to support the quality of Head Start services. Although there is room for improvement, many believe that the quality of Head Start programs compares favorably with that of community child care centers (Chafel, 1992). Quality comes at a cost, however. In 1993, it cost $3,758 for the average child to attend Head Start's part-day 9-month program (U.S. General Accounting Office, 1995c). A national survey conducted in 1990 estimated the average cost of full-day, full-year center-based child care to be just over $3,000 per child per year (Kisker, Hofferth, & Phillips, 1991). Supporters of Head Start justify the program's cost per child by arguing that compensatory education is an important investment in human development that eventually can prevent poverty. Indeed, state-funded prekindergarten programs typically invest significantly more per child than do Head Start programs. In contrast, child care often is viewed by policy makers as nothing more than "a convenience for employed welfare mothers" (Phillips, 1991, p. 161).

Head Start: At What Expense to Parents?

The Head Start program was designed when few mothers of young children were in the labor force, particularly the single mothers living in poverty whose children made up one half the Head Start population by 1990. It made sense in the late 1960s to offer poor children a part-day preschool program, because the presumption was that a parent was home who could easily escort the child to and from the center (most Head Start programs are center based). Even in the 1990s, only about one fourth of participating children attend Head Start for 6 hours per day, 5 days a week. A growing proportion of the families eligible for Head Start, however, have full-time commitments to work or attend school. In 1988, one study showed that 32% of Head Start parents worked full time, and another 19% worked part time or attended school (Hofferth, 1994). If welfare reform efforts succeed, most parents with young children eventually will work outside the home and will find using part-day programs difficult.

Recognizing that the challenge of finding ways to serve employed parents is important, Head Start leaders have initiated demonstration programs to identify promising strategies. Local programs have been urged to arrange full-day care for participating children and to collaborate with other community agencies to link parents to educational and employment opportunities. However, change does not come easily. As one Head Start researcher noted

> The preponderance of part-day or double-sessions services and the lack of full-day child care are universally cited as the number one barrier to Head Start involvement in family-support programs, including JOBS and substance abuse. Some Head Start programs have discovered imaginative ways to overcome those barriers; most have not and will need help. (Collins, 1993, p. 72)

In the interim, the burden of creativity belongs to the parents. Low-income, employed parents whose children attend Head Start must often piece together several child care arrangements to ensure that their preschoolers are cared for before 9 A.M. and after noon. Others may pass up the opportunity to enroll their children in Head Start, because they cannot find wrap-around care or because managing the patchwork arrangements becomes too stressful. Even if Head Start and other preschool programs provide an excellent experience to children during program hours, they may provoke increased stress in poor families, simply because they are designed around the needs of children without regard to the concerns of the children's parents.

FUTURE DIRECTIONS

Both of the policy approaches described here—welfare reform with its associated child care subsidies and the expansion of the Head Start program—were designed to meet critical needs of poor children. On the one hand, children need parents who can work to support them; on the other hand, no one would argue with the fact that children also need stimulating environments that encourage their development and give them access to comprehensive services. Each of the two programs discussed here helps a significant number of children and families, yet frustrates others. Child care subsidies do not ensure that children will experience developmentally appropriate care, and part-day programs, such as Head Start, are logistical nightmares for parents who are trying to hold jobs. Experience with these approaches confirms that it does not work to craft policies that address only one of a child's three critical needs: to live in a family with sufficient income, to have time with nurturing parents, and to develop in a safe, stimulating environment.

The research studies cited earlier in this chapter make it clear that poverty affects children both directly, by placing them in unsafe, chaotic, hostile environments, and indirectly, by bringing out the worst in parents who struggle to manage in often impossible circumstances. Even if child care subsidies enable parents to work, when the only care that is feasible is offered by the overburdened woman who lives in the same deteriorated public housing project as the family, the child will continue to suffer from the limitations of that environment. However, if a child's mother enrolls him or her in a Head Start program, but then either cuts back on her work hours or anxiously relies on a teenager who has dropped out of school to take the preschooler from Head Start to the afternoon babysitter, things are scarcely any better. If policies focusing on poor children and their families are to be truly helpful, they must be designed to work for both the children and their parents.

The extended analysis of these two policy initiatives, child care subsidies linked to welfare reform and Head Start expansion, also demonstrates the inherent weakness of early childhood policy as a response to child poverty. Although both child care subsidies and Head Start mitigate some of the effects of poverty, neither comes close to solving the problem. Enabling families to work in low-wage jobs may keep those families off welfare, but only a few will escape poverty that way. Broader policies are needed to increase family income, including increases in the minimum wage and further expansions of refundable tax credits for families with children. Early childhood policy initiatives also fail to help parents deal with the stresses inherent in entry-level jobs, especially in service industries. One parent interviewed about her child care experience described her goals as follows:

I am working and I want so much to be a normal person as far as my work goes because my fiance comes to my house after he gets off of work and he watches the kids while I go work....I want to work when it is daylight out and come home at a decent hour, cook supper for my kids, eat supper, do baths and bedtime and the whole bit. (Siegel & Loman, 1991, p. 13)

Until policy makers begin to put children's needs squarely in the midst of families' multiple needs, it will be difficult to make this parent's dream a reality. Poverty is a powerful and multifaceted force shaping the lives of families; it is essential that both research and policy responses focused on poor children and families be just as powerful and multifaceted.

REFERENCES

Berrick, J.D. (1991). Welfare and child care: The intricacies of competing social values. *Social Work, 36*(4), 345–351.

Bianchi, S.M. (1993). Children of poverty: Why are they poor? In J.A. Chafel (Ed.), *Child poverty and public policy* (pp. 91–125). Washington, DC: The Urban Institute Press.

Campbell, F.A., & Ramey, C.T. (1994). Effects of early intervention on intelligence and academic achievement: A follow-up study of children from low-income families. *Child Development, 65*, 684–698.

Chafel, J.A. (1992). Head Start: Making "quality" a national priority. *Child and Youth Care Forum, 21*(3), 147–163.

Chafel, J.A. (Ed.). (1993). *Child poverty and public policy.* Washington, DC: The Urban Institute Press.

Chase-Lansdale, P.L., Brooks-Gunn, J., Mott, F.L., & Phillips, D.A. (1991). Children of the NLSY: A unique research opportunity. *Developmental Psychology, 27*, 918–931.

Collins, R.C. (1993). Head Start: Steps toward a two-generation program strategy. *Young Children, 48*, 25–73.

Committee on Ways and Means, U.S. House of Representatives. (1994). *Overview of entitlement programs: 1994 green book.* Washington, DC: U.S. Government Printing Office.

Congressional Research Service. (1995). *AFDC reform: Why again?* Washington, DC: Author. (CRS Report for Congress No. 95-3EPW)

Duncan, G.J. (1984). *Years of poverty, years of plenty: The changing economic fortunes of American workers and families.* Ann Arbor: University of Michigan, Survey Research Center.

Duncan, G.J. (1991). The economic environment of childhood. In A.C. Huston (Ed.), *Children in poverty: Child development and public policy* (pp. 23–50). New York: Cambridge University Press.

Duncan, G.J., Brooks-Gunn, J., & Klebanov, P.K. (1994). Economic deprivation and early childhood development. *Child Development, 65*, 296–318.

Family Support Act of 1988, PL 100-485. (October 13, 1988). Title 42, U.S.C. 1305 et seq: *U.S. Statutes at Large, 92*, 2292–2296.

Galinksy, E., Howes, C., Kontos, S., & Shinn, M. (1994). *The study of children in family child care and relative care.* New York: Families and Work Institute.

Garrett, P., Ng'andu, N., & Ferron, J. (1994). Poverty experiences of young children and the quality of their home environments. *Child Development, 65*, 331–345.

Greater Minneapolis Day Care Association. (1995). *Valuing families: The high cost of waiting for child care sliding fee assistance.* Minneapolis, MN: Author.

Gueron, J., & Pauley, E. (1991). *From welfare to work.* New York: Russell Sage Foundation.

Hernandez, D.J. (1993). *America's children: Resources from family, government, and the economy.* New York: Russell Sage Foundation.

Hofferth, S.L. (1994). Who enrolls in Head Start? A demographic analysis of Head Start–eligible children. *Early Childhood Research Quarterly, 9*, 243–268.

Hofferth, S.L., Brayfield, A., Deich, S., & Holcomb, P. (1991). *National Child Care Survey, 1990.* Washington, DC: The Urban Institute Press.

Huston, A.C. (Ed.). (1991). *Children in poverty: Child development and public policy.* New York: Cambridge University Press.

Huston, A.C., McLoyd, V.C., & Garcia Coll, C. (1994). Children and poverty: Issues in contemporary research. *Child Development, 65,* 275–282.

Institute for Women's Policy Research. (1995). *Research-in-briefs: Few welfare moms fit the stereotypes.* Washington, DC: Author.

Kamerman, S.B., & Kahn, A.J. (1987). *Child care: Facing the hard choices.* Dover, MA: Auburn House.

Kisker, E.E., Hofferth, S.A., & Phillips, D.A. (1991). *A profile of child care settings: Early education and care in 1990* (Vol. 1). Princeton, NJ: Mathematica Policy Research.

Klebanov, P.K., Brooks-Gunn, J., & Duncan, G.J. (1994). Does neighborhood and family poverty affect mothers' parenting, mental health, and social support? *Journal of Marriage and the Family, 56*(2), 441–455.

Klerman, L.V. (1991). *Alive and well? A research and policy review of health programs for poor young children.* New York: National Center for Children in Poverty.

Larner, M., Halpern, R., & Harkavy, O. (1992). *Fair start for children: Lessons learned from seven demonstration projects.* New Haven, CT: Yale University Press.

McLoyd, V.C., & Wilson, L. (1991). The strain of living poor: Parenting, social support, and child mental health. In A. Huston (Ed.), *Children in poverty: Child development and public policy* (pp. 105–135). New York: Cambridge University Press.

Meyers, M.K. (1993). Child care in JOBS employment and training programs: What difference does quality make? *Journal of Marriage and the Family, 55,* 767–783.

Musick, J.S. (1993). Profiles of children and families in poverty. In J.S. Chafel (Ed.), *Child poverty and public policy* (pp. 7–54). Washington, DC: The Urban Institute Press.

National Center for Children in Poverty. (1990). *Five million children: A statistical profile of our poorest young citizens.* New York: Author.

National Center for Children in Poverty. (1995). *Young children in poverty: A statistical update.* New York: Author.

Phillips, D.A. (1991). With a little help: Children in poverty and child care. In A. Huston (Ed.), *Children in poverty: Child development and public policy* (pp. 158–189). New York: Cambridge University Press.

Phillips, D.A., Voran, M., Kisker, E., Howes, C., & Whitebook, M. (1994). Child care for children in poverty: Opportunity or inequity? *Child Development, 65,* 472–492.

Porter, T. (1991). *Just like any parent: The child care choices of welfare mothers in New Jersey.* New York: Bank Street College of Education.

Powell, D.R. (1994). Head start and research: Notes on a special issue. *Early Childhood Research Quarterly, 9,* 241–242.

Sherman, A. (1994). *Wasting America's future: The Children's Defense Fund report on the costs of child poverty.* Washington, DC: Children's Defense Fund.

Siegel, G.L., & Loman, L.A. (1991). *Child care and AFDC recipients in Illinois.* St. Louis: Institute of Applied Research.

Sonenstein, F., & Wolf, D. (1991). Satisfaction with child care: Perspectives of welfare mothers. *Journal of Social Issues, 47*(1), 15–31.

Strawn, J. (1992). The states and the poor: Child poverty rises as the safety net shrinks. *Social Policy Report, VI*(3), 1–19.

U.S. General Accounting Office. (1994a). *Child care: Working poor and welfare recipients face service gaps* (GAO/HEHS-94-87). Washington, DC: U.S. Government Printing Office.

U.S. General Accounting Office. (1994b). *Early childhood programs: Multiple programs and overlapping target groups* (GAO/HEHS-94-4FS). Washington, DC: U.S. Government Printing Office.

U.S. General Accounting Office. (1994c). *Infants and toddlers: Dramatic increases in numbers living in poverty* (GAO/HEHS-94-74). Washington, DC: U.S. Government Printing Office.

U.S. General Accounting Office. (1995a). *Early childhood centers: Services to prepare children for school often limited* (GAO/HEHS 95-21). Washington, DC: U.S. Government Printing Office.

U.S. General Accounting Office. (1995b). *Early childhood programs: Local perspectives on barriers to providing Head Start services* (GAO/HEHS-95-8). Washington, DC: U.S. Government Printing Office.

U.S. General Accounting Office. (1995c). *Low-income families: Comparison of incomes of AFDC and working poor families* (GAO/HEHS-95-63). Washington, DC: U.S. Government Printing Office.

Zigler, E., & Styfco, S.J. (1994a). Head Start: Criticisms in a constructive context. *American Psychologist, 49*(2), 127–132.

Zigler, E., & Styfco, S.J. (1994b). Is the Perry Preschool better than Head Start? Yes and no. *Early Childhood Research Quarterly, 9,* 269–288.

Zill, N., Moore, K.A., Smith, E.W., Stief, T., & Coiro, M.J. (1991). *The life circumstances and development of children in welfare families: A profile based on national survey data.* Washington, DC: Child Trends, Inc.

Zill, N,, & Nord, C W. (1994). *Running in place: How American families are faring in a changing economy and an individualistic society.* Washington, DC: Child Trends, Inc.

Zinnser, C. (1991). *Raised in East Urban: Child care changes in a working class community.* New York: Teachers College Press.

Rita's Story

Rita A. Wilder

One of the experiences that I remember vividly from my early childhood is that I was napping comfortably, nice and snug and warm in an unfamiliar room in a stranger's house. I was no more than 4 or 5 years old at the time. I awoke to see light filtering through the doorway from the hall, and then I saw a man coming into the room. I noticed that he was wearing a dark green or blue uniform with a nametag embroidered in red and white. He started talking to me, but the words he was saying did not make any sense, and I felt danger of some sort. I did not know what this was all about; all I knew was that my heart beat faster and I knew something was wrong, something inside of me felt scared and violated. He started fondling me where little girls should not be touched. I think it was at that moment that I shut down emotionally. Something died inside me that night. Now, 26 years later, I realize that it was my innocence that died.

As I sit here remembering what it was like to be a child in my world, there is great sadness in my heart. One morning when I was 6 years old, I was having breakfast with my older foster brother John. I was eating toast, and the crumbs were getting all over the table. My foster mother came over and started yelling at me that I was a pig because I was making a mess. She asked why I could not be neat like John, who was, I think, a teenager at the time. To punish me, she put some slices of bread in the toaster and toasted them very dark. When she pulled them out of the toaster, they were steaming. She stuffed them in my mouth until I was gagging and choking because she could not fit any more in there. I can still remember the pain and the total humiliation as she made me eat the remaining crumbs off the floor. I felt like an animal. To this day, hot food is a trigger for me, a trigger for pain, shame, rage, and fear.

I hated that foster home and the one after that, and I missed my mother, father, and two sisters very much. It seemed as though people kept coming and going in my life, and I had no control over whether I would see them again. I tried so hard to be good. Even in school, I tried, but I would start daydreaming instead of listening to the teacher, and, when she called on me, I could not answer her question. I thought I was stupid.

Reality has always been very difficult for me to handle. I have lived in a fantasyland for most of my life. When I felt pain, I would run in the opposite direction or zone out in my head. I would do silly things like sing a song to myself or daydream. When those simple things no longer worked to keep the pain at bay, I used alcohol and, finally, heroin to cope with reality.

When my daughter Tiffany was 6 months old, I went out for a drink with my friends, and Tiffany's father took her for a car ride without her carseat. She was hurt when the car crashed into another vehicle. When we arrived at the emergency room, the police and the Department of Social Services were notified. The investigation that started with that incident took more than 6 years to resolve. During that time, I was in and out of long- and short-term rehabilitation centers for my alcoholism; in fact, I was in and out of seven detox facilities in one 3½-month period. I was doing really well at faking that everything was all right with me on the outside. I even fooled myself for a while, until I had to make a very hard decision

---

Rita A. Wilder is a pseudonym.

about open adoption for my daughter. Signing the agreement and surrendering all custody rights to Tiffany was the hardest thing I had ever done in my life, until now, as I struggle to get sober and recover from my addiction and posttraumatic stress disorder.

The day before I signed the adoption agreement, the opportunity to try the best drug in the world—heroin—came knocking on my door, and I did not hesitate, for the pain was just more than I could handle. Although I knew I had made the best decision for Tiffany, I still felt like a failure. I was doing what my own mother had done; I was giving up my child. That guilt started me on the path to heroin addiction, and the rage that followed kept me using, sustaining my addictive behavior through periods of homelessness, helplessness, a serious overdose, and despair.

Today, 5 years later, I have a new baby. I can spend time with Tiffany, and I have a healthy, trusting relationship with a man named Charlie. I am still struggling with my disease, however. I was on methadone maintenance during my pregnancy and have gradually weaned myself off of methadone. I relapsed recently, however, and had to go back to detox. The harder I work on my recovery, however, the longer I can stay in recovery. These past 30 days of sobriety have been the hardest for me, but they have also been the most fulfilling and rewarding. I am taking good care of my baby and myself; I have family and friends to help me on my journey; I have learned to trust people and to begin to trust myself. I am learning to label my feelings and to let them out. I know what I need to do. With the help of a higher power, whom I choose to call God, I can fulfill my own destiny.

Although most of my childhood was unhappy, at some point, I was placed for a short time in a home run by nuns. The nuns treated me with tender, loving care, the first I had ever known. I learned from them and from the nurses in the pediatric hospital that I was lovable. When I was in a group home for older children, student volunteers would come and take us on little trips. I thought I was the luckiest child alive—to go into the square and get an ice cream cone or a muffin with those students. It does not take a lot to make a child feel happy and loved. I learned how to treat my children from those brief encounters with caring people. Although they could not fix or change my life, they showed me a different way of relating to people. I felt what it was like to be treated with respect and affection, and now I can give that to my children.

4

THE IMPACT OF MATERNAL SUBSTANCE ABUSE ON YOUNG CHILDREN

Myths and Realities

Margot Kaplan-Sanoff

Of all the myths and beliefs surrounding the abuse of alcohol and other drugs by women of child-bearing age, perhaps the most pernicious one assumes that if a pregnant woman really loved and wanted her child, she would stop her substance abuse during her pregnancy to protect her child. Indeed, the question most frequently asked by providers is "How could she continue to use when she knew what could happen to her baby?" Questions like this, the "how could she" questions, do little to further our understanding of families and the decisions they make for themselves and their children. Instead, these questions infuse the mother–provider relationship with feelings of anger, frustration, mistrust, and guilt. This chapter examines the many myths and the realities surrounding substance abuse by parents, particularly mothers, and the effects that their addiction can have on their young children. Although this chapter focuses primarily on maternal alcohol and other drug abuse, it should be noted that paternal substance abuse also affects families.

As Rita A. Wilder's story describes so poignantly, in the lives of many women with drug addictions, there exist intricate cycles of childhood trauma and family substance abuse that are complex and interwoven. For many women who abuse substances, their own histories of abusing alcohol and/or other drugs started with a traumatic event(s)—witnessing the continual beating of their mothers; their own childhood physical and/or sexual abuse; or loss of a parent through divorce, murder, incarceration, or foster placement. In an attempt to avoid the painful affect that these incidents arouse, they turn to alcohol and other drugs to numb their feelings and dull their memories. By recognizing this cycle of trauma and addiction, providers can begin to understand many of the puzzling behaviors that children and families affected by substance abuse problems may exhibit in their interactions with the health, education, and social services systems.

THE TRAUMA CYCLE

Research on alcohol abuse suggests that alcoholism runs in families. Sons of fathers who abuse alcohol are four times more likely to abuse alcohol themselves; daughters of mothers who abuse alcohol are three times more likely to abuse alcohol and are also more likely to marry men who abuse alcohol. A biological predisposition to addiction seems to exist in families in which a parent has an alcohol abuse problem. Having a parent who abuses alcohol increases the risk not only for addiction, but also for behavior problems in the children. The Children of Alcoholics Foundation reports that children of alcohol abusers are more likely to report stomachaches, headaches, insomnia, and eating disorders. They also experience more frequent psychosomatic illnesses, depression, and anxiety. Sons of fathers who abuse alcohol had 60% more injuries than and were five times more likely to report emotional problems to their health care providers than sons from families without alcohol abuse problems; daughters of mothers who abuse alcohol were hospitalized three and one half times more often and had three times as many mental health counseling sessions as daughters from families without alcohol abuse problems. Adolescent children of parents who abuse alcohol are more likely to be involved in fights in school and to be referred for reading difficulties or other academic problems.

The National Committee for the Prevention of Child Abuse reports that as many as 80% of all cases of child abuse involve drinking before, during, or after the incident (William Gladden Foundation, 1989). The National Clearinghouse on Domestic Violence states that alcohol use is a factor in approximately one half of all reported cases of domestic violence (William Gladden Foundation, 1989). This association between parental substance abuse and physical maltreatment of children is particularly true in the abuse of very young children. In 1990, almost 90% of those children who died from abuse or neglect were younger than 5 years of age; 53% were younger than 1 year of age (Daro & McCurdy, 1991).

When children are abused physically or sexually or witness domestic violence, they feel powerless and have low self-esteem; they often experience failures in school and with friends. To cope with these painful feelings, many children turn to drugs and alcohol. Retrospective research provides additional insight into the cyclical nature of substance abuse and family violence. In response to a routine inquiry about childhood sexual abuse among women who were treated in an inpatient setting for substance abuse, 75% of the women reported having been sexually abused. For teenage girls in the same setting, the reported rate was 71%–90% (Rohsenow, Corbett, & Devine, 1988). In another study sample of 118 women across the United States who were in treatment for drug abuse, 44% were incest victims. The abuse of drugs and alcohol to mediate the pain of early childhood trauma almost always is the significant contributing factor to addiction for women (Brooks, Zuckerman, Bamforth, Cole, & Kaplan-Sanoff, 1994).

Children of mothers who abuse substances are, therefore, at double risk; they have a biological predisposition for addiction themselves, and they face increased danger of experiencing physical and/or sexual abuse as young children. This opens the door for their own substance abuse as a way of dealing with the trauma of the early maltreatment. The vicious cycle of parental substance abuse and increased risk for physical and/or sexual abuse creates generational patterns of addiction and maltreatment in families.

The characteristics of families who experience addiction and family violence are strikingly similar. Children of parents who are addicted to substances are more likely to become addicted; parents who were abused as youngsters are more likely to abuse their own children. For the many children living with the double risk of parental addiction and family violence, the risks to child development and behavior are greatest (Garbarino & Sherman, 1981). To break the cycle of maltreatment and addiction, intervention must be based on a clear understanding of addiction and its impact on parenting and child development, rather than on the myths perpetuated by the popular press about the hopelessness of the problem. Answers to the "how could she" questions discussed below come from an understanding of addiction and the addicted family system and knowledge of the impact of previous traumatic life events experienced by the woman. Of equal importance is understanding the process of recovery

Addiction: *How could she continue to abuse alcohol or other drugs when she knew she was pregnant?*

"When I found out I was 3 months pregnant I wanted to stop using, but I was afraid to tell anyone and ask for help. What if they took my baby away when she was born?"

The Joint Committee of the National Council on Alcoholism and Drug Dependence and the American Society of Addiction Medicine define addiction as a chronic, progressive, and potentially fatal disease with characteristic signs and symptoms (Morse & Flavin, 1992). The hallmark of addiction is the out-of-control use of substances despite the consequences (Jellinek, 1960). Knowledge of the potentially harmful effects of alcohol and other drugs on the fetus, therefore, does not stop most pregnant women with addictions from abusing alcohol and other drugs. Addiction does not reflect amoral behavior or a lack of willpower. The defining characteristic of the disease is continued abuse of the drug despite adverse consequences. Most women are unable to stop their substance abuse without treatment, no matter how clear their desire to have a healthy child. The extreme guilt brought about by their inability to stop taking drugs triggers shame and anxiety for many women, leading, in turn, to further substance abuse in an attempt to numb the painful feelings. Professionals do not help families by judging parents' actions; judgment merely drives them further away from treatment and results in increased drug abuse to escape the shame and guilt caused by their inability to stop abusing drugs.

Family Systems: *How could she spend the food and clothing allowance on drugs?*

"When I get my check, I know I should save the money for formula, but before I know it, I've used it up on drugs."

Addiction is marked by the compulsive use of a substance; in the late stages of the disease, people with addictions become preoccupied with getting and taking their drugs to the exclusion of all other needs and responsibilities, including taking care of themselves and parenting their children.

To pay for alcohol and other drugs, mothers who are addicted use money that is needed to pay for formula, diapers, and food for the family. Mothers who are addicted to substances have a primary relationship with alcohol and/or other drugs, not with their children (Finkelstein, Duncan, Derman, & Smeltz, 1990).

When mothers are addicted, their primary focus is on their drug of choice, not on their children. Although their lives may seem chaotic and totally bewildering to providers, people with addictions devise elaborate organizational strategies for getting and taking their drugs. Many, however, are not able to organize themselves to get needed health care or educational services for themselves or their children. It is difficult to focus on getting children dressed, fed, and out the door, when one is thinking about how to get the next hit. Although mothers go to extreme lengths to protect their children from their drug abuse, only taking drugs when the children are asleep, for example, the result of their behavior is the same—addiction prevents women from responding to their children's needs (Brooks et al., 1994).

Women with addictions see themselves as bad mothers, and their self-perception frequently is supported by myths in popular culture in which they are portrayed as immoral and deviant (Finkelstein et al., 1990). Providers often hold these same stereotypes of and myths about women who have addictions and communicate their disapproval of these women in both subtle and not-so-subtle ways as they seek to help families. It is impossible, however, to form a therapeutic, supportive relationship with a family within the context of shame and judgment.

Providers must be clear about their own feelings about addiction before beginning any meaningful work with families affected by addiction. A supportive parent–provider relationship can exist only within an atmosphere of mutual trust and respect. For some providers, addiction raises issues within their own families of origin; for others, it raises issues of morality and religion. Providers who work primarily with children often see the children as helpless victims of their mothers' addictions. They feel anger and disapproval toward the mothers and project those feelings onto the mothers, setting them up for failure. The mothers, in turn, sense the anger and disapproval and respond with shame, equal anger, and with attitude. Before providers can forge relationships with women or families, they must examine their own feelings about addiction so that they can meet the families where the families are in their addiction or recovery.

Trauma: *How could she let those little children watch horror movies on TV? How could she leave them alone in the apartment at night?*

"I get so scared at night when I'm alone with the kids. Bad things happened to me at night when I was a little girl. How can I take care of my children? I get so scared, I have to go out and score to get me through the night….I hate myself in the morning."

The majority of women with addictions come from backgrounds fraught with trauma and loss. Rita's story of childhood abuse, serial losses of family and caregivers, and school failure illustrates how patterns of early maltreatment and exposure to substance abuse in the family lead to later addiction and reenactment of the trauma. In many families, there are histories of parental substance abuse, and, usually, siblings are involved in substance abuse as well. Women whose own parents abused alcohol and other drugs are exposed early to addictive experiences, witnessing or participating in criminal behavior to support substance use and witnessing violence, including drug-related deaths. They experience early and frequent disruptions in education and in appropriate social and peer relations. There are family secrets to keep and chronic losses of family members and friends to violence, illness, prison, or foster placement to accept. As adults, these women often unconsciously repeat these earlier traumatic experiences of loss, abandonment, and terror with their own children. Finally, many of these women have had very poor models of parenting; dysfunction seen in a family headed by a parent who abuses substances is not only attributable to the substance abuse or the violence in the home, but it is also related to the lack of a nurturing, supportive, safe relationship in childhood.

Women who have histories of severe trauma experience persistent feelings of depression, low self-esteem, and anxiety and bouts of rage and panic. They have little ability to trust or to develop healthy relationships, and they have no sense of being worthy of love (Sandmaier, 1980). In fact, they experience pervasive feelings of having no control over life events. They have tremendous difficulty identifying feelings or coping appropriately with feelings that arise. Women who are addicted are so disconnected from themselves that their ability to recognize their own needs and feelings, care for themselves, and keep their children safe is severely impaired (Brooks & Rice, in press). They are unable to identify their feelings and, instead, report somatic complaints, such as headaches and stomachaches, in place of the anger, depression, or anxiety that they are experiencing. Severely traumatized women often experience posttraumatic stress disorder (PTSD), which prevents them from exercising good judgment when it comes to their children's needs for protection and safety. As described in Chapter 2, PTSD has a serious impact on parenting ability and family systems.

People who have experienced trauma often are drawn to events that terrify them, such as horror movies. They unconsciously reenact their own trauma through these frightening films in vain attempts to master the overwhelming fears with which they live and the powerful emotions that are triggered by the events in the films. Their trauma and addiction make them unaware of the effects that these films can have on their children. These women are desensitized to their own feelings and are unable to separate their own feelings from those of their children; mothers and their children are locked in this cycle of reenactment of trauma.

Recovery: *She's been through detox and a 28-day treatment program. Why are the children still so angry and out of control?*

"Detox is not a quick fix. Sometimes it's just a 'little vacation,' a time out from the binging and crashing. When you come out, nothing's really changed."

Providers often wonder why mothers' parenting skills or their children's behavior are not improved after completion of a treatment program. But entering a detoxification program or even a day-treatment program does not ensure that women will be able to parent their children appropriately. Recovery is a period of great change for women; it is a developmental process through which women learn not only about staying sober, but also about themselves and their relationships with others (Brown, 1987). Alcohol and other drugs have been such a dynamic part of these women's lives that it takes time for them to learn new ways to behave. They have rarely experienced success in school or in relationships. When asked to describe things that make them happy, they often cannot answer without referring to drug-related behaviors. Recovery is a period for learning new ways to be in relationships with other adults, extended family members, and one's own child or children, all of whom may be angry or resentful at the woman's past behavior or may be missing the person who was "lots of fun" on a binge.

Early recovery is characterized by fatigue, depression, and preoccupation with oneself. Painful, traumatic memories, shame, and anxiety, which might have been numbed by drugs, must now be experienced. Women report feeling extreme guilt and isolation; they feel overwhelmed by the stress of trying to stay sober while dealing with such painful emotions.

But recovery also is a time of hope for women. It is a developmental process through which those aspects of a woman's personality that contributed to her addiction can be changed. People can grow and mature, learn to experience and cope with feelings, feel good about themselves, and learn how to develop positive, meaningful relationships (Brown, 1987). Women in recovery look healthy; they have hope for themselves and their children.

THE IMPACT OF ADDICTION ON CHILDREN

The cycle of trauma and substance abuse directly affects children's daily lives. Children live with the unpredictability and chaos of parents who abuse substances. They learn to take the emotional temperature of the house: who is in the house, who is high or crashing, and who is angry. They live with the effects of maternal depression, which can leave mothers with little emotional energy for nurturing and protecting children. They feel isolated and alone and experience inconsistent care from various caregivers who may frequent the house. They may have several out-of-home placements while their mothers struggle with addictions. This recurring theme of emotional unavailability and abandonment is a potent one for children living with parents who abuse substances.

Children also live with family secrets of guilt, shame, and fear. Many children withdraw, but others express their concerns through rage and aggression. They learn the *don'ts: don't talk* about the drug use, *don't trust* other people with the secret, and *don't feel* anything. Adult children of alcoholics report missing out on childhood because they assumed adult roles of caring for parents who were addicted to alcohol or for younger siblings (Robinson, 1990). A child may assume changing and confusing roles, becoming the parentified child who takes care of the family, the clown who uses humor to cope with the chaos or violence of the home, or the withdrawn child who thinks that if she or he just vanishes, everything will be all right in the family (William Gladden Foundation, 1989). Living with a parent who has an addiction raises significant challenges to the development of trust, attachment, autonomy, and self-esteem and to the modulation of affect for children (Beeghley & Tronick, 1994).

Trust and Attachment

Attachment figures provide consistency, security, and limits for young children. Within the context of the attachment relationship, children develop internalized, integrated structures for the self in relation to others (Miller, 1986). For children struggling with issues of trust brought about by their experiences of abandonment, loss, inconsistency, and lack of boundaries within their families, however, the representative models for attachment become disordered. Children either attach themselves indiscriminately to all adults who pay any attention to them or withdraw from all adults. Children living with parents who have addictions have been described as being very needy and lacking organized, adaptive strategies for forming positive relationships with caregivers. They do not experience a sense of trust within a primary relationship, rather they internalize a model of mistrust and disordered attachment. This disordered attachment often is multigenerational; women who remember their mothers as rejecting are more likely to reject their children (Fraiberg, Adelson, & Shapiro, 1980).

Autonomy and Self-Esteem

Mothers with addictions have difficulty fostering healthy adaptations in their children. They are unable to help their children resolve successfully the salient issues of typical family development, from attachment through autonomy and independence. These children struggle with confusing messages from their mothers who want the children to be independent and take care of themselves and younger siblings when the mothers are under the influence of drugs but want the children to be respectful and attentive when they are sober. These demands place unreasonable burdens on children, leaving them with feelings of inadequacy and self-doubt. Adult children of alcoholics describe feelings of self-loathing and blame themselves for their family dysfunction. As children, they believe that if only they were good/smart/pretty enough, everything would be better. The family secrets that they carry make it difficult for them to connect to adults outside of the family; they feel compelled to refuse potential support from other caregivers, such as teachers and counselors. They worry that their secrets will be betrayed, or worse, that they themselves are part of the secret. They feel unlovable, and they question how anyone could like or respect them. These children have very low self-esteem and, as with most self-fulfilling prophesies, they act out against or withdraw from the very people who could help them—their teachers and counselors.

Modulation of Affect

The self-medication theory of addiction describes how people with drug addictions tend to select their drug of choice based on its effects on their affective or behavior disorders (Khantzian, 1985). Shy, inhibited people turn to alcohol for its ability to break down inhibition; insecure or depressed people use cocaine to feel better about themselves. The main effect of alcohol and other drugs, however, is to alter or numb emotions, leaving most people with addictions unable to identify their feelings or match their affect appropriately to a sad or frightening event. Instead, they use primitive coping mechanisms such as rocking, curling in a fetal position, thumb sucking, or smoking to deal with painful affect or anxiety. Parents with addictions have a very difficult time helping their children understand their own emotions, label their feelings, or deal with their emotions in socially acceptable ways. The children of parents with drug addictions often present as quite volatile, with extreme and unpredictable mood swings. Living in a chaotic environment with a mother with a substance abuse problem and experiencing unpredictable changes in adult presence and behavior make it extremely difficult for children to modulate their own feelings of fear, anger, and sadness.

The impact of addiction on children's behavior can be understood, at least in part, as an environmental or lifestyle effect. Lester and Tronick (1994) use the term *lifestyle* to describe a complex set of interrelated factors including the psychological and social factors that lead women to abuse substances and the family and neighborhood conditions in which children are raised. These conditions may include inadequate and disruptive forms of parenting, poverty, stress, institutional racism, exposure to violence, and a chaotic, disorganized lifestyle. These factors, independent of prenatal drug exposure, can lead to poor developmental outcomes for children. When developmental outcomes are confounded by the pharmacological effects of prenatal drug exposure, the children are at much higher risk for learning and behavior problems.

THE IMPACT OF PRENATAL EXPOSURE ON CHILDREN

In a rush to judgment (Mayes, Granger, Bornstein, & Zuckerman, 1992) immediately following the reported increase in crack cocaine use among poor women of childbearing age, early outcome studies of the effects of prenatal exposure to drugs published in the 1980s focused, for the most part, on biological factors (Chasnoff, Burns, Burns, & Schnoll, 1986; Finnegan, 1982; Zuckerman et al., 1989). These early studies reported that cocaine exposure was associated with a higher risk for spontaneous abortion, shorter gestational age, smaller head circumference, shorter birth length, and lower birth weight. Follow-up studies continue to support these early findings; over time, these growth effects do not appear to diminish. Griffith, Azuma, and Chasnoff (1994) report a lack of catch-up growth in head circumference in children who had been prenatally exposed to drugs with subnormal head size in their 3-year follow-up data. Although these data suggest a strong indicator of potential problems, 3-year head size did not predict intellectual performance, as measured by scores on standardized IQ tests. Subnormal head size may affect more complex forms of learning and reasoning in older children, but those data are not yet available.

Various neurobehavioral effects in infants who had been prenatally exposed to drugs also were reported in the early literature; these included irritability, excessive crying, tremors, jitteriness, abnormal tone, and poor feeding (Brown & Zuckerman, 1991; Coles, Platzman, Smith, James, & Falek, 1992; Weston, Ivins, Zuckerman, Jones, & Lopez, 1989). Findings from these and other studies are limited, however, by serious methodological problems, including inadequate control of confounding variables, case reports, no control groups, and unreliability of identification of people who have substance abuse problems versus people who do not. In addition, research findings of no adverse effects were much less likely to be accepted for presentation and publication, although these studies were, in general, methodologically stronger than were those reporting significant adverse effects (Koren, Graham, Shear, & Einarson, 1989). Bias in favor of accepting only those reports that showed significant adverse effects, therefore, distorted perceptions regarding the real risks associated with prenatal drug exposure.

The long-term effects of prenatal drug exposure are even less well-documented; only a few prospective longitudinal studies report outcome measures (Carta et al., 1994; Phelps & Cox, 1992). The children in the cohort followed by Chasnoff and colleagues were only 4 years old in 1995 (Azuma & Chasnoff, 1993; Chasnoff, Griffith, Freier, & Murray, 1992; Griffith et al., 1994). Results of 3-year follow-up data report that there are no significant mean differences on the Bayley Scales of Infant Development (Bayley, 1993) when children who have been prenatally exposed to cocaine are compared with social class–matched controls. The children who had been prenatally exposed to drugs perform within normal limits on standard IQ tests. More children who had been prenatally exposed to drugs than control children fall outside the normal range, and children who had been prenatally exposed to drugs show lower scores on some subscales, particularly language. As several researchers have suggested (Lester & Tronick, 1994), however, the Bayley Scales of Infant Development provide global estimates of neurobehavioral function, but they may not be suitable to detect the subtle differences or specific areas affected by cocaine. There is a general consensus both within the literature and among clinicians that, when drug effects are observed, they tend to be found in more subtle domains of function rather than along the gross developmental measures usually used to determine differences in populations (Poulsen, 1994).

Prenatal cocaine exposure very well may affect neuroregulatory mechanisms, resulting in disorders in behavioral regulation and may alter patterns of brain metabolism permanently. Inhibited glucose metabolism may account for the difficulty that infants who had been prenatally exposed to cocaine have in regulating states of arousal, which results in hyperactivity and mood instability (Lester et al., 1991). A preliminary study showed some evidence that higher levels of norepinephrine were related to poorer responsivity on the Brazelton Neonatal Behavioral Assessment Scales (Mirochnick, Meyer, Cole, Herren, & Zuckerman, 1991). As hypothesized by Lester and Tronick (1994), these disorders in behavioral regulation can be classified as affecting the four As of infancy: attention, arousal, affect, and action.

Substance abuse can have both a direct acute effect and an indirect long-term effect on child development and behavioral outcomes. Prenatal exposure to drugs poses a potential risk to the infant's biological and neurobehavioral makeup. Exposure to drugs can predispose an infant to self-regulatory vulnerability through a direct pharmacological effect on that child's ability to modulate affect, arousal, attention, and action. Environmental factors can act as long-term regulators or deregulators and as stabilizers or destabilizers of a child's development. Finally, the lifestyle effects associated with addiction can exacerbate the child's neurobehavioral vulnerability. Consider the example of an infant with self-regulatory difficulties in arousal and affect who is cared for by a mother with an addiction who cannot manage her own affect without drugs. The child will have a difficult time developing the coping mechanisms he or she will need to deal with the chaos of living with a mother with a substance abuse problem and may resort to acting-out behavior or withdrawal as a way to manage the tension between his or her neurobehavioral difficulties and the challenges presented by his or her environment. It is this interaction between the infant's neurobehavioral vulnerability and the response of the caregiving environment that determines the outcomes for the child.

INTERVENTIONS FOR CHILDREN AND THEIR FAMILIES

Although few definitive data exist on the long-term outcomes of children affected by maternal substance abuse, these children are not a new breed of children, as they have been portrayed in the media (Griffith, 1992). Some have biological vulnerabilities in neurobehavioral functioning that affect their attention, concentration, modulation of arousal and affect, impulsivity, distractibility, information processing, and other self-regulatory capacities. Some may also have problems that result from environmental factors related to maternal substance abuse. Substance abuse intensifies already well-recognized environmental hazards for mothers and their young children—poverty, violence, abandonment, homelessness, depression, multiple short-term foster placements, and inadequate or abusive parenting. When compared with mothers who do not abuse drugs, mothers who abuse drugs are more likely to have a personal and intergenerational history of trauma and abuse, to have been exposed to violence, and to have experienced more negative life events (Amaro, Zuckerman, & Cabral, 1989). In addition, they are more likely to abuse other drugs, such as alcohol and tobacco (Zuckerman et al., 1989); to consume insufficient nutrients, especially during pregnancy (Frank, Bauchner, Huber, Kyei-Aboagye, Cabral, & Zuckerman, 1990); and to have other medical problems, such as venereal disease (Amaro, Zuckerman, & Cabral, 1989) and depression, personality disorders, and affective disorders (Zuckerman, Amaro, & Beardslee, 1987).

These comorbidities are significant when considering interventions for children. Successful interventions for children with problems of self-regulation, delayed language development, low self-esteem, poor attachment, affective disorders, and PTSD have been developed (Brooks et al., 1994). The best way to help children, however, is not only to address their particular developmental and/or behavior problems, but also to intervene to change the environmental influences that affect the child negatively. In other words, *the best way to help the children is to help the family recover.* Family-focused interventions aimed at helping the mother recover from her addiction provide the most comprehensive and promising approach to avoiding the deleterious outcomes of maternal substance abuse for children and families. For many families, family-focused interventions are, in reality, focused on the mother, who often is a single parent.

Specific Intervention Issues for Children

Interventions for children with language delays, attention disturbances, attachment disorders, and motor problems have been reviewed extensively in the early intervention literature and are very effective for children affected by substance abuse (Coles & Platzman, 1992; Greenspan, 1990; Meisels & Shonkoff, 1990; Schneider, Griffith, & Chasnoff, 1989). The challenge for providers is to understand the child's behavior within the context of the family relationship. Just as mothers are taught to recognize and respond to their infants' cues, providers must be aware of what message a child's behavior may be signaling. Sudden changes in a child's affect or attention may be indicative of changes at home—relapse, family crisis, or domestic abuse. Because children living with parents who abuse substances are at risk for developmental delay and behavior difficulties, their behavior should be carefully monitored and considered within the context of family events. Descriptions of a child's behavior can be used to ask a mother about suspected changes in the family. Instead of confronting a mother with suspicions, a provider can use observations from the child's behavior to talk with the mother about any concerns and questions. Many mothers are able to hear how their behavior and responses to life events negatively affect their children. They can then ask for help with a problem for the sake of the children. The provider can capitalize on the mother's concern for her children to suggest changes in lifestyle that would be beneficial to the whole family, as well as to the child in question.

Early childhood and pediatric health care providers have been trained to analyze confusing or challenging child behavior by reviewing the events immediately preceding the behavior. If, for example, a child has trouble paying attention during circle time, calls out unrelated comments, and hits the child sitting next to him or her, the provider will reflect on variables such as seating arrangements (who the child is seated beside), environmental factors (noise, light, other distractions, what the child is sitting on), and learning style (discussion content that is too advanced, too abstract, or too long for the child). All too often, however, when these questions have been resolved successfully, the confusing behavior persists, leaving the provider feeling powerless and angry at his or her inability to help the child. Providers must be aware that, for some children with neuroregulatory problems like those seen in children who have been exposed prenatally to cocaine or who have PTSD, the event(s) preceding the problem behavior might be driven internally and have little relationship to external factors. Children who experienced prenatal exposure to cocaine can exhibit self-regulatory problems in affect, arousal, and impulsivity. Children with PTSD can have a diminished ability to concentrate because of intrusive thoughts and images. They can experience disordered attachment behavior with significant caregivers and have a nihilistic, fatalistic orientation toward the future, which leads to increased risk-taking behavior (Lyons, 1987). For these children, their behavior may have less to do with the classroom environment than with the internal neurobehavioral mechanisms that control affect, attention, and arousal. This is not to suggest that a provider can do nothing to help a disruptive child or that all challenging children have been prenatally exposed to cocaine or have witnessed domestic violence. Rather, it suggests that providers must think carefully about other influences on a child's behavior, such as parental drug addiction and family and/or community violence. Providers must feel comfortable asking hard questions about family history and child-rearing practices in culturally sensitive ways. One way to approach these questions is to ask a mother about her child: Who does he or she remind you of? Do you think you acted like he or she does when you were in school? The answers to these questions give providers significant insight into how the family sees the child, what expectations the family has for the child's behavior, and what may be affecting the child at home.

Role of the Infant in the Mother's Recovery

"This baby has put everything into perspective." Two months into her recovery from years of cocaine abuse, Gino describes, in *Straight From the Heart: Stories of Mothers Recovering from Addiction*, a videotape produced by Vida Health Communications (1992), how the birth of her child helped her find the strength to acknowledge her addiction and seek help. Children can be a powerful motivating force for women in their struggle toward sobriety. The birth of a child who had been prenatally exposed to drugs can be a window of opportunity, a chance for a woman to examine her substance abuse and seek treatment, perhaps for her child initially and then, later, for herself.

"If I give up my recovery and go out there and use, I'm going to lose myself and I'm going to lose my child." Carol, who also shared her experience in the videotape, describes how the potential loss of her child precipitated a crisis for her and provided a powerful motivating force for her to enter treatment for her cocaine abuse (Vida Health Communications, 1992).

"I was afraid to come in because I didn't want to leave my kids. My kids were my life; they were always there, and they always loved me." In the videotape, DeeDee speaks about how her concern for the care of her children prevented her from seeking treatment for years (Vida Health Communications, 1992). Because DeeDee had no one whom she trusted to care for her children while she was in a residential program, she avoided all forms of treatment until she finally hit bottom. Mothers often report that they want something better for their children and are willing to seek treatment for their substance abuse immediately postpartum, if they can bring their babies with them. Unfortunately, most residential treatment programs do not make provisions to allow women to continue to parent while they work on their recovery. This practice forces mothers to choose between their sobriety and their children, a difficult choice for any parent.

For Gino, Carol, and DeeDee, their children played a significant role in their recoveries. There are valuable lessons to be learned from the experiences these women recount, lessons that can shape approaches to intervention for both women and children. Family-focused intervention for women who abuse substances and for their young children requires a balancing that delicately weighs and considers the needs of the mothers and those of their children. Treatment that focuses on either the mother or the child exclusively ignores the power of the mother–child dyad and the advantages of changing the family system.

For providers and clinicians, the postpartum period also is a window of opportunity to develop a relationship with the family around their shared care and concern for the new baby. The challenge in providing family-focused interventions for women who abuse substances is to get the mothers' attention and to develop therapeutic relationships with them. The provider's ability to succeed in forming those alliances depends on the extent of each mother's drug use, denial, and level of recovery and the presence of concomitant psychiatric disturbance. These problems also interfere with the provider's ability to give information, model behavior, and help the mother provide developmentally appropriate interactions that support the infant's self-regulation, emotional growth, and developmental skills. Pediatricians, clinicians, and providers can join with parents to celebrate a new life and all of the promise it holds for the future, but they must do so within the context of addiction and recovery.

The value of family-focused intervention can be seen at each level of treatment. At the onset of treatment, the mother–child relationship can be the focus of intervention for the mother; the baby's behavior and development can help providers reach the mother and begin to establish a therapeutic relationship with her around her concerns for her child. Infants provide a wealth of behaviors that demonstrate to their parents that they are healthy, happy, and connected to their families. These behaviors include smiling at the sound of their mothers' voices, no longer crying when their mothers pick them up, and playing contentedly with their fingers after feeding. Providers can use all of these signs to show mothers how well they and their children are doing. Pointing out to the mother how central she is in her child's life—"his whole face lights up when he sees you"—supports the dance of attachment and mutual regulation between mother and child.

In addition, children can provide a powerful basis for examining women's life choices and decisions. Simply asking a woman why she has chosen a particular name for her child can provide tremendous insight into her life experiences and family history. As one mother explained, "She's named for my sister who died of AIDS [acquired immunodeficiency syndrome] and for my grandma who raised me after my mother left us." As they talk about their children, women tell the stories of their own life experiences, offering providers the chance to identify with and empathize with traumatizing events, to correct misconceptions, and to support each woman's vision for the future for herself and her child.

Children can be a significant source of pride and self-esteem for their mothers, but they also can be triggers for anger, repressed memories, depression, and relapses. Teaching women about basic child development can better their understanding of why their children behave in certain ways. For example, if a 1-year-old child cries as his or her mother leaves the room, and the mother gets angry, calling the child spoiled and bad, that behavior can be reframed for the mother. With guidance, this mother can come to understand that the child is responding to a scary and painful separation from his or her mother because she is so central to the child's life. Issues of abandonment are often pivotal to the lives of women with addictions; helping these women see their roles in supporting their children's growth toward individuation can enable them to place new meaning on their own lives, on how they interact with and understand their children, and on how they respond to their own losses, pain, and anger.

Finally, children offer hope for a future in which the mothers play a critical role. If a mother can envision a drug-free life for herself and her child or children, then she can begin to change the chaos and crisis that frequently characterize addiction. Recommendations to the mother should be flexible and success oriented. Success measured in small steps—one day at a time—can help the mother sustain a vision for a better life through sobriety and a sense of pride in her accomplishments and those of her child or children.

Parenting in Recovery

The problems of children who are affected by maternal substance abuse may be similar to those of other vulnerable children (Johnson, Glassman, Fiks, & Rosen, 1989), but, unlike other vulnerable children, these children have mothers who have their own significant problems. Addiction interferes with parenting, and the presence of such comorbidities as affective disorder and poverty compounds the impact of addiction. In fact, these comorbidities often continue to interfere with parenting even when the mother is in recovery.

Recovery from addiction is a difficult, challenging, exhausting process for those in recovery and for the providers who work with them. Although there are clearly defined stages of recovery (Brown, 1987), people recovering from addictions seldom move smoothly from one stage to the next. During early recovery, when the risk of relapse is greatest, parenting recommendations, although well intentioned, may lead to frustration and feelings of failure. Interventions always should be as tailored as possible to the realities of a mother's life. For the fragile infant who is having trouble feeding, recommendations to reduce stimulation during feeding must be very specific so that the mother understands what she should try. Suggestions must be concrete, spelling out exactly what to do. For example, the provider should explain to the mother that, before feeding the baby, she should dim the lights, turn down the volume on the television, wrap the baby in a blanket, and hold him or her in a semiupright position so that he or she can see her face. Successfully feeding her child supports the mother's self-image as a parent, provides appropriate nutrition for the baby, and provides a mutually satisfying experience for the mother and the baby to enjoy.

Most providers who work with infants and young children express concern about their ability to intervene with parents, particularly those struggling with addiction or recovery. Although they feel confident setting limits with children, they feel unprepared to set limits with parents. For parents in recovery, however, establishing boundaries between provider and parent and setting limits on behavior is important work. People with drug addictions may have rarely experienced consistency in their own chaotic lives; before they can create consistent, predictable environments for their children, they must experience that sense of predictability themselves. Providers can use the same techniques for limit setting with parents that they use with children.

First, providers can help *modify the environment* for the mother by suggesting drug-free experiences that are pleasurable, such as mother–child recreational activities. Many mothers who have drug addictions are unable to plan activities for their children because they have not experienced these events themselves. Going to a safe park or playground can be an eye-opening adventure for a mother as she learns what her child can do independently, how to set limits for her child's safety, and how to enjoy activities with her child.

Second, providers can *set limits* for parents by reacting to their behaviors appropriately and honestly. Most people with addictions have spent years lying about their substance abuse, and they are skilled at spotting lies in others. Providers must always tell the truth when interacting with parents who are addicted to drugs, even when tempted to ignore a particular situation. When a parent begins to bring his or her child in late, miss appointments, or look disorganized, the provider must address the behavior immediately. The provider should try to help the parent identify what triggered his or her most recent episode of substance abuse. The parent may deny the behavior, but the provider will have signaled his or her concern and willingness to help. A provider should never meet with a parent when he or she is drunk or high. The provider should express concern about the behavior, reschedule the appointment by writing it down for the parent, and arrange for a quiet, private place to meet to talk when no children are around.

Third, providers should *respond to parents' out-of-control behaviors* by helping them get time out from the stress of being with their children full time. Respite care, child care, or temporary foster or kinship care should be offered to parents to help them regain control of their lives before they do something truly dangerous.

The Role of Relapse

Relapse, especially during early recovery, is an expected part of the disease of addiction. Substance abuse specialists see relapse as a potential learning experience to determine what triggered the relapse, what feelings surrounded the relapse, and what strategies can be put in place to overcome those triggers and powerful feelings. For many women, the triggers for relapse are their children. Once they gain some sobriety, they begin to feel extraordinary guilt and shame about what they did to their children when they were abusing alcohol or other drugs. These feelings of shame are so overwhelming that many women relapse to avoid the pain of confronting their emotions.

What may be a critical learning experience for mothers, however, may be a painful, traumatic experience for children because of confusing adult behavior or separation from their mothers. Children may blame themselves for the relapse or for the subsequent separation if their mothers return to detoxification programs. Children must be assured that they were not responsible for the relapse. They need to understand that it is an expected part of their mothers' disease and that the adults are working to solve the problem. Keeping the relapse a secret from the children only adds to their confusion and sense of guilt and loss. Providers must respect the wishes of mothers who do not want to tell their children; they should, however, work with these mothers to help them understand the importance of telling their children, even young children, the truth about their addiction in developmentally appropriate ways.

A provider must not become an enabler of a parent's substance abuse. Denying that the parent has a problem, covering up for the parent, or circumventing the parent by attending to the child's medical needs without involving the parent, are all ways of enabling the parent to continue his or her drug abuse. This is a particularly important lesson for early childhood specialists and pediatricians who have been trained to support parents. In some cases, there is a fine line between supporting parents and enabling their continued drug abuse. Providers should ask for supervision from senior staff or substance abuse specialists when they are unclear about the impact of their interaction with a parent who is abusing drugs or is in early recovery.

Need for Supervision

Family-focused intervention with women who abuse substances is extremely challenging, frustrating work. Substance abuse treatment specialists must learn to cope with the added difficulties that a baby brings to a traditional adult treatment program. Giving careful thought to children's needs during their mothers' treatment can be complicated and time consuming. At the same time, early childhood specialists and pediatricians must acknowledge and deal with their anger at mothers who abuse alcohol and other drugs and their desire to rescue the children. They must learn to develop supportive relationships with these families and to set limits and boundaries within the context of those relationships. They must shift their focus and view the entire family as the client rather than the identified child; they must also consider the mother's issues and concerns, as well as the child's, when planning intervention approaches. Most early childhood educators and pediatricians, however, have not been trained to support women in recovery; similarly, substance abuse treatment specialists have not been trained to consider a woman's role as a mother and, as a result, tend to focus solely on her substance abuse.

To develop and implement successful interventions, providers must first take thorough, private inventories of their feelings and attitudes toward women with addictions and their children. Addiction and trauma have an impact on the lives of many families; providers may come to their work with preconceived ideas and emotional experiences from their own families. Providers are often angry with mothers whose behavior puts their children at risk; (see pp. 81–83 for examples of "how could she" questions that often surface as providers develop plans for children and families). These negative and often punitive feelings create great barriers to intervention. When a mother senses criticism and moral judgment, she will not be able to trust the provider and will be less likely to accept help.

Families affected by drug abuse also tend to experience more chaos and difficulty than do other families; indeed, many affected families use chaos as a way of organizing their lives. When providers begin to get too close, these families may ignite crises to reestablish boundaries that feel less intrusive. In most cases, this is not conscious behavior, but rather the unintentional reenactment of strategies that have worked in the past to isolate these families and confirm parents' beliefs that they are not doing a good job raising their children.

To providers who have invested a great deal of effort and time working with a family, intervention can sometimes feel like continually putting out fires or covering gaping wounds with bandages. Even when mothers are in recovery, providers find that they still must address other psychiatric disturbances or comorbidities. Providers describe the work as a never-ending struggle. They begin to feel as helpless and hopeless as the mothers themselves, mirroring the cost of the struggle. Strategies to support providers in this difficult work must include access to good clinical supervision so that the feelings evoked by these families can be processed and understood. Examining one's own reactions, beliefs, and assumptions about addiction and trauma, particularly those relating to parenting, is critical to providing effective interventions and to developing realistic expectations and goals for these families.

RECOMMENDATIONS

A Comprehensive Program:
Women and Infants Clinic, Boston City Hospital, Boston, Massachusetts

With few exceptions, infants who are prenatally exposed to drugs, particularly cocaine, are routinely sent home from the hospital with their mothers. These mothers usually receive three appointment slips—one for drug treatment, one for a postpartum checkup, and one for a pediatric visit. Not surprisingly, the pediatric visit is the only appointment that most women keep because they believe that all good mothers take their infants to the pediatrician. The Women and Infants Clinic at Boston City Hospital, Boston, Massachusetts, was created in 1990 to capitalize on this trend by providing outpatient drug treatment services for women within the physical structure of the pediatric visit (Kaplan-Sanoff & Leib, 1995; Kaplan-Sanoff & Rice, 1992). This model of one-stop shopping allowed women to come to a single clinic site and receive their drug treatment within the context of their relationships with their babies. By bringing their children to the pediatrician they demonstrated to themselves, their families, and their communities their ability to be good mothers; by receiving drug treatment during that same visit, they attended to their own problems within a nonstigmatizing environment. They did not have to walk through the door of a mental health facility to get help. In addition, everyone involved in the clinic—the pediatrician, early childhood specialist, and substance abuse specialist—already knew of the women's addictions. In that way, the women could openly and honestly address their concerns for their babies. They often asked how their drug abuse had harmed their babies. They were overly concerned about their infants' health; they tended to see every typical childhood ailment from diaper rash to newborn acne to gas as a result of their drug abuse. They were extremely relieved to learn that all babies experienced these conditions and that they could most help their children through their own efforts at sobriety. Rather than seeing the infant and the mother as having different, conflicting needs, the clinic addressed the mother–child dyad as a complex unit, in which each individual needed the other.

Women were supported in their recovery through weekly urine screenings, individual counseling, and a weekly relapse prevention group, with additional support from community Narcotics Anonymous meetings. Children's developmental needs were addressed through a weekly mother–child group that focused on such critical issues as saying goodbye to the babies before leaving for the adult group, understanding children's behavioral signs, and supporting each child's achievements. The goals of the mother–child group were twofold: 1) to form a therapeutic relationship with the mother by sharing in her care and concern for her child and 2) to nurture and support the mother's parenting efforts. The self-esteem of these mothers was so low that they were unable to see themselves as good mothers, and they felt that they could take no responsibility for the progress that their babies made. They stated that their babies were thriving despite them, rather than because of them (Garbarino, Dubrow, Kostelny, & Pardo, 1992; Sameroff, Seifer, Barocas, Zax, & Greenspan, 1987). Much of the work of the clinic team was directed toward helping the women feel good about their efforts at parenting and acknowledge their role in nurturing their children. The group also focused on helping mothers read their children's signals and differentiate their own needs from those of their children. The early childhood specialists made a conscious effort to ask each week how the mothers, and not just the children, were doing. Significant events, such as the child's first steps or first word and the mother's first 60 days of sobriety, were celebrated as accomplishments of both the mother and child. Helping these very disorganized women to acknowledge and celebrate the passage of time, embrace their small successes, and organize their lives around significant life events was an extremely successful intervention strategy for nurturing mothers and supporting their emerging parenting skills.

Comprehensive programs that address the multiple issues of parents and children through services located at a single site offer the best hope for intervention for women and children affected by substance abuse. Health, education, and clinical services can implement more powerful interventions when these approaches are coordinated through a transdisciplinary team of providers working toward mutually agreed-upon goals. There are, however, no magic pills to immunize children to the effects of substance abuse, violence, and poverty. Teachers can no longer just teach children; they must learn to provide true family-focused interventions. Substance abuse treatment programs can no longer ignore the fact that many of the women they serve also are mothers of young children and must attend to the needs of their children while working on their recoveries. Transdisciplinary teams of providers working across agencies, supported by clinical supervision, can make a difference in the lives of women and children struggling with addiction and trauma.

FUTURE DIRECTIONS

Public Policy

In a provocative article, "It's Drugs, Stupid," Joseph Califano (1995) argues that drugs have changed the nature of criminal justice, health care, welfare, and poverty in the United States. He claims that drugs are the greatest threat to family stability, decent housing, public schools, and basic amenities in urban ghettos. Although some politicians and policy analysts might disagree with the expansiveness of his concerns, providers who work with families affected by substance abuse have seen the vicious cycle of poverty, trauma, and addiction take its toll on too many families with young children. Policy recommendations must take into account these cyclical and intergenerational issues of poverty, substance abuse, and trauma (Poulsen, 1994).

Programs Must Address Families' Basic Needs

Families who are struggling with such chronic survival crises as providing food, shelter, and clothing are usually less able to invest in intervention programs for their children, unless those programs also address the basic needs of the family. Poverty forces families to make extremely difficult decisions; mothers may not be able to attend to such critical infant issues as reciprocity and attachment when they are consumed with worry about their children's health and nutrition (Beckwith, 1990). Programs designed for families affected by substance abuse must support families' efforts to attend to their basic survival needs while encouraging supportive, developmentally appropriate interactions with their infants and young children.

Programs Must Effectively Combine
Drug Treatment with Child Development and Family Support

Public policy, often guided by the media portrayal of children who were prenatally exposed to drugs as innocent victims of their mothers' substance abuse, has also prevented drug treatment programs from addressing the role that children can play as a part of the recovery process. Children are, however, a vital part of recovery—they provide the motivation for mothers to begin treatment and the reinforcement to maintain sobriety (Fraiberg, Shapiro, & Cherniss, 1980). Strengthening parenting skills can be a vital part of the recovery process, and recovery is the best way to help mothers parent their children effectively. In traditional drug treatment programs, however, recovery takes precedence over parenting. Addiction counselors believe that abstinence must come first, resulting in a shift in identity, which then makes successful parenting possible. In many programs, women are penalized for infractions in their recovery by losing their privileges to see their children or attend a parenting program. This approach does not address the fact that working on the mother–child relationship also can force the identity shift needed to achieve sobriety (Pawl, 1992). One approach does not take precedence over the other. Each discipline has developed successful interventions, which, when combined, provide more powerful motivation and immediate satisfaction for mothers struggling to overcome addiction and trauma.

Effective Treatment Must Also Include Comprehensive Services for Mothers and Children

Model programs that provide all needed services at one location with trained transdisciplinary staff offer the best hope for family recovery. If a one-stop–shopping approach is not possible, then interagency collaboration becomes critical to program development. Agencies that provide drug treatment must collaborate with early intervention, child care, and educational programs serving the needs of young children; with health care programs providing pediatric and women's health care; and with social services agencies (VanBremen & Chasnoff, 1994). In this era of welfare reform, policy analysts must consider that "all the financial lures and prods and all the job training in the world will do precious little to make employable the hundreds and thousands of welfare recipients who are addicts and abusers" (Califano, 1995, p. 40). Job training and adult literacy programs should be a significant component in drug treatment, but without concomitant drug treatment, these programs are, for many people with addictions, an exercise in futility. Comprehensive programming requires that policies regarding funding streams, eligibility criteria, and length of service provision be revised to consider the unique needs of families affected by substance abuse and to avoid the fragmentation of services that splits mothers, children, and providers into different and, at times, factional, camps.

Training and Supervision of Providers Must Occur Across Agencies

Multiagency cross-training has been recommended by the North American Commission on Chemical Dependency and Child Welfare (1992) as a strategy for implementing a family-centered care mode. Cross-training of staff allows providers from diverse training backgrounds and disciplines to learn from one another, respect one another's practices, and appreciate the frame of reference that each provider brings to decisions about intervention. Community outreach workers with cultural ties in the community can help bridge the gap between providers and the clients they serve. To accomplish that task, funding guidelines across all state agencies must be restructured to provide coordinated services, program continuity, and financial support for staff to attend training and collaborative planning meetings.

Implications for Practice

Addiction, by its very nature, does not exist as an isolated problem. As Rita's story reminds us, the road to addiction is long and circuitous, starting in childhood and progressing through adult crises and life events. Recovery also is a lifelong process, not easily achieved in a 28-day treatment program. In addition, because relapse is an expected part of the disease, mothers who are addicted to alcohol and other drugs need many opportunities to regain their sobriety. As one mother explained her numerous attempts at recovery before finally achieving sobriety, "Maybe you won't make it the first time. God knows, not all of us did. But every time you try, every time, you get closer to the day when something clicks and things that seemed impossible once become possible" (Vida Health Communications, 1992).

Comprehensive programs for women in recovery must offer these women many opportunities to succeed and to learn from their failures over a long period of time. Families need to know that the program will be there for them and that they can return to the program to start again if necessary. Mothers leave drug treatment programs for many reasons, but one reason is their concern for their children who are being cared for by other family members. Sometimes adults uncover early traumatic or abusive events from their childhoods while in treatment and then fear for the safety of their children who are now living with those same individuals who once abused them. Once they leave the program, it is hard for mothers with addictions to reengage in treatment without the support of their counselors. In the current cost-cutting environment of health care reform, many programs today do not have the luxury of open-ended entrance policies. Funders also want to see timely documented changes in behavior, but, unfortunately, recovery is not a quick process. Expectations that women will be able to parent their children after completing a 28-day treatment program or that they will be able to comply with a complex reunification plan after residential treatment are unrealistic and set up mothers to fail. If drug treatment programs are to deal effectively with the complicated issues of addiction and parenting, they must develop new models of long-term treatment that deal realistically with the issues of relapse and a mother's role as a caregiver for a young child.

Changing parenting attitudes and skills in families affected by substance abuse is an extremely challenging task. *For women who have placed their children in foster or kinship care while they focused on their recovery, reentry into the real world of parenting must be planned carefully.* Mothers must experience gradual steps toward reengaging with their children over a fairly long period of time. They may need supervised visits, weekend visits, and, then, aftercare support as they begin to reassert their roles as mothers. Women in recovery tend to romanticize what their new lives with their children will be like, but their children's behaviors often do not match these idealized notions. The children can be confused, angry, resentful, demanding, and mistrustful; they may actively resist the mothers' attempts to reassert their authority just as the mothers are actively attempting to reclaim their roles as parents. Programs must provide carefully planned transitions and aftercare support for mothers and children as they redefine family roles and images.

Finally, in this climate of doom and gloom about the long-term outcomes for children and families affected by substance abuse, *it is important to remember the strengths that each mother brings to the struggle for sobriety and the resilience that young children bring to their growth and development* (Garmezy, 1987; Rutter, 1979; Werner, 1990). Children have a great capacity for change and the flexibility to adapt to change within the context of supportive caregiving relationships. As Rita's story reminds us, children do not require much to feel happy and loved. They have enormous faith in the world and the people around them. Providers may feel that they are not doing enough for the children and families they serve. Professionals cannot change the economic or social environments of the families; professionals cannot make the families' experiences of the world less overwhelming. Professionals can, however, make a difference in the lives of children and families by focusing on their strengths, fostering their resiliency, and supporting parents' visions for the future for themselves and their children.

REFERENCES

Amaro, H., Zuckerman, B., & Cabral, H. (1989). Drug use among adolescent mothers: Profile of risk. *Pediatrics, 84*(1), 144–151.

Azuma, S.D., & Chasnoff, I.J. (1993). Outcomes of children prenatally exposed to cocaine and other drugs: A path analysis of three-year data. *Pediatrics,92*(3), 396–402.

Bayley, N. (1993). *Bayley Scales of Infant Development–Second edition manual.* San Antonio, TX: The Psychological Corporation.

Beckwith, L. (1990). Adaptive and maladaptive parenting: Implications for intervention. In S. Meisels & J. Shonkoff (Eds.), *Handbook of early childhood intervention* (pp. 53–77). New York: Cambridge University Press.

Beeghley, M., & Tronick, E. (1994). Effects of prenatal exposure to cocaine in early infancy: Toxic effects on the process of mutual regulation. *Infant Mental Health Journal, 15*(2), 158–176.

Brooks, C.S., & Rice, K.F. (in press). *Full circle: Understanding and treating families in recovery.* Baltimore: Paul H. Brookes Publishing Co.

Brooks, C.S., Zuckerman, B., Bamforth, A., Cole, J., & Kaplan-Sanoff, M. (1994). Clinical issues related to substance-involved mothers and their infants. *Infant Mental Health Journal, 15*(2), 202–217.

Brown, E., & Zuckerman, B. (1991). The infant and the drug using mother. *Pediatric Annals, 20,* 555–563.

Brown, S. (1987). *Treating the alcoholic: A developmental model of recovery.* New York: John Wiley & Sons.

Califano, J.A. (1995, January 29). It's drugs, stupid. *New York Times Magazine,* 40–41.

Carta, J., Sideridis, G., Rinkel, P., Guimaraes, S., Greenwood, C., Baggett, K., Peterson, P., Atwater, J., McEvoy, M., & McConnell, S. (1994). Behavioral outcomes of young children prenatally exposed to illicit drugs: Review and analysis of experimental literature. *Topics in Early Childhood and Special Education, 14*(2), 184–216.

Chasnoff, I.J., Burns, K.A., Burns, W.J., & Schnoll, S.H. (1986). Prenatal drug exposure: Effects on neonatal and infant growth and development. *Neurobehavioral Toxicology and Teratology, 8,* 357–362.

Chasnoff, I.J., Griffith, D.R., Freier, C., & Murray, J. (1992). Cocaine/polydrug use in pregnancy: Two year follow-up. *Pediatrics, 89*(2), 284–289.

Coles, C.D., & Platzman, K.A. (1992). Fetal alcohol effects in preschool children: Research, prevention and intervention. *Office of Substance Abuse Programs Monograph, 11,* 59–86.

Coles, C.D., Platzman, K.A., Smith, I., James, M.E., & Falek, A. (1992). Effects of cocaine and alcohol use in pregnancy on neonatal growth, and neurobehavioral status. *Neurotoxicology and Teratology, 14,* 23–33.

Daro, D., & McCurdy, K. (1991). *Current trends in child abuse reporting and fatalities: The results of the 1990 annual fifty state survey.* Chicago: National Committee for the Prevention of Child Abuse.

Finkelstein, N., Duncan, S., Derman, L., & Smeltz, J. (1990). *Getting sober, getting well: A treatment guide for caregivers who work with women.* Cambridge, MA: Harvard University Press.

Finnegan, L.P. (1982). Outcomes of children born to women dependent on narcotics. *Advances in Alcohol and Substance Abuse, 1,* 55–101.

Fraiberg, S., Adelson, E., & Shapiro, V. (1980). Ghosts in the nursery: A psychoanalytic approach to the problems of impaired infant–mother relationships. In S. Fraiberg (Ed.), *Clinical studies in infant mental health: The first year of life* (pp. 100–136). New York: Basic Books.

Fraiberg, S., Shapiro, V., & Cherniss, D. (1980). Treatment modalities. In J. Call, E. Galenson, & R. Tyson (Eds.), *Frontiers of infant psychiatry.* New York: Basic Books.

Frank, D., Bauchner, H., Huber, A.M., Kyei-Aboagye, K., Cabral, H., & Zuckerman, B. (1990). Neonatal body proportionality and body composition after in utero exposure to cocaine and marijuana. *Journal of Pediatrics, 117,* 622–626.

Garbarino, J., Dubrow, N., Kostelny, D., & Pardo, C. (1992). *Children in danger. Coping with the consequences of community violence.* San Francisco: Jossey-Bass.

Garbarino, J., & Sherman, D. (1981). High-risk neighborhoods and high-risk families: The human ecology of child maltreatment. *Child Development, 51,* 188–198.

Garmezy, N. (1987). Stress, competence and development: Continuities in the studies of schizophrenic adults and children vulnerable to psychopathology and the search for stress resilient children. *American Journal of Orthopsychiatry, 57,* 159–174.

Greenspan, S. (1990). Comprehensive clinical approaches to infants and their families: Psychodynamic and developmental perspectives. In S. Meisels & J. Shonkoff (Eds.), *Handbook of early childhood intervention* (pp. 150–171). New York: Cambridge University Press.

Griffith, D.J. (1992). Prenatal exposure to cocaine and other drugs: Developmental and educational prognoses. *Phi Delta Kappan,* 30–34.

Griffith, D.J., Azuma, S.D., & Chasnoff, I.J. (1994). Three year outcome of children exposed prenatally to drugs. *Journal of the American Academy of Child and Adolescent Psychiatry, 33,* 20–27.

Jellinek, E.M. (1960). *The disease concept of alcoholism.* New Haven, CT: Hillhouse.

Johnson, H.L., Glassman, M.B., Fiks, K.B., & Rosen, T.S. (1989). Resilient children: Individual differences in developmental outcome of children born to drug abusers. *Journal of Genetic Psychology, 151,* 439–523.

Kaplan-Sanoff, M., & Leib, S.(1995). Model intervention programs for mothers and children impacted by substance abuse. *School Psychology Review, 24*(2), 186–199.

Kaplan-Sanoff, M., & Rice, K.F. (1992). Woman and Infants Clinic: Lessons learned from working with addicted women in recovery and their children. *ZERO TO THREE, 13*(3), 17–22.

Khantzian, E.J. (1985). The self medication hypothesis of addictive disorders: Focus on heroin and cocaine dependence. *American Journal of Psychiatry, 143,* 1255–1264.

Koren, G., Graham, H., Shear, H., & Einarson, T. (1989). Bias against the null hypothesis: The reproductive hazards of cocaine. *Lancet, 2,* 1440–1442.

Lester, B.M., Corwin, M.J., Sepkoski, C., Seifer, R., Peucker, M., McLaughlin, S., & Golab, H.L. (1991). Neurobehavioral syndromes in cocaine-exposed newborn infants. *Child Development, 62,* 694–705.

Lester, B.M., & Tronick, E.Z. (1994). The effects of prenatal cocaine exposure and child outcome. *Infant Mental Health Journal, 15*(2), 107–120.

Lyons, J.A. (1987). Posttraumatic stress disorder in children and adolescents: A review of the literature. In S. Chess & A. Thomas (Eds.), *Annual progress in child psychiatry and development* (pp. 451–467). New York: Brunner/Mazel.

Mayes, L.C., Granger, R.H., Bornstein, M.H., & Zuckerman, B. (1992). The problem of prenatal cocaine exposure: A rush to judgement. *Journal of American Medical Association, 267*, 406–408.

Miller, J.B. (1986). What do we mean by relationships? *(Work in Progress, 22)* Wellesley, MA: Stone Center Working Paper Series.

Meisels, S., & Shonkoff, J. (Eds.). (1990). *Handbook of early childhood intervention.* New York: Cambridge University Press.

Mirochnick, M., Meyer, J., Cole, J., Herren, T., & Zuckerman, B. (1991). Circulating catecholamine concentrations in cocaine-exposed neonates: A pilot study. *Pediatrics, 88*, 481–485.

Morse, R.M., & Flavin, D.K. (1992). The definition of alcoholism. *Journal of the American Medical Association, 268*, 1012–1014.

North American Commission on Chemical Dependency and Child Welfare. (1992). *Children at the front: A different view of the war on drugs.* Washington, DC: Child Welfare League of America.

Pawl, J.H. (1992). Interventions to strengthen relationships between infants and drug-abusing or recovering parents. *ZERO TO THREE, 13*(1), 6–10.

Phelps, L., & Cox, D. (1992). Children with prenatal cocaine exposure: Resilient or handicapped? *School Psychology Review, 22*(8), 710–724.

Poulsen, M. (1994). The development of policy recommendations to address individual and family needs of infants and young children affected by family substance abuse. *Topics in Early Childhood Special Education, 14*(2), 275–291.

Robinson, B. (1990). The teacher's role in working with children of alcoholic parents. *Young Children, 45*(4), 68–73.

Rohsenow, D., Corbett, R., & Devine, D. (1988). Molested as children: A hidden contribution to substance abuse? *Journal of Substance Abuse Treatment, 5*, 13–18.

Rutter, M. (1979). Protective factors to children's responses to stress and disadvantage. In M. Kent & J. Rolf (Eds.), *Primary prevention of psychopathology: Social competence in children* (Vol. 3, pp. 49–74). Hanover, NH: University Press of New England.

Sameroff, A., Seifer, R., Barocas, R., Zax, M., & Greenspan, S. (1987). Intelligence quotient scores for 4-year-old children: Social environmental risk factors. *Pediatrics, 79*, 343–350.

Sandmaier, M. (1980). *The invisible alcoholic women and alcohol abuse in America.* New York: McGraw-Hill.

Schneider, J.W., Griffith, D.R., & Chasnoff, I.J. (1989). Infants exposed to cocaine in utero: Implications for developmental assessment and intervention. *Infants and Young Children, 2*(1), 25–36.

VanBremen, J., & Chasnoff, I.J. (1994). Policy issues for integrating parenting interventions and addiction treatment for women. *Topics in Early Childhood and Special Education, 14*(2), 254–275.

Vida Health Communications. (Producer). (1992). *Straight from the heart: Stories of mothers recovering from addiction* [Videotape]. Cambridge, MA: Producer.

Werner, E. (1990). Protective factors and individual resilience. In S. Meisels & J. Shonkoff (Eds.), *Handbook of early childhood intervention* (pp. 97–116). New York: Cambridge University Press.

Weston, D.D., Ivins, B., Zuckerman, B., Jones, C., & Lopez, R. (1989). Drug-exposed babies: Research and clinical issues. *ZERO TO THREE, 9*(5), 1–7.

William Gladden Foundation. (1989). *Children from alcoholic families.* York, PA: Author.

Zuckerman, B., Amaro, H., & Beardslee, W. (1987). Mental health of adolescent mothers: The implications of depression and drug use. *Developmental and Behavioral Pediatrics, 8*, 111–116.

Zuckerman, B., Frank, D., Hingson, R., Amaro, H., Levenson, S., Kayne, H., Parker, S., Vinci, R., Aboagye, K., Fried, L., Cabral, H., Timeri, R., & Bauchner, H. (1989). Effects of maternal marijuana and cocaine use on fetal growth. *New England Journal of Medicine, 320*, 762–768.

Meeting the Challenge of Environmental Illness

One Family's Journey

Anne Raymer

My husband and I are the parents of three children with environmental illness (EI), a combination of extreme allergies and chemical sensitivities. Symptoms of EI can include typical allergies or hay fever, as well as hyperactivity, attention-deficit/hyperactivity disorder, depression, chronic infections, irritability, asthma, sleeping disorders, and learning disabilities. Our children fall into the more severe range; they have serious health and behavior problems.

Although EI is an inherited tendency, no one in either of our families had exhibited such problems. From our first days as parents, my husband and I knew that something was wrong. Both of us had worked with young children, and neither of us had ever seen an infant act like ours. For brief periods, our son was happy and calm; but we spent most days dealing with a fretful, clingy, frustrated little boy who rarely felt well. When our second child was born with similar difficulties, we knew that there was a serious problem: This was not simply our lack of parenting experience showing.

This situation was like nothing we had ever seen or imagined of parenthood. Our children's health and behavior problems took over our lives. Our oldest son, from birth on, awoke 5–6 times a night and screamed until he fell asleep from exhaustion, only to repeat the scene an hour later. Nothing we did comforted or helped him. This pattern continued for more than 2 years, waking our neighbors night after night. We feared that we would be evicted from our apartment or that someone nearby, hearing the awful noise, would report us for child abuse.

Along with their impossible behavior, it seemed as though our children were constantly ill. We lived with chronic ear infections, went through operations for ear tubes and adenoidectomies, and spent so much time at our pediatrician's office that the nurses joked about renting us a room.

We tried to make our lives feel more normal and tried to spend time alone together or with friends, but more often than not, we ended up canceling our plans so that we could stay home and care for our sick children. When they did occur, get-togethers with friends and family were strained. Our children were clingy, whiny, and uncontrollable: We were embarrassed and constantly found ourselves the center of attention and the recipients of unwanted advice.

As one of our children grew older, his temper tantrums increased in frequency and seriousness—something as small as a broken cookie might trigger a bout of screaming and destruction that could last all morning. We started to fear for his future—we worried that eventually he would be diagnosed as mentally ill. What else could explain the long, violent tantrums; the unprovoked aggression toward us; and the wild swings in mood and personality, from angry and out of control to irritatingly silly and hyperactive?

Sometimes, catching a glimpse of a father walking, holding hands and talking with his small son, would bring tears to my eyes. It seemed as though we would never be able to relate to our children in such a relaxed, effortless way and simply enjoy being with them.

Most of the time, we functioned in what my husband called survival mode, simply trying to get through each day. We felt increasingly isolated. We were reluctant to burden friends with our strange situation. Our families, who live in different states, meant well and wanted the best for us, but they seemed to believe that we were overreacting and making hypochondriacs of our children.

All this time, I was searching for some kind of explanation for our problems, going to support group meetings for new parents, and reading everything I could find. We tried numerous doctors—an ear, nose, and throat specialist; various pediatricians; a sleep specialist; and a child psychologist. Although we followed all of the directions they gave us (as well as all of the advice we received from family and friends), little seemed to help. My husband and I were exhausted, burnt out, and scared, and, at this point, we began looking into family therapy. We tried not to think beyond that.

When our children were ages 5 years, 3 years, and 7 months, we finally learned the underlying cause of all of our problems. It has been almost 6 years now since we began going to a wonderful pediatric allergist who specializes in environmental medicine, and our lives have taken an extraordinary turn for the better. With the use of a precise form of allergy testing called provocation/neutralization, this allergist finally was able to identify the cause-and-effect relationship between our children's environment and the problems with their behavior and health. Ragweed pollen caused our toddler's screaming, thrashing on the floor, and refusal to be touched. Cucumbers and milk made our oldest son extremely irritable and negative. Potatoes caused our middle son to become silly and uncooperative. Molds caused asthma, stomachaches, and runny noses. Exposure to school cleaning supplies resulted in spaciness and an inability to concentrate in our oldest son. It was instantly clear, watching this testing, that we had found the bizarre cause of our children's lifelong problems, and we were thrilled to learn that we could turn off the symptoms simply by giving our children drops of allergy extract under their tongues. The change we saw truly was a miracle: We had three bright, sweet-tempered, creative, healthy children.

It is not easy to maintain our sons' health; we live with a complicated and expensive regime of organic food, special vitamins, and allergy extract, and our sons must undergo retesting several times a year. We withdrew them from school for health reasons and have been homeschooling for 3 years. Nevertheless, it has been well worth it. They are healthier than they have ever been, and they are now able to go to an occasional birthday party, play ball, or go sledding without feeling and acting awful. Our family is beginning to feel more like a regular family. Our children may have to contend with EI throughout their lives, but at least we now know how to manage it.

One of the obstacles we faced in trying to get to the bottom of our situation was the confusing nature of EI. Hyperactivity, irritability, and aggression, which can easily be misinterpreted as the results of poor parenting, led to much misunderstanding on our part and understandably negative reactions from others. At present, little accurate information exists about EI. Most doctors do not recognize or understand the pattern of symptoms, and children like ours often end up in special education classes, labeled as having learning disabilities, behavior disorders, or attention-deficit/hyperactivity disorder; psychiatry and Ritalin are commonly prescribed. Family situations such as ours often result in broken homes. We feel fortunate to have avoided all of these scenarios.

Despite the obvious and dramatic improvement in our children, we are faced with what may be a permanent emotional wall separating us from our families. For 11 years, they told us repeatedly that we were crazy to put our family through all of this medical and financial nonsense. Now, we are glad for the miles between us and the privacy that distance gives us. We know that our families can never understand what our lives have been like or our fears for our children's health, emotional well-being, and futures; as a result, we keep the details of our struggles to ourselves. Our religious faith was a source of strength and comfort to us throughout this time, and we believe that we were guided to solutions to these challenges in response to our prayers.

We are thrilled with our children's progress, and we feel so fortunate that their health problems can be reversed by our efforts. We try to live each day as it comes and not worry about what lies ahead. On our bad days, we grieve for the lost times and the limits that EI has placed on our children and our family; on our good days, we remind ourselves how very far we have come.

5

Unsuspected Environmental Causes of Health and Learning Problems

Doris J. Rapp and Karen Kochanski

Environmental allergic illness is a major unsuspected, frequently missed cause of chronic health and learning problems in children (Rapp, 1991, in press; Rapp & Bamberg, 1986). Many children do not reach their full potential because teachers and physicians are not trained to consider environmental causes of learning and health difficulties. Environmental illness and food and chemical sensitivities can affect any child. Environmental illness also can be a part or all of the cause of diverse learning problems, such as attention deficit disorder, attention-deficit/hyperactivity disorder, Tourette syndrome, and autism. The following is a representative history of an environmentally ill child.

KELLY'S ENVIRONMENTAL ILLNESS

When Kelly was 12 years old she was examined to determine the role of allergies and environmental illness in her health and behavior problems. Many of her relatives had typical allergies. As an infant, she experienced constipation, colic, and sleeplessness. She was a restless and unhappy baby. It is interesting to note that she started drinking cow's milk at 6 months of age and began having ear problems 2 months later. All of her symptoms were classic for an infant who is sensitive to milk.

By the time she was a toddler, she demonstrated classic nose rubbing each spring. In addition, her eyes became red, itchy, and watery, which is a common symptom of hay fever. This pattern follows the typical progression of allergy.

After Kelly started school in 1992, she developed some symptoms that were typical of a "prolonged flu." This flu often is a misdiagnosis for chemical sensitivity. We sought to uncover any changes in her environment. We learned that, the summer before Kelly began to attend school, the school building had undergone extensive remodeling. When school began that year, new carpets still were being installed just days after they had been manufactured. The adhesive that was used to secure the carpets had a very strong odor. By October, Kelly's teachers complained that she seemed to be excessively wiggly, irritable, restless, and hyperactive. Kelly developed a tight feeling in her throat and chest, blurred vision, headaches, painful muscle aches, tight joints, dizziness, fatigue, and difficulty sleeping; some other students and some teachers also developed similar symptoms. She had difficulty breathing in one room in particular; it was in this room that other students and one of the sickest teachers had similar complaints. Kelly felt better when the windows were open. Her ankles and knees hurt so much that it was difficult for her to walk. In addition, she cried easily and had emotional ups and downs. At times, she seemed very depressed and she demonstrated inexplicable changes in behavior. All of these symptoms diminished at night and on weekends. The symptoms persisted until Christmas vacation; over the break she felt and behaved much better.

When school resumed, however, in January 1993, Kelly's symptoms worsened. This pointed to school exposure because more chemicals had been introduced into the building over the holiday break. In addition, Kelly could no longer attend church because the odor from perfumes gave her headaches. In addition, Kelly's skin was itchy, and she seemed unusually pale. Her mother said she changed so much "she became the kid from hell." At school she became very combative, slammed doors, and exhibited a total reversal of her normal, pleasant attitude. She complained of numbness and tingling of her fingers and toes, which suggested possible changes in her peripheral nervous system. Her joints caused her so much pain that she stated they were "killing me."

Her grades gradually fell from Bs to unsatisfactory because she had difficulty concentrating. It is unclear if this difficulty arose because she did not feel well or because her brain was adversely affected by the chemicals. (Other children and teachers in that school who had similar complaints were found to have experienced changes in blood flow to the brain and brain function on single photon emission computed tomography tests; Kelly's family could not afford his type of test.)

By May 1993, Kelly had to leave school and be taught at home. After only 5 days, Kelly's mother noticed a definite improvement in her disposition. Kelly herself was surprised because she was so much better that she could, at times, walk without any joint or muscle pain. Her emotional mood swings diminished, and she was no longer restless. She continued to improve over the summer. By then she also had undergone P/N allergy skin testing (a precise method of testing single allergenic substances in which one concentration provokes a response [P], and another neutralizes that response [N]). These tests revealed that she had a definite sensitivity to a few foods, dust, molds, grass, glycerine, and formaldehyde. Her blood studies showed changes that were consistent with chemical exposure as well as with typical allergies. She also had developed antibodies against parts of her own nervous system. When a regime of allergy extract injection therapy, home and diet changes, and supplemental nutrients was begun, Kelly's condition improved by 75%–85%.

What does Kelly's history demonstrate? She had a number of complaints suggestive of classic allergies that dated back to her infancy and toddlerhood. By 10 years of age, she exhibited many of the symptoms frequently noted in children with environmental illness and chemical sensitivity. Her allergic tendency set the stage for possible future problems that were manifested clearly when she was exposed to an environmentally unsound, chemical-laden school. No one can predict how long Kelly's chemical sensitivity will last, but the progression of her illness indicates she needs additional medical help. It is anticipated that Kelly's symptoms will subside slowly. She has returned to school, but she continues to experience stomachaches and behavior problems.

It has been estimated that, like Kelly, approximately 15%–20% of the population has allergies and at least another 20% has environmental illness (Rapp, 1991). Those children who have allergies themselves or who have family members with allergies are most apt to manifest illnesses related to foods and chemicals. The challenge is to recognize this medical possibility as early as possible for each child. If this potential illness can be identified by the time a child enters kindergarten or earlier, a child's learning potential should be enhanced. A number of clues typically are evident before the age of 5 years, and these clues tend to expand and intensify with time.

PHYSICAL CLUES THAT SUGGEST POSSIBLE ENVIRONMENTAL ALLERGIC ILLNESS

Many children have unsuspected and unrecognized forms of environmental allergic illness that cause recurrent symptoms from infancy through adulthood. Physical clues are often present in these children. These characteristic changes in appearance include some combination of the following:

1. Allergic salute, rubbing the nose upward with the palm of the hand
2. Allergic nose wrinkle, horizontal crease across the bridge of the nose, caused by pushing upward on the nose with the hand
3. Persistent runny or stuffy nose
4. Open mouth with dry lips from mouth beating
5. Sneezing several times in a row
6. Clucking throat sounds or throat clearing
7. Dark blue, black, or pink eye circles
8. Wrinkles below the eyes
9. Swollen eyelids
10. Bags below the eyes
11. Glassy, glazed eyes associated with sudden behavior changes
12. Extremely red earlobes and/or cheeks
13. Constant movement of the legs
14. Marked abdominal distension
15. Dry itchy skin patches on body and/or arm and leg creases

Exposure to allergens also can result in behavior changes in children. These behavior patterns often include some combination of the following:

1. Reluctance to remain dressed (especially in children ages 2–4 years)
2. Dislike of being held, hugged, or touched (in infancy and beyond)
3. Crawling under furniture or into dark corners
4. Intermittent or constant difficulty writing, drawing, or speaking
5. Extreme negativity or irritability (e.g., threatening to kill)
6. Racing about aimlessly
7. Inability to sit through a story, meal, or television program
8. Extreme drowsiness

9. Sudden unexplained aggression or violence
10. Problems falling asleep or staying asleep or frequent nightmares
11. Poor school performance on a daily or intermittent basis
12. Depression; feeling unloved; and/or, at times, wanting to die or to kill

Symptoms of environmental illness or allergies also tend to vary with a child's age (Rapp, 1991, in press; Rapp & Bamberg, 1986). Typical age-specific symptoms are as follows. Infants who have environmental illness or allergies engage in prolonged screaming and crying; require multiple formula changes because of numerous intestinal complaints (e.g., colic, diarrhea, constipation, excess spitting, vomiting); demonstrate a nonstop need to be fed, an inability to sleep, a desire to be bounced up and down, self-injurious behavior, extreme crib rocking, reluctance to be cuddled, infrequent smiling, irritability, recurrent ear infections, nose or chest congestion, eczema, excessive drooling, and extreme perspiration; and often walk before 10 months of age. Affected toddlers' symptoms include temper tantrums, intestinal complaints, leg pain, earaches, hyperactivity, behavior problems, fatigue, stuffy noses, throat clearing, chronic coughs, asthma, headaches, crawling in dark corners, and refusal to be touched. Children who have environmental illness or allergies experience hay fever, clucking throat sounds, asthma, headaches, leg pain, intestinal complaints, sudden mood and behavior changes (e.g., hyperactivity, fatigue, depression, irritability, aggression), erratic school performance, inability to write or draw, hives, eczema, recurrent infections, or bedwetting after 5 years of age. Affected adolescents and adults have symptoms that include fatigue, depression, irritability, aggression, moodiness, excessive crying, intermittent poor memory, chronic asthma, hay fever or sinusitis, intestinal complaints (e.g., bloating, diarrhea, constipation, gas), chronic bowel disease, bad breath, hives, obesity, and alcoholism (Rapp, 1991).

Although all of the above-mentioned conditions may have many other medical causes, undetected allergies sometimes play an unsuspected role. Environmental allergic illness should be considered in children who display the above-described physical signs and in those who have relatives with allergies. For a list of conditions that may be allergy related, see Table 5.1.

Table 5.1. Conditions in which environmental illness or diet may play an unsuspected role

Recurrent ear infections
Excessive bloating, gas, or abdominal discomfort
Headaches
Depression
Inappropriate behavior or delinquency
Restless legs
Bedwetting or frequent or urgent need to urinate
Attention deficit disorder or attention-deficit/hyperactivity disorder
Tourette syndrome
Learning disabilities
Joint tightness
Obesity

Teachers can identify affected children on the basis of sudden inexplicable changes in activities or behavior or an inability to learn. Affected children often are described as having Dr. Jekyll/Mr. Hyde personalities. If a child usually behaves well all morning but routinely or frequently returns from lunch with bright red ears and starts to hit other children, disrupts the class, or falls asleep at his or her desk, the cause may be something he or she eats for lunch. If such behavior changes routinely occur before lunch, hypoglycemia may be the cause. If a child always becomes tearful in a dusty classroom, the cause may be an allergy to dust in that room. If a straight A student repeatedly fails exams given on rainy days, he or she may have a mold allergy. If a child acts inappropriately after using the school lavatory, he or she may have an allergy to cleaning chemicals or disinfectants. It is imperative that, when sudden changes in behavior occur, a teacher stops and asks what was different just before the change. Answers often are found that simply. Teachers should try to identify, in particular, those children who have a combination of typical allergies, erratic learning ability, and the physical manifestations of environmental allergies or chemical sensitivities.

CAUSES OF ALLERGIC REACTIONS

When a sudden change in how a child looks or behaves is observed, it is important to ask "What has that child just eaten, touched, or smelled?" Could the cause be something inside or outside the school, a food, or a chemical? It is important to remember that it is not how long or how often the child is exposed, but how sensitive he or she is, that determines whether a reaction occurs. When the causes of these problems are explored, parents and teachers often notice patterns of response that help identify previously hidden sensitivities. If no one asks why a behavior or physical change occurs, cause-and-effect relationships can remain elusive for years.

The physical signs of allergy can occur daily or intermittently, depending on how often a child is exposed to an allergen. A given child can be allergic to almost any substance to which he or she is exposed. Environmentally allergic children usually have multiple sensitivities; these can include several common foods, dust, mold spores, grass, weed and/or tree pollen, pet dander, and chemical odors. Molds and dust routinely are causative factors in older buildings. Children who are sensitive to mold tend to be symptomatic on damp, rainy days, whereas children who are sensitive to chemicals can have difficulty after the slightest exposure to various odors.

Allergic reactions can be caused by anything a person eats, touches, or smells. Food allergies often are caused by junk foods, but many nutritious foods also can cause allergies. Allergies to foods, such as milk, wheat, corn, and apples, to name a few, are common. Major suspect foods can easily be identified by listing the five foods that a child "loves" or "hates" (Rapp, 1991). Foods that individuals crave or to which they feel addicted are likely to cause allergies in those individuals. For example, if a person hates milk but loves cheese, he or she may have a milk allergy. If someone absolutely loves or hates all dairy products, they may have a milk allergy. If, however, someone is indifferent to dairy products, it usually indicates no problem with this food group (Rapp, 1991). All food-related sensitivities are not allergies; foods can contain natural or mold toxins, as well as various synthetic chemicals.

It is simple to determine whether a single suspect food actually causes a reaction (Boris & Mandel, 1994; Egger, Carter, Graham, Grumley, & Soothill, 1985; Egger, Stolla, & McEwen, 1992; O'Shea & Porter, 1981; Rapp, 1978, 1979, 1991, in press; Rapp & Bamberg, 1986). First, the food should not be eaten in any form for 4–7 days. This abstinence allows time for the food to be eliminated from the body entirely. For example, if milk is suspected, all dairy products must be stopped for a full 4–7 days. (This includes cheese, yogurt, ice cream, casein, milk powder in packaged foods, and luncheon meats and soups because they frequently contain caseinate or whey.)

The best way to do a single food elimination trial is for a child's parents to stop serving the suspect food from Monday through Friday. Teachers can help to ensure that the child does not cheat by trading lunches or snacks with other children. Parents then should add the single food back into the diet after school on Friday and watch for any change in how the child looks, acts, feels, or behaves over the weekend. The child's teacher should be informed when a test food causes a reaction.

If many foods are thought to cause symptoms, a multiple food elimination allergy diet may be tried (Rapp, 1991, in press; Rapp & Bamberg, 1986). In part 1 of this two-part diet, the most commonly offending foods are eliminated for 1 week. The following week, in part 2, foods are added back one by one each day for 1 week, and all symptoms are recorded. Typically, a child with food allergies will begin to feel better between days 4 and 7 of the first week. This part of the diet detects the food allergy; the second week often helps pinpoint the exact source(s) of a child's health, emotional, or learning problems.

After troublesome foods have been detected, children who have been diagnosed with multiple food allergies should follow a rotation diet (Powell, 1989). This diet allows them to eat very gradually increasing amounts of problem foods at 4-day intervals. Rotating foods is thought to help desensitize the body, so that existing food allergies will lessen. A child on this type of diet must take packed lunches to school to maintain the rotation plan. Teachers who have such children in their classes must be made aware of their dietary restrictions. Teachers and parents should communicate about the dos and don'ts of the child's diet and discuss ways to encourage acceptance among the child's classmates. A casual attitude and the de-emphasis of a child's special needs can be most helpful in this regard: A teacher should allow a child to eat his or her special foods or leave for the health office with as little attention or comment as possible.

Individuals with diagnosed or suspected food allergies are encouraged to eat simply; meals and snack should consist of only a few foods. Eating in this way makes it easier to determine the specific cause of any allergic reactions that may occur. Foods ideally should be organic or less contaminated by pesticides or antibiotics, because these so often cause allergic reactions. In general, artificial coloring (especially red), sweeteners, additives, preservatives, sugar, popcorn, and dairy products should be avoided. For healthful snack ideas for schools, see Table 5.2.

Table 5.2. Healthful snacks for children

Whole grain crackers made from a single grain such as wheat, rye, or rice
Rice cakes
Pretzels (made from wheat, corn, yeast, or soy)
Dried fruit (unsulphured, available at health food stores)
Fresh fruits or vegetables
100% fruit juices made from a *single* fruit (e.g., apple, grape, orange)
Nut butters, such as peanut, cashew, or almond, on crackers or rice cakes

Note: All of these snacks should be organic whenever possible and should be ingested only if they do not cause symptoms of allergy, sensitivity, or illness.

CHEMICAL SENSITIVITIES

Chemicals can affect individuals regardless of whether they have allergies, although individuals who have allergies are more susceptible (Ashford & Miller, 1989). Frequently, children will react, at least initially, when exposed to only one particular odor or chemical. Once an individual has developed a major sensitivity to a single chemical, it is not unusual for him or her to develop multiple chemical intolerances. This means that exceedingly small amounts of many chemicals that previously had caused no difficulty become capable of causing a reaction. Once this common spreading phenomenon has been established, treatment becomes very challenging, because it is nearly impossible for a person to avoid the plethora of chemicals that pervade present-day society.

Newly built or remodeled schools or child care centers tend to create chemically related problems, because construction materials, such as plywood and wall paneling, frequently are laden with formaldehyde. Especially during the first months after construction, these chemicals can be released into the air and inhaled by the children and adults who spend many hours inside such buildings. This process of chemical contamination is known as outgassing, which means the chemical odors are released from the furniture, clothing, carpets, and so forth, as time passes. Within a few months or years after construction, most chemicals will have been released. In rare cases, however, carpets have outgassed enough chemicals to present a potential cause of illness for up to 20 years. New carpets are one unsuspected source of outgassed chemicals in schools (Beebe, 1991). Carpets and carpet adhesives usually contain a vast array of chemicals; some of these are known to cause people to become very ill. Some carpets contain only a few offending chemicals and cause no symptoms in people. Other carpets can cause mild-to-severe symptoms, which can cause chemical sensitivities or worsen preexisting sensitivities. Although the worst carpets can adversely affect many students and teachers in a given school, carpets are not always identified as a source of school-related health or academic problems.[1]

Problems related to outgassed chemicals are compounded by the poor ventilation that often exists within school buildings; this condition has been termed *sick building syndrome.* It was first noted in the 1970s and

[1]To determine whether a carpet contains potentially harmful chemicals, send a 10-inch carpet square to Anderson Laboratories, 773 Main Street, West Hartford, VT 05084-0323.

resulted from a strong movement to make buildings more energy and cost efficient. The energy crisis in the United States prompted the closure of intake vents, and, as a consequence, much less air entered school buildings. In addition, design changes, such as windows that do not open, added insulation, doors designed to exclude outside air, and artificial air circulation systems, combined to create poor-quality indoor air. These modifications are effective ways to keep out the cold in winter and the heat in summer, but they have caused ever-increasing amounts of dust, mold, and chemical pollution to be retained in the air in school buildings. Students, teachers, and other staff who spend time in these "tight" buildings often have health complaints related to chemical or other indoor air pollution. It is now widely known and accepted that indoor air often is more toxic or contaminated than is outside air.

Symptoms of chemical exposure from carpets or others sources vary. They often include the following: headache, fatigue, weakness, confusion or memory loss, inability to concentrate, breathing problems, muscle and joint pains, twitching, numbness or tingling of the face or extremities, peculiar taste in the mouth, irritation of the throat and eyes, sensitivity to light, swelling, hoarseness, dizziness, depression, nausea, rashes, anxiety, and abdominal pain. On occasion, individuals experience only one symptom; however, a combination of symptoms is more common. Such complaints often are initially misdiagnosed as flu; when these medical problems persist or intensify, a second misdiagnosis is often made suggesting that the affected person has a functional or psychological illness.

There is one clue that aids in identifying chemically sensitive individuals: They usually are the ones who have the keenest senses of smell and can perceive odors that others do not detect. They will be the first to develop symptoms when a chemical odor is barely apparent, and their complaints should not be taken lightly. They are often unable to tolerate exposure to malls, lavatories, restaurants, and/or churches. Chemically sensitive students can alert teachers so that potentially serious chemical problems within classrooms are more quickly detected. Correcting or eliminating the source of a problem before others become ill always is the best form of treatment (Berthold-Bond, 1990; Dadd, 1990; Maberly & Anthony, 1992a, 1992b). (For a list of features that would exist in the ideal environmentally safe school, see Table 5.3.)

The following is an example of how a teacher's illness should have alerted school administrators to a problem; she was not believed, however, until a student also became ill.

ONE TEACHER'S SCHOOL-RELATED ILLNESS

W.S., a middle-age teacher, had had many typical allergies as a child. She became ill when she was assigned to a different classroom; she was ill for 4 years. Before her reassignment, she had been healthy, but after this change, she began to be sick every year from October to May. She had congestion, colds, laryngitis, and constant upper respiratory infections. She started each day by sniffling and coughing up mucus. Her chest felt heavy. When she was not in school, she felt better. W.S. learned that the teacher who

Table 5.3. The ideal environmentally safe school

Building

10–20 years old and neither dusty nor moldy

Proper ventilation—intake and exhaust vents adequately open, windows that
open

Odor-free paints

Wood or hard vinyl tile floors

Safer cleaning agents, disinfectants, and deodorants[a]

Classrooms

No unnecessary clutter

Air purifier in each room to remove dust, pollen, molds, and chemicals

Enclosed bookcases

Easily cleaned cotton curtains

Furniture made of metal or genuine wood (not plywood)

No plastic or other synthetic materials

Odor-free art supplies, crayons, and marking pens

No pesticides, plants, or pets with fur or feathers

Full-spectrum shielded lighting

Teachers and students

No scented personal products (e.g., perfume, after-shave, cosmetics, hair spray)

No tobacco use

Food

As plain as possible

Organic

No artificial colorings, preservatives, additives, artificial sweeteners, and sugar

A balanced menu with a wide variety of fresh foods

[a]*Sources:* Berthold-Bond (1990); Dadd (1990); Gorman (1993).

had previously been assigned to that classroom had experienced such
severe headaches that she would lie on the floor behind her desk during
school hours.

W.S. was embarrassed because she always was complaining about feeling ill. Her list of medical complaints became progressively longer and
more severe by the end of the school year. Her voice was so hoarse, she
could barely whisper. She could not speak for a full month. She eventually
discovered that the combination of closed ventilation ducts, an extremely
old carpet, lavatory disinfectants, and pollinating grass was simply more
than her body could tolerate.

W.S.'s health improved that summer and she felt well, as she did
whenever there was a school vacation. By October, however, she had
returned to the same classroom and her usual infections returned. She had
so many symptoms that the school principal joked to others about her
"complaint of the week." Few believed her endless array of "psychosomatic" symptoms. Her excruciating migraine headaches made her feel as if her
head would explode because of the throbbing, stabbing pain. She had
intestinal problems and excessive abdominal gas. She had ringing and a
feeling of fullness in her ears. Her muscles ached, and her feet felt numb.
Her eyes burned and teared, and she had intermittent problems seeing and
breathing.

Because she felt ill at school and better at home, she realized something in her school building must be the cause of her illness. At about the time that W.S. made this connection, a school superintendent not only listened, but also took appropriate action. This change in attitude, however, did not happen until a student also became ill in her classroom. A teenage boy became so fatigued that he could no longer play sports. His most unusual and inappropriate behavior in W.S.'s classroom helped convince the principal and the superintendent that the teacher's complaints might be genuine. By this time, W.S. was so ill that she would develop a flushed face and severe shortness of breath within minutes after entering her classroom.

The superintendent wisely decided to investigate the school's heating/ventilation/air conditioning system. All of the ventilation ducts were opened (for years, only two had been open). New filters were installed. Odorous chemicals were removed from every classroom and environmentally safer cleaning agents and disinfectants were used instead. Air purifiers were placed in W.S.'s room and in all of the affected boy's classrooms. Before purchasing new carpet, school officials exposed the student to several carpet samples to see which one he seemed to tolerate best. Initially, school officials carpeted only one room, and when this boy did not become ill in that room, this more expensive carpet was purchased for the entire building.

W.S.'s health improved further after she consulted an environmental medical specialist. She made changes in her own home, similar to those made in the school. She began to drink pure, glass-bottled, spring water and tried to eat organic foods. She took nutrients to help strengthen her immune system and to aid her body in detoxifying chemicals. She became more knowledgeable about when and why she was ill. She learned to pinpoint and avoid the probable causes of her symptoms more quickly, before she became very ill. At present, she is well unless she is accidentally exposed to some chemical; this exposure is much less frequent now because her classroom, school building, and home all are more environmentally sound.

When W.S. was provoked during P/N allergy testing with an extract made from her school air and the original school carpet, she suddenly developed a hoarse voice and breathing difficulty, similar to the difficulty she had noted so frequently in her own classroom. These symptoms were relieved in a few minutes when the correct dilution of the school air allergy extract, the neutralizing dose, was administered. She also was found to be sensitive to other typical allergenic substances.

After the necessary changes were made, W.S.'s experience during the next school year was entirely different. For the first time, she did not develop her typical pattern of repetitive illness that had been so evident during the previous 4 years. Not only did her health improve, but others who were in her classroom appeared to be healthier. Unlike other teachers who have become sick from exposure to chemicals at school, W.S. did not become a prisoner in her own home. She did not have to apply for worker's compensation or Social Security benefits, and there was no need for litigation. The school administrators' approach was practical, sensible, and farsighted.

They have a teacher who is able to work and does not need to be replaced. They have a child who feels better, can remain in school, and does not need to receive home schooling. They also have helped other children and teachers who had less obvious symptoms and illnesses related to the same daily school exposures. This school administration and school board chose very wisely. This situation illustrates how a few sensible, necessary changes and precautions can defuse a potentially serious medical and legal powder keg.

WAYS TO EASILY IDENTIFY POSSIBLE CAUSES OF ALLERGIC REACTIONS

Once someone suspects that an allergy or chemical sensitivity is causing symptoms in one or more students or teachers, further investigation is necessary. The following commonsense approach requires no medical expertise and often pinpoints the specific cause of allergic reactions. If individuals can learn to think like medical detectives, they often will succeed in their search for meaningful answers.

Some ways to identify allergic reactions, including recognizing the typical changes in how affected children feel, look, act, behave, and learn, were mentioned previously. Another method to detect allergic reactions is to monitor a child's ability to write or draw. A teacher who suspects that a classroom is contaminated can ask a child or entire class to write or draw at the beginning and end of class. If there is deterioration in a student's penmanship during art class, for example, it may mean that the child was allergic to something he or she touched or smelled in that class (provided that he or she had nothing to eat). Changes in writing can include letters that are upside down, large, sloppy, and backward. For younger children, a sudden inability to color within the lines can occur (see Figure 5.1).

An additional way to spot allergic reactions applies to children with asthma. Asthma should be suspected when a teacher or parent notices a child wheezing or experiencing prolonged coughing after laughter, exercise, or exposure to cold air. Children older than 5 years of age can check their lungs by blowing as forcefully as possible into a plastic tube called a peak flow meter before and after each meal or each class. If the gauge on the instrument drops 15% (or from 300 to 255), it is possible that something present in a room or a food that was eaten recently has caused asthma. Find and eliminate the cause, and asthma should no longer be evident. If the cause is not found, the need for asthma drugs can persist for a lifetime. Whenever possible causative factors are identified, they should be shared with the child's parents and doctor.

The final indicator of environmental illness is a change in a child's pulse. The pulse functions like an alarm within the body. When an allergenic substance enters the body, an alarm often goes off, and the pulse goes up. A rise in pulse rate greater than 20 beats per minute is significant in a resting child. For example, a teacher or parent might suspect that a child is sensitive to something in the science classroom. The child's pulse in other classrooms averages approximately 80 beats per minute; after science class, however, the child's pulse routinely rises to 110 beats per minute. Assuming the child was at rest for both readings, such a change would

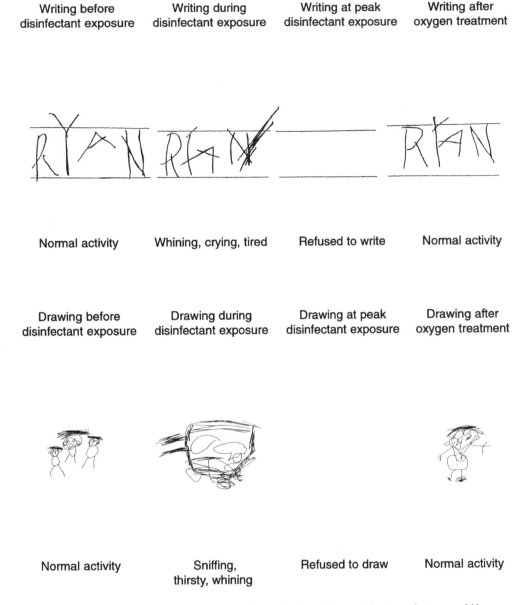

Writing before disinfectant exposure	Writing during disinfectant exposure	Writing at peak disinfectant exposure	Writing after oxygen treatment
Normal activity	Whining, crying, tired	Refused to write	Normal activity

Drawing before disinfectant exposure	Drawing during disinfectant exposure	Drawing at peak disinfectant exposure	Drawing after oxygen treatment
Normal activity	Sniffing, thirsty, whining	Refused to draw	Normal activity

Figure 5.1.   Disinfectant aerosol exposure causes changes in the writing and drawing of a 4-year-old boy.

indicate a probable environmental reaction. Another example would be the child who seems fine until naptime. If this child's pulse suddenly increases or the child coughs or sneezes, perhaps he or she has a sensitivity to the molds and dust in a carpet on which he or she is resting. At rest, the pulse should go down, not up. Any of these changes would be especially significant when associated with red ears, dark eye circles, restless legs, or a change in attitude, behavior, or writing.

In summary, five possible helpful clues to spot an allergic reaction are 1) a change in the child's appearance (e.g., red ears, dark eye circles, spacey eyes, restless legs, nose rubbing); 2) a change in how the child feels, acts, or behaves (e.g., angry, irritable, hostile, tired, hyperactive, vulgar); 3) a change in the child's writing or drawing; 4) a change in the child's breathing (e.g., coughing, wheezing, fast breathing, a drop of greater than 15% on a peak flow meter); and 5) a rise in the child's pulse rate of 20 beats or more per minute. (A normal pulse rate is 80 or fewer beats per minute.)

HOW TO KEEP RECORDS

To find the cause(s) of environmental allergic reactions, a child's teacher or parent probably will need to keep some records (Rapp, 1991). For example, if a child is hyperactive shortly after lunch, someone should make a note of what he or she ate. By keeping a list of foods on "bad" days and a second list of foods eaten on "good" days, possible suspect foods can be identified easily. The foods common to both lists should be crossed off, and those that remain on the "bad" list are the possible culprit(s). The teacher can then share this list with the parent (or vice versa) and possibly suggest books and videos about food allergies or environmental illness to read and view.

Once a suspect food has repeatedly caused the same type of allergic reaction, either that food can be eliminated from the diet or the parents can seek the help of an environmental medical specialist who knows how to treat most food sensitivities with allergy extracts.[2] These physicians, unlike most others, know how to test for and treat most food allergies. The help of an environmental medical specialist is especially necessary when a child is found to be sensitive to many foods or to dietary staples, such as milk, wheat, corn, eggs, and/or sugar. Unfortunately, many general allergists do not believe that multiple food allergies occur and can be treated with allergy extracts or that foods can affect a child's actions or behavior.

The following sections present examples that further illustrate how teachers can help identify environmentally allergic reactions and find their causes. The key always is to ask what the child ate, smelled, or touched just before the symptom(s) began. Could the problem be caused by something inside or outside the school, a food, or a chemical (Rapp, 1991; Rapp & Bamberg, 1986)?

THE NEW CARPET IN MS. JONES'S CLASSROOM

Ms. Jones noted a deterioration in the school performance of the students in her second-grade class shortly after a new carpet had been installed in her classroom. Many of the students complained of headaches and stomachaches late in the day. Ms. Jones also noticed she suddenly needed to take aspirin almost daily to relieve her own headaches. Because these complaints began shortly after the carpet had been installed, Ms. Jones suspected that the carpet was the cause. To test her theory, she had all of her students write their names and draw pictures before they entered the class-

---

[2]For information about finding an environmental medical specialist, contact the Environmental Allergy Center at (716) 875-5578 or the American Academy of Environmental Medicine at (913) 642-6062.

room in the morning. She also asked whether any of them felt sick, noted whether they looked or behaved unusually, and recorded their comments. She then allowed the children to sit and play on the carpet for 1 hour. Afterward, she again asked them to write their names, draw pictures, and tell her how they felt, and she recorded their new complaints. Ms. Jones then reported which children showed significant changes in these variables to the parents and other teachers so that steps could be taken to resolve the problem.

BILLY'S SENSITIVITY TO APPLE JUICE

Two of the students in Ms. Griffin's morning kindergarten class intermittently wet their pants in school. She noted that one of the students, 5-year-old Billy, invariably had bright red ears on the days he had accidents. Suspecting a sensitivity to something, Ms. Griffin asked Billy what he had for breakfast each day for a week. It quickly became apparent that Billy's red ears and wet pants only occurred on days when he drank apple juice for breakfast. She advised Billy's mother of her suspicion and Billy's mother eliminated apple juice from his diet for the week. Billy did not wet his pants again until his mother gave him apple juice again on a Saturday. Billy, his mother, and Ms. Griffin were all glad to discover the cause of this problem.

MELISSA'S CHEMICAL SENSITIVITY

Every Thursday morning, Mr. Hopper noticed that one of his brightest students, 9-year-old Melissa, could not sit still in her seat. She fidgeted constantly. This problem lasted most of the morning and did not reappear until the following Thursday. Mr. Hopper knew that Melissa also had allergy symptoms in pollen season, so he suspected that her Thursday morning behavior change might, in some way, be caused by a sensitivity to something. One week he had happened to come to school early on a Thursday to put up new decorations. He ran into the janitor who was cleaning the desktops in his room with a strong-smelling cleaning product. Mr. Hopper inquired and found out that the janitor routinely cleaned the desks every Thursday morning. To test for this suspected chemical sensitivity, some of this cleaning product was sprayed on Melissa's desk before school on Friday. Melissa's pulse rate was 76 beats per minute before she entered the class. After an hour of fidgeting at or near her desk, her pulse rate rose to 100 beats per minute. The school began to use a hypoallergenic cleaning product, and Melissa's Thursday fidgeting and pulse changes did not recur.

JONATHAN'S ALLERGY TO POLLEN

Jonathan seemed to be one of the brightest and most outgoing children in the toddler classroom of the early childhood center he attended. In April, however, his teachers noticed a drastic change. In addition to physical symptoms, including a pale appearance, dark eye circles, and a runny nose, his personality seemed to change almost overnight. He became very quiet and withdrawn. On the first day that the classroom windows were opened, he crawled under a desk and refused to be touched. His parents also noticed these changes and took Jonathan to see an allergist. After he started allergy extract treatment for grass pollen, Jonathan returned to his former, cheerful self.

Most teachers are much too busy to become part-time physicians, but sometimes they have no choice. They sometimes spend more time with the children than do their parents. On occasion, it is impossible to teach a class when one hyperactive child is disrupting everyone. The *who* is easy to identify, but the *what, why, where,* and *how* only become evident when a caring educator develops an increased awareness about environmentally related illness. With a little insight, the answers can be so obvious that teachers wonder how they missed spotting the cause-and-effect relationships for so long.

FUTURE DIRECTIONS

The recognition of food and environmental sensitivities as significant but frequently undetected causes of illness, behavior, and learning difficulties in children must be enhanced at many levels. Parents, teachers, school administrators, and health care providers all should become much more aware of the diverse ways in which environmental factors can adversely affect some children. As Anne Raymer's essay illustrates, the effects of environmental illness can profoundly change the lives of children and their parents.

One factor impeding progress is the lack of readily available, simple, inexpensive treatments for environmental illness. If large numbers of affected children were helped, then it would be hard to dispute the existence of this problem. The reality is that many doctors, as well as teachers, have never been taught how to recognize or treat food allergies despite the attention devoted to this topic from the 1920s to the 1970s (Rinkel, 1944a, 1944b; Rinkel, Randolph, & Zeller, 1950; Rowe, 1922, 1925, 1928, 1931, 1932a, 1932b; Rowe & Rowe, 1972; Speer, 1970). Although present-day effective allergy extract treatment for food sensitivities is expensive, invasive, and time consuming, it is effective.

Environmental medicine is a comprehensive, expansive, and detailed approach to treating allergies. It entails extensive patient education, and, therefore, is time consuming. Only those parents with children who are significantly ill (such as the Raymers) will seek and find the physicians who treat environmental medical illness. Some Americans prefer the faster, easier approach of daily symptomatic medication. A rapidly expanding segment of parents, however, now desires to understand why their children need drug treatment not simply which drug provides the best temporary relief.

Research must be directed to investigate faster, easier, less expensive, more effective treatment modalities. Several promising techniques exist, but these must be evaluated thoroughly to ensure they are both safe and effective. The larger medical community must acknowledge that the answer to all illness is not a better, more sophisticated drug, but the detection and elimination of the cause of an illness or a learning problem. To bring about this change in philosophy, much more in-depth education is required at all levels. Sources of funding must be obtained to investigate newer, possibly more successful, approaches to resolve certain school-related illnesses. In 1996, there seems to be much more emphasis on scientific studies to validate the efficacy of drugs than on studies to investigate inexpensive, simple diets to resolve a child's problem. If a 1-week diet results in an improvement of almost 70% in 4–7 days, why is it not tried before activity-modifying drugs, such as Ritalin, are prescribed?

Research is also needed to determine which common childhood disorders may respond to diets or allergy treatment; for example, autism, on very rare occasions, appears to subside entirely when a child is placed on a totally dairy- or wheat-free diet (Reichelt, Ekrem, & Scott, 1990). Every child with autism should be placed on such a diet. Research to determine the percentage of children with autism who can be helped in this way is imperative. Rare success stories in the treatment of autism also have been reported after allergy treatment by using a technique called enzyme-potentiated desensitization. Other studies have found B_6 nutritional supplementation helpful for children with autism (Rimland, 1964, 1988).

Another priority should be the study of preschool history forms similar to that shown in Figure 5.2. If this preschool history form is validated, it might enable us to ascertain if it is indeed possible to preselect which children might develop learning problems in the future. Earlier proper medical intervention might prevent many secondary learning, social, and psychological sequelae. Such identification and intervention may enable those who care for and educate young children to truly help those children who are environmentally ill to learn at a level more comparable to their ability.

Additional biochemical studies are needed to determine whether nutrients are deficient in affected children (Krohn, 1991). If cellular nutritional deficiencies are recognized and treated, the body should be better able to withstand the onslaught of chemicals that are so pervasive and damaging to our immune systems and that can lead to allergies and sensitivities in children and to much more serious illnesses in adults.

Finally, additional studies should be conducted to compare the effects of diet, exposure to environmental factors, such as dust and molds, and exposure to chemicals. It is absolutely necessary that all of these factors be considered simultaneously. How well some children (and teachers) feel, act, behave, and perform in the school environment is determined by their total exposure. If the combined effect of foods, dust, molds, and chemicals is more than an individual can tolerate, some adverse change will be evidenced. The aim, therefore, is to decrease one or all of these factors, so the total exposure is not at a level that will cause illness.

The responsibility has been placed on educators to help recognize children whose learning is affected by environmental factors. Educators' efforts will be rewarded because they will be able to teach children who will be able to learn, and they and their students will be healthier. Sometimes a child's entire future depends solely on the degree of a caring teacher's concern and awareness. If cause-and-effect relationships can be detected and corrected early, many children's lives can be redirected so they can reach their highest potential.

Name _____   Date _____

Fetal history (in utero)

Excessive hiccups	Yes _____	No _____
Excessive kicking	Yes _____	No _____
Too active	Yes _____	No _____
Too quiet	Yes _____	No _____

Infant history

Prolonged screaming and crying	Yes _____	No _____
Colic after 6 months	Yes _____	No _____
Excessive diarrhea	Yes _____	No _____
Constipation	Yes _____	No _____
Excessive spitting	Yes _____	No _____
Excessive vomiting early in infancy	Yes _____	No _____
Nonstop need to be fed	Yes _____	No _____
Inability to sleep	Yes _____	No _____
Self-injurious behavior	Yes _____	No _____
Crib rocking	Yes _____	No _____
Irritability	Yes _____	No _____
Recurrent ear infection by 8 months	Yes _____	No _____
Congested nose or chest	Yes _____	No _____
Eczema	Yes _____	No _____
Excessive drooling	Yes _____	No _____
Excessive perspiration	Yes _____	No _____
Walking before 10 months	Yes _____	No _____
Bronchiolitis or wheezy chest	Yes _____	No _____
Inability to drink milk formulas	Yes _____	No _____
Inability to drink soy formulas	Yes _____	No _____

Childhood history

Nose

Nose symptoms	Yes _____	No _____
warm months	Yes _____	No _____
cold months	Yes _____	No _____
all year	Yes _____	No _____
Stuffy nose	Yes _____	No _____
Noisy breathing	Yes _____	No _____
Watery, runny nose	Yes _____	No _____
Sneezes several times in a row	Yes _____	No _____
Rubs nose upward	Yes _____	No _____
Crease across nose	Yes _____	No _____
Wiggles nose	Yes _____	No _____
Picks nose	Yes _____	No _____
Clears throat often	Yes _____	No _____
One cold after another	Yes _____	No _____
but not sick	Yes _____	No _____
how often per month	_____	

(continued)

Figure 5.2.   Suggested preschool history form.

Figure 5.2. *(continued)*

Nosebleed (excessive)	Yes _____	No _____
how often	_____	
Number of facial tissues used per day	_____	

Ears

Recurrent ear problems	Yes _____	No _____
Fluid in eardrums	Yes _____	No _____
Intermittent hearing difficulty	Yes _____	No _____
Ear popping	Yes _____	No _____
Flushed, red ear lobes	Yes _____	No _____
Dizziness	Yes _____	No _____
Ringing in ears	Yes _____	No _____

Chest

Wheezing or asthma (whistle in chest)	Yes _____	No _____
with infection	Yes _____	No _____
at other times	Yes _____	No _____
Coughing	Yes _____	No _____
with laughter	Yes _____	No _____
with exercise	Yes _____	No _____
with exposure to cold air	Yes _____	No _____
when drinking cold drinks	Yes _____	No _____
at night	Yes _____	No _____
when damp outside	Yes _____	No _____
Excessive chest infections	Yes _____	No _____
Unclear voice	Yes _____	No _____
Chronic laryngitis	Yes _____	No _____

Eyes

Itchy	Yes _____	No _____
Red	Yes _____	No _____
Watery	Yes _____	No _____
Puffy, baggy	Yes _____	No _____
Wrinkles under eyes	Yes _____	No _____
Blue, black, or red circles under eyes	Yes _____	No _____
Burning	Yes _____	No _____
Painful	Yes _____	No _____
Sensitive to light	Yes _____	No _____
Excessive squinting or frowning	Yes _____	No _____
Excessive rubbing	Yes _____	No _____
Glassy	Yes _____	No _____

Skin

Pale complexion	Yes _____	No _____
Eczema or atopic dermatitis	Yes _____	No _____
Itchy rash on body	Yes _____	No _____
Itchy rash in arm or leg creases	Yes _____	No _____
Itchy round spots on skin	Yes _____	No _____
Itchy skin—no rash	Yes _____	No _____

(continued)

Figure 5.2.   *(continued)*

Extremely wrinkled palms	Yes _____	No _____
Dry, scaly spots on skin	Yes _____	No _____
Cracked toes or fingertips	Yes _____	No _____
Hives or welts	Yes _____	No _____
Easy bruising	Yes _____	No _____
Tender, sore spots	Yes _____	No _____
Swollen face, feet, lips, or eyes	Yes _____	No _____
Puffy fingers or hands	Yes _____	No _____

Intestines

Swelling of face or lips	Yes _____	No _____
Sore edges of lips	Yes _____	No _____
Irritation of mouth corners	Yes _____	No _____
Excessive drooling	Yes _____	No _____
Frequent lip licking	Yes _____	No _____
Cracked, dry lips	Yes _____	No _____
Mottled "bald" patches on tongue	Yes _____	No _____
Deep grooves or fissures in tongue	Yes _____	No _____
Excessive throat mucus	Yes _____	No _____
Excessive throat clearing	Yes _____	No _____
Itchy roof of mouth	Yes _____	No _____
Canker sores (ulcers on gums or inside cheeks)	Yes _____	No _____
Bad breath	Yes _____	No _____
Frequent stomachaches	Yes _____	No _____
Frequent nausea	Yes _____	No _____
Excessive rectal gas or belching	Yes _____	No _____
Bloated abdomen	Yes _____	No _____
Frequent diarrhea	Yes _____	No _____
Frequent constipation	Yes _____	No _____
Itchy rectal area	Yes _____	No _____
Ulcers—gastric or peptic	Yes _____	No _____
Colitis	Yes _____	No _____

Behavior

Constant restlessness	Yes _____	No _____
Irritability	Yes _____	No _____
Hyperactivity, restlessness	Yes _____	No _____
Moodiness	Yes _____	No _____
Clumsiness—poor coordination	Yes _____	No _____
Listlessness, tiredness	Yes _____	No _____
Hostility—fights a lot	Yes _____	No _____
Temper tantrums	Yes _____	No _____
Frequent or easy crying	Yes _____	No _____
Unhappiness	Yes _____	No _____
Nervousness	Yes _____	No _____
Behavior problem	Yes _____	No _____
Emotional unresponsiveness	Yes _____	No _____

(continued)

Figure 5.2.　*(continued)*

Poor balance	Yes _____	No _____
Fainting	Yes _____	No _____
Barking or making strange noises	Yes _____	No _____
Vulgarity in speech or actions	Yes _____	No _____
Looking "spaced out"	Yes _____	No _____
Looking "demonic"	Yes _____	No _____
Talking nonsense	Yes _____	No _____
Talking too much	Yes _____	No _____
Repeating self	Yes _____	No _____
Sleeping poorly	Yes _____	No _____
Nightmares	Yes _____	No _____
Sleepy and tired in A.M.	Yes _____	No _____
Sleepy after eating	Yes _____	No _____
Sleepy after napping	Yes _____	No _____
Unexplained depression	Yes _____	No _____
Tics or twitching	Yes _____	No _____
Seizures	Yes _____	No _____
Stuttering	Yes _____	No _____
Good vocabulary but inability to read	Yes _____	No _____
Poor language development	Yes _____	No _____
Inability to draw, print, or write	Yes _____	No _____
Poor concentration or attention span	Yes _____	No _____
Dislike of loud noises	Yes _____	No _____
Dislike of bright lights	Yes _____	No _____
Dislike of certain odors	Yes _____	No _____

Bladder or Kidney

Wet pants in daytime	Yes _____	No _____
Frequent daytime urination	Yes _____	No _____
Wet bed at night	Yes _____	No _____
How many times per week	1　2　3　4　5　6　7	
Up at night to urinate	Yes _____	No _____
Recurrent bladder infections	Yes _____	No _____
Other kidney/bladder problems	Yes _____	No _____
Blood in urine	Yes _____	No _____
Urine burns	Yes _____	No _____
Rushing to urinate	Yes _____	No _____
Difficulty starting urination	Yes _____	No _____
Difficulty stopping urination	Yes _____	No _____
Spraying bathroom when urinating	Yes _____	No _____
Urinary problems recurring at specific times each year	Yes _____	No _____

Miscellaneous

Headaches	Yes _____	No _____
Growing pains	Yes _____	No _____
Muscle aches	Yes _____	No _____
Neck or shoulder pain	Yes _____	No _____

(continued)

Figure 5.2. *(continued)*

Backaches	Yes _____	No _____
Leg cramps	Yes _____	No _____
Weak legs	Yes _____	No _____
Joint aches	Yes _____	No _____
Tight joints	Yes _____	No _____
Tingling in arms or legs	Yes _____	No _____
Excessive perspiration	Yes _____	No _____
Extreme sensitivity to cold	Yes _____	No _____
Excessive infections	Yes _____	No _____
Frequent fever without infection	Yes _____	No _____
Vaginal itching or irritation	Yes _____	No _____
Irregular heartbeat	Yes _____	No
Sudden rapid heartbeat	Yes _____	No _____
Unusual body or hair odor	Yes _____	No _____
Excessive thirst/appetite	Yes _____	No _____

REFERENCES

Ashford, N., & Miller, C. (1989). *Chemical sensitivity: A report to the New Jersey Department of Health.* (Available from Practical Allergy Research Foundation, P.O. Box 60, Buffalo, NY 14223)

Beebe, G. (1991). *Toxic carpet III.* (Available from Practical Allergy Research Foundation, P.O. Box 60, Buffalo, NY 14223)

Berthold-Bond, A. (1990). *Clean & green.* (Available from Practical Allergy Research Foundation, P.O. Box 60, Buffalo, NY 14223)

Boris, M., & Mandel, F.S. (1994). Foods and additives are common causes of the attention deficit hyperactivity disorder in children. *Annals of Allergy, 72,* 462–468.

Dadd, D.L. (1990). *Nontoxic, natural, and earthwise.* Los Angeles: Jeremy P. Tarcher.

Egger, J., Carter, C.M., Graham, P.J., Grumley, D., & Soothill, J.F. (1985). Controlled trial of oligoantigenic treatment in the hyperkinetic syndrome. *Lancet, 1,* 540–545.

Egger, J., Stolla, A., & McEwen, L. (1992). Controlled trial of hyposensitization in children with food-induced hyperkinetic syndrome. *Lancet, 339.*

Gorman, C. (1993). *Less toxic living.* Texarkana, TX: Optima Graphics.

Krohn, J. (1991). *The whole way to allergy relief and prevention.* Point Roberts, WA: Hartley & Marks Publishers.

Maberly, D.J., & Anthony, H.M. (1992a). Asthma management in a "clean" environment. I. The effect of challenge with foods and chemicals of peak flow rate. *Journal of Nutritional Medicine, 3,* 215–223.

Maberly, D.J., & Anthony, H.M. (1992b). Asthma management in a "clean" environment. II. Progress and outcome in a cohort of patients. *Journal of Nutritional Medicine, 3,* 231–248.

O'Shea, J.A., & Porter, S.F. (1981). Double-blind study of children with hyperkinetic syndrome treated with multi-allergen extract sublingually. *Journal of Learning Disabilities, 14*(4), 189.

Powell, D. (1989). *Why 5? A complete allergy guidebook.* (Available from Practical Allergy Research Foundation, P.O. Box 60, Buffalo, NY 14223)

Rapp, D.J. (1978). Does diet affect hyperactivity? *Journal of Learning Disabilities, 11,* 56–61.

Rapp, D.J. (1979). Food allergy treatment for hyperkinesis. *Journal of Learning Disabilities, 12,* 42–50.

Rapp, D.J. (1991). *Is this your child? Discovering and treating unrecognized food allergies.* New York: William Morrow and Co. (Also available from Practical Allergy Research Foundation, P.O. Box 60, Buffalo, NY 14223)

Rapp, D.J. (in press). *Is this your child's world?* New York: Bantam Doubleday.

Rapp, D.J., & Bamberg, D.L. (1986). *The impossible child—in school, at home.* (Available from Practical Allergy Research Foundation, P.O. Box 60, Buffalo, NY 14223)

Reichelt, K.-L., Ekrem, J., & Scott, H. (1990). Gluten, milk proteins and autism: Dietary intervention effects on behavior and peptide secretion. *Journal of Applied Nutrition, 42*(1), 1–11.

Rimland, B. (1964). *Infantile autism: The syndrome and its implications for a neural theory of behavior.* New York: Appleton-Century-Crofts.

Rimland, B. (1988). Controversies in the treatment of autistic children: Vitamin and drug therapy. *Journal of Child Neurology, 3,* 568–572.

Rinkel, H.J. (1944a). Food allergy. I. The role of food allergy in internal medicine. *Annals of Allergy, 2,* 115.

Rinkel, H.J. (1944b). Food allergy. II. The technique and clinical application of individual food tests. *Annals of Allergy, 2,* 504.

Rinkel, H.J., Randolph, T.G., & Zeller, M. (1950). *Food allergy.* Springfield, IL: Charles C Thomas.

Rowe, A.H. (1922). Recent advances in the diagnosis and treatment of hay fever and asthma. *California State Journal, 20,* 94.

Rowe, A.H. (1925). The treatment of bronchial asthma. *Journal of the American Medical Association, 84,* 1902.

Rowe, A.H. (1928). *A handbook for the diabetic.* New York: Oxford University Press.

Rowe, A.H. (1931). *Food allergy: Its manifestations, diagnosis, and treatment.* Philadelphia: Lea & Febiger.

Rowe, A.H. (1932a). Food allergy in the differential diagnoses of abdominal symptoms. *American Journal of Medical Science, 183,* 529.

Rowe, A.H. (1932b). Uterine allergy. *American Journal of Obstetrics and Gynecology, 24,* 333.

Rowe, A.H., & Rowe, A., Jr. (1972). *Food allergy, its manifestations & control, & the elimination diets—a compendium: With important consideration of inhalant, drug, and infectant allergy.* Springfield, IL: Charles C Thomas.

Speer, F. (1970). *Allergy of the nervous system.* Springfield, IL: Charles C Thomas.

RESOURCES

The following resources[3] are available from Doris J. Rapp, M.D., F.A.A.P., F.A.E.M., at the Practical Allergy Research Foundation, Post Office Box 60, Buffalo, NY 14223, (800) 787–8780.

The video *Allergies Do Alter Activities & Behavior* is a supplement to the book *The Impossible Child—in School, at Home;* this three-part video runs 43 minutes.

The video *Impossible Child or Allergic Child?* runs 20 minutes.

The video *Why a Clean Classroom?* is a supplement to *Is This Your Child? Discovering and Treating Unrecognized Food Allergies* and runs 60 minutes.

The multiple food elimination allergy diet and tips sheet.

The single food elimination diet.

---

[3]Publication of this resource list does not constitute endorsement by Paul H. Brookes Publishing Co.

VISIONS FOR THE NEW MILLENNIUM

WHAT WOULD AN IDEAL WORLD LOOK LIKE FOR YOUNG CHILDREN AND THEIR FAMILIES?

Julie Blackman

The ideal world would be safe. No child would fear the upraised hand of an adult, no child would live with the pain of trust betrayed by a violent adult, no child would transform this pain into rage, and no child would become dangerous in his or her own right.

Drug abuse, poverty, and homelessness impair parenting. All of these promote a reliance on violence that would be reduced were drug abuse, poverty, and homelessness ended. In the millennium, no one would abuse drugs, no one would be poor, and no one would be homeless.

Attitudes toward children would be different. "I brought you into this world. I can take you out": My son, standing on the sidelines during a soccer game, heard a parent say this to his son. It is a shocking but succinct statement of a view of children that mocks the millennium.

Children are entitled, simply because they are children, to good and fair treatment. Often, however, children's rights are violated by adults who pass along the sad legacy of their own rights denied.

Children would not be abused and neglected in an ideal world. Instead, parents would respect their children, learn their children's unique qualities and proclivities, and use that knowledge to shape their child-rearing practices. Parents would neither insult their children verbally nor neglect them by placing their own needs above the needs of their children. They would not hit their children and, instead, would teach them by example of the many nonviolent, creative, and constructive alternatives to hitting.

In the millennium, the awful by-products of poverty would not be advanced as culture nor would the justification that it is part of African American culture for parents to hit their children. From a highly educated, African American elementary school principal to the women I interview in jail cells because they have killed their tormentors, I have heard an advocacy for violence in African American families. The principal said

> You could walk into any classroom in this building and hear African American children talk about getting "beat" at home. All African American parents beat their children. Sometimes, the best thing you can do is beat your kid. You don't understand black families.

One woman, who killed her mother after years of physical and sexual abuse, said, "When I didn't hit my son, my neighbors would say, 'What are you trying to do? Do you want him to grow up white?'"

Recently, I interviewed a woman who killed her boyfriend. She said, "I got hit a lot as a kid. I just figured that's how blacks were."

This is not to say that parents of other colors do not hurt their children; they do, of course. Even so, touting violence against one's own children as a defining aspect of one's culture frightens me. I think it is a sign of a kind of self-hatred that endangers those who possess it and those they touch.

In the millennium, all parents, of every color, will be attentive and loving. All will eschew the use of violence for any purpose whatsoever. No one will speak of violence positively or proudly; no one will claim violence as part of his or her culture.

In the millennium, children will not pack guns along with peanut butter and jelly sandwiches. Mothers will not send their children to school with bruises on their backs and bellies full of anger. Fathers will not worry that their children will be killed by their peers.

In ideal classrooms populated by children of different races, ethnicities, cultures, and abilities, no child will be distinguished for his or her capacity to do harm. In 1996, classes created by the politics of inclusion are controversial. Certainly, the dangerous child poses the greatest threat to the view that all children should be educated together.

To the extent that schools can and do identify children who are abused and dangerous in this pre-millennial era, important questions remain about what to do. Efforts to remove children from violent homes are beset by problems. Keeping children in historically violent families and offering supportive services seems to be a better approach but requires more long-term, attentive support services than the United States, as a society, ever has elected to provide.

In the millennium, schools will be envisioned more clearly as adjuncts to families and will focus on meeting emotional as well as academic goals; they also, of course, will be adequately funded. Class sizes will be small, and children will experience their classrooms as family-like environments, with countless daily opportunities to be loved and taught.

I have tried to focus on the question put to me: "What would an ideal world look like for young children and their families?" Before concluding, I must add that this essay has been difficult to write because it has required me to deny the reality of 1996. In my work as a forensic social psychologist, I traverse the legion space across social classes daily—from my upper middle-class home in the New Jersey suburbs to my office on the 49th floor of a New York City skyscraper to an airless cell used to interview prison inmates in the Bronx Supreme Court Building.

My idealistic thoughts of the millennium are tempered by reality, as families dissolve before our eyes, poverty increases, and millions of teenagers give birth to millions of babies. The hope for social change that I felt 20 years ago is faded. Alongside that hope are nightmares of what I have seen in the most devastated and dangerous of families. In the millennium, there will be no fear of violence within families.

CREATING AN IDEAL WORLD FOR CHILDREN

Valora Washington

Creating an ideal world for children and families can only begin when we all, as individuals, neighbors, and citizens, strengthen our sense of community. It is necessary but not sufficient that our caring embraces our own children. All children are *our* children. Together, these children represent the wealth of diversity and strength that exists in the United States.

Many of us know the African proverb "It takes the whole village to raise a child." To create an ideal world for children and families, I would add "It takes all of us working together to make the village."

The 1980s and 1990s have brought important advances that have expanded and improved the options available to families to support child well-being. Many of the advances were initiated and are sustained by child care professionals and providers. Early childhood experts contribute their efforts to improve the child care system by articulating standards of professional practice through professional membership groups such as the National Association for the Education of Young Children, working directly with children in child care and preschool programs, training teachers and caregivers in institutions of higher learning, and striving to make the fragmented child care system more comprehensible to parents through child care resource and referral agencies.

The efforts of professionals, however, must be joined by increased support for children from other sectors of society with innovative efforts by pioneers in business, government, and philanthropic and human services organizations. In addition, the best efforts of all of these groups must be joined and amplified by citizens in local communities, at the state level, and in Washington, D.C. The late 1980s and early 1990s have brought rapid changes and new investments in child care, Head Start, and preschool programs. New research studies and strategic thinking by professionals have highlighted methods for building high-quality programs throughout the early child care system. In many states and communities, these years have been a time of creative ferment, during which new ideas, approaches, and systems have been envisioned and put into place. Opportunities and challenges usually come hand in hand, however, and creativity must be matched by persistence and commitment to the hard work of implementation and long-term support. Innovative programs and investments in children have the best chances for success when they are supported by a consensus within the broader community that children and families are a top priority. Only then will community members in the public and private sectors alike devote the time, energy, and resources required to create a truly caring community for children.

CLOSING THE GAP BETWEEN WHAT WE KNOW AND WHAT WE DO

Creating community consensus and public will is essential to our efforts to make our world ideal for children. The importance of public will is highlighted by the gap between what we *know* through research and practice and what we actually *do* to promote optimal child outcomes. We know better than we do. It is clear that, since the 1960s, research has greatly enriched the knowledge that we use to define the characteristics of ideal settings for children. Nonetheless, typical arrangements for the care and nurturance of children and families have not kept pace with the lessons we have learned. We are applying what we know very poorly.

Many effective strategies that work for children, families, and communities have been used throughout the United States. The time has come to build on these successes and establish comprehensive, coordinated policies and practices that work efficiently and effectively. By doing so, we can make a lasting difference for children and families. What works and is available for some must be brought to scale and made available for all.

A WORLD OF CARING

To create an ideal world for children, caring must be a central value. Caring relationships are the soul of productive human existence. It is through these relationships that most individuals thrive, learn, and grow.

My value as a professional is to create or enhance relationships that encourage the growth of competent, caring, loving, and lovable people: parents who care about their children, teachers who care about their students, families who care about their neighborhoods, children who care about their elders, and institutions that care about the communities around them and vice versa. These are important caring relationships that are critical to our continued survival.

In an ideal world

> Every child should be
> cherished in families,
> supported by communities,
> considered holistically,
> nurtured with care.

This is a vision of a world in which caring is valued. In this ideal world, we would build on our record of success in serving children and families and our considerable knowledge base, bring to scale the policies and practices that have proved to be effective, and leverage our skills and expertise into the broader systems changes that would strengthen both families and our society as a whole.

Is this ideal world possible? Absolutely! Margaret Mead inspires us: "Never doubt that a small group of thoughtful, committed citizens can change the world; indeed it is the only thing that ever has." Margaret Mead realized that it takes all of us working together as partners to meet the challenge of change.

All of us in our local communities and states should view ourselves as committed citizens who can create change. Collectively, even now, we are becoming stronger voices for families and the professionals who serve those families. Building on the phenomenal growth and success of the entire array of professions and groups that address family issues, we are well positioned to effectively influence public policy, advance knowledge in the field, and strengthen professional practice.

To create an ideal world for children, we must

1. Create and strengthen a broader network of new and existing leaders to build a coherent, integrated message about our values and vision for children and families
2. Share lessons from model projects or initiatives that demonstrate that the vision is possible
3. Engage in processes focused on both local capacity-building issues and statewide visions
4. Foster a climate for improving public policy at all levels of government

Albert Einstein advised us that "the significant problems we face cannot be solved at the same level of thinking we were at when we created them." To create the ideal world for children, we will need to resist the temptation to simply develop new programs or change procedures; rather, we will need to address, fundamentally, our values and our basic sense of community.

II

CARE AND EDUCATION
ISSUES IN EARLY CHILDHOOD

Everything I Have Learned About Education, I Learned Through My Son

Janet M. Krumm

When our son Joseph was born 9 years ago, I knew with certainty that my husband and I would need assistance traveling down the road of life with him. Two mornings after we tearfully received the tentative diagnoses of Down syndrome and tetralogy of Fallot, I sat on the side of my bed in my private hospital room, my gaze lingering on the parking lot outside, trying to figure out how I could find those agencies in Grand Forks, North Dakota, that could help us. My immediate thought was the telephone book, and I resolved to do this research as soon as we left the hospital.

Within a few hours, a social worker at the hospital came into my room and put into my hands a list of all of the agencies that offered help to families like mine. She spent a little time explaining which ones we might want to contact first and the kind of help each offered. My surprised amazement turned quickly into gratitude. I found myself on first base without even having to swing the bat!

When Joseph was 6 months old, we moved from the Great Plains to the Granite State. Our move to New Hampshire was necessitated by two pressing realities—Joseph's need for major heart surgery and the approaching end of my husband Jack's tour of duty at Grand Forks Air Force Base. By researching which medical center had the lowest mortality rate for the type of surgery Joseph needed as well as which nearby Air Force base was located in a state offering early intervention services (not all states did at that time), we decided that New Hampshire was the place to be. A little less than a year after Joseph's surgery, Jack separated from the Air Force, and we now call New Hampshire home.

In the 9 years since Joseph's birth, we have met many social workers, therapists, and educators. Joseph has been enrolled in three early intervention programs, two child care programs, a community preschool, and a special education preschool and is now in elementary school. He missed out on kindergarten because the private Catholic program to which we had applied decided at the last moment that he really was not welcome after all.

Through all of this I have learned a lot about early education for children with disabilities. One lesson, however, stands out: The single most powerful factor in any effort to educate a child like my son is the belief of the educator.

When Joseph was in early intervention (all three programs), the attitude of each service provider was that he could and would accomplish what any other child could—he would just take a little longer to do it. Home visits were very supportive, encouraging, and celebratory, as well as informational. I learned a lot about child development, but most important, I learned that I was not alone in believing in a positive future for my son.

I was hungry for information, and early intervention was a resource. The only dark spots during this time were the compulsory 6-month written evaluations. Ongoing verbal reports always emphasized the positive—what Joseph had accomplished. Participants in the team evaluations always tried to be positive, but whatever efforts they made were negated by the written reports, which documented the growing gap between Joseph's development and so-called normal development. I can remember leaving those meetings completely devastated. I came to view them as ordeals I had to endure, the price I had to pay for continued assistance.

Our family's first major philosophical disagreement with early intervention came when Joseph graduated to a toddler group. At the age of 2 years, he became part of a group of other toddlers, all of whom had a disability or were at risk for developing one. What disturbed me most about this arrangement was that, even here, in what already could be viewed as a segregated group, Joseph was segregated even further.

For some of the children in this group, their only disability was a delay in their speech and language development—motor coordination and problem-solving abilities were good. For instance, they could cut with scissors with no problem; Joseph could not. As a result, Joseph was put into a small group with only one other child, another child with Down syndrome. Scissors never found their way into this group.

In addition, the room was organized in such a way that the children had no access to any of the toys. Decisions about which toys the children could play with, how they could play with them, and for how long they could engage in the play were all adult directed. There was no freedom of choice or building on children's interests.

After fruitless discussions with the director of the program about learning theory and what I thought was most beneficial for my son, I decided to take him out of the early intervention program and find a more challenging community program. Having rejected the kind of support the early intervention program was willing to offer, I received no additional assistance from them.

Fortunately, I did have the support of our area agency, which, in New Hampshire, is the regional service delivery system. This agency also had philosophical differences with the early intervention program in our area, and the director of the agency saw assisting me as a way to influence the kind of services offered to families of young children.

My search for a community preschool began; it culminated in Joseph's enrollment in the preschool program run by the University of New Hampshire Child and Family Center. Joseph was the first child with a disability accepted into their program. Nobody had had any experience with a child like Joseph before, so everything was a learning process. I can remember walking up the path toward the Child and Family Center on that first morning, holding my son's hand, and being scared to death.

I spent the entire morning there, teaching the teachers about Joseph, and helping him participate in the activities. Those 3 hours were an emotional rollercoaster ride for me—one minute I was convinced I had made a huge mistake, and the next I was certain that this was the best thing I could have done. That morning, I left physically and emotionally exhausted and literally climbed into bed upon returning home.

Joseph spent 3½ years at the Child and Family Center. Those years were full of challenges and opportunities that were not offered in the special education preschool program. I know this because he was also enrolled in our district's program for most of that time. I would have preferred that he spend a full day at the Child and Family Center, but theirs was only a half-day program. So, we split his time between the University's program and the school district's program.

What made his experience at the Child and Family Center so successful despite the staff's inexperience with children with disabilities was their overriding conviction that this was the right thing to do. They held a strong and unshakable belief that my son belonged in that program, that he had as much right as any other child to be there. That belief eliminated all the time and energy that would otherwise have been expended debating his right to participate along with the other children. Instead, the team put all their effort into figuring out how to make it work on a daily basis.

Joseph's success at the Child and Family Center paved the way for him to be integrated into the general classroom in the elementary school he attends. He had a *history* of success that could not be denied; and that success was continually put into the context of what typically developing preschoolers were doing. It was a wonderful support to me during school district team meetings, when the emphasis by special educators was on Joseph's weaknesses, to hear the early childhood professionals from the Child and Family Center emphasize his strengths and accomplishments. They did so consistently by pointing out how Joseph's skill level fit into the range of skills exhibited by typically developing children. It made me feel like Joseph was a part of this group, not apart from it.

Sometimes I think that the challenges in Joseph's life are not what he himself faces as much as the challenges he presents to those responsible for his development, whether they be his parents, his teachers, his therapists, his dentist, his playground supervisors, or his priest on Sunday mornings. Joseph is simply a little boy who destroys all illusions that life is governed by normalcy. His basic premise in life appears to be that life is good; people are, for the most part, caring; and everything is open to investigation. He forces those who interact with him to see the world from a different vantage point, which may mean perching precariously on a ledge far above familiar terrain.

Because how people react to Joseph depends largely on the value system within which they operate, new situations hold the potential for devastation as much as for exhilaration. We have experienced our share of rejection of our little boy. That history has taught us to be wary, to always be on the alert for the sucker punch. That caution has served us well in certain instances, but also has created unintended consequences when communication was shaky.

Now that Joseph is in elementary school and does not learn like most children, the challenges he presents to teachers are compelling. Only those teachers who are confident enough in their ability to figure things out, humble enough to admit their lack of knowledge, committed enough to the moral right of my son's inclusion, and flexible enough to discard methods that just do not work are equipped to create a welcoming, positive, and challenging climate in which my son (and his classmates) will flourish. That is a tall order.

How can society help with this task? First, we must educate our administrators. A big part of the reason for Joseph's success in elementary school is the exceptional principal he has. John O'Connor is committed to children and to what is best for each child. His commitment provides the support that is necessary to the incredible effort that is exerted every day by the teachers and support staff who work with Joseph. Mary Jane Moran of the Child and Family Center was the grounding support of Joseph's past team of preschool professionals.

Second, we must educate our educators. Some of the greatest obstacles to our desires for Joseph were the convictions of the special educators, who were unable and unwilling to see a picture that differed from the one they were taught. In addition, although we have been fortunate to have teachers in Joseph's school who were willing and happy to have Joseph in their classes, I know of other teachers who are convinced that it is not their job because they were not trained to teach such children.

Although it is critical to change the college training for teachers, that is only part of the picture. There are many teachers out there who have already finished their training and have no desire to venture into unfamiliar territory. We must give major incentives to teachers to rethink their competencies and stretch their professional abilities.

Finally, we must develop mechanisms to reduce the adversarial tensions that exist between parents and educators. As good as the relationship I now have with my school district is, I am still viewed as a demanding mother with yet another off-the-wall idea when I walk into a meeting. If educators took more initiative in coming up with alternatives for parents instead of simply waiting in uneasy anticipation of and reacting to parents' demands, I, for one, would be happy to relinquish part of this heavy responsibility I carry: the feeling of having to be knowledgeable about every new theory and method so that my child can have a fighting chance for a quality education.

It boils down to belief and trust. I can trust someone who really believes in my child. (For that matter, why should any parents trust educators who do not believe in their children, typically developing or not?) More important, Joseph will flourish under that loving care and grow into a capable, contributing citizen of our community. As for me, every time I grow weary of the tremendous effort it takes to ensure Joseph is on the right path in life, I remember that the positive tomorrow I want so passionately for my son begins with every decision I make today.

6

THE PARADOX OF DIVERSITY
IN EARLY CARE AND EDUCATION

Rebecca S. New and Bruce L. Mallory

Early childhood education professionals approach the beginning of the 21st century with a sense of hope tinged with trepidation. This ambivalence is well justified; members of our field have much to acclaim, even as we aspire to overcome the negative conditions cited in Chapters 2, 3, and 4. Early childhood educators have made substantial progress in promoting the professional status of the field and gaining at least the verbal support of some U.S. leaders for the critical importance of high-quality early child care and education. Children, specifically, and the field, in general, have benefited from the availability of new advances in medical treatment, educational technology, and professional development. These signs of progress coexist, however, with social conditions that are testing the field and placing children at risk in unprecedented and urgent ways.

A central feature of these social conditions is the increasing economic, cultural, and developmental diversity that now characterizes U.S. society. Over the last quarter of this century, the distance in material wealth between those who have and those who have not has grown consistently in the United States (Center on Budget and Policy Priorities, 1987); and children represent an increasing proportion of the population living in poverty. At the same time, more children are being born to U.S. families of racial and ethnic minority groups, and more ethnically diverse families are emigrating into the United States. Children of these families are overrepresented in the poverty rate (Huston, McLoyd, & Garcia Coll, 1994). It is estimated that, by the year 2000, one third of the U.S. population will be African American, Hispanic, or Asian American (House Report 102-198, 1991). During the first half of the next century, these groups will constitute a majority of the U.S. population. In addition, increasing numbers of young children are being identified as having significant disabilities (Office of Special Education Programs, 1993). In essence, the diversity of the child population is growing in both type and number—a phenomenon that will most certainly challenge assumptions about diversity and the meaning of minority status. Given the insufficient scope of resources to meet the needs of this diverse population of children, the language of the early childhood field—especially in the area of early intervention—has

---

The authors shared equal responsibility for this chapter.

become the language of triage, in which professionals attempt to allocate chronically insufficient resources for a broad range of pressing needs. (See Janet M. Krumm's essay for a parent's perspective.)

These circumstances present early childhood professionals with new opportunities as well as new challenges, all of which must be confronted and accommodated. Choosing effective responses to meet the needs of contemporary young children necessitates a reexamination of basic assumptions regarding our goals and roles as they affect *all* young children in society. That the clarity of the task remains elusive is surely a result of the seemingly inextricable correlations among socioeconomic status (see Chapter 3), race, ethnicity, childhood illness and disability, exposure to violence (see Chapter 2) and substance abuse (see Chapter 4), family stress, and developmental sequelae. This confounding of variables also precludes any singular interpretation of the diversity that now characterizes America's early childhood settings, hence the title and topic of this chapter.

Responses to diversity among early childhood educators have included our earlier call for an "ethic of inclusion which embraces the physical, psychological, and social aspects of diversity in our society" (New & Mallory, 1994b, p. 11). Yet a fundamental paradox is inherent in this effort to embrace diversity in a society that continues to discriminate against those who are different. Therefore, the general aim of this chapter is to move beyond our plea for more inclusive ideology and to begin the task of deconstructing the concept of diversity. We have argued previously that the concept of diversity—and any subsequent analysis of its meaning—applies to two overlapping populations of young children—those who represent culturally diverse populations and those who exhibit diverse developmental sequelae and outcomes (New & Mallory, 1994b). In either case, a requisite first step in the "unpackaging" (Whiting, 1976) of a variable such as diversity is a consideration of the cultural context within which the term has evolved and is currently understood. Such an analysis is necessary for the subsequent distinction between forms of diversity that are intrinsic to individuals—those characteristics that require respect, tolerance, and fair treatment—and the sort of *ad*versity that results from oppressive or inequitable social conditions. This critical stance is essential to an improved understanding of the diversity inherent within human behavior and development and to the design of more effective, equitable, and efficient educational programs that meet the needs of all children in our society.

This chapter begins with a discussion of the American cultural context in which diversity is both cause for celebration and basis for discrimination. This section includes a brief description of the history and the nature of the more adverse consequences of diversity for the lives and educational opportunities of American children who are culturally or developmentally different. This analysis concludes with a review of the present state of social and institutional responses to such differences among children, as well as the theoretical and ideological paradigms that have supported and perpetuated those responses.

The next section of this chapter builds on the premise that, because diversity is an inevitable characteristic of U.S. culture, it should be reflected in our social institutions and empirical understanding of human development. A review of changing policies and exemplary practices in the fields of early childhood education and early childhood special education is considered in relation to recent interpretations of social constructivist theory, all of which contribute to the possibility of more inclusive early childhood programs. A central bias that motivates the chapter is that multiple expressions and pathways of development can provide educators with rich and complex challenges and opportunities to make early education truly responsive to the present and future lives of young children (see Janet M. Krumm's essay).

THE CULTURAL CONTEXT OF RESPONSES TO DIVERSITY

It is well established that responses to racial and developmental diversity are culturally situated (Farber, 1968; Mallory, 1993; Myrdal, 1944; Super, 1987). In the American context, the transaction between our unique history as a nation of immigrants and the competing demands of a pluralistic society heightens the tensions associated with determining appropriate responses to the diversity among us. It is also the case, as noted previously, that many of the advances, as well as the troubling trends, associated with the lives of young children and their families are specific to the United States. Therefore, the contemporary paradox regarding cultural and developmental diversity that daily confronts teachers and caregivers of young children is bound to the American sociopolitical context. This phenomenon has been interpreted as a crisis with respect to both "handicapism" and racism in educational settings (Bogdan & Biklen, 1977; Silberman, 1970). It is reassuring at this point to acknowledge that the Chinese symbol for *crisis* incorporates both challenge and opportunity. This duality aptly describes both the enthusiastic and the problematic responses of our field and the United States as a whole to human diversity.

On the one hand, Americans celebrate the differences manifested in the multiple languages, customs, and rituals expressed in the diverse ethnic and racial groups that compose U.S. citizenry. We take pride in the symbolic meaning of the Statue of Liberty and in the pluralism that characterizes our society. Citizens of the United States have Constitutional and legislated protections that are found nowhere else in the world for people who differ by virtue of race, age, gender, ethnicity, religion, or ability. Mainstream publishing companies, school boards, and professional educational associations attest to the need for and value of multicultural curricula and materials. On the surface, at least, it appears that, as a nation and as a profession, we welcome and foster diversity, through both formal and informal means. Indeed, we have historically measured our success as a nation by our ability to knit together diverse people into a cohesive and stable community—*E pluribus unum.*

On the other hand, it is now widely recognized that some forms of diversity carry with them social penalties that result in marginalization and disenfranchisement. Although the etiologies and contexts often differ dramatically, there is a striking similarity in the patterns and effects of discrimination experienced by those with ethnic differences (including racial and/or linguistic markers) and by those with developmental differences. As a culture, the United States has a long history of both acknowledging and denying the endemic racism that permeates our social institutions and arrangements. Disability also constitutes an "unexpected minority" status (Gleidman & Roth, 1980), as evidenced by social attitudes and treatment that unnecessarily preclude full participation in society. Furthermore, cultural discrimination has been found to contribute to developmental disparities. The U.S. Congress has acknowledged that transactional relationship by declaring

> Minority status and poverty are highly correlated with poor maternal, pre- and post-natal care and nutrition, which in turn, lead to health problems and developmental delays. These sociobiological factors may be exacerbated by institutional inequities which taken together elevate the incidence of disabilities among minorities and the poor. (House Report 102-198, 1991, p. 11)

Unfortunately, it seems that, despite our best democratic intentions, we have often been unable to overcome the pervasive forms of meritocracy and discrimination found in U.S. social institutions.

Many in the field of early education have tried to counter these prevailing social norms through efforts to acknowledge, respect, and respond appropriately to manifestations of diversity as they appear in the classroom. When differences are defined as deviances, however, and efforts to assist children deny their dignity, educational interpretations of diversity demand amelioration rather than celebration. Furthermore, when diversity results from or leads to discriminatory treatment toward particular individuals or groups, teachers must move beyond their classrooms to challenge these societal responses. These interpretations place new demands on the discipline of early childhood education. Efforts to rectify classroom and social inequities for children who are different will be more successful if we first understand the historical context that has contributed to these circumstances.

Diversity as Adversity: Historical Perspectives

Punitive Responses to Poverty, Disability, and Cultural Difference

Since the earliest stages of U.S. history, state and local governments have provided (sometimes demanded) substitute care for young children whose families live in conditions of poverty and disenfranchisement. Although marginalization from a group or society can be based on any number of idiosyncratic interpretations of diversity, poverty consistently has been a concomitant characteristic of many people in U.S. society who differ as a function of race, ethnicity, language, or (dis)ability. Poverty has been viewed as a sign of moral and intellectual deficiency, and poor people have been viewed as threats to the stability and welfare of the larger community. In the early 19th century, as a result of these attitudes, poor adults and children often were separated from their own families and communities, placed in state-run almshouses and orphanages, and, in many cases, required to perform indentured labor in compensation for society's benevolence.

Views on the treatment of very young children reflected prevailing attitudes about poverty, class, and religion. Organizations such as the Society for the Religious and Moral Instruction of the Poor, which was active in the 1820s, were instrumental in instigating public primary education in

Boston, Massachusetts, and elsewhere (Beatty, 1995). The aims of such education were clearly articulated in the Society's name. For children of the aristocracy and emerging middle class, the necessity of being at home under a mother's care was advocated by some, whereas others called for the creation of infant schools, where children's natural capacities and dispositions could be nourished. Foreshadowing later patterns, poor children were perceived as objects of intervention whereas advantaged children were regarded as competent, if immature, individuals who would benefit from a natural, nonacademic experience before being exposed to the rigors of primary school (Beatty, 1995).

Although poverty remains one of the most difficult dimensions to disentangle from the construct of diversity, other social and historical factors have also contributed to the deleterious consequences of being different. Antebellum laws that prohibited slave children (and adults) from acquiring literacy (Lightfoot, 1978) set a precedent that subsequently contributed to differential treatment for children of minority racial or ethnic membership. Later in the 19th century, during periods of rapid urbanization and massive immigration from Europe and Asia to the United States, children who were poor, uneducated, or ethnically diverse continued to be removed from mainstream society and/or forced to work in oppressive and dangerous conditions (Harrington, 1984). As a result of these interrelated patterns, minority children were viewed as less capable of benefiting from an education and, therefore, deserving of only the most meager level of support to survive in unconscionable conditions.

Throughout the 19th century, people with disabilities were also subject to discriminatory treatment for a variety of reasons, some of which are similar to those cited previously. Disability was viewed as a sign of both moral and genetic inferiority. Children and adults with seizure disorders, cerebral palsy, and severe mental retardation, for example, were warehoused in large institutional settings, initially to protect them from society but ultimately to protect society from them. Although individuals with disabilities were viewed as being incapable of benefiting from education, they often were expected to contribute to their own maintenance by participating in institutional labor. Impoverished citizens with disabilities were particularly likely to be singled out for such treatment due to prevailing beliefs about both the causes of disability (and poverty) and the necessity of segregation as an effective means of treatment and control (Gleidman & Roth, 1980).

At the turn of the 20th century, the precepts of social Darwinism, the new economies of mass production, and Weber's model of efficient bureaucracy had become accepted social truths. These beliefs, masquerading as science, provided a common frame of reference that rationalized differential treatment of the disabled, the poor, and the linguistically or culturally diverse. This social context was further influenced by the growing availability and acceptability of measures of so-called innate intelligence to legitimize systematic efforts to separate, track, and control children who were not part of the core culture (Katz, 1975; Tropea, 1987). By the early 1900s, a cycle of discrimination, poverty, and social and educational disparities associated with diversity seemed to be well underway. Public education and social welfare agencies were charged with dealing with the unsavory and marginalized "others," albeit with no recognition of the government's responsibility to reduce the institutional inequities and exclusionary practices that contributed to this marginalization in the first place. (An excellent discussion that expands on this brief history of schooling and institutional treatment for those who were "behaviorally and culturally deviant" is found in Richardson, 1994, p. 710.)

Government as Active Agent: A New Thrust

The devastating and widespread effects of the Great Depression acted as a significant catalyst for rethinking the purposes and possibilities of U.S. social policy. As a result, over the course of the 1930s and 1940s, the reluctance to acknowledge the responsibility of government in the reduction of social inequities eventually dissipated. The recognized need to intervene and offer assistance when necessary ultimately combined with an emerging ideology of government activism to justify the interventionist policies of the New Deal. The concept of universal protection for the unemployed, the retired, and the most destitute first became codified through PL 74-271, the Social Security Act of 1935, and then through single-purpose programs such as job training, subsidized public housing, and child care for children whose parents worked in wartime industries. Unlike later initiatives, these programs were not aimed explicitly at particular demographic subgroups that had experienced chronic economic and educational disadvantage. Rather, New Deal programs were intended to benefit the large numbers of children and adults throughout the country who were affected by acute economic and military crises.

The prosperity of the United States in the period following World War II initially masked the continuing problems faced by those who remained out of the social mainstream. In Harrington's (1962) terms, the "other America" remained invisible to the thriving middle class majority. Within a short time, however, new norms began to emerge with respect to both disability and racial equality. This ideological shift ultimately led to significant changes in educational policies and practices. The national consensus regarding the need to honor and rehabilitate war veterans with disabilities required the public to rethink its attitudes toward disability in general. The birth of the parent advocacy movement, evidenced by the formation of the National Association for Retarded Children, gave further impetus to the call for special educational services. The monumental impact of the *Brown v. Board of Education* decision in 1954 laid the groundwork for major policy reform in the fields of both general and special education. These legal and attitudinal changes co-occurred with the beginning of a paradigmatic shift in the field of child development. New evidence of the plasticity of early development for all children, including those with disabilities (Kirk, 1958), was joined by a growing awareness of the implications of Jean Piaget's work with young children, especially those living in poverty (Hunt, 1961). These intellectual and social developments established the foundation for arguments in support of compensatory education programs.

By the early 1960s, the civil rights movement and new views about the malleability of human development contributed to a political ideology that emphasized the need for a federal response to the poor and disenfranchised (Harrington, 1962). These forces converged in the form of national aspirations to achieve The Great Society by waging a war on both poverty and discrimination. Reflecting these aims, interventions of the 1960s and 1970s emphasized equal opportunity and access for all citizens, regardless of race, ethnicity, gender, or ability. Immediate and direct consequences for the field of early childhood resulted from these initiatives. Targeted and categorical programs began to evolve, often aimed at young children who were from low-income families or at those who had specific educational disabilities. Head Start, designed initially as an 8-week summer preschool program, was conceived as an essential tool to break the cycle of exclusion and school failure that had become so entrenched for impoverished American children. Similarly ambitious goals characterized the First Chance Network, the first national early intervention program aimed at preschool-age children with disabilities. The prevailing assumption seemed to be that short-term, narrowly focused efforts would boost children who were poor and/or disabled into mainstream society and allow them to remain there as productive, participating citizens.

Other categorical and targeted programs were begun in the decade between 1965 and 1975, including the Women, Infants, and Children Supplemental Nutrition Program (WIC) and the Early and Periodic Screening, Diagnosis, and Treatment (EPSDT) program. PL 94-142, the Education for All Handicapped Children Act of 1975 (subsequently reauthorized as PL 101-476, the Individuals with Disabilities Education Act [IDEA] of 1990), also mandated categorical services, in this case, for children with disabilities. Although serious concerns about categorical approaches to education and social policies were raised by the end of this first wave of War on Poverty initiatives (e.g., Hobbs, 1975), narrowly targeted, single-purpose programs have continued to represent the dominant approach to social policy for children who are economically and educationally disadvantaged up to the mid-1990s.

Contemporary Complexities

It is unfortunate for the targeted population of children, as well as for U.S. society as a whole, that the multifaceted efforts that began in the 1960s have proved inadequate to the task of social reform. At this point in history, there is a legal framework that delineates the rights of all children, including those who are disabled and ethnically diverse, to participate in core social institutions such as public schools. Nonetheless, as a field and a nation, we continue to struggle with the dilemma of achieving pluralistic schools and communities in which the integrity of diverse individuals and groups is respected. There are a number of explanations for why nationwide efforts have failed to mitigate against discrimination and social inequities, not the least of which is that the task itself has expanded in complexity as well as in size.

First and foremost, the number and variety of programs that have been put into place since the 1960s were neither large enough nor sustained enough to achieve the broad goals of ending poverty and discrimination. Notwithstanding the good intentions of most interventionist policies, the resultant programs have failed to reach a sufficient number of children and families to significantly alter the incidence or experience of either poverty or disability. Despite the plethora of federal programs aimed at young children who are disenfranchised in some way or another (more than 90 programs were reported by the U.S. General Accounting Office in 1994), many have consistently reported long waiting lists. For example, until recently, Head Start programs have served only 20%–30% of the eligible population; most young children who are economically disadvantaged still do not participate in any form of preschool program. Children with disabilities have been equally underserved. Federal special education funding has provided less than one third of the amount initially authorized, which, itself, was only 40% of the average cost of educating children without disabilities.

To summarize thus far, the number of programs and resources put into place since the 1960s has been inadequate to meet the chronic economic, educational, and social welfare needs of children who are poor, members of minority groups, and/or disabled. What is worse, many of these programs, as currently legislated and implemented, may exacerbate the very problems they were designed to ameliorate. Richardson (1994) has summarized the potential detrimental effects of categorical programs, arguing that

> the elaboration of these [categories] exposes a paradox: Reforms that seek to incorporate groups that have been historically excluded or exempted reinforce cultural and socioeconomic differences. As an attribute assigned by law for purposes of jurisdiction, legal status carries with it a "fixed quota of capacities and incapacities" (Graveson, 1953, p. 55) to act within the limits imposed by the classification. The capacities and incapacities of statuses are incidents that are imposed on incumbents. While the sources of incapacity may stem from real differences in social and economic circumstances, an added source comes from the legal classification structure itself, which imposes a legal personality on incumbents. (p. 714)

These concerns have serious implications for the field of early childhood education, particularly in light of the conservative political climate that characterizes the close of the 20th century. An urgent and pressing need exists for our field to acknowledge both its capacity and its responsibility to address the adverse consequences of diversity. As educators and as citizens, we cannot ignore the inadequate coverage of programs for children whose special needs require government intervention. This ethical imperative requires a stronger advocacy role on the part of all early childhood professionals. At the same time, we must be willing to assume a more critical stance regarding our own policies and practices. In particular, we need to consider the extent to which these much-needed programs contribute to the social fragmentation that has existed throughout our nation's history.

Separate Still Isn't Equal

One of the primary ways in which targeted categorical programs may perpetuate the continued disenfranchisement of certain populations is by institutionally separating these populations from the core culture. It is a tautology that families with incomes at or below the poverty level are most likely to use publicly controlled and subsidized child care. The proportion of children who are members of minority ethnic groups in such programs also is typically high; averages of 46% for African American children and 40% for Hispanic children were cited in one national study

(Phillips, Voran, Kisker, Howes, & Whitebook, 1994). In one widely known, longitudinal, center-based early intervention program (the Carolina Abecedarian Project), fully 98% of the enrolled children were African American (Campbell & Ramey, 1994). Head Start programs reflect this pattern of isolating culturally diverse families. Because only 10% of the children who attend this broadly conceived program are in families that have incomes above the federal poverty level, Head Start enrollments include a disproportionately high number of children who represent racial and linguistic minorities (Administration for Children, Youth, and Families, 1990). These figures are in stark contrast to the demographic makeup of programs that serve middle- and upper-income families, which often enroll a disproportionate number of Caucasian children compared with the general population. The principles of an integrated society, which should be reflected in an inclusive education, are therefore not being realized for *any* children, whether poor or middle income, minority or Caucasian.

The tradition of segregated services for children with economic and cultural differences has corollaries regarding children with disabilities. Institutionalized segregation can result from the application of special education law, because judicial and administrative interpretations have often favored separate instruction over inclusion. Federal and state special education laws emphasize both appropriate education and placement in the least restrictive environment. At times, disputes have arisen between parents and professionals that have required a choice between these two definitions of preferred educational placement. In general, especially when such disputes have been formally adjudicated, the decisions have been weighted toward the nature of the specialized treatment rather than the social context and consequences.

Not only are children who are different by virtue of ability, socioeconomic status, and culture kept apart as a result of social policy design, but the types of programs and services provided also vary as a function of child and family characteristics. For example, within and between income-segregated (and, therefore, often racially segregated) programs, quality varies considerably, as was observed in the 231 Head Start programs included in the study by Phillips et al. (1994). Consistent with the results of previous studies (e.g., Kagan, 1991), Phillips et al. found a curvilinear relationship between the family incomes represented in early childhood programs and certain indices of quality. On one hand, subsidized programs serving low-income families and private programs serving upper-income families had a higher quality of care in terms of program structure (e.g., group size, adult–child ratios, staff turnover) than did programs serving middle-income families. On the other hand, more discrete analyses focusing on teacher–child interactions within the same study revealed a linear relationship between family income and interpretations of program quality, such as responsiveness rates and instructional styles (Phillips et al., 1994).

Normative Theories and Approaches to Difference

Questions about the nature and consequences of those program differences, particularly when they are viewed as determinants of quality, are linked conceptually to debates within and between the fields of early childhood education and special education (Mallory & New, 1994a). These debates are in no small part related to the theories that have guided educators' understandings of and responses to young children. Developmental theories that reflect the core culture and the practices these theories have spawned assume a limited range of normal cognitive, linguistic, and social development (New, 1994). When young children demonstrate characteristics that are outside this presumed range of normalcy, they present both theoretical and practical dilemmas for the social institutions with which they come in contact. As a result, in the applied fields of both special education and compensatory education, there has been a prevailing assumption that different theories of development and learning are necessary for different populations of children (Mallory, 1992; New & Mallory, 1994a). This mindset has contributed to and been reinforced by the continuing separation of diverse children as described in this chapter.

For young children with disabilities, clinical approaches based on diagnostic/prescriptive and behavioral models of intervention have been dominant. These models isolate discrete areas of deficit to be remediated and rely on distinct professional competencies for therapeutic treatment. Therefore, speech-language pathologists work to overcome communicative impairments, physical therapists focus on gross motor problems, occupational therapists target fine motor control, and teachers and psychologists take on cognitive impairments and anything else that is left over. The increased use of clinical diagnoses for poorly defined learning problems (e.g., attention deficit disorder) and the concomitant reliance on medication to alter behavior provide additional evidence of this trend. The fragmentation or splintering of the child that results from such clinical approaches often is mirrored in classroom arrangements in which the curriculum is *dis*integrated into arbitrary segments or time blocks and children are grouped according to the diagnostic categories to which they have been assigned.

Similar problems occur in compensatory education, which, by definition, assumes that something critical is missing. Paradigms of "cultural disadvantage" that informed program design beginning in the 1960s have continued to affect early childhood practice, even as the old term has been discarded in favor of contemporary references to "disenfranchisement" and "marginalization." Throughout this time, assumptions of deprivation have contributed to various instructional models, some of which assume opposite places on the continuum of academic versus child-centered curricula. Therefore, numerous early programs for so-called culturally disadvantaged children include instructional models that assign a passive role to the child as learner. In these models, direct instruction, often given in separate settings for at least part of the day, is seen as essential to the acquisition of mainstream knowledge, behaviors, and dispositions. Alternative models, typically classified as play based or child centered, eschew academic goals in favor of promoting children's linguistic and social competencies. In all of these models, the aim is to enrich young children's experiences so that they might obtain attributes and attitudes similar to those of the core culture. None of these approaches acknowledges the dual possibility that culturally diverse children have the need and the right to acquire mainstream skills and knowledge, while bringing with them useful knowledge, ways of learning, and patterns of behavior that should be included in the culture of the classroom (Phillips, 1994).

Another theoretical influence on inclusionary practices (or the lack thereof) draws on the readiness model. Rooted partly in the Gesellian maturational framework, notions of readiness perpetuate exclusionary practices that keep children who are different out of both private and public early childhood settings. When young children arrive at preprimary or primary classrooms with obvious differences related to race, language, or visible disabilities, assumptions about ability and readiness may be made. Ample evidence exists that skin color, the condition of clothing, or the presence of a wheelchair or other prosthesis can lead to predictions of incompetence in the eye of the beholder (e.g., Alston & Mngadi, 1992; Goffman, 1963; Stone, Stone, & Dipboye, 1992). When a child has not yet mastered standard English or learned requisite skills, such as anticipating and responding to toileting needs, attending to adult direction for an extended period of time, or resolving conflicts verbally, he or she is said to be not yet ready to benefit from the classroom environment, whether or not a developmental disability label has been assigned. Such variations from the expected norms, which may result from diverse cultural or developmental patterns, often lead to the recommendation that a child defer program entry or attend a more specialized setting characterized by clinical approaches aimed at correcting the child's difference. As well intentioned as the readiness model may be, it has served to exclude rather than include children with developmental and cultural differences. As long as the option of exclusion exists, children who represent diverse ways of behaving and learning are at risk for separation and isolation when they enter into formal early education programs.

The readiness approach to diversity represents a continued allegiance to linear, sequential models of learning and instruction that discourage divergent or novel paths to development (Biddel, 1992). Not only does the readiness model have short-term exclusionary effects, it also undermines long-term goals of inclusion. Although readiness classes typically are intended to serve as transitions to more integrated settings, this early exclusionary experience is not likely to be a one-time-only occurrence. Research has shown clearly that preprimary and primary school programs often begin a pattern of tracking and segregation based on socioeconomic status or cognitive ability that continues throughout school and into adulthood (Oakes, 1985).

Many educators claim that these segregated services—whether defined as clinical, compensatory, or readiness—are not only well intended, but are also essential to the adequate provision of specialized services to children who would not otherwise benefit from more traditional educational programs. It is our contention, however, that, to the extent to which separate programs continue to exist for separate populations, the field is perpetuating the problem of a segregated society rather than adequately addressing children's needs.

The preceding sections have argued that, from both historical and more contemporary perspectives, traditional sociocultural paradigms continue to affect our beliefs and actions. In addition to the ethical problems associated with segregated services, problems of limited access remain because of the insufficient scope of coverage and variations in quality across programs for children from low-income and middle-class families. It is no wonder, then, that early childhood professionals remain uncertain about how best to advocate for the children and families for whom they work. The paradox of diversity undoubtedly is exacerbated by our historical tendency to find differences among children and to use those differences to justify separation and differential treatment. Rarely have professionals attempted to find those commonalities and strengths among children that might inspire the design of educational programs that reflect the diversity and range of young children's development. Yet, as Martin (1988) asserted, "Public education can only succeed when all children are accepted equally as contributors to the classroom community and when teachers work together, trusting themselves and children to learn" (p. 501).

Programs intended to care for and educate young children can be designed in such a way that they foster the positive aspects of diversity without perpetuating the adversities associated with minority status or developmental disability. To accomplish this, the immediate need is to direct sufficient public resources and attention to the most economically disadvantaged and socially disenfranchised members of our society *without* perpetuating further separation as a result of the regulations governing those resources. A more distant goal is to reduce those conditions that create disadvantage and disenfranchisement in the first place. The policy challenge inherent in achieving these aims is to develop a framework for scaling up successful early intervention programs in a way that includes a broad range of young children and affects not only their individual learning, but also acts as a catalyst for broader structural changes in society. This challenge is particularly salient in the final decade of this century as conservative political forces attempt to dismantle the social support apparatus explicitly aimed at families with young children who are poor and disabled.

PROMISING POLICIES, PRACTICES, AND PARADIGMS

In the previous section, we identified a pattern of differential treatment for diverse groups of young children that reflects a history of social and institutional discrimination. It was also argued that this treatment is the result of the application of divergent theoretical paradigms about young children's learning and development; these paradigms contribute to and result from such children being classified as deviant in some way—developmentally, culturally, or experientially. Having identified some of the constraints to inclusive early childhood education, our attention now shifts to signs of hope. There is an opportunity in the present historical moment to take advantage of the transactions among emergent policy, theory, and practice to strengthen our advocacy for all young children. In particular, a new congruence in ethical, social, and psychological understanding presents early childhood professionals with the conditions needed to move toward a more inclusive praxis in the field of early education.

Addressing Diversity in Social Policies

Attempts to create more inclusive policies that address the full range of cultural and developmental differences in young children are found in federal legislative actions that took place in the early 1990s. Examples from special education law, the 1994 Head Start reauthorization, and the first national education goal, codified in 1994, are used to illustrate these initiatives. Each of these examples marks some important policy developments that have significant consequences for young children.

Special Education Legislation

The most significant legislation affecting young children with developmental differences is PL 99-457, the Education of the Handicapped Act Amendments of 1986. In these amendments, Part H was added to the law to define services and make available funding for children younger than school age who have disablties or who are at risk for disability as a result of environmental, biological, or medical factors. The amendments require all states to provide a free, appropriate, public education for children with disabilities or developmental delays beginning at 3 years of age and to create a discretionary incentive program for states to extend this entitlement to newborns. The amendments also allow states, at their option, to use the noncategorical eligibility label *developmental delay* for children who are 3–6 years old, a classification that was previously allowed for infants and toddlers only. In addition, federal special education law places a significant emphasis on family involvement, such that infants and toddlers who receive services under Part H must have an individualized family service plan (IFSP) aimed at supporting families in their caregiving responsibilities. In this way, the law bolsters the movement toward family-centered services that has been underway for some time in the early intervention field (Dunst, Trivette, & Deal, 1988).

Federal law was further amended by PL 102-119, the Individuals with Disabilities Education Act Amendments of 1991. These amendments are significant for at least two reasons. First, the 1991 amendments to Part H added an explicit reference to the principle of inclusion by calling for early intervention services that, "to the maximum extent appropriate, are provided in natural environments, including the home, and community settings in which children without disabilities participate" (Section 12 (G)). Although this language still allows for the use of restrictive settings by including the caveat "to the maximum extent appropriate" in the opening phrase, it reflects the growing conviction that early intervention for all children, including the youngest, should take place in heterogeneous contexts.

Second, the 1991 amendments explicitly recognized the particular needs of families who are not members of the core culture. Beginning in fiscal year 1992, states were required to assure the U.S. Department of Education that they had adopted policies and practices that foster the involvement of "traditionally underrepresented groups, including minority, low-income, and rural families, in the planning and implementation of all the requirements of this part and...that such families have access to culturally competent services within their local areas" (Section 678 (b)(7)).

Here, then, is recognition that some families face the double threat of disability and cultural exclusion. This recognition is bolstered by a mandate that states take explicit steps to minimize the adverse consequences associated with this status.

Head Start Reauthorization of 1994

When Congress enacted PL 103-252, the Head Start Reauthorization of 1994, it extended the life of the Head Start program for an additional 3 years. Since the 1960s, Head Start has been the primary means for improving the educational and economic opportunities for young children and their families who live in conditions of significant poverty. In PL 103-252, Congress emphasized the need to address issues of cultural diversity by mandating the provision of "linguistically and culturally appropriate services to non-English language background children and their families" (Section 614 (A)). Published regulations governing the delivery of Head Start services require all programs to have a curriculum that "is relevant and reflective of the needs of the population served (bilingual/bicultural, multi-cultural, rural, urban, reservation, migrant, etc.)" as well as to have staff who reflect the racial and ethnic characteristics of the families who are enrolled, "including persons who speak the primary language of the children and are knowledgeable about their heritage" (45 CFR Part 1304.2-2 (c)).

Although parent participation in program policy making has always been part of the Head Start program, parent involvement was added to the list of mandated and defined services in 1994. This increased emphasis on the rights and roles of parents with respect to their children's education may also be found in new requirements to provide family literacy services (in conjunction with federally funded Even Start programs when possible). Finally, in recognition of the changing circumstances of Head Start families, the reauthorization legislation requires the U.S. Secretary of Health and Human Services to conduct investigations into the effectiveness and feasibility of full-day and full-year Head Start programs. Each of these initiatives has implications for the inclusion of culturally and developmentally diverse children. They are aimed at enhancing families' capacities, increasing program access and quality, and attending to the needs of children with diverse characteristics.

A related development in federal social policy affecting young children is found in PL 103-382, the Improving America's Schools Act of 1994 (which amended PL 89-10, the Elementary and Secondary Education Act of 1965). Among the provisions added in 1994 is a requirement that all schools providing preschool services under the law must operate those services according to Head Start Performance Standards. This means that school-based programs for children younger than school age must now incorporate the comprehensive educational, social, health, and parent involvement components of Head Start. Unfortunately, the law makes no provision for expanded funding for these services.

The First National Goal

The policies described above were implemented in a changing social and political climate that recognized the critical importance of the lives of *all* children to the well-being of society at large. This change is perhaps nowhere as evident as in PL 103-227, Goals 2000: Educate America Act of 1994. The first of these national education goals addresses the comprehensive needs of young children before they enter school and includes among its objectives the provision of high-quality preschool programs for all children, parental support and involvement in early education, adequate nutrition, and health care. Notwithstanding efforts to repeal the entire Goals 2000 Act, the significance of this particular goal and its preeminent status among the eight national goals should not be overlooked.

In essence, the first national goal marks a shift from emphasizing discrete programs, such as Head Start and Part H, to asserting a national policy statement that applies to *all* children. Recent interpretations of the first national goal acknowledge the need for a universal approach in policy even as they emphasize institutional responsibilities for responding to children's differences. Boyer (1991) reiterates these points in noting that, "While we get all children ready for school, we must, of course, get school ready for children—ready to accept with hope and enthusiasm *every* child who comes to the schoolhouse door" (p. 6, *emphasis added*).

Ironically, this broad-aim social policy denoting an expanded national responsibility for all young children has collided with contemporary manifestations of historical prejudices. Implementation of the first national goal has been confounded by efforts to repeal the entire Goals 2000 Act, given increasingly divergent attitudes regarding public responses to socioeconomic inequities associated with cultural and developmental differences. These attitudes are embodied in the debates that took place in 1995–1996 in the 104th Congress, as the Act became a target of the implicit racism and elitism of the "Contract with America." The Act has also been a victim of more general resistance to inclusive social welfare and educational programs at state and local levels.

To return to the theme of this chapter, at a time when many educators and policy makers are calling for broader efforts to assist *all* children and families, conservative political and religious leaders are emphasizing personal responsibility as a rationale for eliminating categorical educational and family assistance policies. The movement away from targeted programs that contribute to segregated services thus reflects two very different political and philosophical perspectives. For some within American society, diversity continues to represent a threat to the nostalgic image of the melting pot and is, therefore, an attribute that should not be perpetuated through public policies and programs. For numerous others, ourselves included, both the human assets and the sociohistorical liabilities associated with diversity must be acknowledged, distinguished, and responded to within a variety of inclusive contexts.

Inclusion and Classrooms

Concomitant with large-scale policy initiatives, changes at the classroom level reflect a growing recognition of the benefits of inclusion and the theoretical and practical interpretations that sustain those benefits. As has been the case with policy changes at the national level, however, the movement toward more inclusive educational practice has not occurred without controversy, even among those who argue for more equitable treatment of children who are different. Some professionals in the field of special education argue that separate programs continue to constitute one form of least restrictive environments (e.g., Fuchs & Fuchs, 1994). Indeed, the notion of "requiring *all* disabled children to be included in mainstream classrooms" has been described as "replacing one injustice with another" (Shanker, 1995, pp. 18–19). Recent analyses of the impact of inclusion on children who are deaf (Cohen, 1994) and on African American children (Ogbu, 1992; Paley, 1995) raise important questions about the educational and social consequences of some forms of inclusion, especially when mainstream norms continue to dominate. Reflecting these concerns, separate classes and schools dedicated to particular populations, including those distinguished by gender alone, continue to be supported and implemented in settings across the United States. Nonetheless, there is growing consensus among parents, professionals, and policy makers that fully integrated and inclusive programs, classrooms, and services represent a central principle of ethical and effective educational practice (e.g., Taylor, 1988; Wang & Walberg, 1988).

Professional arguments counter to the inclusion movement are distinguished from those representing the political divisions of American society and, in fact, are based primarily on criticisms that we share of current educational practice. In examining the experiences and empirical support that are called upon in both sides of the debate, it seems increasingly apparent that, although including all children in classroom demographics is a necessary step in the right direction, it is surely not a sufficient solution to the challenges of educating an increasingly diverse population of young children. Issues of identity, assimilation, achievement, and community cohesion are crucial concerns, especially when integrated services and inclusive programs are coerced or superficially implemented, whether through special education laws or mandated school desegregation policies. As noted previously, when young children with cultural or developmental differences are placed in early childhood programs in which curricula continue to be predicated on mainstream cultural norms, these children remain at risk for being identified as deviant or disabled. It is also the case that when culturally and developmentally diverse children are placed in environments that fail to meet even the needs of the so-called typically developing children, the number of alienated learners and educational failures increases rather than declines. What is needed is a vision of teaching and learning that incorporates the needs, interests, and abilities of *all* children and *each* child. (See Chapter 8 for a more detailed discussion.)

Again, the dialectical tensions associated with the paradox of diversity become evident. The challenge, simply put, is to respect and respond appropriately to children's individual differences in a manner that acknowledges their shared membership in society. This principle is reflected in the image of an inclusive classroom that functions as a community of learners. This interpretation is consistent with recent theoretical advances of the 1990s, which are, in turn, receiving substantial empirical and practical support in the fields of early education and early childhood special education.

The reliance by the field of early education on developmental norms that reflect the core culture has been described previously (New, 1994). Evidence for the dominance of these norms is found in the first edition of the guidelines for developmentally appropriate practice (DAP) published by the National Association for the Education of Young Children (NAEYC) (Bredekamp, 1987). Purported to represent the collective voice of members of the NAEYC, DAP guidelines have brought national attention to the issue of high-quality early childhood programs. The guidelines have also served to promote educational practices that acknowledge the particular developmental characteristics of young children as a function of age and individual differences, even as the document itself has been the target of both thoughtful and random criticisms. In particular, because the original DAP guidelines largely ignored differences associated with developmental and cultural diversity, numerous critiques have found fault with this narrow perspective (Carta, Schwartz, Atwater, & McConnell, 1991; Mallory & New, 1994a; Walsh, 1991).

Acknowledging that the intent of the original document was never to mandate particular practices for all children (Bredekamp, 1995), NAEYC—the largest early childhood professional organization in the United States—has again taken up the challenge of articulating principles of practice that respect children's unique and shared educational goals and capabilities. The revision process has focused extensively on the interface between children's development and the sociocultural contexts within which they live, as well as the need for teachers to assume and share more of the decision-making responsibility in the determination of developmentally appropriate practices. The revised guidelines will emphasize the need for teachers to expand their repertoire of teaching strategies to accommodate the various learning styles and needs of children, including those who are culturally and/or developmentally diverse. These ongoing revisions of guiding principles for developmentally appropriate practices reflect more than shifting social tides regarding the inevitability of human diversity. As noted previously (Mallory & New, 1994b), changing theoretical paradigms both contribute to and draw upon social norms and experience. It is, therefore, no coincidence that social constructivist theory is a target of interest across a broad field of educators, anthropologists, and developmental and cultural psychologists.

Social Constructivism as a Tool for Accommodating Diversity

The theoretical paradigm of social constructivism reflects a growing body of inter- and multidisciplinary thought and empirical study on the relationship between children's learning and development and the sociocultural context in which such growth takes place. Social constructivist theory, which has much in common with contemporary interpretations of constructivism (Brooks & Brooks, 1993), builds on earlier models of cognitive interactionism and social learning theory. The appellation *social* acknowledges the theoretical heritage of Vygotskian and neo-Vygotskian thinking. Late 20th century understandings of the social and cultural contexts of learning and development have also benefited from interpretations and elaborations by numerous scholars (e.g., Bruner, 1986; Forman, Minick, & Stone, 1993; Rogoff, 1990; Wertsch, 1985, 1991). This work, in turn, joins recent thinking in cultural psychology, which underscores the inextricable nature of culture and development (Shweder, 1990). Common themes across this array of theoretical conceptions include

The role of the sociocultural context in assigning value and meaning to
educational content

The contributions of social activity, including peer collaboration, direct
instruction, and sociodramatic play, in the display and elaboration of
skills, knowledge, attitudes, and concepts

The significance of sociocognitive conflict as a source of motivation to
identify and subsequently address problems that are emotionally and
intellectually significant

The zone of proximal development as a means of conceptualizing the
readiness state of the learner and as a focus for guided assistance in the
development of emerging competencies

The active construction of knowledge through a process that begins with
socially situated and shared activity and is ultimately internalized by
the individual learner

The transactional relationship between the development of individuals
and the development of the larger sociocultural context(s)

Some scholars have cautioned against attempts to apply this theory of
learning and development to a theory of instruction, especially given its
reliance on social mediation within specific cultural contexts in the determination of what is worth knowing and how it ought to be learned. Yet
numerous pedagogical implications are apparent for educators wishing
to utilize this knowledge of the processes of learning and development
on behalf of young children. If children are likely to learn what is valued
by a community, then the classroom environment—as a community of
learners—has much to contribute to the importance children assign to
their learning tasks and opportunities. To the extent that children benefit
from the opportunity to explore, explain, and expand their understandings
through the course of their interactions with others, then teachers would
do well, as Forman and Cazden (1985) noted, to take advantage of the fact
that classrooms are typically dense social settings. Given the importance
children assign to problems of personal significance, including those that
are moderately beyond their ability to resolve by themselves, then curriculum goals and objectives might be best met if they are incorporated into
learning activities that respond to children's questions, ideas, concerns,
and interests and that require children of differing abilities to work col-
laboratively. If children are expected to benefit from the classroom culture, then they ought also to be expected and allowed to contribute to that
culture.

As such, social constructivist theory offers a framework for the conceptualization of inclusive educational practices that are worthy of being
called appropriate—that is, they are designed to address the social, educational, and developmental needs of *all* young children. (See Mallory &
New, 1994b, for a more detailed discussion.) The convergence of this theoretical paradigm with particular sociocultural values, beliefs, and educational objectives is demonstrated in two long-term and carefully
documented programs for young children—the preprimary program in
Reggio Emilia, Italy, and the Kamehameha Elementary Education Program
(KEEP) in Hawaii.

The Reggio Emilia Approach

Since World War II, the citizens of Reggio Emilia have devoted considerable economic and social resources to building a municipally funded program of infant-toddler centers and preprimary schools that have now garnered worldwide attention and acclaim (New, 1990). Relatively wealthy and demographically homogeneous, Reggio Emilia appears to have little relevance for educators attempting to respond to the challenges of cultural and developmental diversity extant in America's pluralistic society. This Italian example of early care and education has much to offer, however, if only as an inspiration to the conceptualization of an inclusive education. Characteristics of the Reggio Emilia approach include the use of long-term projects based on children's interests and adult observations of children's social and intellectual development; the fostering of children's many symbolic languages to maximize the wide variety of their creative and intellectual capabilities; the use of the physical and social environments to identify and promote educational aims, and an emphasis on the benefits of collaboration as a means of working with and learning from both adults and children of diverse interests and abilities. (See Edwards, Gandini, & Forman, 1993, for a more complete description, including chapters by Reggio Emilia educators, of this Italian approach to early child care and education.)

Typically developing children are not the only ones to benefit from this approach to early care and education. In Reggio Emilia, children with special needs are described as having special rights and are given priority enrollment in the oversubscribed schools. Children with developmental disabilities are included in general classrooms, and therapists, auxillary staff, and teachers work with small groups on projects in which the child with special needs is included. The expressed image of the child is one of possessing competence and rights, including the right to be supported, challenged, and regarded as a contributing member of a caring community of learners. It is difficult to imagine an environment that is more philosophically and conceptually harmonious with the interpretation of inclusive early education expressed in this chapter (New & Mallory, 1994a).

KEEP

An inclusive approach to education within the United States that shares many of these same characteristics but serves a culturally diverse population of older children is KEEP. This project was initiated in 1969 in Honolulu, Hawaii, as a research and development program for at-risk students belonging to ethnic minorities. The project eventually expanded to serve more than 3,000 students in elementary schools in three states; the students represented multiple cultures, languages, and abilities. The intent of KEEP was to examine and improve the relationship among diverse cultural settings, processes of teaching, and children's educational success. Based on a synthesis of Vygotskian and neo-Vygotskian principles, two fundamental tenets of KEEP are 1) that teaching must be redefined as assisted performance, and 2) that children's schooling must be a continuation of their sociocultural context (Tharp & Gallimore, 1988).

Drawing upon observations and extended investigations of characteristics of children's home environments and patterns of work, play, and social interactions, numerous elements of KEEP were modified to reflect both cultural values and culturally established ways of promoting children's development. Thus, learning centers are designed to maximize opportunities for coparticipation and instructional conversation with peers as well as teachers. The concept of assisted performance is emphasized as teachers work with children within their zones of proximal development, often coparticipating actively with them. The concept of shared meaning is acknowledged as teachers seek correspondence between curriculum objectives and children's particular social goals and intellectual aims.

KEEP has had a remarkable degree of success in reversing generations of school failure for large percentages of children who belong to ethnic minorities since its inception. Much of this success likely results from the belief that all members of the school community are learners *and* teachers. This premise—that effective schools support the learning of adults as well as children—is also shared by Reggio Emilia educators; and it is perhaps this contribution from programs on opposite sides of the globe that is the most necessary element of an inclusive education for culturally and developmentally diverse children. (For a more complete description of both the KEEP program and the theoretical and philosophical premises associated with this approach to schooling, see Tharp & Gallimore, 1988.)

These two notable approaches are not the only examples of the practical benefits of social constructivist theory. This approach to children's learning is consistent with recent empirical work in the field of special education (e.g., Harris & Graham, 1994). Among those methods that are consistent with this theoretical interpretation of sound educational practice and are most often associated with children's educational successes are the following:

Attending to the assets as well as the difficulties of individual learners
Recognizing the diverse learning styles, interests, and dispositions of young children
Soliciting parental views and advice about their children's social and intellectual needs and capacities
Forming closer alliances among teachers, parents, and other community members
Engaging in contextualized and meaningful problem solving
Encouraging peer collaboration in small heterogeneous groups and pairing children with more capable peers in the mastery of discrete tasks
Using authentic performance-based assessment, with multiple assessment strategies as a means for planning individual and group instruction

The benefits of these pedagogical features are not limited to a particular population or cultural setting. In fact, the above-enumerated strategies are compatible with the more general school reform movement underway in the 1990s (Sarason, 1990).

The second half of this chapter provides examples of inclusive policy and practice, both of which are supported by theoretical advances that acknowledge the variable and transactional nature of human development within sociocultural contexts. The examples of inclusive policy and practice build upon the lessons learned (both positive and negative) from previous responses to diversity. The challenge faced in 1996 is not so much to decide what to do, but to marshall the will and the resources to do it. To the extent that classroom practice can demonstrate effective means to respect and foster the positive aspects of diversity, then social policies can also become less categorical and social integration more likely. The point is not so much *where* to begin, as it is *to* begin. There is much to be gained by maximizing the transactional and mutually reinforcing nature of theory, research, policy, and practice. As such, the press for inclusion serves to improve the educational experiences of all young children.

CONCLUSION

It seems fitting to draw upon a United Nations declaration of children's rights to conclude this discussion of the challenges and the paradox of diversity in early education. This declaration was embodied in the United Nations Convention on the Rights of the Child, adopted in 1989, and ultimately ratified by 154 countries as of early 1995. Sections of the Convention speak directly to the issue of developmental and cultural diversity and inclusion in early childhood practices, as excerpted below.

> Article 23, part 1: States Parties recognize that a mentally or physically disabled child should enjoy a full and decent life, in conditions which ensure dignity, promote self-reliance and facilitate the child's active participation in the community...in a manner conducive to the child's achieving the fullest possible social integration and individual development, including his or her cultural and spiritual development.
>
> *Article 29, part 1:* States Parties agree that the education of the child shall be directed to (a) the development of the child's personality, talents, and mental and physical abilities to their [sic] fullest potential; (b) the development of respect for human rights and fundamental freedoms...; (c) the development of respect for the child's parents, his or her own cultural identity, language, and values, for the national values of the country in which the child is living, the country from which he or she may originate, and for civilizations different from his or her own; (d) the preparation of the child for responsible life in a free society, in the spirit of understanding, peace, tolerance, equality of sexes, and friendship among all peoples, ethnic, national, and religious groups and persons of indigenous origin. (United Nations, 1989)

As straightforward as the concept of children's rights might appear, the fact remains that the United States (along with such countries as Iraq, Somalia, and Singapore) has not yet ratified the Convention, thereby attesting to the continued uncertainty in the United States about the value of children and the need to recognize their full membership in society.

The interpretation of children's rights as a form of political expression supports our contention that neither theory, research, nor equitable policies and practices will completely remove the *adversity* from children's experiences with diversity. Rather, the elimination of prejudice and discrimination requires a change of heart as well as mind. In the words of Beth Harry (1992), "The challenge facing American schools is to reverse not only assumptions, reputations, and instructional methodologies but also the essential ethos that conveys to students and their families that power and right reside only in the culture of mainstream America" (p. xviii). In this light, the paradox of diversity requires us to acknowledge the inextricable nature of our personal and professional lives, our moral and our intellectual selves. As such, this vision of inclusion expands both the possibilities and the responsibilities inherent in our work with young children.

REFERENCES

Administration for Children, Youth, and Families. (1990). *Project Head Start statistical fact sheet (fiscal year 1990).* Washington, DC: Author.

Alston, R.J., & Mngadi, S. (1992). The interaction between disability status and the African American experience: Implications for rehabilitation counseling. *Journal of Applied Rehabilitation Counseling, 23*(2), 12–16.

Beatty, B. (1995). *Preschool education in America: The culture of young children from the colonial era to the present.* New Haven, CT: Yale University Press.

Biddel, T.R. (1992, June). *The constructive web: Diversifying conceptions of development.* Paper presented at the annual meeting of the Jean Piaget Society, Montreal, Quebec.

Bogdan, R., & Biklen, D. (1977). Handicapism. *Social Policy, 7*(5) 14–19.

Boyer, E.L. (1991). *Ready to learn: A mandate for the nation.* Princeton, NJ: The Carnegie Foundation for the Advancement of Teaching.

Bredekamp, S. (Ed.). (1987). *Developmentally appropriate practice in early childhood programs serving children from birth through age 8.* Washington, DC: National Association for the Education of Young Children.

Bredekamp, S. (1995, April). *What's appropriate about developmentally appropriate practices?* Paper presented at the annual meeting of the American Educational Research Association, San Francisco.

Brooks, J.G., & Brooks, M.G. (1993). *In search of understanding: The case for constructivist classrooms.* Alexandria, VA: Association for Supervision and Curriculum Development.

Brown v. Board of Education, 347 U.S. 483 (1954).

Bruner, J. (1986). *Actual minds, possible worlds.* Cambridge, MA: Harvard University Press.

Campbell, F.A., & Ramey, C.T. (1994). Effects of early intervention on intellectual and academic achievement: A follow-up study of children from low-income families. *Child Development, 65,* 684–698.

Carta, J.J., Schwartz, I.S., Atwater, J.B., & McConnell, S.R. (1991). Developmentally appropriate practice: Appraising its usefulness for young children with disabilities. *Topics in Early Childhood Special Education, 11*(1), 1–20.

Center on Budget and Policy Priorities. (1987). *Gap between rich and poor widest ever recorded: Poor grow poorer.* Washington, DC: Author.

Cohen, L.H. (1994). *Train go sorry: Inside a deaf world.* Boston: Houghton Mifflin.

Delpit, L.D. (1988). The silenced dialogue: Power and pedagogy in educating other people's children. *Harvard Educational Review, 58*(3), 280–298.

Dunst, C.J., Trivette, C.M., & Deal, A.G. (1988). *Enabling and empowering families: Principles of guidance for practices.* Cambridge, MA: Brookline Books.

Education for All Handicapped Children Act of 1975, PL 94-142. (August 23, 1977). Title 20, U.S.C. 1401 et seq: *U.S. Statutes at Large, 89,* 773–796.

Education of the Handicapped Act Amendments of 1986, PL 99-457. (October 8, 1986). Title 20, U.S.C. 1400 et seq: *U.S. Statutes at Large, 100,* 1145–1177.

Edwards, C., Gandini, L., & Forman, G. (Eds.). (1993). *The hundred languages of children: The Reggio Emilia approach to early childhood education.* Norwood, NJ: Ablex.

Elementary and Secondary Education Act of 1965, PL 89-10. (April 11, 1965). Title 20, U.S.C. 2701 et seq: *U.S. Statutes at Large, 79,* 27–58.

Farber, B. (1968). *Mental retardation: Its social context and social consequences.* Boston: Houghton Mifflin.

Forman, E.A., & Cazden, C.B. (1985). Exploring Vygotskian perspectives in education: The cognitive value of peer interaction. In J.V. Wertsch (Ed.), *Culture, communication, and cognition: Vygotskian perspectives* (pp. 323–347). New York: Cambridge University Press.

Forman, E.A., Minick, M., & Stone, C.A. (Eds.). (1993). *Context for learning: Sociocultural dynamics in children's development.* New York: Oxford University Press.

Fuchs, D., & Fuchs, L.S. (1994). Inclusive schools movement and the radicalization of special education reform. *Exceptional Children, 60,* 294–309.

Gleidman, J., & Roth, W. (1980). *The unexpected minority: Handicapped children in America.* New York: Harcourt Brace Jovanovich.

Goals 2000: Educate America Act of 1994, PL 103–227. (March 31, 1994). Title 20, U.S.C. 5801, *U.S. Statutes at Large, 108,* 125–280.

Goffman, E. (1963). *Stigma: Notes on the management of spoiled identity.* New York: Simon & Schuster.

Harrington, M. (1962). *The other America: Poverty in the United States.* New York: Macmillan.

Harrington, M. (1984). *The new American poverty.* New York: Holt, Rhinehart & Winston.

Harris, K.R., & Graham, S. (Eds.). (1994). Implication of constructivism for students with disabilities and students at risk: Issues and directions [Special issue]. *The Journal of Special Education, 28*(3).

Harry, B. (1992). *Cultural diversity, families, and the special education system: Communication and empowerment.* New York: Teachers College Press.

Head Start Reauthorization of 1994, PL 103-252. (May 18, 1994). Title 42, U.S.C. 9831 et seq: *U.S. Statutes at Large, 108,* 623–673.

Hobbs, N. (1975). *The futures of children.* San Francisco: Jossey-Bass.

House Report 102-198. (1991, September 11). *Providing a comprehensive delivery system for children birth through five years of age and their families.* Washington, DC: U.S. Government Printing Office.

Hunt, J.M. (1961). *Intelligence and experience.* New York: Ronald Press.

Huston, A.C., McLoyd, V.C., & Garcia Coll, C. (1994). Children and poverty: Issues in contemporary research. *Child Development, 65,* 275–282.

Improving America's Schools Act of 1994, PL 103-382. (October 20, 1994). Title 20, U.S.C. 630 et seq: *U.S. Statutes at Large, 108,* 3518–4062.

Individuals with Disabilities Education Act (IDEA) of 1990, PL 101-476. (October 30, 1990). Title 20, U.S.C. 1400 et seq: *U.S. Statutes at Large, 104,* 1103–1151.

Individuals with Disabilities Education Act Amendments of 1991, PL 102-119. (October 7, 1991). Title 20, U.S.C. 1400 et seq: *U.S. Statutes at Large, 105,* 587–608.

Kagan, S.L. (1991). Examining profit and non-profit child care: An odyssey of quality and auspices. *Journal of Social Issues, 47,* 87–104.

Katz, M. (1975). *Class, bureaucracy, and schools: The illusion of educational change in America* (Exp. ed.). New York: Praeger.

Kirk, S.A. (1958). *Early education of the mentally retarded.* Urbana: University of Illinois Press.

Lightfoot, S.L. (1978). *Worlds apart.* New York: Basic Books.

Mallory, B.L. (1992). Is it always appropriate to be developmental? Convergent models for early intervention practice. *Topics in Early Childhood Special Education, 11*(4), 1–12.

Mallory, B.L. (1993). Changing beliefs about disability in developing countries: Historical factors and sociocultural variables. In D. Woods (Ed.), *Traditional and changing views of disability in developing societies: Causes, consequences, and cautions* (pp. 1–24). (Monograph No. 53). Durham: University of New Hampshire and World Rehabilitation Fund.

Mallory, B.L., & New, R.S. (Eds.). (1994a). *Diversity and developmentally appropriate practices: Challenges for early childhood education.* New York: Teachers College Press.

Mallory, B.L., & New, R.S. (1994b). Social constructivist theory and principles of inclusion: Challenges for early childhood special education. *Journal of Special Education, 28*(3), 322–337.

Martin, A. (1988). Screening, early intervention, and remediation: Obscuring children's potential. *Harvard Educational Review, 58*(4), 488–501.

Myrdal, G. (1944). *An American dilemma: The Negro problem and modern democracy.* New York: Harper & Row.

New, R.S. (1990). Excellent early education: A town in Italy has it. *Young Children, 45*(6), 4–10.

New, R.S. (1994). Culture, child development, and developmentally appropriate practices; Teachers as collaborative researchers. In B.L. Mallory & R.S. New (Eds.), *Diversity and developmentally appropriate practices: Challenges for early childhood education* (pp. 65–83). New York: Teachers College Press.

New, R.S., & Mallory, B.L. (1994a, November). *Implications of Reggio Emilia for inclusive early childhood education.* Paper presented at the annual meeting of the National Association for the Education of Young Children, Atlanta.

New, R.S., & Mallory, B.L. (1994b). Introduction: The ethic of inclusion. In B.L. Mallory & R.S. New (Eds.), *Diversity and developmentally appropriate practices: Challenges for early childhood education* (pp. 1–13). New York: Teachers College Press.

Oakes, J. (1985). *Keeping track: How schools structure inequality.* New Haven, CT: Yale University Press.

Office of Special Education Programs. (1993). *To assure the free appropriate public education of all children with disabilities: Fifteenth annual report to Congress on the implementation of the Individuals with Disabilities Education Act.* Washington, DC: U.S. Department of Education.

Ogbu, J.U. (1992). Understanding cultural diversity and learning. *Educational Researcher, 21*(8), 5–14.

Paley, V.G. (1995). *Kwanzaa and me: A teacher's story.* Cambridge, MA: Harvard University Press.

Phillips, C.B. (1994). The movement of African-American children through sociocultural contexts: A case of conflict resolution. In B.L. Mallory & R.S. New (Eds.), *Diversity and developmentally appropriate practices: Challenges for early childhood education* (pp. 137–154). New York: Teachers College Press.

Phillips, D.A., Voran, M., Kisker, E., Howes, C., & Whitebook, M. (1994). Child care for children in poverty: Opportunity or inequity? *Child Development, 65,* 472–492.

Richardson, J.G. (1994). Common, delinquent, and special: On the formalization of common schooling in the American states. *American Educational Research Journal, 31*(4), 695–723.

Rogoff, B. (1990). *Apprenticeship in thinking: Cognitive development in social context.* New York: Oxford University Press.

Sarason, S. (1990). *The predictable failure of school reform: Can we change course before it's too late?* San Francisco: Jossey-Bass.

Shanker, A. (1995). Full inclusion is neither free nor appropriate. *Educational Leadership, 52*(4), 18–21.

Shweder, R. (1990). Cultural psychology—What is it? In J.W. Stigler, R.A Shweder, & G. Herdt (Eds.), *Cultural psychology: Essays on comparative human development* (pp. 1–43). New York: Cambridge University Press.

Silberman, C. (1970). *Crisis in the classroom.* New York: Random House.

Social Security Act of 1935, PL 74-271. (August 14, 1935). Title 42, U.S.C. 301 et seq: *U.S. Statutes at Large, 15*, 687–1774.

Stone, E.F., Stone, D.L., & Dipboye, R.L. (1992). Stigmas in organizations: Race, handicaps, and physical unattractiveness. In K. Kelley (Ed.), *Issues, theory, and research in industrial/organizational psychology* (pp. 385–457). Amsterdam: North-Holland.

Super, C.M. (Ed.). (1987). *The role of culture in developmental disorder.* San Diego, CA: Academic Press.

Taylor, S.J. (1988). Caught in the continuum: A critical analysis of the principle of the least restrictive environment. *Journal of The Association for Persons with Severe Handicaps, 13*(1), 41–53.

Tharp, R.G., & Gallimore, R. (1988). *Rousing minds to life: Teaching, learning, and schooling in social context.* Cambridge, UK: Cambridge University Press.

Tropea, J.L. (1987). Bureaucratic order and special children: Urban schools, 1890s–1940s. *History of Education Quarterly, 27*, 29–53.

United Nations. (1989, November 20). *United Nations Convention on the Rights of Children.* New York: Author.

U.S. General Accounting Office. (1994). *Early childhood programs: Multiple programs and overlapping target groups* (GAO/HEHS 95 4TS). Washington, DC: U.S. Government Printing Office.

Wang, M.C., & Walberg, H.J. (1988). Four fallacies of segregationism. *Exceptional Children, 55*(2), 128–137.

Walsh, D.J. (1991). Extending the discourse on developmental appropriateness: A developmental perspective. *Early Education and Development, 2*(2), 109–119.

Wertsch, J.V. (Ed.). (1985). *Culture, communication, and cognition: Vygotskian perspectives.* Cambridge, England: Cambridge University Press.

Wertsch, J.V. (Ed.). (1991). *Voices of the mind: A sociocultural approach to mediated action.* Cambridge, MA: Harvard University Press.

Whiting, B.B. (1976). The problem of the packaged variable. In K. Riegel & J. Meacham (Eds.), *The developing individual in a changing world* (pp. 303–309). Chicago: Aldine.

A Mother's Search for Child Care

Emma Tolbert

A single mother with three children, a 3-year-old and a set of 18-month-old twins, moves to Massachusetts to make a life for them. Should this woman expect to find resources, child care, and help?

Does this seem too outrageous? Not to me. My name is Emma Tolbert, and I am that woman. I was born in Sumter, South Carolina, where I spent my elementary and part of my middle school years. I came to Massachusetts to reunite with my parents and to finish school. However, because of my family situation, I had to drop out of school in the 10th grade to work. I knew that an education would make my life better, so, I went to night school and earned my general equivalency diploma by the time I was 19 years old. I returned to South Carolina. There, I got married and, by the time I was 21 years old, had my first baby. When I returned to Massachusetts, I was a single mother of three. My child care dilemma had begun.

It was hard to determine which options were available for me and my children. I was not familiar with the Massachusetts social services system. I did not know anything about welfare or the type of assistance, if any, it would provide me. Where would I find affordable child care for three children that was both accessible to my home and workplace and provided the quality and the hours I needed? At that time, the only assistance provided to me was a shelter. After living in a shelter for 1 month, I was fortunate to find a furnished apartment for myself and my children.

After 3 months, I was not satisfied with staying at home all day. I needed work and, naturally, child care. I found two suitable programs: One provided transportation for my oldest child; I walked the twins to the other program. Although the programs were adequate, the child care hours did not meet my work schedule, so I was forced to quit. In the meantime, I had to return to welfare for assistance. I took this opportunity to further my education until the twins entered first grade.

I was anxious for the twins to begin school because I was excited about returning to work. It was difficult to find after-school care for three children. I sought help from the only resource available to me, the welfare system, but it was not equipped to help me find after-school care. Then, in the newspaper, I read an ad placed by a person who would watch children after school. The child care arrangements were far from perfect. I was responsible for transporting the children from school to the person's home. This, of course, meant leaving and returning to work twice each day. There was not surround care for children as I know it today.

My situation improved for a time. For 1 year, I received assistance with child care, health care benefits, food stamps, and so forth, but then the next stumbling block appeared. All of the assistance provided to me was totally cut off. A pay raise put me over the financial limit for assistance. It was difficult for me to pay for everything on my salary. I applied for assistance to help me pay for child care because more than half of my salary was needed to cover my child care costs. I was rejected because my monthly earnings were $100 more than the limit. A subsidized child care system did not exist. Again, I was faced with the prospect of quitting my job and returning to the welfare system. This was not a preferred option for me. I decided to try to survive with the little bit of money I earned.

I wanted help, needed help, but could not get help. All I could do was continue to look to the future and hope that things would get better for me and my children. After all, this was America, the land of opportunity and jobs. I did not have my children so that I could receive a welfare check. I wanted to be a positive role model in my children's lives, a hardworking woman who tried to be a good mother and provider.

Those first 11 years of life as a mother opened my eyes to child care and the lack thereof. I could not believe how unimportant child care was to U.S. society. In the 1970s, a woman was expected to stay home and watch her children. But people like me, divorced with children, did not have that option. It was a difficult time, not something I wanted my children to experience. My children are all adults now, but I still feel the need to do something so that women in situations similar to mine will not have to suffer as I did.

I became involved in an organization called Parents United for Child Care (PUCC). I liked their mission statement: "PUCC is a membership organization of low and moderate income parents dedicated to increasing the supply of quality, affordable child care in Massachusetts." PUCC educates parents about child care advocacy so that those parents feel empowered to talk to their elected officials about their situations. Because of my involvement with this organization, I have become a registered voter. I pay attention to the identities of elected officials and how they vote on child care issues. I am concerned with making a difference in the state budget, lobbying legislators, and getting more parents involved in the whole process. I try to express my feelings on child care issues as well as the views of other parents. I work on committees that plan actions and make changes in the lives of all families.

I believe that I have a right to share information that I receive. PUCC translates political jargon into parent-friendly language so that all parents can understand what new laws or suggested changes will mean to families. Without this knowledge, I would not be able to advocate for the needs of families. I feel stronger, because I know which avenues or networks to turn to get the services I need. All of this involvement leads to wanting to know as much as possible. Education is the key to change.

If the proper resources to address my situation had been available in the 1970s, I would not have gone through so much adversity. The only person available to help me was a welfare case worker. I did not know anyone who had conquered the obstacles I was facing and who was familiar with the agencies. Unlike today, resource and referral agencies, which provide parents with information on child care and how to gain access to it, did not exist. In addition, the information available to parents should be self-explanatory. Many agencies use abbreviations instead of the words, which can be confusing. Imagine being told, "You need to go to DSS because you are not eligible for a DPW voucher because EOHHS didn't give us enough money in the CC account for you." Someone new to Massachusetts or its welfare system would not know the meaning of these letters.

The United States must take a better look at child care. PUCC's Public Action Committee has developed the following "Principles for a Legislative Initiative Child Care Delivery System in Massachusetts," which establish that child care should be

Affordable—no family should pay more than 10% of its gross income for child care

Accessible—child care should be easily available to parents in a manner that fits well with their family backgrounds, schedules, and geography

Of high quality—child care should enhance children's well-being through the development of their intellectual, social, and psychological resources

The principles also advocate the following:

High standards—high standards and adequate salaries should be established so that staff/providers earn livable wages

Parental involvement—parents should be involved at all levels of the child care delivery system to ensure that it meets their own and their children's needs

These principles can help Massachusetts create one of the best child care delivery systems in the United States and serve as a model for other states.

Unfortunately, it seems as though the child care situation worsens as technology improves. Children's issues are not a top priority of the U.S. government. When a budget cut is made, it is usually made in an area that will affect children and families. I believe that all elected officials should live the same lifestyle of those their decisions will affect for at least 1 month. By this, I mean they should live in households with fixed incomes (no credit cards or extra money) and experience plenty of social services agency interaction. If legislators were to experience the impact of their laws on an individual level, things might change for the best.

All parents should have access to high-quality child care choices. No one should be able to tell the difference between a child care program in an inner city and one in an affluent suburban town. This is not to imply that all child care programs should be identical; rather, a variety of high-quality flexible programs should be made available to all families.

These are some of the specific problems facing Massachusetts's child care delivery system, but they are problems families grapple with across the United States. With welfare reform on everyone's agenda and many parents forced to work long hours to support their families, it is imperative that U.S. society address the needs of children. High-quality child care will prepare children to learn when they reach elementary school. We must make this happen.

7

THE COMPLEXITIES OF CHILD CARE

Jerlean Daniel

Among researchers, a growing tendency exists to define all programs serving young children in classrooms, such as Head Start programs, nursery schools, and preschools, generically as centers (Galinsky & Friedman, 1993). Others, including the Census Bureau (Casper, Hawkins, & O'Connell, 1994), have grouped all such delivery systems, including family child care homes, into one category, calling them either child care or early childhood programs. For the purposes of this chapter, however, child care refers to the nonparental provision of early care and education in programs designed primarily to meet the needs of parents who work or attend school. The complexities of child care programs are illustrated by differences in the auspices of the programs and states' regulatory practices.

DIFFERENCES AMONG CHILD CARE PROGRAMS

Auspices

Whether located in centers or homes, child care programs generally operate 10–12 hours a day Monday through Friday. Child care programs exist under the auspices of for-profit and nonprofit sponsors and are classified as sectarian or nonsectarian programs. Helburn et al. (1995) found little difference in program quality between programs operated by for-profit sponsors and those operated by nonprofit sponsors. Among nonprofit programs, sectarian programs displayed more of the characteristics of for-profit programs and had the poorest quality programs (Helburn et al., 1995). Where child care programs are physically housed does not necessarily indicate the auspices under which they operate. For example, numerous child care facilities are located in churches. It is not unusual, however, for a center located in a church to be run by a nonsectarian nonprofit entity that receives the majority of its funding from a local, state, or federal government agency. Notwithstanding the range and combinations of sponsoring child care agencies, many parents continue to have a rather limited range of child care choices because of factors such as income level and the types of services available in a given community.

State Regulatory Practices

During the early 1980s, the Federal Interagency Day Care Regulations (FIDCR) were set aside. A general sentiment existed among several states' officials that the FIDCR were too strict. The states' officials argued persuasively that meeting the FIDCR made the cost of operating too expensive and, therefore, discouraged potential new service providers, leaving states without enough care to meet their growing child care needs. In addition, the FIDCR were alleged to intrude on the states' rights to create their own regulations based on the needs of both families and the business community. In the absence of the FIDCR, each state developed its own regulations, and, as a result, regulations vary widely from state to state. The variance in state regulations has contributed considerably to differences in the quality of programs available throughout the United States.

Although many parents depend on relatives for child care, state monitoring of care delivered by relatives varies from state to state. Most states regulate child care, not based on the relationship of the caregiver to the child or children, but rather based on the actual number of children in care. Therefore, some relative-provided child care situations are unregulated. It is also possible for a child care program to operate as a legally unregulated facility in the private sector. In some states, for example, facilities operated under sectarian auspices are legally exempt from regulation. In many states, the number of children, including the caregiver's own children, that a family child care provider can serve will determine whether the caregiver is legally required to be monitored by the state. This variance means that many children receive unmonitored child care.

In addition, child care regulations vary from state to state as to whether providers are monitored through licensure or registration (an officially sanctioned listing of service providers). State regulations also vary with regard to the level of training required of an individual child care provider. Preservice and in-service training requirements also are within the purview of the states. For additional information on the content of state regulations, review the extensive documentation compiled by the Career Center for Early Care and Education at Wheelock College (Morgan et al., 1993). For the purposes of this chapter, it is important to understand that decentralization of state child care regulations has contributed to tremendous differences in program policies, substance, and quality. With these differences in mind, the author examines some of the critical child care issues addressed in Emma Tolbert's essay.

CRITICAL CHILD CARE DELIVERY ISSUES

Emma Tolbert's poignant essay offers a parent's view of child care delivery issues. Although many communities now have the resource and referral services that were not available to Tolbert in the 1970s, many of the issues she faced continue to plague the system. The basic issues of eligibility, affordability, accessibility, and quality of service remain unresolved. To be certain, some attempts have been made to address these issues. For example, PL 101-508, the Child Care and Development Block Grant of 1990 (CCDBG) attempted to reinforce the child care delivery system infrastructure (quality, accessibility, and affordability). Much remains to be done, however, to produce an effective child care delivery system that addresses the needs of parents and children, including children with special developmental needs. The benefits of child care services sought by Tolbert continue to be out of reach for far too many parents.

Child care is part of the early care and education array of programs offered to families with young children. An ongoing debate exists within and outside the early care and education profession regarding whether child care programs are educational or not. Contributing significantly to these divergent views are two major competing expectations for child care. One major expectation of child care is to provide parents with opportunities for self-sufficiency: Child care programs serve as places for children to be while parents go to school or work. The second major expectation of child care focuses on enhancing the child's emotional, social, physical, cognitive, and developmental needs. Historically, the U.S. public has been divided on the degree to which child care is a substitute for, partner of, or disruptive intrusion into parenting (Powell, 1987). A cohesive child care delivery system that addresses both of these conflicting goals is needed.

Tolbert's essay demonstrates the clear need for the child care delivery system to address simultaneously a young mother's desperate desire for self-sufficiency and the developmental needs of her children. Tolbert found two suitable programs that met the needs of her children, but the program hours conflicted with her work hours. Because of this scheduling conflict, she was forced to quit her job and rely on the welfare system until her children reached school age. At that time, she found another job but lost her child care subsidy when she earned a raise that changed her eligibility status. A $100-per-month increase was too much money to allow her to continue to receive the subsidy but not enough to pay for child care and other essential household expenses. In the absence of a social policy that integrated all aspects of the child care delivery system, Emma Tolbert was unable to find a program that would meet her children's developmental needs and allow her to achieve self-sufficiency. Emma Tolbert's case is by no means an isolated example.

Meeting the Needs of Mothers and Children

In 1991, 31 million mothers in the U.S. workforce had children younger than 15 years of age (Casper et al., 1994). In the United States, mothers of infants younger than 12 months increased from 38% of the workforce in 1980 to 54% in 1992 (Casper et al., 1994). These figures represent a significant increase in the number of mothers in the workforce, including 9.9 million mothers of children younger than 5 years of age (Casper et al., 1994). Of course, not all of these mothers rely on welfare assistance to meet their child care needs; a substantial number do, however.

Despite repeated calls to reform the welfare system that Tolbert and others like her have tried to avoid, the issue of child care has not always been a consistent part of the welfare reform dialogue. In 1996, this inconsistent consideration of child care issues remained the case despite the fact that a major component of the welfare reform efforts is to put parents who receive welfare to work. The incentives to work or continue one's education lose their luster if by doing so one loses access to affordable, high-quality child care. If we are to simultaneously address the needs of children and aid people such as Emma Tolbert in their quests for self-sufficiency, then it is essential that we maintain and strengthen programs such as Head Start.

Head Start is a federally funded program charged with meeting the needs of parents and children. On the one hand, it offers a comprehensive developmental program for children. On the other hand, it offers employment opportunities and community development skills through the parent involvement dimension of the program. Since the 1980s, Head Start has won substantial political support. Although Head Start can legitimately cite many success stories (Lombardi, 1990; Washington & Greene, 1995), in the early 1990s, members of Congress and others began to raise questions regarding the quality of the program. Indeed, some of the concerns were valid, because not enough attention had been paid to enhancing the Head Start infrastructure designed to address the developmental needs of young children. In addition, the number of eligible children served by Head Start and other child care agencies remained an issue.

Quantity versus Quality of Services

The debate over increasing the quantity of services versus improving the quality of existing services has been an ongoing social policy dilemma. Typically, policy makers have chosen to make resources available to serve more eligible families. The CCDBG, however, is an example of federal legislation that added quantity by improving affordability and also set aside 25% of the funds to improve quality.

Eligibility and program purpose are additional dimensions of the quantity-versus-quality debate. Emma Tolbert's additional $100 per month made her ineligible for the subsidy that made child care affordable for her. A social policy known as categorical funding adds to the difficulty parents and professionals alike have in gaining access to programs for which families are eligible. As Tolbert notes, the acronymic shorthand used for the funding streams further confuses the situation. To clarify, categorical funding outlines the purpose of the funds, the eligible population, the implementation regulations, and federal department auspices. Table 7.1 was prepared by the Public Affairs Division of the National Association for the Education of Young Children (NAEYC) in July 1994. It details the array of federally funded programs with child care provisions. Note, however, that Table 7.1 lists programs in place before block grants began to be awarded to states and before the elimination of some programs proposed by Congress in 1995.

An examination of the statements of purpose of child care programs reveals some overlap among the services to children with disabilities and among child care services in general. The Title IV-A purposes, however, appear to build on each other. Services to children with disabilities include one program that serves children through 8 years of age and two additional programs for children younger than 8 years of age. Smith and Rose (1993) advised that changes at the federal level are required to alleviate many of the conflicting eligibility statutes among programs meant to serve children categorized as disabled, at risk, and so forth. In addition, Smith and Rose (1993) found that misinterpretation of policies within bureaucracies is a serious problem and is perpetuated over time, which creates the perception that barriers to services exist. A similar problem of perception plagues the child care funding streams: Money can be earmarked for a number of purposes within one funding source. For example, some funds in a CCDBG can be used for resource and referral, and some can be used to fund before- and after-school care. The Dependent Care and Development Grant is a source for similar funding. The self-sufficiency goal for child care is reflected in the purposes of the Title IV-A funds. The purposes of the other programs listed in Table 7.1 reflect either a care or an education intent.

Conflicting child care goals aside, early care and education are inextricably interwoven (Kagan, 1994). Young children learn actively across their developmental domains in integrated, experiential ways. The cognitive domain is expanded and enhanced by experiences occurring in the social and physical domains. Developmentalists view care and education as one in the same in programs serving young children (Daniel, 1995a).

Critical Components of High-Quality Child Care

High-quality, center-based child care consists of several powerfully resonating research-based components. These components include the following:

Appropriate staff-to-child ratios—staff available to specific numbers of children
Small group sizes
Teaching staff with specialized training—child development certificate and/or bachelor degree
Adequate compensation—wages and benefits
Caregivers consistently available to the children—low staff turnover and primary caregiver assignments
Safe environment with a range of choices for children—developmentally appropriate according to the age and individual needs of children

State child care regulations determine the standards for several of the known quality components. Helburn et al. (1995), in a four-state study of 400 centers, found that states with more stringent regulatory standards had a higher incidence of high-quality centers. Effective licensing standards usually regulate group sizes, staff-to-child ratios, staff qualifications, and health and safety standards. In addition, Helburn et al. (1995) found that centers that adhered to standards that were higher than minimal licensing requirements also provided higher quality programing. Examples of standards that are higher than state licensing criteria for family child care and child care center are accreditation standards required by the National Association for Family Day Care (NAFDC) and NAEYC, respectively. Staff-to-child ratios, for example, are higher in the NAEYC accreditation standards. All of the standards are included in the Helburn et al. (1995) definition of good quality, which meets basic health and safety standards, provides warm and nurturing adult–child interactions for all children, and encourages a variety of learning opportunities.

At its most basic level, high-quality child care is characterized by small group sizes (Phillips & Howes, 1987) and the presence of college-

Table 7.1. Overview of federal child care and early education programs

Programs	Features			
	Authorization	Funding for fiscal year 1995	Purpose	Federal agency
CCDBG	PL 101-508, PL 102-586	$934.7 million[a]	To help states provide, expand, and improve child care services for children and families	Child Care Bureau, ACF, DHHS
Title IV-A at-risk child care	PL 101-508	Capped entitlement, $300 million	To provide funds to parents who do not receive AFDC, but who depend on child care to work and are at risk of becoming dependent on AFDC if they lose their child care	Child Care Bureau, ACF, DHHS
Title IV-A AFDC child care	PL 97-35, PL 97-248, PL 97-300, PL 98-369, PL 100-485	Open-ended entitlement	To provide child care to enable parents who receive AFDC to participate in education and job training or work	Child Care Bureau, ACF, DHHS
Title IV-A transitional child care	PL 100-485	Open-ended entitlement	To continue AFDC child care benefits for up to 1 year for families in which parents moved from welfare to work	Child Care Bureau, ACF, DHHS

Adapted by permission from National Association for the Education of Young Children Public Affairs Division.

Abbreviations: ACF, Administration for Children and Families; ACYF, Administration on Children, Youth, and Families; AFDC, Aid to Families with Dependent Children; CFR, Code of Federal Regulations; DOE, Department of Education; DHHS, Department of Health and Human Services.

[a]75% for direct services or quality improvement and 25% for early childhood development and before- and after-school care (75% of 25%), quality improvement (20% of 25%), and other uses at each state's discretion (5% of 20%).

Match (Yes/No)	Regulations/ rules	Eligibility	Fees (Yes/No)	Training provisions	Licensing requirements
No	45 CFR, Parts 98 and 99	Low-income, working (or in training) families that do not receive AFDC with children younger than 13 years of age	Yes, sliding scale	Yes	Yes
Yes	Final Regulation, *Federal Register,* August 4, 1992	Low-income, working families that are at risk for AFDC dependency with children younger than 13 years of age	Yes, sliding scale	No	No
Yes	*Federal Register,* October 13, 1989	Families that receive AFDC and include working parents and children younger than 13 years of age and those that include parents who participate in approved education/training or JOBS activities and children younger than 13 years of age	No	No	No
Yes, 50% state match	*Federal Register,* October 13, 1989	Families that received AFDC in 3 of the last 6 months and that include children younger than 13 years of age, but that no longer are eligible for AFDC	Yes, sliding scale	No	No

(continued)

Table 7.1. *(continued)*

Programs	Features			
	Authorization	Funding for fiscal year 1995	Purpose	Federal agency
Title I (formerly Chapter 1) programs	PL 89-10, PL 103-382	$6.7 billion	To provide compensatory education, including preschool services, to children who are educationally deprived (approximately $800 million is earmarked for preschool services)	Compensatory Education Programs, Office of Elementary and Secondary Education, DOE
Comprehensive child development centers[b]	PL 100-297, PL 103-252	Funds were not appropriated	To provide grants to model programs for intensive, comprehensive, supportive services for infants, toddlers, and preschoolers from low-income families	ACYF, ACF, DHHS
Dependent care and development grants	PL 101-501, PL 103-252	$12.8 million[c]	To provide funds to states for before- and after-school child care and resource and referral systems	Children's Bureau, ACF, DHHS
Even Start	PL 89-10	$102 million	To provide early childhood education to children who are educationally deprived and to provide literacy education to their parents	Compensatory Education Programs, Office of Elementary and Secondary Education, DOE

[b]As of fiscal year 1995, incorporated into a birth-to-3 initiative included under Head Start.
[c]60% for care for school-age children and 40% for resource and referral services.

		Features *(continued)*			
Match (Yes/No)	Regulations/ rules	Eligibility	Fees (Yes/No)	Training provisions	Licensing requirements
No	34 CFR 200	Preschool- and school-age children who are educationally deprived and who live in low-income areas	No	No	No
Yes, 20% agency match	No regulations codified in 45 CFR, Part 1300	Infants, toddlers, and preschoolers from low-income families, their families, and other family members	No	No	No
Yes, 25% match	No specific program regulations apply	Families that include children ages 17 years and younger for resource and referral services, and families that include children ages 3–13 years for before- and after-school programs	N/A	Yes	No
No	34 CFR 212	Children, 1–7 years of age, who are educationally disadvantaged and their families	No	Yes	No

(continued)

Table 7.1.   *(continued)*

Programs	Features			
	Authorization	Funding for fiscal year 1995	Purpose	Federal agency
Head Start	PL 97-35, PL 100-297, PL 101-501, PL 103-252	$3.53 billion	To provide educational, social, health, and nutritional services primarily to preschool-age children from low-income families and to provide other services to their parents	Head Start Bureau, ACYF, ACF, DHHS
Social Services block grant	PL 97-35, PL 98-8, PL 98-473, PL 100-203, PL 100-485	Capped entitlement, $2.8 billion	To provide grants to states for social services activities, including child care	Office of Community Assistance, Division of State Assistance, ACF, DHHS
Temporary child care and crisis care nurseries	PL 99-401, PL 100-403	$11.8 million	To provide temporary care to children who have disabilities and are seriously ill and to provide crisis nurseries for children who are abused, neglected, or at risk for abuse	Children's Bureau, ACYF, ACF, DHHS
Services for children with disabilities				
Early education for children with disabilities	PL 98-199, PL 99-457, PL 100-630, PL 101-476	$25.2 million	To expand and improve early intervention and special education services for children with disabilities from birth through age 8	Special Education Programs, Office of Special Education and Rehabilitative Services, DOE

[a]At least 10% of enrollment opportunities must target children with disabilities.

		Features *(continued)*			
Match (Yes/No)	Regulations/ rules	Eligibility	Fees (Yes/No)	Training provisions	Licensing requirements
20% local match (in-kind)	45 CFR 1301-05	Primarily families with incomes below the federal poverty level, although up to 10% of children enrolled may be from families with incomes above the poverty level[d]	No	Yes, training: T/A	N/A
No	45 CFR 96	State, county, or local agency determines eligibility	Yes, state option	Yes	Yes, state option
Yes, 25% state grantee match	No regulations codified in 45 CFR, Part 1300	Families that include children who are chronically ill and/or have disabilities and children who are abused and neglected or who are at risk for abuse and/or neglect	Temporary child care: Yes; Sliding scale crisis care nurseries: No	No	No
Yes, 10% grant recipient match	34 CFR 309	Infants, toddlers, and children with disabilities, ages 8 years and younger	No	Yes	N/A

(continued)

Table 7.1. *(continued)*

Programs	Features			
	Authorization	Funding for fiscal year 1995	Purpose	Federal agency
Grants for infants/tod-dlers with dis-abilities	PL 91-230, PL 99-457, PL 100-630, PL 101-476	$281.6 million	To assist states in developing and imple-menting statewide sys-tems of early intervention services	Special Educa-tion Pro-grams, Office of Special Education and Rehabilitative Services, DOE
Preschool grants	PL 94-142, PL 99-457, PL 100-630, PL 101-476 PL 101-497,	$360.3 million	To assist states in providing spe-cial education and services to children, ages 3–5 years, who have disabili-ties	Special Educa-tion Pro-grams, Office of Special Education and Rehabilitative Services, DOE

educated teachers/caregivers (Helburn et al., 1995). Research demonstrated that specialized training is particularly important for teachers/caregivers of infants (Whitebook, Howes, & Phillips, 1989). In addition, a positive relationship has been found between teachers/caregivers who have more education and higher quality programs that adhere to higher standards (Helburn et al., 1995;Whitebook et al., 1989). Because many providers in both early childhood and early intervention programs have very little training in their field (Kontos & File, 1993), and because turnover rates are high, overall program quality is often lower than it should be. Helburn et al. (1995) determined that 85% of center care was beneath good quality, and, specifically, 40% of the infant and toddler care was beneath minimal quality.

Family child care also has been the subject of quality-defining research. Galinsky, Howes, Kontos, and Shinn (1994), in a study of nonrelative and relative care in homes, identified several factors that affect the quality of home care; these include regulations, ratios, group sizes, and training—the same factors that are associated with high quality in centers. Galinsky et al. (1994) identified the following two additional indicators of the quality of home care: 1) whether the family child care provider was interested in working with children as a career and 2) whether the provider was part of a network of providers. Finally, higher compensation and parent fees served as indicators of high-quality child care.

Attitudes toward compensation and parent fees demonstrate the dependence of program quality on available resources. The Helburn et al. study (1995) found that "even mediocre-quality care is costly to provide" (p. 5). When fees are increased to provide adequate compensation for teachers/caregivers, the services become less affordable to people like Emma Tolbert and the full-time employed, single parents who participated in the study by Helburn et al. (1995) and who earned $21,000 before taxes

Match (Yes/No)	Features *(continued)*		Fees (Yes/No)	Training provisions	Licensing requirements
	Regulations/ rules	Eligibility			
No	Final Regulations, *Federal Register,* June 22, 1989; August 19, 1992	Infants and toddlers with disabilities, from birth through 2 years of age	No	Yes	N/A
No	34 CFR 301	Children with disabilities, ages 3–5 years	No	Yes	N/A

in 1993. The average cost of child care per child per year in the Helburn et al. (1995) study was $4,940. Because the cost of child care is such a strain on families, child care program administrators fear that raising fees will price their programs out of the market. Furthermore, Culkin, Helburn, and Morris (1990) describe child care as a young and volatile industry, suffering intense pressure from the unregulated side of the market. Unregulated child care providers start with the fiscal advantage of having no regulatory compliance costs. Culkin et al. (1990) also state that the principle of supply and demand does not work in child care as it does in more traditional markets. Child care is described as a merit good of high value to society, but it is not recognized as such by society. For society to get full value from child care, public support is necessary (Culkin et al., 1990). The general lack of resources means that teachers/caregivers are compensated poorly.

Indeed, inadequate compensation is the single most important factor contributing to the high turnover rates found among staff of center-based child care programs. In a four-state study, Whitebook et al. (1989) found a turnover rate of 41%, which is nearly double the average turnover found in the rest of the U.S. workforce. In states with stricter regulations and, therefore, higher child care quality, child care staff still do not earn wages commensurate with their levels of education and responsibilities; they are, however, paid at a rate closer to their market value (Helburn et al., 1995). When staff attrition is high, and staff are not consistently available to the children, then children's fundamental need to feel attached to their caregivers/teachers is thwarted, and quality is undermined.

Research on how children learn has found that children thrive when they are connected to their caregivers/teachers by a warm and nurturing relationship. Children learn in an integrative fashion, building on the experiences they have across all of the growth domains (emotional, social, physical, and cognitive) (Bredekamp, 1987). Greenspan and Porges (1984) discussed the importance of relational development to the cognitive, emotional, and social development of infants and toddlers. Daniel and Shapiro (in press) expanded on Greenspan's concept of relational development as it pertains to the transition of infants and toddlers from their homes to center-based child care programs. Erickson (1963) plotted the emotional and social development of the child, weaving in its implications for the child's approach to cognitive development. Piaget's work on the cognitive development of the child described the process by which everyday social experiences interact to build a substantial cognitive case (Bredekamp, 1993). It is through social interaction that the child eventually learns that others have perspectives that differ from his or her own. Such a developmental achievement is a prerequisite for the sophisticated, abstract, cognitive manipulation of ideas.

A crucial quality factor is the consistency of the nurturing relationship for the child in a child care environment, which is manifest in both the availability of a central or primary caregiver and the number of core team caregivers. Group sizes, staff-to-child ratios, staff training, staff turnover, and compensation all determine the existence of consistency and the quality of that consistency. Through the National Academy of Early Childhood Programs' accreditation guidelines, NAEYC has established a set of nationally recognized standards for staff-to-child ratios based on the ages of the children and the sizes of the groups. A sample of the optimal standard ranges is listed in Table 7.2.

When appropriately trained staff are available to children in sufficient numbers, staff have increased opportunities to interact with the children, which enhances the quality of the child care program. The interim report on the Florida Child Care Quality Improvement Study (Howes, Smith, & Galinsky, 1995) examined the Florida licensing standards when they were changed to improve the staff-to-child ratio from 1:6 to 1:4 for infants and from 1:8 to 1:6 for toddlers and to require that at least one staff person in each classroom have a Child Development Associate (CDA) Certificate (a college-level certificate program) or the equivalent. Classrooms of teachers who had bachelor degrees and advanced training had the highest overall quality score, but the rooms staffed by CDA certificate holders showed the most significant improvement.

The relationship between the knowledge base of staff members and program quality is a serious dynamic that plagues the entire early care and education field. In preparation for the Child Care Aware Campaign to raise the U.S. public's consciousness about the importance of child care, very revealing parent focus group meetings were held. Parents' descriptions of a high-quality child care environment focused on staff–child interactions.

Table 7.2. Staff-to-child ratios recommended by NAEYC

Age	Group size	Staff-to-child ratio
Birth–1 year	6–8	1:3–1:4
2 years	8–10	1:4–1:5
3 years	14–18	1:7–1:9
5 years	16–20	1:8–1:10

Warmth, enjoyable learning experiences, and individual attention were high on the parents' list. Parents did not, however, recognize the caregiver's/teacher's training as a determinant of quality (Child Care Action Campaign, 1991).

Emma Tolbert's definition of high-quality child care mirrors that of the focus group parents. During a panel presentation, Tolbert told the audience that her expectation for child care was that it not scar her children. She explained that she wanted her children to be happy, whole, learning, and living to capacity (E. Tolbert, personal communication, August 1994). Although professionals would use slightly different language, such as nurturance and developmentally appropriate practice (DAP), professionals and parents seem to agree on the definition of high-quality care, except for the critical issue of training. Research indicates that parents' expectations cannot be met in a group child care program without the presence of trained staff.

Developmentally Appropriate Practice

The knowledge base that is critical to the positive enhancement of the growth and development of the child is an understanding of the developmental needs across the emotional, social, cognitive, and physical domains. Bredekamp (1993) described the basis for DAP as follows:

> Learning environments, teaching practices, and other program components should be planned based on what is generally to be expected of children of various ages and stages, but adaptations should be made for the wide range of differences between individual children. NAEYC's statement reflects a constructivist, interactive approach to learning and teaching, strongly influenced by Piagetian theory, emphasizing play and active, child-initiated learning. (p. 261)

In a developmentally appropriate environment, a child is given a range of choices of activities that allow him or her to repeat known skills as well as to learn something new. In a developmentally appropriate environment, children also are given sufficient time to manipulate the environment across all domains so that the experience is comprehensive, holistic, and integrated into the context of their daily experiences. The teacher is a facilitator who has prepared the physical environment through room arrangement and selection and placement of materials. The teacher also facilitates the learning environment by guiding the social dynamics of the group, including peer relationships and how adults interact with individual children and the group.

One significant area of the social dynamics of group care and education is culture. "Cultural differences in how children are socialized in the home significantly affect a child's response to the teaching techniques used by teachers" (Chang & Sakai, 1993, p. 19). One criticism of DAP is that it does not clearly take into account the cultural differences among groups of people. DAP itself is criticized as being culture specific. NAEYC has decided to reexamine DAP in light of the significance of the cultural dynamic and how it can best be approached to maximize the growth and development of all children enrolled in early care and education programs.

Some misunderstandings between the fields of early childhood education and early childhood special education have arisen with regard to DAP.

The misunderstandings center on the degree to which activities are teacher directed or child initiated. Bredekamp (1993) notes that it is not a simple matter of either one or the other, rather it is a matter of determining the appropriate degree based on each child's individual needs. Bredekamp (1993) noted several areas in which early childhood education and early childhood special education could build on each other's knowledge bases and, thereby, enhance programming for all children. Areas on which to build include family-centered approaches, planning and assessment, interdisciplinary team collaborations, transitions to new settings, and advocacy (Bredekamp, 1993). McLean and Odom (1993) discussed issues and practices that exist in early childhood education and early childhood special education and concurred with those listed by Bredekamp. McLean and Odom (1993) delineated the emphases placed by each field on the discussion points. They also discussed service delivery models, including the inclusion model. In fact, if the least restrictive environment provision required by PL 94-142, the Education for All Handicapped Children Act of 1975 (subsequently reauthorized as PL 101-476, the Individuals with Disabilities Education Act [IDEA] of 1990), and PL 99-457, the Education of the Handicapped Act Amendments of 1986 (subsequently reauthorized as PL 102-119, the Individuals with Disabilities Education Act Amendments of 1991), and by inclusion is to be successful, each field must build on the assets of the other's theory and practice base.

In 1988, Strain succinctly outlined what is known about the outcomes for children in least restrictive, inclusive environments (Smith & Rose, 1993). Such integrated, planned, and frequent interactive services produce positive social outcomes both for children with disabilities, regardless of the severity of the disabling conditions, and for typically developing children. Children with disabilities use and maintain new skills more often when they participate in inclusive settings. Because inclusive settings benefit all children, it is critical that early care and education and special education professionals collaborate extensively across traditional field boundaries, building on points of agreement.

One point of agreement is that both early care and education professionals and early childhood special education professionals value the natural approach to early learning. Early childhood special educators are perhaps more consciously planful (Wolery, 1994b) in their attempts to maximize the opportunities for growth and learning in a natural environment (see Chapter 9). The two fields differ in their emphases in this area of curriculum and in their intervention strategies; early childhood educators stress the psychological and thinking processes of children, and special education professionals place a greater emphasis on building skills, such as self-help and communication skills (McLean & Odom, 1993). Concerning special education, Wolery (1994b) wrote, "it means that the team realizes that every interaction and activity should be done for a purpose; the team is able to describe that purpose and organizes the child's opportunities for interaction so that those purposes are met" (p. 152).

Each of the emphases requires different intervention behaviors from the teachers involved. To engage in DAP, the teacher would assess the child's development across all domains and offer the child activities that allow for the maximization of growth, recognizing that all children develop unevenly across the domains. Children with disabilities very often have complex developmental needs, because they typically have more than one disability. Wolery (1994a) identifies assessment as a critical component of programming for children with disabilities. Assessment begins with the initial screening of the child's abilities and is used to determine appropriate placement, planning of the individualized education program (IEP), and the monitoring and evaluation process (Wolery, 1994a). By law, parents are key partners with the interdisciplinary team in the programming decisions made for children with disabilities. In comparison, parents are far less involved in the programming decisions made in typical child care programs.

PARENT INVOLVEMENT

Powell (1987) echoed Tolbert's concern when he wrote that matching child care services with the needs of the family is important to overall family functioning: "A critical family life issue today is how to find and maintain a high-quality day-care arrangement" (p. 130). Tolbert described the after-school arrangement for her twins as far from perfect. According to Powell (1989), her far-from-perfect experience is not uncommon. Powell reviewed the research on family involvement in early childhood programs. The fit between families and programs depends on variables such as the values, education levels, social classes, and ethnicities of the people involved. Differences in child-rearing styles also arise from such variables. Powell's assessment of the literature on the effects of discontinuity between families and programs was that, "the differences appear to be greatest for children whose parents are non-Anglo and not middle class" (1989, p. 49). His review, however, indicated that there are more questions than answers in this area of investigation. Early childhood professionals have long assumed a positive theoretical basis for parent involvement.

Historically, educators have attempted to involve families in various activities in early childhood programs. Typically, parents have been involved as volunteers in classrooms and on boards as sources of and recipients of information, but not as real decision makers regarding curricular issues. Although the practice of parent involvement historically has been associated with programs considered to be of high quality, Powell (1989) found that very little empirical research has been undertaken to substantiate the validity of that practice. Powell noted the impressive theoretical basis for the presumption that family involvement is beneficial, such as Bronfenbrenner's work on interrelated systems, but called for researchers and practitioners to collaborate in an effort to construct an empirical basis for effective practice.

Parent involvement in fundamental decision making is mandated by law in programs that serve children with disabilities. Parents of children with disabilities and other advocates waged an intensive campaign for several years that finally established the pivotal place of parents in the process of making decisions about the integration of educational and related services for children with disabilities. Families determine the parameters of the least restricted environment on the basis of their differing needs, values, resources, and so forth—in other words, on the basis of their individualized social context (Winton, 1993). Winton (1993) noted that the evolution of the family support movement, building on family strengths rather than limitations, has changed the assumptions on which the special education field operates: "The assumptions include the following: 1) family support should be a primary goal of early intervention, and 2) families' values, interests, and priorities should guide intervention" (p. 65). It is clear that the traditional role of the professional as the expert must change to one of partner or facilitator in assisting the parents in their pivotal decision-making role (Powell, 1989).

Barr and Cochran (1992) suggested that the proper role definition for human services professionals is that of transformer. Cochran (1989) explained that this is in contrast with the role professionals play in the deficit model:

> The "deficit" model indirectly encourages parents and caregivers to vie for limited quantities of self-esteem, money, and children's affection. The empowerment process allows for partnerships to develop in which parents and caregivers can work together for better living and working conditions, such as good nutrition and education, a safe, healthy living environment, parental leave policies, and good salaries and working conditions. (p. 9)

The transformer is a politically astute professional who understands the power dynamic of human interaction, is fully aware of his or her role in the decision-making process, and knows when to step back so that others can maximize their involvement in the process. The transformer participates in large part by enabling others, such as parents, to build on the strengths they bring to the situation (Barr & Cochran, 1992). This newly defined professional assists parents in becoming advocates for their children.

Parent Advocacy

Emma Tolbert's parent advocate voice resonates clearly. Her involvement with Parents United for Child Care has provided her with a set of family-supportive, quality-enhancing principles and a means of having a cohesive impact on both of the child care delivery system goals. A merit good, such as child care, requires such focused attention, backed by research, if the needs of all children and parents are to be met. The effectiveness of the combined advocacy of parents and professionals is evidenced by the mandates in statute, for example, individualized education programs, for early childhood special education programming for young children and their families. Although both parents and professionals are strong advocates for high-quality programs for young children and their families, the social agenda priority of the United States will not change until a wider segment of society believes inherently in the value of high-quality early care and education programs. In fact, the single recommendation made by Helburn et al. (1995) was that the United States commit to the provision of high-quality child care for all children. Helburn et al. (1995) wrote, "across all levels of maternal education and child gender and ethnicity, children's cognitive and social development are positively related to the quality of their child care experience" (p. 4). A massive public education campaign focused on the value of high-quality early care and education is the central recommended strategy for accomplishing that goal.

FUTURE DIRECTIONS

Because misinformation usually spreads more quickly than do thoughtful analysis and accurate information, it is assumed that the woefully misguided set of circumstances surrounding child care in 1996 will continue in the future. Therefore, the fundamental recommendation for the resolution of the complexities of child care for all children is broad communication to the general public, to policy makers, and among professionals in the early child care and education fields.

Within the fields of early care and education, including special education, the need for cross-disciplinary preparation of professionals is critical. Segregated early childhood caregiver/teacher preparation undermines the interdisciplinary approach needed for successful inclusion (Bruder, 1994; Smith & Rose, 1993; Winton, 1993). Smith and Rose noted that collaboration requires "skill trading among participants," a circumstance in which participants share information freely (1993, p. 61). Early child care and education professionals also have called for greater infusion of other disciplines, such as sociology, in teacher preparation programs (Daniel, 1994). Both emerging and established professionals strive to be effective in their work. Professionals recognize the immediacy of the need to alter their professional perspectives to meet the needs of families who are part of the rapidly changing demographics of the United States.

The continued collaboration between the two major professional organizations, NAEYC and the Division for Early Childhood of the Council for Exceptional Children (DEC), as well as that among other such organizations, will continue to be crucial to the accurate interpretation of information, the setting of high-quality practice standards, and advocacy to ensure cohesive social policies for inclusive services that meet the needs of all children.

Many of the future successful advocacy efforts of professionals, parents, and others will depend on the availability of accurate information. Early care and education service delivery is increasingly informed by research that queries the complexities of child care. Many questions remain to be answered. For example, what is the best method of serving a diverse population? Tolbert suggests that, in terms of quality, one should not be able to ascertain the affluence of the neighborhood in which a program is located by looking inside the center. At the same time, however, she recognizes the need for programs to be sensitive to the family backgrounds of children. What are the best methods of teacher preparation that allow for an effective interdisciplinary approach to DAP? What are viable funding mechanisms for a child care delivery system that meets the developmental needs of all children and supports parents' need for self-sufficiency? What are the components that constitute an effective, inclusive child care delivery system?

It has been suggested that "early care and education has become a laboratory for the use of service integration as a strategy for systemic reform" (Kagan, Goffin, Golub, & Pritchard, 1995, p. 9). Numerous U.S. communities have rallied around the National Governors' Association's first national education goal, which is that all children will enter school ready to learn. The pursuit of that deceivingly simple goal has focused communities to look more holistically at children's developmental needs and the needs of their families. Readiness is a function of numerous developmental elements, such as health and social development, that are affected by other variables, such as poverty and lack of opportunity. In fact, attempts to achieve the readiness goal are resulting in a cohesive, more inclusive policy climate, which may help to fuse the two goals of child care—serving parents and serving children. The guiding principle that provides the most hopeful climate for forging a cohesive, inclusive child care delivery system is that of enhancing family support. This principle builds on family strengths and welcomes parents as informed decision-making partners.

As mentioned earlier, however, U.S. society does not place the appropriate value on the benefits it receives from high-quality early child care and education programs. A cross-section of society must first own the complex issues involved in child care for there to be a community will to commit the necessary resources to build a high-quality, inclusive delivery system. Community support for an inclusive delivery system is critical if professionals are to be free to involve families more creatively in the decision-making process (Winton, 1993). Effective human services delivery system changes will have the best chance for success if the family support movement can be taken to scale, expanded beyond demonstration projects. Couched in the notion of building on the strengths of families is the potential to shift the paradigm that stereotypes too many people by race, ethnicity, education, income, and class.

Several watershed social trends are likely to increase the tendency to stereotype groups of people negatively. Shrinking resources and perceived increased levels of crime can cause people to be fearful and to act in noninclusive ways. Other social trends include the following: an increasing number of children in the United States who live in poverty; a child population in the United States that is growing increasingly diverse in color, language, and social class; health care that is costly and unattainable for some families; and the belief that the federal government and its broadbased solutions are not as effective as local solutions (Daniel, 1995b). The circling of wagons that is the classic response when people feel besieged and attacked will be counterproductive to resolving the complex issues Emma Tolbert faced. Nothing short of a reordering of U.S. priorities will alleviate the complexities involved in finding and affording appropriate, convenient high-quality child care.

Parents should be offered a selection of inclusive high-quality early care and education choices. Their choices should be part of an accessible comprehensive network of services, including health, housing, employment and training opportunities, and education, that respects differences and builds on family strengths. The extension of the definition of quality beyond individual classrooms or family child care homes to a comprehensive network of collaborative services offers the best chance of bringing some balance to the dual goals of child care. High-quality programming for children and self-sufficiency for parents must be delivered simultaneously. The needs of each of the two populations should not compete with each other, but rather should be addressed as a complex family system in need of balance, thoughtful management, and shared, nonduplicative financing.

REFERENCES

Barr, D., & Cochran, M. (1992). Understanding and supporting empowerment: Redefining the professional role. *Networking Bulletin, 2*(3), 9–10.

Bredekamp, S. (Ed.). (1987). *Developmentally appropriate practice in early childhood programs serving children from birth to age 8* (Exp. ed.). Washington, DC: National Association for the Education of Young Children.

Bredekamp, S. (1993). The relationship between early childhood education and early childhood special education: Healthy marriage or family feud? *Topics in Early Childhood Education, 13*(3), 258–273.

Bruder, M. (1994). Working with members of other disciplines: Collaboration for success. In M. Wolery & J. Wilbers (Eds.), *Including children with special needs in early childhood programs* (Research Monograph Vol. 6, pp. 45–70). Washington, DC: National Association for the Education of Young Children.

Casper, L., Hawkins, M., & O'Connell, M. (1994). *Who's minding the kids? Child care arrangements: Fall 1991* (Current Population Reports P70-36). Washington, DC: U.S. Government Printing Office.

Chang, H., & Sakai, L. (1993). *Affirming children's roots: Cultural and linguistic diversity in early care and education.* San Francisco, CA: California Tomorrow.

Child Care Action Campaign. (1991). *Choosing quality child care: Top line findings.* Unpublished manuscript, Child Care Action Campaign, New York.

Child Care and Development Block Grant of 1990, PL 101-508. (November 5, 1990). Title 42, U.S.C. 9858 et seq: *U.S. Statutes at Large, 104.*

Cochran, M. (1989). Child care/empowerment. *Networking Bulletin, (1)*1, 1–9.

Culkin, M., Helburn, S., & Morris, J. (1990). Current price versus full cost: An economic perspective. In B. Willer (Ed.), *Reaching the full cost of quality in early childhood programs* (pp. 9–26). Washington, DC: National Association for the Education of Young Children.

Daniel, J. (1994). New with something more to learn: Commentary on the skills necessary for entry into an early childhood classroom as a competent teacher. In S. Goffin & D. Day (Eds.), *New perspectives in early childhood teacher education: Bringing practitioners into the debate* (pp. 63–66). New York: Teachers College Press.

Daniel, J. (1995a). Advancing the care and education paradigm: A case for developmentalists. *Young Children, 50*(2), 2.

Daniel, J. (1995b). NAEYC's contractual commitment to children. *Young Children, 50*(3), 2.

Daniel, J., & Shapiro, J. (in press). *Infant transitions: Home to center based care. Child and Youth Care Forum.*

Education for All Handicapped Children Act of 1975, PL 94-142. (August 23, 1977). Title 20, U.S.C. 1401 et seq: *U.S. Statutes at Large, 89,* 773–796.

Education of the Handicapped Act Amendments of 1986, PL 99-457. (October 8, 1986). Title 20, U.S.C. 1400 et seq: *U.S. Statutes at Large, 100,* 1145–1177.

Erikson, E. (1963). *Childhood and society.* New York: Norton.

Galinsky, E., & Friedman, D. (1993). *Education before school: Investing in quality child care.* New York: Scholastic.

Galinsky, E., Howes, C., Kontos, S., & Shinn, M. (1994). *The study of children in family child care and relative care: Highlights of findings.* New York: Families and Work Institute.

Greenspan, S., & Porges, S. (1984). Psychopathology in infancy and early childhood: Clinical perspectives on the organization of sensory and affective-thematic experience. *Child Development, 55*(1), 49–70.

Helburn, S., Culkin, M., Howes, C., Bryant, D., Clifford, R., Cryer, D., Peisner-Feinberg, E., & Kagan, S. (1995). *Cost, quality, and child outcomes in child care centers: Executive summary.* Denver, CO: University of Denver.

Howes, C., Smith, E., & Galinsky, E. (1995). *The Florida child care quality improvement study: Interim report.* New York: Families and Work Institute.

Individuals with Disabilities Education Act (IDEA) of 1990, PL 101-476. (October 30, 1990). Title 20, U.S.C. 1400 et seq: *U.S. Statutes at Large, 104,* 1103–1151.

Individuals with Disabilities Education Act Amendments of 1991, PL 102-119. (October 7, 1991). Title 20, U.S.C. 1400 et seq: *U.S. Statutes at Large, 105,* 587–608.

Kagan, S. (1994). Readying schools for young children: Polemics and priorities. *Phi Delta Kappan, 76*(3), 226–233.

Kagan, S., Goffin, S., Golub, S., & Pritchard, E. (1995). *Toward systematic reform: Service integration for young children and their families.* Falls Church, VA: National Center for Service Integration.

Kontos, S., & File, N. (1993). Staff development in support of integration. In C.A. Peck, S.L. Odom, & D. Bricker (Eds.), *Integrating young children with disabilities into community programs: Ecological perspectives on research and implementation* (pp. 169–186). Baltimore: Paul H. Brookes Publishing Co.

Lombardi, J. (1990). Head Start: The nation's pride, a nation's challenge. *Young Children, 45*(6), 22–29.

McLean, M., & Odom, S. (1993). Practices for young children with and without disabilities: A comparison of DEC and NAEYC identified practices. *Topics in Early Childhood Special Education, 13*(3), 274–292.

Morgan, G., Azer, S., Costley, J., Genser, A., Goodman, I., Lombardi, J., & McGimsey, B. (1993). *Making a career of it: The state of the states report on career development in early care and education.* Boston, MA: Wheelock College.

National Association for the Education of Young Children. (1984). *Accreditation criteria and procedures of the national academy of early childhood programs.* Washington, DC: Author.

Phillips, D., & Howes, C. (1987). Indicators of quality child care: Review of the research. In D. Phillips (Ed.), *Quality in child care: What the research tells us?* (Research Monograph Vol. 1., pp. 1–19). Washington, DC: National Association for the Education of Young Children.

Powell, D. (1987). Day care as a family support system. In S. Kagan, D. Powell, B. Weisbourd, & E. Zigler (Eds.), *America's family support programs* (pp. 115–132). New Haven, CT: Yale University Press.

Powell, D. (1989). *Families and early childhood programs.* Washington DC: National Association for the Education of Young Children.

Smith, B., & Rose, D. (1993). *Administrator's policy handbook for preschool mainstreaming.* Cambridge, MA: Brookline Books.

Washington, V., & Greene, S. (Eds.). (1995). *Head Start works!* Alexandria, VA: National Head Start Association.

Whitebook, M., Howes, C., & Phillips, D. (1989). *Who cares? Child care teachers and the quality of care in America, executive summary, national child care staffing study.* Oakland, CA: Child Care Employee Project.

Winton, P. (1993). Providing family support in integrated settings: Research and recommendations. In C.A. Peck, S.L. Odom, & D.D. Bricker (Eds.), *Integrating young children with disabilities into community programs: Ecological perspectives on research and implementation* (pp. 65–80). Baltimore: Paul H. Brookes Publishing Co.

Wolery, M. (1994a). Assessing children with special needs. In M. Wolery & J. Wilbers (Eds.), *Including children with special needs in early childhood pro-*

grams (Research Monograph Vol. 6., pp. 71–96). Washington, DC: National Association for the Education of Young Children.

Wolery, M. (1994b). Implementing instruction for young children with special needs in early childhood classrooms. In M. Wolery & J. Wilbers (Eds.), *Including children with special needs in early childhood programs* (Research Monograph Vol. 6., pp. 151–166). Washington, DC: National Association for the Education of Young Children.

Inclusion and Opportunity

Walter Thies

My son Keith, who is 6 years old, just might be headed for the Olympics. At the playground, Keith hangs upside down from jungle gyms, and he rollerskates at breakneck speed. At the local laundry, he might dangle from a countertop or clamber into a washing machine. At home, he scales tables, chairs, and bunkbeds, and, when no equipment is at hand, he climbs on me.

I love Keith, so I am proud of his high-flying exploits even when they provoke consternation in others. I think, however, that Keith's physical prowess excites wonder in children and anxiety in adults in part because Keith has low vision and is deaf.

I certainly do not deny that Keith is unique, nor do I deny that his disability introduces a degree of complexity not usually present when planning how to meet the educational needs of a typically developing child. I do not believe, however, that consideration of the characteristics that make Keith unique constitute, in and of themselves, cause for assigning him to a self-contained special education class.

In early 1994, I asked the New York City Board of Education (the Board) to provide Keith with special education services in a general education class in our neighborhood. By June, the Board had recommended a school, and that school had selected a class for Keith to join. Keith visited the class, and his designated teacher visited Keith at his school for children who have multiple disabilities. Keith and I met with representatives of the Board and administrators of the designated school to discuss the implementation of Keith's program, and representatives of the school made plans to attend a conference that addressed issues concerning individuals who are deaf-blind. Then, in July, the Board informed me that the school had abruptly decided against receiving Keith as a student.

I requested an impartial hearing, expecting that the school's administrators simply would be made to see that Keith, like any child, had to be accorded an opportunity to attend the school. After learning, however, that the administrators, despite offering no justifiable rationale for their rejection, resolutely opposed receiving Keith as a student, I began to question whether litigation offered the best hope for relief. Due process probably would have secured Keith a place in the school, but I was less certain whether it also could have overcome the attitudes that caused the administrators to reject Keith in the first place. Mortified as I was to learn that Keith's individualized education program was viewed, not as a mandate, but as a suggestion to be implemented voluntarily, if at all, I accepted the Board's proposal that Keith enroll in a kindergarten class at a different school. In October of 1994, Keith began attending a special program housed in a general education school in our neighborhood.

Keith's class was a general education/special education blend in which an early childhood teacher and a special education teacher instructed 24 students. Despite the fact that Keith's class was touted as inclusive, it actually perpetuated several practices typical of self-contained special education classes. Neither in terms of numbers nor in types of special education needs did Keith's classmates reflect the incidence of disability encountered in the general population. Approximately one third of the students in Keith's class received special education services, and, except for Keith, those who did were selected to enroll in this class according to the types of services they required. Moreover, because Keith's class comprised two roughly homogenous categories of students—those who received intervention for mild language problems and those who did not—and, because Keith fit neatly into neither group, he often worked at parallel rather than integrated lessons. For example, while his classmates were reading together, Keith often was in another part of the room or even in another room altogether working with a specialist or a paraprofessional. Finally, some of the children who received special education services traveled from distant neighborhoods. As the year progressed, it became evident that these students probably would attend different schools for first grade, because their blended class was not going to be extended. At least two children were referred to self-contained classes, and Keith's school began to oppose his continued placement there.

In June of 1995, the Board referred Keith back to a self-contained class. I resolutely opposed this referral, which still was pending at the end of the calendar year. I also insisted that, as long as Keith remained at his current school, the Board had to take steps to provide him with an appropriate education. As a start, in October, I obtained an interim order from an impartial hearing officer that the Board provide Keith's school with 15 hours per week of technical assistance from an expert named by me.

I am reasonably confident that the Board will fail in its efforts to remove Keith from his school, and I am cautiously optimistic that, in time and given adequate support, Keith's school will come to share my belief that Keith's educational needs can be met in a general education class. For the present, however, we remain very far from bringing this vision to life.

Implementing any high-quality inclusion program might be expected to present challenges; I believe, however, that the primary obstacle in Keith's case is reliance on two faulty assumptions about education: 1) the educational goals of typically developing children will be subverted when their classes include a limited number of students who receive special education services, and 2) students who have disabilities can receive adequate special education services only when they are grouped according to shared characteristics. In fact, grouping children according to type or severity of disability can inhibit learning. For example, children like Keith, who require intensive intervention if they are to develop peer social skills, are at a marked disadvantage if they encounter only children who also require intensive intervention. Rather than learning standard social skills, those children may learn values specific to their classrooms, values that may serve them ill in the community. Conversely, thoughtful diversification of classes accompanied by a free exchange of information among professionals and families can expand learning opportunities for all children. A child who reads well may continue to improve his or her literacy skills and learn something about homelessness when he or she tutors a child who lives in a shelter, or a child experiencing delays in the acquisition of communication skills may discover an aptitude for sign language and help a child who is deaf-blind learn to make choices. Best of all, every child would have the opportunity to learn to be a friend.

Fortunately, because all communities already contain students of diverse backgrounds and abilities and educators of broad training and experience, we already have abundant resources with which to work. Does this mean that inclusion is easy? My experience tells me no, at least not so far. But regardless of whether inclusion is easy to achieve, we have a responsibility as individuals and as a society to confront challenges to fundamental rights squarely and in good faith.

The laws of the United States promote equal opportunity, but, by thoughtlessly relegating children to self-contained special education classes, Americans have institutionalized segregation in schools and restricted access to opportunity. Simply by enabling all children to participate meaningfully in their communities' most fundamental institutions—especially neighborhood schools—inclusion extends opportunity to all to both contribute to and benefit from community life. Just as surely as I believe that inclusion holds the promise of a more secure place in his community for Keith, I also believe that Keith's community will be a richer place for his being there.

8

THE PROMISE AND CHALLENGE OF SUPPORTING ALL CHILDREN IN NATURAL ENVIRONMENTS

Elizabeth J. Erwin

Since the passage of PL 94-142, the Education for All Handicapped Children Act of 1975, subsequently reauthorized as PL 101-476, the Individuals with Disabilities Education Act (IDEA) of 1990, interest in providing meaningful experiences for children with disabilities, like Keith, together with typically developing age-mates has grown dramatically. As early as the 1920s, many professionals had begun to question the logic of providing specialized services to children with disabilities in environments that were inconsistent with life in the real world (Wang, 1989). Since the mid-1970s, the movement toward educating children with and without disabilities together has gained strong momentum and continues to grow.

By 1996, this practice, known as *inclusion*, had gained significant national attention and acceptance in the United States among early childhood professionals (Fewell & Neisworth, 1990; Peck, Odom, & Bricker, 1993). In this chapter, inclusion is defined as a philosophy that fosters the belief that all children, regardless of their (dis)abilities, can and should participate fully in natural community-based environments. (Inclusion is defined in greater detail later in this chapter.) This chapter examines how the philosophy and practice of inclusion has evolved and explores which aspects of inclusion contribute to high-quality early care and education for all children.

THE INFLUENCE OF KEY LEGISLATION ON EARLY CHILDHOOD INCLUSION

The concept of bringing together young children with and without disabilities is not new to early childhood education. Since the late 1970s, advocates have strongly supported the idea of integrating or including youngsters with disabilities with their age-appropriate peers (Cooke, Ruskus, Apollini, & Peck, 1981; Guralnick, 1978; Vincent, Brown, & Getz-Sheftel, 1981). Because the philosophical and educational rationales for including children with disabilities with their age-appropriate peers have been reviewed previously (see Bricker, 1978; Odom & McEvoy, 1988; Vincent et al., 1981), these discussions are not repeated here. Rather, this section illustrates the impact of key legislation on service delivery practices in early childhood.

Values play an important part in the development and implementation of legislation. Turnbull (1990) noted that a values-based approach should guide and mirror advocacy efforts and legislation:

> Law and legal interpretation follow values; sometimes they precede values, and at other times they reflect values. Because there is an inextricable connection between law, values, and results for infants, toddlers, and families, advocates should argue on the basis of values and principles. (p. 31)

Values have been instrumental in securing legislation for young children, particularly with regard to the inclusion of children with disabilities in natural, community-based environments. Often it seems as though clear and well-conceived reasons form the grounds for legislation; in reality, values, not logic, frequently guide policy (Gallagher, 1992).

Federal legislation supports the value that young children with disabilities should have access to opportunities within natural environments and with their typically developing peers. In the early 1970s, amendments to Head Start legislation (PL 92-424, the Economic Opportunity Amendments of 1972, and PL 93-644, the Community Services Act of 1974) mandated that children with disabilities comprise at least 10% of Head Start's program enrollment. Although these amendments were some of the first legislative efforts to integrate youngsters with and without disabilities, Mallory (1994) suggested that they may have had unintended, detrimental results: They isolated or ghettoized children from low-income families and children with disabilities, because the majority of Head Start children are from ethnically and culturally diverse backgrounds (see Chapter 6). Therefore, although the intent of the Head Start program was to integrate children, it actually may have promoted the segregation of children of color and children with disabilities.

The passage of PL 99-457, the Education of the Handicapped Act Amendments of 1986, extended the rights and provisions of PL 94-142 to children with disabilities from birth to 5 years of age. The amendments, subsequently reauthorized as PL 102-119, the Individuals with Disabilities Education Act Amendments of 1991, entitle children with disabilities to a free and appropriate public education beginning at 3 years of age (Part B). PL 102-119 also provides states with incentives to develop, implement, and evaluate statewide systems of early intervention for infants and toddlers with disabilities and their families (Part H).

One of the most striking aspects of PL 99-457 is that values played a vital role in defining how and where services should be provided. It is clear that values have driven the conceptualization of this legislation. For example, PL 99-457 was instrumental in providing young children with disabilities and their families access to support and services within natural community-based settings in which children without disabilities are present. This provision reflects the value that children with disabilities should remain in, not be removed from, the natural environments in which they would participate if their disability were not present.

PL 101-336, the Americans with Disabilities Act (ADA) of 1990, also has influenced the inclusion of children with disabilities into community-based programs. This law ensures that individuals are not discriminated against because of their disabilities. Program directors must make efforts to adapt existing facilities and practices to accommodate individuals with disabilities. Making such accommodations might include installing a wheelchair-accessible ramp leading to the building's front entrance, placing braille labels throughout the school, and installing a flashing light to indicate when the fire alarm rings. One of the key implications of PL 101-336 is that early childhood programs may not discriminate against children with disabilities by refusing to enroll them. PL 101-336 is grounded in the value that all children have a fundamental right to equal opportunity. It is clear that values have played a significant role in the development of legislation for young children with disabilities.

THE NATURE AND POLITICS OF INCLUSIVE EDUCATION

Inclusion often provokes impassioned debates. One reason for this strong reaction is that people complicate the concept of inclusion by attaching inconsistent meanings and outcomes to it. Therefore, before the status of inclusion in 1996 is examined in this chapter, the social and political history of inclusion is explored. In an effort to gain a comprehensive perspective on this topic, the focus of the following discussion is not limited to early childhood issues, but instead addresses inclusive education as it relates to all age ranges and abilities.

Inclusive Education as a Value

Inclusion is a value and a belief, not a setting in which children are placed. Understanding inclusion as a value is the first step toward conceptualizing this idea within an educational framework. Values can be thought of as sets of beliefs that guide actions. Guralnick (1990) suggested that early childhood inclusion is grounded firmly in a value system that guides program design, implementation, and analysis. The Division for Early Childhood (1993) provides a clear definition in its position statement on inclusion

> Inclusion, as a value, supports the right of all children, regardless of their diverse abilities to participate actively in natural settings within their communities. A natural setting is one in which the child would spend time had he or she not had a disability...DEC believes in and supports full and successful access to health, social service, education, and other supports and services for young children and their families that promote full participation in community life.

This position statement has been endorsed by the National Association for the Education of Young Children.

The concept of inclusion recognizes that all children are unique and, therefore, have different interests, priorities, gifts, and strengths. The underlying assumption is that practitioners can successfully adapt environments to accommodate the needs and interests of all children, instead of requiring children to conform to meet the demands of their environments. Supports can be provided within natural environments (e.g., home, child care center, car, playground) to ensure full participation and membership for all children. Natural supports are discussed later in this chapter.

Peace, democracy, and a sense of community are concepts that are reflected consistently in daily practices within inclusive settings.

As a value, inclusion transcends the educational environment. According to some parents, children with disabilities are active and valued members within their family networks, religious communities, and neighborhoods, but, ironically, not within their schools (Biklen, 1992; Erwin & Soodak, 1995). It is imperative that schools accept completely children with disabilities and learn how best to do so from exemplary programs in which such acceptance already occurs. In programs that promote an inclusive philosophy, professionals address children's priorities in both educational and noneducational settings (e.g., birthday parties, recreational activities, shopping malls). Consistently meeting the needs of children in multiple natural environments greatly enhances the potential to achieve two important outcomes: 1) acquisition, maintenance, and generalizability of critical skills and 2) full and meaningful participation in the real world. In short, inclusive environments are driven by a vision that recognizes that everyone belongs and has an important contribution to make.

Tolerance for Segregation

It is important to examine the social and political climate that has driven profound changes in education, such as the move toward inclusive education. Like other underserved groups in the United States, individuals with disabilities have not always had full and equal access to opportunity. Most groups in the United States who have been oppressed (e.g., people who are economically disadvantaged, people of color, people with disabilities) have had to struggle to gain access to an integrated education (Stainback, Stainback, & Bunch, 1989). As recently as the 1950s, the educational system of the United States was based on the premise that isolation and separation are acceptable conditions.

Many educators, policy makers, and parents continue to confront assumptions regarding separate or segregated education for children with disabilities. The lessons learned from the civil rights movement in the United States have served to maintain attention on the need for equal opportunity and access. The landmark *Brown v. Board of Education* (1954) civil rights case provided strong support for the inequality of segregated education. The tenet "separate is inherently unequal," which initially was applied to African Americans in the Brown case, has been applied to other groups, including women, individuals who are economically disadvantaged, and, most recently, individuals with disabilities. More than 20 years after *Brown v. Board of Education*, PL 94-142 and the least restrictive environment (LRE) principle served as the legal mandate to educate children with disabilities within the mainstream.

Segregated systems of education were established as a means of accommodating a particular group of underserved children. These systems were instituted, however, with no critical analysis of the short- or long-term implications of segregation. Stainback, Stainback, and Jackson (1992) suggested that "for reasons that seemed good at the time, we fragmented our system to ensure appropriate support to everyone (special education, intelligence quotient tests, labels). Over time, this small empire has turned into a support system for segregation" (p. xvi). As a result, educators, parents, and other advocates aim to rectify this situation by welcoming back all children who traditionally have been excluded from the mainstream of society.

THE EVOLUTION OF THE INCLUSION IDEOLOGY

Inclusive education has emerged as a result of the fervent advocacy for the rights of children with disabilities; this advocacy spanned several decades. Approaches to bringing children with and without disabilities together have, however, changed greatly over time. This section highlights and compares some of the key elements that have guided service delivery for students with disabilities in settings with their typically developing peers.

Normalization

The terms *mainstreaming, integration,* and *inclusion* often are used interchangeably; their meanings vary greatly, however. These terms represent applications of the concept of *normalization* (also referred to as *social role valorization*), a principle that initially was brought to the United States from Scandinavia and was advocated for by, among others, Wolfensberger (1980), who defined normalization as "the use of culturally valued means in order to enable people to live culturally valued lives" (p. 80). In other words, individuals with disabilities can participate in normalized activities and lead the most normal lives possible. Mainstreaming, integration, and inclusion all are grounded in the normalization principle; these concepts differ, however, in why and how they are used to ensure that children with disabilities participate in natural environments (i.e., educational, community, recreational, vocational) within society. The LRE principle put forth in PL 94-142 prompted national discussion in the United States regarding educating children with disabilities with their age-appropriate peers.

Least Restrictive Environment

PL 94-142, with its LRE mandate, has been in effect since the 1970s, and yet, considerable controversy regarding some of its key principles continues. For example, despite explicit language in PL 94-142, differences abound across the United States in how states define and implement the LRE principle (Lipsky & Gartner, 1989). The LRE principle is based on the least restrictive alternative, a constitutionally based doctrine that holds that if a state or local government provides a service for its citizens (i.e., fostering public health, regulating commerce, providing public education), it must provide that service in a way that does not infringe on the civil rights of any of its citizens (Turnbull, 1990). Although the intent behind the LRE principle is to ensure that children with disabilities are placed in educational environments with their peers who are typically developing to the maximum extent appropriate, serious problems arise in the interpretation of the LRE principle as a policy directive for developing services for children with disabilities.

Taylor (1988) identified several key flaws related to the LRE principle including the following:

The LRE principle confuses intensity of services with segregated environments. A false assumption is made that integrated settings provide fewer and less intensive services for people with disabilities.

The LRE principle is based on a readiness model that implies that children with disabilities must prove that they are ready by meeting certain eligibility requirements before entering an integrated setting. This implies that children must earn the right to be included. In addition, students with significant disabilities would be excluded for most, if not all, of their lives, because they may never reach the desired performance level.

The LRE principle supports the role of the professional as the primary decision maker, which suggests that professional judgment, and not social values and ethics, guides the placement decision.

The LRE principle focuses more on physical environments than on the services and supports children with disabilities require to be integrated.

Taylor challenged the education field to rethink some of its assumptions about the LRE and the continuum of services and "to move toward a vision of society based on enduring human values like freedom, community, equality, dignity, and autonomy" (1988, p. 51). Although debate is healthy and necessary for the progression of ideas, more consensus about the paramount role of social values in contemporary U.S. society might mean less time spent on *whether* and more time spent on *how* to afford high-quality, individualized education for all students.

Mainstreaming, integration, and inclusion, although separate and distinct concepts, have in common the purpose of bringing together children with and without disabilities. Each of these concepts builds on the others to ensure more active and meaningful participation by and acceptance of children with disabilities in natural environments. Although mainstreaming, integration, and inclusion are separate concepts, the practices and policies embraced by schools and programs do not always reflect a clear distinction among the three. Table 8.1 highlights and contrasts several key assumptions guiding mainstreaming, integration, and inclusion.

Mainstreaming

Mainstreaming, a term that is not present in the text of PL 94-142, is used to describe the process of providing opportunities for students with disabilities who are in self-contained special education settings to spend part of their time in general education environments with their typically developing peers (Lipsky & Gartner, 1989; McLean & Hanline, 1990; National Association of State Boards of Education, 1992). Children usually are selected to attend a general education setting for a specified time period on the basis of the probability that they will make it in this type of environment. Students chosen for mainstreaming visit the general education classroom for social or academic purposes for part or all of the day and are often accompanied by an assistant or aide during this time.

Table 8.1. Comparison of general assumptions underlying service delivery approaches for children with disabilities

Approach	Placement criteria	Program parameters
Mainstreaming	Child is a good candidate; high probability child will succeed in general education.	Special education system is responsible for child.
	Placement is generally for academic instruction or social purposes.	There are few curricular modifications in general education.
	Time can range from 1 activity/week to 2–3 periods/day in general education classes or activities.	Classroom teacher receives little or no support.
		Related services are delivered exclusively on a pull-out basis.
		Little or no communication exists among general educator, special educator, and related services staff.
		Individualized education program goals are primarily carried out in self-contained environments.
		Family members attend individualized education program meetings.
Integration	Child needs opportunities to interact with age-appropriate peers.	Some program components are modified.
	Child fits nicely into the classroom or other general education setting.	Special education system is responsible for child.
	Placement can range from half day to full day.	Some training is available for general educators.
	Number of children with disabilities who are integrated can range from one student to one half of the class.	Related services generally are on a pull-out basis.
		Goals are facilitated in the general education classroom by special education or related services personnel.
		Periodic informal and formal communication occurs among most team members.
		Family members attend team meetings and provide input for child's program.
Inclusion	Child belongs in natural settings within educational, community, and family contexts, regardless of the nature or severity of his or her disability.	General education system is responsible for child.
	Child is a full-time member of the general education classroom.	Program accommodates all children with and without disabilities.
	Participation extends beyond education to encompass all aspects of life.	Family is an active and integral part of the planning process.

(continued)

Table 8.1. *(continued)*

Approach	Placement criteria	Program parameters
Inclusion *(continued)*	Number of students included per class is either one or no more than 10% of the total class size.	Consistent and frequent meetings involving all team members are held. All staff, including administrators, receive ongoing training and support. Goals are facilitated by all team members in natural environments (i.e., classroom, cafeteria, hallway, playground).

The concept of mainstreaming was developed to promote greater acceptance of and participation by children with disabilities in natural settings; resultant practices, however, might have fostered just the opposite. In practice, mainstreaming tends to perpetuate the separateness of children with disabilities from their peers. New and Mallory (1994), for example, argued that mainstreaming practices tend to focus on the physical proximity of children with disabilities to typical children and the amount of time that these children spend together. This focus excludes more child-driven variables, such as the children's priorities, interests, abilities, and lifestyles.

As a result of its limited focus, mainstreaming presents more challenges than it does benefits. Children with disabilities are viewed neither as members of the general education setting they visit nor as members of the self-contained special education setting, because they so often are removed for mainstreaming (National Association of State Boards of Education, 1992; Schnorr, 1990). Ironically, isolation from the mainstream, which decreases the probability that children will return to general education (Lipsky & Gartner, 1989), is inherent in the concept of mainstreaming.

Integration

Integration is perhaps one of the most difficult concepts to define, because it often is misinterpreted as mainstreaming or inclusion. On the most basic level, integration is the process of actively bringing together children with and without disabilities (McLean & Hanline, 1990; Odom & McEvoy, 1988). Taylor (1988) described integration as "the elimination of social, cultural, economic, and administrative barriers to community integration" (p. 51). Moving away from the good candidate criterion used in mainstreaming, the rationale for integrating children with and without disabilities centers around ethical and moral principles.

In an integrated environment, 50% of the children in a given classroom may have disabilities or there may be fewer children with disabilities than children without disabilities. In either case, the program would be regarded as an integrated setting, because children with and children without disabilities would be together in one environment. In general, a classroom in which there are more children with disabilities than children without disabilities is considered a reverse mainstreaming model. Limitations exist regarding integration, however, because the conceptual framework and educational practices of integration condone the premise that the special education system ultimately is responsible for children with disabilities. For example, Salisbury (1991) suggested that when one group is viewed as the mainstream and the other is not, an underlying assumption reinforces the practice of excluding some individuals from certain activities and events on the basis of their (dis)ability. Salisbury (1991) further explained that "while integration is considered to be philosophically and educationally superior to segregation, such 'push in' arrangements remain inherently hierarchical and unequal" (p. 147).

Staffing patterns in integrated environments may or may not include a special educator in the role of head teacher, team teacher, or consultant, although usually there is some degree of training for staff, particularly the general education teacher involved in the integration effort. It is important to recognize that, although inclusion has emerged as the favored philosophy, some people prefer the term integration, because integration is more closely associated with the civil rights struggle for racial equality. (See Chapter 6 for a more detailed discussion of perspectives on integrating individuals who are culturally, economically, and developmentally diverse.)

Inclusion

Although some schools still refer to mainstreaming and integration, most have shifted toward the term inclusion. Stainback et al. (1992) suggested several reasons for this shift including the fact that the term inclusion better reflects the spirit of *including* children in their educational communities, whereas integration implies that they are returning to environments from which they had been excluded previously. Both mainstreaming and integration imply that children must fit into the existing environment; inclusion, in contrast, focuses on building a community that addresses the diverse needs and contributions of everyone in that community.

Guided by a strong philosophical framework, inclusive educational environments refer to the provision of natural services and supports to all students in general education classes in ways that promote a strong sense of community (Giangreco & Putman, 1991; Stainback et al., 1992). In inclusive environments, all children are valued as full-time members of their classrooms, schools, neighborhoods, and communities. The concept of partial inclusion simply is not possible.

Because the concept of inclusion is embedded so deeply in a value system that recognizes the civil rights of all children, the field continues to be challenged to create learning environments in which the individuality and talents of all children are respected and nurtured. The issue that professionals address when they are serious about welcoming all children into their programs is *how* to do it not *why* (Biklen, 1992; Guralnick, 1990).

RECOGNIZING THE UNIQUENESS OF EARLY CARE AND EDUCATION

The philosophical framework for inclusion remains the same whether those being included are adults, adolescents, or young children. There are, however, differences in service delivery approaches that distinguish the focus and implementation of education for young children from that for older children. Unique considerations regarding infants, toddlers, pre-schoolers, and early elementary school-age children differ from the consid-erations regarding older children. These unique considerations naturally have an impact on the way services are established and provided in natural environments.

One reason that service delivery approaches used with young chil-dren differ from approaches used with older children is that the natural environments in which the children may spend a good portion of their days differ. Natural environments can be defined as all community set-tings in which the majority of participants are individuals without disabil-ities (Noonan & McCormick, 1993). Infants, toddlers, and preschoolers may spend a good portion of the day in widely varied natural environ-ments, whereas older children typically spend the day at school. One rea-son for the wider range of service delivery options for young children with disabilities than for older children with disabilities is that public schools typically do not offer programs for infants, toddlers, or preschoolers. Some natural, community-based settings in which young children with disabili-ties may receive services include, but are not limited to, homes, kinder-gartens, Head Start programs, preschools, community play groups, and child care centers. Some self-contained environments in which services are provided for young children with disabilities include neonatal inten-sive care units, early intervention centers, and other hospital-based set-tings. Bailey (1989) noted that although numerous settings exist in which young children with disabilities receive early intervention, staff who deliver these services require specialized training in early childhood. Although families of younger children may have many options in select-ing environments in which services are provided, it is imperative that the staff who provide those services are qualified and competent to serve young children. The range of natural environments, therefore, is one dis-tinction between the approaches to service delivery in early childhood and those in later childhood.

The high degree of family involvement during the early childhood years is another factor that distinguishes the care and education of infants and young children from that of older children. It is clear from his essay that Walter Thies, Keith's father, plays a highly visible role in advocating and planning for his son's education. Bredekamp (1993) noted that, as chil-dren grow older and are considered less vulnerable, the emphasis on the family decreases. In young children's lives, however, families play a promi-nent role, thereby making collaboration between families and profession-als vital. According to the National Association for the Education of Young Children report on developmentally appropriate practice, which provides clear and distinctive standards to the field of early childhood education, "to achieve individually appropriate programs for young children, early childhood teachers *must* [italics added] work in partnership with families and communicate regularly with children's parents" (Bredekamp, 1991, p. 12). Although home–school partnerships are necessary regardless of chil-dren's ages, it is during the early developmental stages when the family, particularly a parent or caregiver, is the primary source of attention, love, security, and learning.

Finally, service delivery practices in early childhood are unique, because young children have their first experiences with peers during these formative years. Peer encounters generally are among the first meaningful interactions young children experience outside of their families. Corsaro (1988) noted that, when young children initially enter preschool or kindergarten, significant changes occur in their lives, such as encountering many adults who are not their parents and meeting numerous peers for the first time. Early experiences with peers influence children's acquisition of the necessary social interaction skills that serve as a foundation for positive relationships within a peer group (Odom & Brown, 1993; Ramsey, 1991). Because early peer interactions lay the foundation for future social experiences, it is vital that children's initial introductions to and encounters with peers are both natural and positive.

In summary, the three primary factors that differentiate approaches to service delivery in early childhood versus later childhood are 1) the range of natural environments, 2) the necessity for and degree of family involvement, and 3) the critical nature of initial experiences with peers. These elements have an impact on program structure, professional development and training, and the provision of services to young children and their families.

PERSPECTIVES ON INCLUSION IN EARLY CHILDHOOD

As the interest in and awareness of inclusion in early childhood care and education continue to grow, the knowledge base also expands. The following discussion sheds light on perspectives on inclusion for young children and includes a summary of existing professional literature on the topic, an explanation of challenges and barriers regarding implementation, and a synthesis of quality indicators for early childhood programs.

Growing Knowledge Base on Early Childhood Inclusion

It is difficult to read the professional literature in early childhood and not find information on inclusive early childhood efforts. There are chapters on theory and practice (e.g., Hanson & Hanline, 1989; Mallory, 1994; Odom & McEvoy, 1988); special topical issues in professional journals (Fewell & Neisworth, 1990; Odom & Strain, 1989); and textbooks addressing issues, challenges, and effective practices of including children with disabilities in community-based settings (Allen, 1992; Noonan & McCormick, 1993; Peck, Odom, & Bricker, 1993; Safford, 1989). In addition, professional journal articles reflect numerous aspects of early childhood inclusion and integration, such as developmental and behavioral outcomes (e.g., Buysse & Bailey, 1993; Cole, Mills, Dale, & Jenkins, 1991; Fewell & Oelwein, 1990); social competence and interactions (e.g., Guralnick & Groom, 1987; Hanline, 1993; Kohl & Beckman, 1984); recommendations for practice (e.g., Brault, 1992; Erwin, 1991; Wolery, Strain, & Bailey, 1992); parent perspectives (e.g., Bailey & Winton, 1987; Green & Stoneman, 1989; Miller et al., 1992); professional perspectives (e.g., Eiserman, Shisler, & Healey, 1995; Marchant, 1995); and attitudes of and outcomes for typically developing peers (e.g., Diamond, 1993; Esposito & Reed, 1986; Odom, DeKlyen, & Jenkins, 1984). These and other works suggest that young children with and without disabilities can have successful and fulfilling experiences when they are included in natural environments and provided with the necessary support.

Despite the steady increase of empirical literature on children's social interactions and competence in integrated or inclusive environments, precautions should be taken when comparing research studies because differences between study participants and settings may limit comparisons. Although many benefits of including children with disabilities in settings with typically developing peers have been found, numerous differences exist across research investigations, including the definition of social interaction, types of children with disabilities served, chronological ages of study participants, levels of teacher preparation, program quality, and research methods (Buysse & Bailey, 1993; Odom & McEvoy, 1988). Furthermore, program philosophies, service delivery approaches, and degrees of family participation also may have an impact on the comparison of research findings. Strain (1990) suggested that no controlled studies have found segregated early childhood programs to be superior to integrated programs and noted that programs that include children with disabilities also demonstrate exemplary service delivery practices in areas such as family collaboration, appropriate curricula, and child-centered outcomes. Although empirical findings have demonstrated successful outcomes for children with and without disabilities in inclusive environments, the generalizability of these findings should not be assumed.

Scant information exists about early childhood policy development and the availability of inclusive environments in the United States from a national perspective. This is the case, in part, because disability categories reported for preschool placements are the same as those for school-age populations, although placement options for young children vary (U.S. Department of Education, 1993). The National Early Childhood Technical Assistance System (1993) reported that, in 1993, 31 state education agencies (SEAs) had developed or were in the process of developing policies or mission statements leading to inclusion. Twenty-eight SEAs have LRE policies (PL 101-476, Part B), but local districts are responsible for determining how policies are implemented for preschoolers. In addition, in 1993, 37 SEAs were in the process of developing or were using data collection tools to monitor preschool services in the LRE. It seems as though state and local education agencies have begun to reevaluate and redefine approaches to service delivery for young children with disabilities.

Although the knowledge base on early childhood inclusion continues to grow, unanswered questions and issues remain. For example, the availability and accessibility of community-based settings serving children with and without disabilities throughout the United States is unclear. Furthermore, it is not known to what extent existing programs reflect high-quality practices (see Chapter 7). This knowledge could serve as an important bank of information at the national, state, and local levels. In addition, the level and quality of training available to early childhood educators and other disciplines across the United States is not known. In the absence of effective professional training, efforts to serve children with and without disabilities in the same environments would be futile.

In an effort to address these and other issues, Wolery et al. (1993) surveyed a randomly selected sample of early childhood personnel representing higher education programs, Head Start agencies, community child care centers, preschools, and kindergartens to ascertain the status of inclusive practices in natural environments. Results revealed that, in the 1985–1986 school year, only 38% of early childhood programs enrolled children with disabilities; this percentage increased to 74% of programs during the 1989–1990 school year. Wolery et al. (1993) reported that 57.5% of these programs enrolled children with speech and language impairments, and 31% enrolled children with developmental delays, but less than 15% of the programs enrolled children who had mental retardation, visual impairments, hearing impairments, or autism. Although efforts to include children with disabilities have increased, it seems as though children with certain disabilities, such as sensory impairments, autism, and significant intellectual disabilities (i.e., populations often considered to be of low prevalence in nature), may not have ready access to community-based natural environments.

Wolery et al. (1993) also found that, although training was available to some child care professionals, a great need remained to prepare professionals from various disciplines with the skills and competencies they need to work with all children. Through this study, Wolery et al. (1993) provided some important insights into the growing trend to integrate children with disabilities, identified children who were excluded from this trend, and demonstrated the need for better preparation and collaboration of early childhood personnel to meet this increased demand.

Identifying Challenges and Barriers to Inclusion in Early Childhood

Providing high-quality professional development and preparation is perhaps one of the most important challenges facing the field of early childhood education and early childhood special education. In addition, other challenges that affect the success or failure of inclusion, such as the adequacy of resources (Peck, Furman, & Helmstetter, 1993), philosophical differences (Odom & McEvoy, 1990), and resistance to change (Kontos & File, 1993; Peck, Furman, & Helmstetter, 1993), have been identified. It seems as though individual perspectives and beliefs often are at the root of these issues. Perhaps many professionals are reluctant to change or seek new solutions because of their existing attitudes, which often mirror directly the beliefs, values, and experiences that they have collected over many years.

A study by Rose and Smith (1993) reported that attitudes were a frequent barrier to integrating children with and without disabilities. Specifically, they found that barriers resulted from turf issues, restricted professional preparation, communication problems, and obstacles to collaboration, as identified by early childhood professionals and parents (Rose & Smith, 1993). Rose and Smith (1993) suggested that "the teachers' new learning can lead to changes in child outcomes, and improved child outcomes should lead to changes in teachers' beliefs and attitudes" (p. 62). Inclusion should be viewed as an interactive process in which both teachers and children learn and change together.

Challenges associated with providing children and their families with high-quality services always will exist. The key to addressing any barrier is to recognize it as a challenge and then find creative and collaborative solutions to meet it. When meeting challenges it is important to remember that it is not *what* happens, but rather *how* one chooses to deal with it that determines success.

Quality Indicators of Inclusive Early Care and Education

As a result of advancements in the provision of services to young children with disabilities and their families in community-based settings, there also has been an increase in programs that label themselves inclusive. It is important, however, to look beyond a program's description or brochure to determine whether it actually embraces an inclusive philosophy.

Environments that include young children with disabilities also must meet standards for early child care and education. Standards set forth by the National Association for the Education of Young Children (Bredekamp, 1991) recommend high-quality early childhood practices in areas such as program design, adult–child interactions, professional–family interactions, curriculum, and staffing. In addition, the Division for Early Childhood has recommended practices (Division for Early Childhood Task Force on Recommended Practices, 1993) that provide indicators of quality for various settings that serve young children with disabilities and their families; some of these indicators include sound assessment, meaningful family participation, a meaningful individualized family service plan or individualized education program, effective service delivery models, appropriate curricula and intervention strategies, and systematic program evaluation. These guidelines, set forth by leading professional organizations for young children with and without disabilities, provide a solid beginning for recognizing high-quality programs and practices in early childhood education and early childhood special education.

Despite these standards, the need remains for clear and integrated guidelines for community-based environments that serve children with and without disabilities. Table 8.2 illustrates indicators of quality for inclusive early childhood environments. These guidelines have been adapted and synthesized from the existing literature on early care and education for children with and without disabilities in natural settings. These guidelines are applicable to *all* children, including those with unique needs (i.e., children who are linguistically diverse, children who are considered to be at risk for developmental delays, children who were prenatally exposed to drugs, children who are economically disadvantaged).

The guidelines in Table 8.2, which are by no means exhaustive, highlight some of the practices that can be found in exemplary models of inclusive early childhood care and education. Two basic tenets drive these quality indicators. The first is a program philosophy that demonstrates a clear commitment to create a place in which all children and their families belong. Inherent in this philosophy is a complementary value that children and families come first. The program philosophy should be shared by all

Table 8.2.   Guidelines for community-based environments serving young children with and without disabilities

Program features	Quality indicators
Philosophy and mission	Program philosophy, which is clearly articulated and communicated, exemplifies a values-based approach to early care and education.
	Program goals reflect identified early childhood practices and principles.
	Program is family- and child-driven, not fiscally or politically driven.
	Heterogeneity, diversity, and membership are valued.
	Children's choices, abilities, priorities, and talents are respected and nurtured.
	Children are viewed within the context of their families, cultures, and communities.
Structure and organization	Leadership is strong and supportive.
	Program philosophy is reflected in policies and daily practice.
	Ongoing training and staff development are provided.
	Ample time, resources, training, and technical assistance are allocated.
	Expertise and resources are shared among team members.
	A system for program evaluation and modification is in place.
	Program structure is very flexible so that family choices and preferences are addressed.
Curriculum and instructional strategies	Curriculum is comprehensive, individualized, community based, generalizable, and age appropriate.
	Individual goals are facilitated naturally through daily activities and routines.
	Heterogeneous groupings and cooperative learning are promoted.
	Natural supports and accommodations are provided as warranted.
	Classroom reflects antibiased and multicultural curriculum, materials, attitudes, activities, and practices.
	Active and meaningful participation is promoted consistently.
	Children are provided ample and consistent opportunities to make meaningful choices.
	A variety of social interactions and friendships are encouraged.
	Principles of democracy are fostered.
Collaboration and teaming	Collaborative teamwork, integrated therapy, and transdisciplinary teaming approaches are used.
	Families are full partners in decision making, if they choose to be.
	Family members are integral and valued members of the team and/or school community.
	Systematic and frequent communication occurs among team members.
	Clearly defined procedures for conflict resolution and negotiation are established and implemented.

Sources: Bredekamp (1991); Bruder (1993); Division for Early Childhood Task Force on Recommended Practices (1993); Derman-Sparks (1992); Diamond, Hostenes, & O'Connor (1994); Koralek, Colker, & Dodge (1993); McDonnell & Hardman (1988); Noonan & McCormick (1993); Peck, Furman, & Helmstetter (1993); Safford (1989); Salisbury (1991).

staff members and should be demonstrated clearly in program decisions, policies, and daily practices.

The second tenet is the flexible nature of community-based settings that serve all children. These programs are designed to meet the interests, priorities, and preferences of all children and families, so usually there is a range of options from which to choose, including the type and degree of family involvement and the frequency and duration of program attendance (e.g., 5 half days per week, 3 full days per week). In these programs, children also have numerous opportunities throughout the day to make meaningful decisions about issues that affect their lives (e.g., materials, activities, time, playmates). As a rule, directors and staff of these programs not only are responsive to program evaluation, but willing and prepared to make changes as necessary.

When professionals consider how to address the unique situations of young children (i.e., abilities, ethnicities, cultures, socioeconomic backgrounds), it is important to recognize that regardless of their differences, all children are, first and foremost, children. All children have in common the need for unconditional love, emotional and physical health, dependable security and safety, a cultivated self-concept, positive interpersonal interactions, and independence. Wolery et al. (1992) suggested that, because of these and other commonalities, professionals who work with children with disabilities must not only understand the development of typical children, but also must be competent in addressing the unique requirements of children with specific needs.

CREATING EARLY CHILDHOOD
COMMUNITIES THAT VALUE ALL OF THEIR MEMBERS

When one thinks of community, an image of a neighborhood or town may come to mind. A community also can be a group of individuals who come together because of shared interests, characteristics, and beliefs (e.g., religious communities, the deaf community). In the 1990s, increased attention has been paid to the notion of building community within schools (Sailor, 1991; Sapon-Shevin, 1992; Stainback et al., 1992). A community is created when all children feel valued, accepted, and supported by peers and other members of the school community. Early childhood settings (i.e., classrooms, child care arrangements, hospital-based programs) can be conceptualized as communities—each with its own set of members, rules, routines, rituals, and relationships. Because each member is a valued part of the community, it becomes necessary to examine *how* to provide natural support so that all children have the opportunity to participate actively, make important decisions, and contribute in meaningful and individual ways.

Supporting All Children in Natural Environments

Providing appropriate support in natural settings is the key to ensuring successful experiences and outcomes for all children. Support usually involves sustaining, maintaining, strengthening, and promoting. It should be noted that support is a highly individualized and complex concept. Providing support to a young child does not necessarily mean that the support was requested, appropriate, or even needed. York, Giangreco, Vandercook, and Macdonald (1992) suggested that genuine support occurs when

> 1) the receipt of support perceives that he or she has been helped; 2) the responsibility for achieving desired student outcomes is shared among team members...; 3) the goal of meeting diverse needs of students is better accomplished;

4) the effort required for collaboration is worth the outcomes; and 5) priority outcomes for students at school, at home, and in the community are achieved. (p. 103)

Natural support systems, which include peer tutoring, cooperative learning groups, buddy systems, and other methods of linking children together in positive and collaborative ways (Stainback et al., 1992), are particularly useful for providing children with consistent and meaningful learning experiences. The development, implementation, and evaluation of natural supports is an ongoing process. For young children in particular, who may not have sophisticated systems of communication, it is imperative that adults observe and interpret signs of communication carefully before, during, and after support is provided. This attention will help to determine whether a specific support was desired by the child and/or the family, and whether that support was adequate for the demands of the situation.

The types and degrees of support needed by young children may vary across time and may result from various factors (e.g., dealing with the divorce of parents, encountering racism, needing physical assistance with a task). Typically, adults shadow students with disabilities and erroneously think that they are providing a valuable service. There are, however, numerous ways to provide support to children both naturally and nonintrusively. Some examples of natural support are arranging or modifying the environment, adapting materials or activities, encouraging peers to support one another, and providing natural and consistent opportunities for skill acquisition or generalization. Natural supports can and should be facilitated by people who come into a child's life on a consistent basis (i.e., family members, bus driver, babysitter). Respect for children's choices in meaningful decisions that affect their lives can be even more important than the type of support provided.

The key to providing support is knowing when to provide it and when not to. Input from children and their families is essential for the success of the support plan. Some fundamental questions professionals must consider when designing support plans include the following: Are the child's and family's concerns and priorities represented? Will the support foster independence, competence, and health? Will the support enhance the child's status and promote meaningful participation?

There are additional questions that early child care and early childhood special education professionals can begin to think about to support the independence and competence inherent within all children. The following questions, adapted from McCracken's (1993) educational goals for children, serve as a beginning point for supporting and nurturing all children:

Are children learning to love and loving to learn?

Are children learning to see themselves as competent problem solvers, decision makers, discoverers, and communicators?

Are children learning to negotiate and collaborate in democratic and peaceful ways?

Are children learning to understand and appreciate our world's rich diversity of culture, heritages, abilities, and interests?

In addition to ensuring that their support addresses these questions, educators must ensure that their support is desired by the children: Support is useful only when it is wanted. To create early childhood environments that support all children and value their contributions, it is useful to understand the significance of becoming a member of the peer culture within a classroom community.

Membership and Peer Culture

The notion of learning about young children within the context of their peer culture has gained momentum steadily since the mid-1980s. During early childhood, peer culture is "a joint attempt by children to acquire control over their lives through the establishment of a collective identity" (Corsaro, 1985, p. 75). Children's joint attempts at forming a group identity are accomplished through repeated and shared social experiences between and among peers; this group identity is used to respond to, organize, and even challenge information about the adult world.

Corsaro's contributions to the understanding of peer culture in early childhood have had a substantial influence on the growing knowledge base on children's social rules, group formation, and peer relationships. Before the publication of Corsaro's research (1979), attention to peer interactions essentially was limited to older children and their social cognitive abilities (Elgas, Klein, Kantor, & Fernie, 1988). Corsaro (1988) maintained that the peer culture of young children is markedly different from the culture of older children or that of adults. The peer culture of preschoolers is defined by the routines and activities that they share. By establishing routines and an eventual group identity, young children learn to cooperate, create, interact, problem-solve, and gain independence (Ramsey, 1991). In addition, children may become more compassionate, tolerant, benevolent, and secure as they become active participants within a familiar social network of their peers. Becoming members of the peer culture is perhaps one of the most important social experiences young children encounter in their early lives.

Many routines and activities are customary across early childhood environments, but, many rituals and themes are unique to individual environments. For example, in one preschool program, a ritual was established during outside free play by a 3-year-old boy with visual impairments and his classmates. One child would drive up to the "Burger King window" on a tricycle, place an order for food with another peer who was posing as a Burger King employee, receive the order, and then drive away. This same routine was played out on a daily basis for most of the school year. In this ritual, children imitated a familiar activity, which led to an ongoing social encounter. Some other routines and rituals can include humor (i.e., using specific nonsense words, repeating each other's words), approach–avoidance (i.e., running and chasing), and greeting rituals (i.e., imitating greetings by media celebrities) (Corsaro, 1985; Ramsey, 1991). These routines and rituals serve an important function in establishing a group's identity.

How can learning about peer culture assist early childhood service providers? By understanding the dynamics of peer culture, providers can begin to appreciate more fully the significance of classroom rituals, games, rules, and networks in the lives of young children. Service providers can then use this information to respect groups' needs to establish their own identities and to create opportunities that will foster peer cultures within early childhood environments. Adults can support and encourage peer cultures naturally by facilitating group problem solving, creating activities designed to promote social interactions, demonstrating consistently that everyone has important talents and contributions, and respecting children's seemingly silly games by not interrupting or discouraging them. In addition, when service providers are aware of peer cultures, they may be more sensitive to individual children who are at risk for social isolation and may better develop and implement specific interventions to promote acceptance and meaningful participation.

Becoming a member of any group not only provides a sense of belonging, but also fosters a meaningful connection to and responsibility for a larger social context. Numerous investigations on the social interactions of young children with and without disabilities have been undertaken (Buysse, 1993; Erwin, 1993; Guralnick & Groom, 1987; Jenkins, Odom, & Speltz, 1989; Kohl & Beckman, 1984; Peterson, 1982); there is, however, a dearth of literature on membership and social dynamics of the peer culture within inclusive environments. In one investigation on membership and peer culture regarding a child with disabilities, Schnorr (1990) discovered that a boy with Down syndrome, who was mainstreamed into first grade for part of the day, was not considered to be a member of the class by his peers, because he did not share the same experience of first grade as the rest of the class did. For example, classmates perceived membership in this first-grade class as depending on what you do (i.e., work, projects), where you belong (i.e., assigned teacher, grade), and with whom you play (i.e., status, playmates). Not only did the student who was mainstreamed have limited opportunities to participate in class activities and rituals, but he also was not viewed as a valued or important member of the class by the teacher, which further influenced how the other children viewed him.

Membership within a peer culture can be influenced by many factors, including teacher perceptions, shared experiences and expectations, and a social network of peers. Although there are many dimensions of the peer culture, the area of friendship and social interaction has continued to receive consistent attention.

Formation and Maintenance of Friendships and Other Relationships

Like adults, most young children have a range of peer relationships that grow and change over time. Like family members, peers serve an instrumental role in the lives of young children. Because of the prominent roles that peers play, it is necessary to explore the nature of friendships and other peer relationships that exist within the peer culture.

Through careful examination of social interactions in early childhood peer culture, Corsaro (1985) found that few stable core groups or cliques existed; rather, children tended to maintain some stable relationships with several playmates. This finding is consistent with other works that suggest that preschoolers tend to have brief or inconsistent peer interactions, but they also tend to play with a smaller range of playmates over time

(Howes, 1983; Ladd, Price, & Hart, 1990; Rubin 1980). This change suggests that preschoolers may become more discriminating about their playmates over time.

Discovering how early friendships and other relationships evolve is a complex process. One aspect of children's relationships, entry into existing activities, has captured more attention than has any other social behavior, because it serves as an initial step before a child can actually engage in a peer interaction (Putallaz & Wasserman, 1990). Although young children depend on a variety of strategies to attempt to gain entry into existing peer activities, the most frequently used rituals (i.e., nonverbal entry, disruptive entry, circling the area) are not necessarily the most successful (Corsaro, 1979). Corsaro suggested that peer encounters in a preschool are extremely delicate and that "children *protect* interaction in ongoing episodes by discouraging most initial attempts at access by other children" (1979, p. 330). If such interactions between typically developing children are considered fragile, what are the implications for children with disabilities who are members of community-based natural environments, given that these children may not possess sophisticated social competence or experience in gaining independent access to existing peer activities? It is difficult to answer this question empirically because of the variety of factors that affect outcomes for children in inclusive early childhood environments.

As discussed earlier in this chapter, the empirical base on social interactions between young children with and without disabilities has been instrumental in increasing understanding of some of the dynamics that exist in specific contexts. The variability across research studies (e.g., definitions, population, program quality), however, challenges the generalizability of these findings.

In short, it is necessary to understand the dynamics of peer culture and the importance of children's membership within that culture. Although children tend to encounter a range of early relationships with peers, interest remains strong in studying friendships among typically developing young children (Ladd, 1990; Park, Lay, & Ramsay, 1993; Ramsey, 1991; Rubin, 1980) and those among children with disabilities (Buysse, 1993; Raupp, 1985). Therefore, careful attention must be devoted to the types of environments and practices that foster the formation and maintenance of peer relationships, particularly friendships, and how to nurture these relationships within peer cultures.

FUTURE DIRECTIONS

This chapter provides a context for understanding both the legal, political, and philosophical roots of inclusive early care and education and some thoughts on how programs can welcome all children. Although progress regarding the education of young children with disabilities has been steady since 1975, certain questions continue to challenge both professionals and families; these questions include the following: How can families of young children who desire inclusive early care and education environments gain ready access to them? How can high-quality services be made affordable for all young children and their families? What responsibility does society have to improve early care and education for all children?

Although these questions may not have simple solutions, service providers can begin to address them to achieve positive and immediate change. Providers also must consider the following questions: How can early childhood professionals encourage friendships and other peer rela tionships within natural environments? How can professionals promote membership within the classroom community and peer culture? How can professionals foster peace, acceptance, and democracy within early childhood settings? Service providers raise such questions and seek their answers every day. Perhaps more attention should be paid to understanding children within the contexts that are most familiar to them. Qualitative research, or ethnography (i.e., the study of a group of individuals and their tools, beliefs, knowledge, behavior), which provides an excellent means to learn about children with and without disabilities within natural contexts, continues to gain credibility as an acceptable educational research model (Bogdan & Biklen, 1992; Walsh, Tobin, & Graue, 1993). Future directions for early childhood research must include qualitative investigations to capture a contextually rich picture of young children, their families, and the environments in which they live and play.

Researchers and practitioners must continue to explore the variables that make meaningful differences in the quality of young children's lives. In addition, U.S. society must take responsibility for the images that are presented of people with disabilities, because often these very images fos ter misconceptions and stereotypes. The limited number of people with disabilities who appear in advertisements and hold visible positions of power continues to reinforce the exclusion of people with disabilities in U.S. society. In the 1980s and 1990s, the visibility of individuals with disabilities increased in politics and in popular television, theater, and motion pictures (e.g., *Life Goes On, Children of a Lesser God, Rain Man, My Left Foot, Forrest Gump*). The need remains, however, for an unwavering commitment by the systems within all communities (e.g., media, business, industry, religion, law, education, medicine) to ensure that people with disabilities are included and respected within the mainstream of U.S. society. All members of society should have role models and heroes with disabilities. Within community-based environments, all young children, particularly those with disabilities, must have role models and positive interactions with adults and older children who have disabilities: Although it is important that Keith and other young children like him grow up with role models and heroes who experience the same disabilities as they do, it is equally important that Keith's typically developing peers have these same positive images so that they come to understand and value the contributions of all members of society. The intent behind inclusion is not to distance people, but to bring them closer together.

REFERENCES

Allen, K.E. (1992). *Mainstreaming in early childhood education.* Albany, NY: Delmar.

Americans with Disabilities Act (ADA) of 1990, PL 101-336. (July 26, 1990). Title 42, U.S.C. 1201 et seq: *U.S. Statutes at Large, 104,* 327–378.

Bailey, D.B., Jr. (1989). Issues and directions in preparing professionals to work with young handicapped children and their families. In J.J. Gallagher, P.L. Trohanis, & R.M. Clifford (Eds.), *Policy implementation and PL 99-457: Planning for young children with special needs* (pp. 97–132). Baltimore: Paul H. Brookes Publishing Co.

Bailey, D.B., Jr., & Winton, P.J. (1987). Stability and change in parents' expectations about mainstreaming. *Topics in Early Childhood Special Education, 7*(1), 73–88.

Biklen, D. (1992). *Schooling without labels: Parents, educators, and inclusive schooling.* Philadelphia: Temple University Press.

Bogdan, R.C., & Biklen, S.K. (1992). *Qualitative research for education.* Needham, MA: Allyn & Bacon.

Brault, L.M. (1992). Achieving integration for infants and toddlers with special needs: Recommendations for practice. *Infants and Young Children, 5*(2), 78–85.

Bredekamp, S. (1991). *Developmentally appropriate practice in early childhood programs serving children from birth through age eight.* Washington, DC: National Association for the Education of Young Children.

Bredekamp, S. (1993). The relationship between early childhood education and early childhood special education: Healthy marriage or family feud? *Topics in Early Childhood Special Education, 13*(3), 258–273.

Bricker, D.D. (1978). A rationale for the integration of handicapped and nonhandicapped preschool children. In M.J. Guralnick (Ed.), *Early intervention and the integration of handicapped and nonhandicapped children* (pp. 3–26). Baltimore: University Park Press.

Brown v. Board of Education, 347 U.S. 483 (1954).

Bruder, M.B. (1993). The provision of early intervention and early childhood special education within community early childhood programs: Characteristics of effective service delivery. *Topics in Early Childhood Special Education, 13*(1), 19–37.

Buysse, V. (1993). Friendships of preschoolers with disabilities in community-based child care settings. *Journal of Early Intervention, 17*(4), 380–395.

Buysse, V., & Bailey, D.B., Jr. (1993). Behavioral and developmental outcomes in young children with disabilities in integrated and segregated settings: A review of comparative studies. *The Journal of Special Education, 26*(4), 434–461.

Cole, K.N., Mills, P.E., Dale, P.S., & Jenkins, J.J. (1991). Effects of preschool integration for children with disabilities. *Exceptional Children, 58*(1), 36–46.

Community Services Act of 1974, PL 93-644. (January 4, 1975). Title 42, U.S.C. 2701 et seq: *U.S. Statutes at Large, 88,* 2291–2330.

Cooke, T.P., Ruskus, J.A., Apollini, T., & Peck, C.A. (1981). Handicapped preschool children in the mainstream: Background, outcomes, and clinical suggestions. *Topics in Early Childhood Special Education, 1,* 73–83.

Corsaro, W.A. (1979). We're friends, right?: Children's use of access rituals in nursery school. *Language in Society, 8,* 315–336.

Corsaro, W.A. (1985). *Friendship and peer culture in the early years.* Norwood, NJ: Ablex.

Corsaro, W.A. (1988). Peer culture in the preschool. *Theory into Practice, 27,* 19–24.

Derman-Sparks, L. (1992). Reaching potentials through antibias, multicultural curriculum. In S. Bredekamp & T. Rosegrant (Eds.), *Reaching potentials: Appropriate curriculum and assessment for young children* (pp. 114–127). Washington, DC: National Association for the Education of Young Children.

Diamond, K. (1993). Preschool children's concepts of disability in their peers. *Early Education and Development, 4*(2), 123–129.

Diamond, K.E., Hostenes, L.L., & O'Connor, C.E. (1994). Integrating young children with disabilities in preschool: Problems and promise. *Young Children, 49*(2), 68–75.

Division for Early Childhood. (1993). *DEC position on inclusion.* Pittsburgh, PA: Author.

Division for Early Childhood Task Force on Recommended Practices. (1993). *DEC recommended practices: Indicators of quality in programs for infants and young children with special needs and their families.* Reston, VA: Council for Exceptional Children.

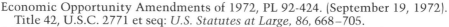

Economic Opportunity Amendments of 1972, PL 92-424. (September 19, 1972). Title 42, U.S.C. 2771 et seq: *U.S. Statutes at Large, 86,* 668–705.

Education for All Handicapped Children Act of 1975, PL 94-142. (August 23, 1977). Title 20, U.S.C. 1401 et seq: *U.S. Statutes at Large, 89,* 773–796.

Education of the Handicapped Act Amendments of 1986, PL 99-457. (October 8, 1986). Title 20, U.S.C. 1400 et seq: *U.S. Statutes at Large, 100,* 1145–1177.

Eiserman, W.D., Shisler, L., & Healey, S. (1995). A community assessment of preschool providers' attitudes toward inclusion. *Journal of Early Intervention, 19*(2), 149–167.

Elgas, P.M., Klein, E., Kantor, R., & Fernie, D.E. (1988). Play and the peer culture: Play styles and object use. *Journal of Research in Childhood Education, 3*(2), 142-153.

Erwin, E.J. (1991). Guidelines for integrating young children with visual impairments in general education settings. *Journal of Visual Impairment and Blindness, 85,* 138–142.

Erwin, E.J. (1993). Social participation of young children with visual impairments in specialized and integrated environments. *Journal of Visual Impairment and Blindness, 87,* 138–142.

Erwin, E.J., & Soodak, L.S. (1995). "I never knew I could stand up to the system": Parents' perspectives on pursuing inclusive education. *Journal of The Association for Persons with Severe Handicaps, 20*(2), 136–146.

Esposito, B.G., & Reed, T.M. (1986). The effects of contact with handicapped persons on young children's attitudes. *Exceptional Children, 53,* 224–229.

Fewell, R.R., & Neisworth, J.T. (Eds.). (1990). Mainstreaming revisited [Special issue]. *Topics in Early Childhood Special Education, 10*(2).

Fewell, R.R., & Oelwein, P.L. (1990). The relationship between time in integrated environments and developmental gains in young children with special needs. *Topics in Early Childhood Special Education, 10*(2), 104–116.

Gallagher, J.J. (1992). The role of values and facts in policy development for infants and toddlers with disabilities and their families. *Journal of Early Intervention, 16*(1), 1–10.

Giangreco, M.F., & Putnam, J.W. (1991). Supporting the education of students with severe disabilities in regular education environments. In L.H. Meyer, C.A. Peck, & L. Brown (Eds.), *Critical issues in the lives of people with severe disabilities* (pp. 245–270). Baltimore: Paul H. Brookes Publishing Co.

Green, A., & Stoneman, Z. (1989). Attitudes of mothers and fathers of handicapped children toward preschool mainstreaming. *Journal of Early Intervention, 13,* 293–304.

Guralnick, M.J. (Ed.). (1978). *Early intervention and the integration of handicapped and nonhandicapped children.* Baltimore: University Park Press.

Guralnick, M.J. (1990). Major accomplishments and future directions in early childhood mainstreaming. *Topics in Early Childhood Special Education, 10*(2), 1–7.

Guralnick, M.J., & Groom, J. M. (1987). The peer relations of mildly delayed and nonhandicapped preschool children in mainstreamed playgroups. *Child Development, 58,* 1556–1572.

Hanline, M.F. (1993). Inclusion of preschoolers with profound disabilities: An analysis of children's interactions. *Journal of The Association for Persons with Severe Handicaps, 18*(1), 28–35.

Hanson, M.J., & Hanline, M.F. (1989). Integration options for the very young child. In R. Gaylord-Ross (Ed.), *Integration strategies for students with handicaps* (pp. 177–193). Baltimore: Paul H. Brookes Publishing Co.

Howes, C. (1983). Patterns of friendship. *Child Development, 54,* 1041–1053.

Individuals with Disabilities Education Act (IDEA) of 1990, PL 101-476. (October 30, 1990). Title 20, U.S.C. 1400 et seq: *U.S. Statutes at Large, 104,* 1103–1151.

Individuals with Disabilities Education Act Amendments of 1991, PL 102-119. (October 7, 1991). Title 20, U.S.C. 1400 et seq: *U.S. Statutes at Large, 105,* 587–608.

Jenkins, J.R., Odom, S.L., & Speltz, M.L. (1989). Effects of social integration of preschool children with handicaps. *Exceptional Children, 55*(5), 420–428.

Kohl, F.L., & Beckman, P.J. (1984). A comparison of preschoolers' interactions across classroom activities. *Journal of the Division for Early Childhood, 8,* 49–56.

Kontos, S., & File, N. (1993). Staff development in support of integration. In C.A. Peck, S.L. Odom, & D.D. Bricker (Eds.), *Integrating young children with disabilities into community programs: Ecological perspectives on research and implementation* (pp. 169–186). Baltimore: Paul H. Brookes Publishing Co.

Koralek, D.G., Colker, L.J., & Dodge, D.T. (1993). *The what, why, and how of high-quality early childhood education: A guide for on-site supervision.* Washington, DC: National Association for the Education of Young Children.

Ladd, G.W. (1990). Having friends, keeping friends, making friends and being liked by peers in the classroom: Predictors of children's early school adjustment? *Child Development, 61,* 1081–1100.

Ladd, G.W., Price, J.M., & Hart, C.H. (1990). Preschoolers' behavioral orientations and patterns of peer contact: Predictive of peer status? In S.R. Asher & J.D. Coie (Eds.), *Peer rejection in childhood* (pp. 90–115). New York: Cambridge University Press.

Lipsky, D.K., & Gartner, A. (Eds.). (1989). *Beyond separate education: Quality education for all.* Baltimore: Paul H. Brookes Publishing Co.

Mallory, B.L. (1994). Inclusive policy, practice, and theory for young children with developmental differences. In B.L. Mallory & R.S. New (Eds.), *Diversity and developmentally appropriate practice* (pp. 44–62). New York: Teachers College Press.

Marchant, C. (1995). Teachers' views of integrated preschools. *Journal of Early Intervention, 19*(1), 61–73.

McCracken, J.B. (1993). *Valuing diversity: The primary years.* Washington, DC: National Association for the Education of Young Children.

McDonnell, A., & Hardman, M. (1988). A synthesis of "best practice" guidelines for early childhood services. *Journal of the Division for Early Childhood, 12*(4), 328–341.

McLean, M., & Hanline, M.F. (1990). Providing early intervention services in integrated environments: Challenges and opportunities for the future. *Topics in Early Childhood Special Education, 10*(2), 62–77.

Miller, L.J., Strain, P.S., Boyd, K., Hunsicker, S., McKinley, J., & Wu, A. (1992). Parental attitudes toward integration. *Topics in Early Childhood Special Education, 12,* 230–246.

National Association of State Boards of Education. (1992). *Winners all: A call for inclusive schools.* Alexandria, VA: Author.

National Early Childhood Technical Assistance Systems. (1993). *A profile of Part B-Section 619 services* (4th ed.). Chapel Hill, NC: Author.

New, R.S., & Mallory, B.L. (1994). The ethic of inclusion. In B.L. Mallory & R.S. New (Eds.), *Diversity and developmentally appropriate practice* (pp. 1–13). New York: Teachers College Press.

Noonan, M.J., & McCormick, L. (1993). *Early intervention in natural environments: Methods and procedures.* Pacific Grove, CA: Brooks/Cole Publishing.

Odom, S.L., & Brown, W.H. (1993). Social interaction skills interventions for young children with disabilities in integrated settings. In C.A. Peck, S.L. Odom, & D.D. Bricker (Eds.), *Integrating young children with disabilities into community programs: Ecological perspectives on research and implementation* (pp. 39–64). Baltimore: Paul H. Brookes Publishing Co.

Odom, S.L., DeKlyen, M., & Jenkins, J.R. (1984). Integrating handicapped and nonhandicapped preschoolers: Developmental impact on nonhandicapped children. *Exceptional Children, 51*(1), 41–48.

Odom, S.L., & McEvoy, M.A. (1988). Integration of young children with handicaps and normally developing children. In S.L. Odom, & M.B. Karnes (Eds.), *Early intervention for infants and children with handicaps: An empirical base* (pp. 241–267). Baltimore: Paul H. Brookes Publishing Co.

Odom, S.L., & McEvoy, M.A. (1990). Mainstreaming at the preschool level: Potential barriers and tasks for the field. *Topics in Early Childhood Special Education, 10*(2), 48–61.

Odom, S.L., & Strain, P.S. (Eds.). (1989). Integration of young children with and without disabilities [Special issue]. *Journal of Early Intervention, 13*(4).

Park, K.A., Lay, K.K., & Ramsay, L. (1993). Individual differences and developmental changes in preschoolers' friendships. *Developmental Psychology, 29*(2), 264–270.

Peck, C.A., Furman, G.C., & Helmstetter, E. (1993). Integrated early childhood programs: Research on the implementation of change in organizational contexts. In C.A. Peck, S.L. Odom, & D.D. Bricker (Eds.), *Integrating young children with disabilities into community programs* (pp. 187–206). Baltimore: Paul H. Brookes Publishing Co.

Peck, C.A., Odom, S.L., & Bricker, D.D. (Eds.). (1993). *Integrating young children with disabilities into community programs.* Baltimore: Paul H. Brookes Publishing Co.

Peterson, N.L. (1982). Social integration of handicapped and nonhandicapped preschoolers: A study of playmate preferences. *Topics in Early Childhood Special Education, 2*(2), 56–69.

Putallaz, M., & Wasserman, A. (1990). Children's entry behavior. In S.R. Asher & J.D. Coie (Eds.), *Peer rejection in childhood* (pp. 60–89). New York: Cambridge University Press.

Ramsey, P.G. (1991). *Making friends in school: Promoting peer relationships in early childhood.* New York: Teachers College Press.

Raupp, C. (1985). Approaching special needs children's social competence from the perspective of early friendships. *Topics in Early Childhood Special Education, 4*(4), 32–46.

Rose, D.F., & Smith, B.J. (1993). Preschool mainstreaming: Attitude barriers and strategies for addressing them. *Young Children, 48*(4), 59–62.

Rubin, Z. (1980). *Children's friendships.* Cambridge, MA: Harvard University Press.

Safford, P.L. (1989). *Integrated teaching in early childhood.* White Plains, NY: Longman Inc.

Sailor, W. (1991). Community school: An essay. In L.H. Meyer, C.A. Peck, & L. Brown (Eds.), *Critical issues in the lives of people with severe disabilities* (pp. 379–385). Baltimore: Paul H. Brookes Publishing Co.

Salisbury, C.L. (1991). Mainstreaming during the early years. *Exceptional Children, 58*(2), 146–155.

Sapon-Shevin, M. (1992). Celebrating diversity, creating community: Curriculum that honors and builds on differences. In S. Stainback & W. Stainback (Eds.), *Curriculum considerations in inclusive classrooms: Facilitating learning for all students* (pp. 19–36). Baltimore: Paul H. Brookes Publishing Co.

Schnorr, R.F. (1990). "Peter? He comes and goes...": First graders' perspectives on a part-time mainstream student. *Journal of The Association for Persons with Severe Handicaps, 15*(4), 231–240.

Stainback, S., Stainback, W., & Jackson, H.J. (1992). Toward inclusive classrooms. In S. Stainback & W. Stainback (Eds.), *Curriculum considerations in inclusive classrooms: Facilitating learning for all students* (pp. 3–17). Baltimore: Paul H. Brookes Publishing Co.

Stainback, W., Stainback, S., & Bunch, G. (1989). Introduction and historical background. In S. Stainback, W. Stainback, & M. Forest (Eds.), *Educating all students in the mainstream of regular education* (pp. 3–14). Baltimore: Paul H. Brookes Publishing Co.

Strain, P.S. (1990). LRE for preschool children with handicaps: What we know, what we should be doing. *Journal of Early Intervention, 14*(4), 291–296.

Taylor, S.J. (1988). Caught in the continuum: A critical analysis of the principle of the least restrictive environment. *Journal of The Association for Persons with Severe Handicaps, 13*(1), 41–53.

Turnbull, R.H. (1990). *Free appropriate public education: The law and children with disabilities* (3rd ed.). Denver, CO: Love Publishing Co.

U.S. Department of Education. (1993). *Fifteenth annual report to Congress on the implementation of the Individuals with Disabilities Education Act.* Washington, DC: Author.

Vincent, L.J., Brown, L., & Getz-Sheftel, M. (1981). Integrating handicapped and typical children during the preschool years: The definition of best educational practice. *Topics in Early Childhood Education, 1*(1), 17–24.

Walsh, D.J., Tobin, J.J., & Graue, M.E. (1993). The interpretive voice: Qualitative research in early childhood education. In B. Spodek (Ed.), *Handbook of research on the education of young children* (pp. 464–476). New York: Macmillan.

Wang, M.C. (1989). Implementing the state of the art and integration mandates of PL 94-142. In J.J. Gallagher, P.L. Trohanis, & R.M. Clifford (Eds.), *Policy implementation and PL 99-457: Planning for young children with special needs* (pp. 33–57). Baltimore: Paul H. Brookes Publishing Co.

Wolery, M., Holcombe-Ligon, A., Brookfield, J., Huffman, K., Schroeder, C., Martin, C.G., Venn, M.L., Werts, M.G., & Fleming, L.A. (1993). The extent and nature of preschool mainstreaming: A survey of general early educators. *Journal of Special Education, 27*(2), 222–234.

Wolery, M., Strain, P.S., & Bailey, D.B. (1992). Reaching potentials of children with special needs. In S. Bredekamp & T. Rosegrant (Eds.), *Reaching potentials: Appropriate curriculum and assessment for young children* (pp. 92–113). Washington, DC: National Association for the Education of Young Children.

Wolfensberger, W. (1980). The definition of normalization. In R.J. Flynn & K.E. Nitsch (Eds.), *Normalization, social integration, and community services* (pp. 71–115). Baltimore: University Park Press.

York, J., Giangreco, M.F., Vandercook, T., & Macdonald, C. (1992). Integrating support personnel in the inclusive classroom. In S. Stainback & W. Stainback (Eds.), *Curriculum considerations in inclusive classrooms: Facilitating learning for all students* (pp. 101–116). Baltimore: Paul H. Brookes Publishing Co.

We All Work Together as a Team

Garrett Silveira and Betsy Silveira

Our son Ryan was born on March 6, 1990. At birth, Ryan was diagnosed with ectodactyl, ectodermal dysplasia, cleft, and urinary tract (EECUT) syndrome. (He did not, however, have clefting.) When Ryan was 2 months old, we were advised that both of his retinas were abnormal and totally detached and that, as a result, he would have no vision; when he was 4 months old, we learned that his skull was closing prematurely (craniosynostosis); and, when he was 8 months old, he was diagnosed with esophageal reflux and failure to thrive. All told, Ryan had five operations and had been fed through a nasal tube for 5 months by the time he was 15 months old.

Ryan became known as our little bundle of surprises, because, naturally, we were shocked and dismayed each time we learned of a new medical problem. Fortunately, we found a source of strength and endurance in our geneticist. He was communicative, accessible, and positive and assumed the roles of medical coordinator and parent–physician liaison to help us navigate a storm of medical procedures as well as all of the questions and concerns that besiege parents in such situations. For the first 2 years of Ryan's life, this geneticist maintained close contact with us, calling to check on Ryan's progress and the coordination of events and remaining available whenever we called him. He has continued to touch base with us every 6 months and has proved to be a wonderful resource because he is knowledgeable about every aspect of our son. We have also been blessed with a remarkable pediatrician, who has come to know us very well, to understand Ryan, and to ensure that Ryan receives high-quality medical care.

As a result of Ryan's medical conditions, he requires various early intervention services. Since the age of 4 months, Ryan has received vision, physical, occupational, rehabilitation and orientation, and feeding therapies. The arrangements for and coordination of all of these therapies have proved to be the most daunting and frustrating tasks. The agencies providing Ryan's early intervention services were grossly uneducated and misinformed about their obligations and were ill-prepared to arrange for and coordinate services. Several agencies seemed to be more concerned with rules and regulations than with providing Ryan with the educational and related services he needed and was legally entitled to receive; this bureaucratic focus often resulted in long breaks in the provision of services. Initially, for example, our local agency had no certified vision teacher on staff and lacked any sense of urgency in locating a qualified individual. In addition, we were told that all services must be obtained through a single provider, which severely limited our options and, for a time, required Ryan to be in a peer group that did not include typically developing children.

When Ryan reached preschool age, we wanted him to attend a general education school and receive necessary services in the classroom. We wanted him to interact with his typically developing peers and to experience everything a child without disabilities would experience. Before preschool age, Ryan received services on a one-to-one basis either at home or at a local institution. The time consumed, the paperwork required, and the effort we as parents had to expend to obtain the services Ryan needed and was legally entitled to seemed wasteful and caused great frustration.

Relief from the confusion and frustration involved in obtaining early intervention services for Ryan has come only recently; now, Ryan's educational needs are met and coordinated through the local school district by knowledgeable professionals who have contact with the necessary resources and support parents' decisions and choices. Ryan now attends a private preschool program with his typically developing peers. At his preschool, Ryan receives vision and occupational therapies (feeding therapy takes place in our home), and there are both a teacher and a full-time assistant in his classroom. The classroom teacher, assistant, and therapists communicate with one another and coordinate Ryan's services. We also are an integral part of this process.

We firmly believe that the frustration we experienced and the time we spent to gain initial access to services were entirely unnecessary and served only to heighten our stress. We are pleased and very relieved that we have created the perfect program for Ryan. We all work together as a team and are able to watch Ryan grow and experience life just as his typically developing classmates do. Ryan has attended his preschool program since the age of 3 years, and he has progressed beautifully. We are so pleased with this inclusive program that we have enrolled Ryan in the school's kindergarten.

9

Partnerships for Collaboration

Building Bridges in Early Care and Education

Elizabeth J. Erwin and Beverly Rainforth

To achieve natural environments in which all children belong and hetero-geneity and diversity are valued, collaboration must be the foundation on which all else is built. Frequent and regular coordination with other systems, agencies, and personnel is required to maximize the scope and quality of services to the families of young children like Ryan. Furthermore, young children and their families in the United States face a multitude of challenges, including poverty (see Chapter 3), violence (see Chapter 2), inadequate housing, parental substance abuse (see Chapter 4), and poor health and nutrition. Because, typically, these problems occur in clusters rather than singly, resources to ameliorate these issues must be coordinated and multidimensional. The involvement of multiple systems or individuals often is necessary to achieve desired outcomes fully (see Chapter 7). Failure to coordinate these multiple elements will likely lead to fragmentation and duplication of services as well as to unsuccessful outcomes for children and their families.

In this chapter, *collaboration* is defined as "organizational and interorganizational structures where resources, power, and authority are shared and where people are brought together to achieve common goals that could not be accomplished by a single individual or organization independently" (Kagan, 1991, p. 3). This definition highlights several important aspects of collaboration, including the notion of *sharing,* which implies the existence of joint planning, control, and responsibility for resources among key players. This concept of collaboration among adults parallels the recommended practices of turn taking, responsiveness, and active participation that are appropriate and necessary during adults' interactions with young children (Bredekamp, 1991). Early childhood programs, therefore, require a collaborative culture in which adults practice and model the same interactions that they encourage in young children.

This chapter explores the importance and nature of collaboration when working with young children and their families. This chapter also provides a synthesis of the research and literature on the challenges of and approaches to collaboration and teaming within early childhood contexts.

FRAMING COLLABORATION WITHIN AN EARLY CHILDHOOD CONTEXT

Although the concept of collaboration is not new to education, increased attention to and interest in collaborative efforts within early childhood care and education have been noted. Kagan and Rivera (1991) suggested that the popularity of early childhood collaboration in the 1990s emanates from sources both inside and outside the field. One outside influence is the growing emphasis on collaboration in the corporate world, fostered by the realization that the merging of resources has fiscal advantages. Within the field of early child care and education, one of the most influential forces behind the enhanced interest in collaboration is the advancement in policy and legislation that began in the 1980s.

Influence of PL 99-457 on Collaboration

When it was passed, PL 99-457, the Education of the Handicapped Act Amendments of 1986, was considered landmark legislation because of "the promise it held for young children with disabilities and their families as well as the values and beliefs it reflected" (Safer & Hamilton, 1993, p. 17). PL 99-457 assisted states in developing statewide, comprehensive, coordinated, multidisciplinary, and interagency systems of early intervention for infants and toddlers with disabilities and their families. It also mandated a free and appropriate public education for children with disabilities ages 3–5 years.

PL 99-457 influenced the expansion of services for infants, toddlers, and preschoolers with disabilities to community-based natural environments. In addition to the legislative mandate, strong philosophical, ethical, and educational reasons are behind the efforts to include young children with disabilities in community-based settings with their age-appropriate, typically developing peers (Bricker, 1978; Odom & McEvoy, 1988). (For a more detailed discussion about providing services and supports in early childhood community-based environments, see Chapter 8.) This shift prompted the field to examine more closely the innovative and integrated efforts in early childhood program development, service provision, and professional preparation and training.

PL 99-457 had far-reaching implications for collaboration in early childhood. Whereas alliances between health care and educational communities generally had been complex and fragmented (Shonkoff & Meisels, 1990), PL 99-457 provided a strong framework for enhancing collaboration among agencies and among personnel. Several ways in which collaboration was valued and encouraged within this early childhood legislation include, but are not limited to, recognizing

1. That services often are provided to young children with disabilities by personnel from various disciplines and agencies
2. The need for a service coordinator who can facilitate the integration and implementation of services and supports
3. The need for an individualized family service plan (IFSP) that produces an integrated framework for the delivery of services
4. The need to develop an interagency coordinating council consisting of parents and professionals

5. The need for a central directory of services, resources, experts, and research
6. The need for transition services for children moving to new programs
7. The need for grants to demonstrate and disseminate information about exemplary models and practices in early education, including interdisciplinary models and practices

Although PL 99-457 encouraged collaborative efforts between agencies and personnel, Harbin and McNulty (1990) noted that the legislation did not specify why or how to accomplish this collaboration. The authors further asserted that how states achieved coordination and collaboration depended on how well the rationale, implications, and methods were understood (Harbin & McNulty, 1990).

In addition to its impact on collaboration across agencies and personnel, PL 99-457 had a profound impact on partnerships between families and professionals. In interactions with families, professionals often had assumed the role of experts who assessed situations, predicted realistic expectations, and prescribed solutions. Since the passage of PL 99-457, this type of expert role, in which professionals solve problems *for*, rather than *with*, parents and other team members, no longer is considered satisfactory (Bailey, 1987; Biklen, 1992; File & Kontos, 1992; Turnbull & Turnbull, 1990).

PL 99-457 gave parents the freedom and authority to choose which services they wanted and needed and to determine their role in the IFSP. As a result of PL 99-457, families have a much more instrumental role in the development, implementation, and evaluation of educational programs that affect their children than they had in the past. In this way, PL 99-457 has had an impact on the way families are viewed by professionals.

PL 99-457 provided the foundation for initiating discussion and subsequent action about early childhood collaboration on both interagency and interpersonal levels. In essence, PL 99-457 challenged the field to redefine relationships as well as systems. In 1991, PL 99-457 was reauthorized as PL 102-119, the Individuals with Disabilities Education Act Amendments of 1991, thereby, reaffirming the importance of collaboration in early child care and education. One way to better understand early childhood collaboration from a policy and practice perspective is to explore the rationale behind personnel, program, and home–school collaborations.

Rationale for Collaboration Across Professionals and Programs

Changes in the provision of services to young children with and without disabilities have drawn increased attention to collaboration in early child care and education. Dramatic shifts in the demand for and nature of early child care and education have been demonstrated since the mid-1980s (Children's Defense Fund, 1992; Elkind, 1987; Honig, 1990; Kontos, 1992; Mitchell, Seligson, & Marx, 1989). As a result, many new early childhood programs and arrangements have been developed and/or expanded. Because numerous agencies monitor programs for young children and their families (e.g., Head Start; child care licensing; social services, welfare, health, and education departments), there is an immediate challenge to ensure coordination across and within programs (Mitchell et al., 1989).

In general, early childhood programs encounter challenges when they attempt to interface with other systems that may or may not have similar agendas. Bruder and Bologna (1993) suggested several factors that inhibit interagency collaboration including competitiveness among programs (e.g., turf or political issues), poor or lacking organizational structure (e.g., conflicting philosophies, poor planning), technical factors (e.g., resources, logistics), and personnel (e.g., attitudes, resistance to change). Unfortunately, Ryan's parents, like so many others, experienced firsthand the lacking or limited coordination among and within systems. Although challenges to collaboration can exist among systems, barriers also can exist among personnel within those systems.

Numerous factors contribute to feelings of isolation in early childhood care and education professionals; these include diversity in race, ethnicity, religion, income level, funding, and policies (Galinsky, Shubilla, Willer, Levine, & Daniel, 1994). The need to create meaningful connections among individuals, as well as systems, remains one of the greatest challenges facing professionals in early child care and education.

Despite the many challenges, early childhood collaborative efforts have a positive impact on services to children, standards and conditions for service providers, and collaboration among systems and personnel (Kagan & Rivera, 1991). In a study of collaboration across the United States in the early child care and education field, respondents from national, state, and local organizations identified several beneficial outcomes of collaboration, including higher quality of services, increased utilization of resources, expanded training opportunities, advancements in legislation, and development of exemplary programs and practices (Kagan & Rivera, 1991). When systems and the personnel within those systems are coordinated effectively, the risks of duplication, fragmentation, and inferior services are greatly reduced or eliminated.

A vital need for partnerships among systems, personnel, and families exists, regardless of the ages of the children involved or the environments in which services are provided. When an infant who is medically fragile is ready to be discharged from a hospital, a smooth and successful transition from hospital to home requires intensive collaboration efforts among family members, infant follow-up program staff, primary health care providers, community health nursing professionals, and early intervention specialists (Gilkerson, Gorski, & Panitz, 1990). As the Silveiras describe, medical personnel provided invaluable support and guidance by skillfully coordinating the wide array of services that Ryan needed during his first year of life.

Likewise, special education and related services (e.g., occupational therapy, physical therapy, vision services, feeding therapy) were integrated carefully into Ryan's daily routines and activities when he began attending a private preschool program. All school staff who have contact with Ryan (e.g., classroom teacher, teacher assistant, therapists, specialists) continue to collaborate with one another and with Ryan's parents on a regular basis to ensure an integrated and individualized plan for Ryan. The benefits of collaboration in early care and education, therefore, affect children, their families, and the individuals who are responsible for providing services and support.

Rationale for Home–School Collaboration

Educational collaboration often is assumed to mean professional collaboration. Parents and, more recently, other family members, have, however, also been recognized as valuable and necessary collaborators in early child care and education.

Why Collaborate with Parents and Families?

The question is not why professionals should collaborate with parents and families, but rather, why parents should collaborate with professionals. Many parents, particularly those of children with disabilities, have experienced a long history of feeling ignored, blamed, labeled, and treated like submissive recipients of professional decisions by educators (Biklen, 1992; Fine & Gardner, 1994; Lipsky, 1989; Safford, 1989; Turnbull & Turnbull, 1990). The ways professionals view parents most likely are reflected in the ways professionals treat parents.

   Attention to home–school partnerships has increased significantly during the 1990s. Perhaps one reason for this interest is that parent–family collaboration has been linked closely to early childhood program quality and effectiveness (Children's Defense Fund, 1992; Division for Early Childhood Task Force on Recommended Practices, 1993; Koralek, Colker, & Dodge, 1993). The focus of collaboration with professionals shifted from mothers to parents and from parents to families. This shift is grounded in the family systems theory, which asserts that families not only are competent and resourceful, but can provide unique and necessary contributions to home–school collaborative relationships (Galinsky & Weissbound, 1992; Turnbull & Turnbull, 1990). Turnbull and Turnbull maintain that a family systems framework is based on the idea that

> An understanding of family characteristics, interaction, functions, and life cycle can serve as the basis of meaningfully individualizing parent–professional relationships for the benefit of all concerned—the child, parents, other family members, and professionals. Furthermore, we can begin to consider *family*–professional relationships rather than merely *parent*–professional relationships. (1990, p. 19)

This approach illustrates that family members other than parents (e.g., siblings, extended family members, stepparents) are integral members of a family system and, therefore, make important contributions to overall family dynamics.

   Advances in federal policies and programs affecting families result in part from new governmental views on the paramount role of families in children's lives (Safer & Hamilton, 1993). Changes in the 1980s reflected an emerging assumption about family competence and values that was not present during the 1960s and 1970s, when the prevailing assumption was that federal programs for children, independent of the influence of families and communities, could ameliorate social challenges. The latest shift from parent-only participation to family participation reinforces the idea that all family members, not just parents, play extremely important roles in the lives of young children.

RECOMMENDED PRACTICES IN EARLY CHILDHOOD COLLABORATION

Although the need to empower parents has been demonstrated clearly by advocates involved with Head Start, early intervention, and health care for children with chronic illnesses (Pizzo, 1993), a discrepancy often exists between recommended practice and reality. The importance of parental involvement in early care and education has long been widely recognized, yet only recently have practitioners begun to seek ways to actively include parents (Morrison, 1991). In fact, despite the widely held assumption that collaboration is an important part of working with young children and their families, there is a dearth of empirical evidence on collaborative efforts in early childhood settings (Hanson & Widerstrom, 1993). Future research efforts, therefore, must focus on strategies that foster family and professional partnerships. This section summarizes key elements and advancements in collaboration in early child care and education.

Families as Partners in Early Child Care and Education

Parental involvement in young children's education has long been valued in the early childhood education field (Bredekamp, 1993; Honig, 1975). Although this value is reflected in Head Start legislation, PL 101-476, the Individuals with Disabilities Education Act (IDEA) of 1990, has redefined the ways parents participate in the development, implementation, and evaluation of early childhood special education and related services. When parents and families are viewed as partners with professionals, the underlying assumption is that parents know their children best and are capable of making meaningful decisions.

In the late 1980s and early 1990s, discussions centered on how to promote *equal partnerships* between professionals and parents and/or families, instead of how to simply involve parents in the care and education of their children (Bricker, 1989; Erwin & Soodak, 1995; Gelfer, 1991; Morrison, 1991; Salisbury, 1992). Erwin and Soodak (1995) noted that "parent input is only meaningful in a school system that values parents as partners" (p. 13). The underlying assumptions are that parent contributions to home–school collaborations only can be realized fully when professionals within a system have healthy attitudes about parents and their ability to make decisions and that the practices within a system foster this decision-making process. True collaboration between professionals and families occurs when families receive the support they need to make informed decisions.

Merely inviting a parent to a function or corresponding on a weekly basis, for example, does not necessarily constitute active or meaningful parent participation or demonstrate a partnership between home and school. Equal partnerships, which usually are created to achieve mutually agreed-upon outcomes, can be thought of as interactive relationships based on respect, sharing, and joint authority. Partnerships between homes and environments in which services are provided to young children and their families (e.g., child care centers, hospitals, community programs, Head Start programs, social services agencies) are essential. These partnerships can enable families to make informed decisions that reflect the values, supports, resources, and priorities that they have identified as important. Empowering families with the authority to make meaningful decisions does not preclude the participation of professionals. Instead of instructing families as to what to do, professionals share information that will assist families when making their own decisions.

Fostering a Family-Centered Approach

When services to children and their families are based on a professional's perception of a family's priorities, conflicts over values, beliefs, and expectations may arise. In a family-centered approach, families are recognized as the constant and chief influence in young children's lives (Association for the Care of Children's Health, 1989; Brown, Thurman, & Pearl, 1993; Dunst, Johanson, Trivette, & Hamby, 1991). This approach, clearly reflected in PL 99-457 and PL 101-476, acknowledges not only that families are unique and resourceful, but also that they are competent to make important decisions that affect their lives. A family-centered approach does not eliminate the need for professional expertise or input (Westby & Ford, 1993); rather, it broadens the need for professional support in ways that are identified by the family.

Although family-centered practices receive much support, conflicts may arise when parents and professionals seek different outcomes for young children (Powell, 1994). For example, if parents want their neighborhood preschool to teach their child to read by the age of 3 years, the preschool teachers likely will have conflicting ideas about how children develop and what they should learn. In such a situation, early childhood educators are responsible for informing parents about what constitutes high-quality early child care and education so that parents can make knowledgeable decisions. Professionals may not, however, know how to make joint decisions with parents. Powell (1994) noted

> the call for parents to share in decisions about their children's care and education is a one-sentence recommendation, and the [Developmentally Appropriate Practice in Early Childhood Programs (Bredekamp, 1991)] report offers no concrete examples of how this practice is to be implemented or specifically how teachers show respect for parents' alternative point of view. (p. 176)

It is, therefore, imperative that professionals learn to distinguish between situations in which parents need more information to make better decisions and those in which parents simply have a different perspective, which must be respected. It is equally important that professionals learn skills to support, collaborate with, and negotiate with parents, as well as other professionals, who have different points of view. Balancing these considerations is a challenge but can produce worthwhile benefits for all involved.

Building Partnerships Among Professionals

In a discussion of collaborative teamwork, it is useful to examine briefly some attributes of exemplary models and some weaknesses of traditional models of services. The general consensus is that no single discipline can meet the needs of children with disabilities and those of their families, and that services from many disciplines are more efficient and effective when they are well coordinated.

Coordination among service providers reduces duplication and contradictions (Bricker & Campbell, 1980), rendering teams more effective and reducing stress on families. When professionals truly work as a team, rather than as a collection of individuals, they also become more attuned to the interests and needs of families (Garshelis & McConnell, 1993). Unfortunately, most professionals have not been taught to collaborate with professionals from other disciplines, and, as a result, they struggle with their roles as team members. Some professionals define roles in terms of turf held by each discipline; others assume that their discipline can meet all or most student and family needs or that the team revolves around their discipline (Feeg, 1987). Exemplary services, in contrast, are characterized by professionals working together with families as equals to establish a shared philosophy, identify needs and priorities, and determine roles and relationships required to address those priorities efficiently and effectively. A review of literature from many disciplines involved in early childhood and special education reveals that every discipline has practiced some aspect of exemplary services that contribute to models of collaborative teamwork.

Transdisciplinary Teaming

Starting around 1970, the United States Cerebral Palsy Associations sponsored a series of projects, first, in residential institutions for children and adults with developmental disabilities and, later, in community programs for infants and young children with disabilities and their families (Hutchison, 1978). One important outcome of these projects was the conceptualization of a transdisciplinary team approach, in which team members practice role release (Patterson et al., 1976). In this model, all team members expand their knowledge and skills in their own disciplines, teach others relevant information and skills traditionally associated with their disciplines, learn from one another, and work in various roles to provide services to children.

Teachers of young children often are the educational synthesizers (Bricker, 1976) who receive, integrate, and apply much of the training from other team members. Likewise, parents often assume the role of primary interventionist (Patterson et al., 1976) for their young children. Some professionals feared that the transdisciplinary approach would reduce accountability and violate professional ethics through abdication of responsibility, but these fears reflect misconceptions of both intent and recommended implementation (York, Rainforth, & Giangreco, 1990). Unfortunately, much of the early literature about transdisciplinary teamwork was theoretical rather than practical. In the late 1980s and early 1990s, several authors offered explicit strategies for implementing these transdisciplinary teams for those who work with infants, toddlers, and young children with disabilities in their homes, preschools, and public school programs (Linder, 1993a, 1993b; Rainforth & Salisbury, 1988; Rainforth, York, & Macdonald, 1992). Although PL 101-476 does not call for a transdisciplinary approach by name, it does call for the practices that are hallmarks of this approach.

Integrated Therapy

Another aspect of collaborative teamwork was first described in the special education literature as integrated therapy (Sternat, Messina, Nietupski, Lyon, & Brown, 1977). In this approach, therapists provide their services during natural routines and activities as children need to develop component skills. An occupational therapist, therefore, might teach dressing skills during arrival or departure, when children are taking off or putting on coats, or address sensory–perceptual needs during free play at a preschool, rather than pulling children out of their classes for therapy that consists of artificial tasks, expectations, and environments. When integrated therapy is combined with transdisciplinary teamwork, team members collaborate to identify individual children's needs within natural routines, design intervention strategies to address those needs, share and learn relevant strategies from one another's disciplines, and teach children throughout daily routines using team-developed strategies.

Collaborative Consultation

The transdisciplinary-integrated therapy approach is similar to the collaborative consultation model recommended for teams of general education classroom teachers, special educators, and school psychologists who serve school-age children with disabilities (Idol, Nevin, & Paolucci-Whitcomb, 1994; Pugach & Johnson, 1995). This approach grew out of the recognition that classroom teachers did not follow the advice of expert consultants. Because the consultant and classroom teacher had a hierarchical relationship, the consultant missed opportunities to integrate the classroom teacher's expertise, expectations, and constraints. In collaborative consultation, however, when classroom teachers find that routine instruction is not effective for individual children (with or without disabilities), team members work as equals to identify more satisfactory methods.

The literature on collaborative consultation stresses the communication and collaborative problem-solving skills required for effective teamwork. To a lesser extent, the literature describes the roles of participants in collaborative consultation. One role involves team teaching, in which team members plan lessons jointly and teach those lessons to a large group together or to smaller groups concurrently. Team teaching is advocated as a means toward curriculum reform and instructional improvement, as well as professional support to improve working conditions (Pugach & Johnson, 1995).

Although these approaches to collaborative teaming are described in the special education literature, some aspects, such as team teaching, have roots in general education (Pugach & Johnson, 1995). Several aspects parallel the developmentally appropriate practice recommended in early childhood education (Bredekamp, 1991). Examples of developmentally appropriate practice (which parallel recommended teaming practices in special education) include the following:

Specialists work with classroom teachers, rather than provide parallel, episodic instruction (just as in collaborative consultation).
The curriculum is embedded into natural routines, and skills from many domains are integrated (just as in integrated therapy).
The number of caregivers or teachers is limited (just as in the transdisciplinary model).

Finally, both the special education literature and early childhood education literature advocate interagency collaboration to coordinate the range of services that many children receive (Bredekamp, 1991; Division for Early

Childhood Task Force on Recommended Practices, 1993; Graff & Ault, 1993; Hansen, Holaday, & Miles, 1990).

When individuals and groups commit themselves to these forms of collaboration, team effectiveness and satisfaction are greatly influenced by their ability to resolve conflicts. It is not so much that collaboration creates conflict, but rather, that collaboration compels professionals to face the conflicts that have always existed. Whether conflict is expressed, suppressed, or ignored in less collaborative models, it does not only affect professionals. Too often, children and families have been affected directly by the conflict, and families are left to handle the consequences by themselves.

COLLABORATION FOR EARLY CHILDHOOD PROFESSIONAL DEVELOPMENT

Despite some fundamental differences between the fields of early childhood education and early childhood special education, leaders in both fields recognize extensive similarities (Bredekamp, 1993; McLean & Odom, 1993). Educators have called for professional unification to display a serious commitment to the philosophy and practice of including all children (Burton, Haines, Hanline, McLean, & McCormick, 1992; Miller, 1992; National Association for the Education of Young Children [NAEYC], 1994). Professional associations of therapists also advocate collaboration across disciplines to a greater extent than ever before (American Occupational Therapy Association, 1987; American Physical Therapy Association, 1990; American Speech-Language-Hearing Association, 1991). Model programs in which early childhood educators, early childhood special educators, and related services providers collaborate to provide services for young children with disabilities have been developed (Bruder, 1993; Hanline, 1990). Despite such attention, many professionals remain uninformed about exemplary practices in collaboration; others are informed, but fail to use the teaming practices they consider to be ideal (Effgen & Klepper, 1994).

The similarities across disciplines are further reflected by collaborative efforts in the licensure and preparation of early childhood professionals. The Division for Early Childhood of the Council for Exceptional Children, NAEYC, and the Association of Teacher Educators (1994) have developed a joint position statement on personnel standards for early education and early intervention. This position paper reinforces and expands on the ideas set forth by previous efforts to articulate standards for professionals who work with young children and their families. In addition, NAEYC (1994), in conjunction with other groups, has developed a position statement that describes a conceptual framework for understanding early childhood professional development within the broader service delivery system.

Recommendations for integrated personnel preparation (Bredekamp, 1992; Miller, 1992; Odom & McEvoy, 1990) reflect the notion that pooling resources and expertise from various sources committed to young children will lead to more successful and cohesive outcomes. In the mid-1990s, however, personnel preparation programs in early childhood were as diverse as the components of the early childhood service delivery system (NAEYC, 1994), and a continued need exists to strengthen the gap between knowledge and practice in early childhood training programs (Katz, 1987; NAEYC, 1994; Perry, 1990). Inadequate personnel training contributes significantly to resistance and failure to provide high-quality integrated programs (Peck, Hayden, Wandschneider, Peterson, & Richarz, 1989). Although efforts to promote integrated personnel preparation have been made, an unmet need to further address this vital aspect of early childhood teacher education remains.

Although personnel preparation programs generally advocate teamwork, few provide experiences that effectively teach collaboration. Typically, professionals enter the field with a strong disciplinary identity, which may overshadow their understanding of or curiosity about the potential contributions of other disciplines. Often, these professionals work in educational or other systems that do not support or promote teamwork directly, particularly transdisciplinary teamwork. When in-service training occasions about teamwork are offered, they likely consist of 1-day events without follow-up sessions. As a result, staff members have no real opportunities to develop the strategies required for effective collaboration. Furthermore, when a group decides to adopt a collaborative team approach, the resultant role changes may be too taxing or unsettling for some group members to endure the transition. Even when the need for change is evident, professionals may opt for the more familiar (and secure) individual or unidisciplinary roles. Although collaboration among professionals and families is advocated here, it is challenging to formulate solutions to these and other issues.

The above-described situations point to personnel preparation and staff development needs for team members, as well as for the program administrators who arrange the structures that either support or undermine teamwork. To achieve successful collaboration, program administrators must afford ongoing opportunities for staff members to learn about effective teaming and must provide adequate professional time to collaborate (West, 1990). Before personnel preparation programs can train practitioners in collaborative teamwork effectively, higher education must reconceptualize and restructure programs so that faculty members model collaboration successfully.

To prepare professionals for collaborative teaming, higher education must address four broad areas: competence in the discipline; collaborative roles (i.e., how to work together to assess, plan, implement, evaluate); communication, including collaborative problem solving and conflict resolution; and cultural competence.

Competence in the Discipline

Personnel preparation programs simultaneously face challenges of increasing specialization and increasing generalization. In the late 1980s and early 1990s, many states still offered only one certification to teach children of all ages with all disabilities (Putnam & Habanek, 1993). Preschool teachers, however, have identified that some significantly different competencies are required to work with infants and toddlers than are required to work with young children (McCollum, 1987). In recognition of the uniqueness of the early developmental stages, NAEYC has identified different practices as developmentally appropriate for infants, toddlers, preschoolers, and elementary school–age children (Bredekamp, 1991).

The fields of early childhood education and early childhood special education are in agreement that distinct differences exist among infants, toddlers, preschoolers, and elementary school–age children and that the learning and developmental characteristics of children from birth to 8 years of age are quite different from those of older children. Consistent with this viewpoint, a core knowledge base has been recommended for personnel who work with all young children from birth to 8 years of age with and without disabilities (Bredekamp & Willer, 1992; NAEYC, 1994). Table 9.1 provides a summary of these recommendations.

Because related services personnel usually are prepared to serve a broader clientele (children and adults with more varied abilities and disabilities), specialization is more desirable, but also more challenging, for these individuals (Bagnato, Neisworth, Paget, & Kovaleski, 1987; Effgen, 1988). For example, pediatric physical therapy is a very small (i.e., relatively unpopular) specialization within the field of physical therapy, physical therapy in educational settings is a subset of that specialization, and early childhood special education is an even smaller unit of that subset. At the same time that specialization is recommended, so is interdisciplinary preparation to develop a common core of beliefs, knowledge, and skills (Odom & McEvoy, 1990). Unfortunately, this generalized preparation among disciplines and more specialized preparation within each discipline face the following similar barriers: too few faculty with appropriate expertise, curricula that already are ponderous (often to meet entry-level licensure requirements), and personnel shortages that limit incentives for advanced training (Bailey, Simeonsson, Yoder, & Huntington, 1990; Wolery et al., 1993).

Despite the challenges associated with early childhood professional development, mastering a core content in early child care and education and developing a specialization are fundamental to basic competence and

Table 9.1. Core content for early childhood professionals

Demonstrate a basic understanding of child development and apply this knowledge in practice.

Establish and maintain an environment that ensures children's safety and their healthy development.

Plan and implement a developmentally appropriate program that advances all areas of children's learning and development, including social, emotional, intellectual, and physical competence.

Establish supportive relationships with children and implement developmentally appropriate techniques of guidance and group management.

Establish positive, productive relationships with families.

Support the uniqueness of each child, recognizing that children are best understood within the contexts of their families, cultures, and societies.

Demonstrate a basic understanding of the early childhood profession and make a commitment to professionalism.

Observe and assess children's behavior for use in planning and individualizing teaching practices and curricula.

Source: Bredekamp & Willer (1992).

effectiveness in early childhood settings. Teachers, who enter the profession with coursework and field experience in early childhood education, should have this core competence before employment. Related services professionals, who typically specialize after entering the field, should begin appropriate continuing education immediately after employment.

For teams to function properly, team members representing various disciplines must be competent in their disciplines. Furthermore, the team must look beyond discipline labels to see the unique competencies that each individual possesses. These competencies can vary tremendously, depending on professional preparation programs, continuing education, work experience, and individual interests. Unfortunately, as a result of personnel shortages people who have the required license, but who lack knowledge and experience relevant to young children with and without disabilities, sometimes are hired or assigned to teams. Licensed profession als are responsible for developing and maintaining competencies in their disciplines that are appropriate to the populations they serve. Program administrators share this responsibility, which they can exercise through hiring decisions, supervision, and staff development.

Collaborative Roles

Early childhood special educators and higher education faculty often report inadequate preparation in the interdisciplinary process and recommend that training be increased (Bailey et al., 1990; Hanson & Lovett, 1992). It is unclear, however, which aspects of the process are being assessed. Furthermore, related services personnel trained in medical settings may learn hierarchical models of interdisciplinary teamwork that are inappropriate in educational settings.

Educational team members assume various roles and need program structures to support those roles when, together, they conduct assessments, develop individualized education programs (IEPs) and IFSPs, and plan and provide instruction. It often is assumed that when individuals share a philosophy and communicate effectively, they automatically will perform their functions as a team. When team members merely share information about their parallel work, however, minimal collaboration is achieved. Higher education programs that prepare students to work with young children with disabilities must address the roles that team members assume, the strategies they use, and the administrative supports required to perform these roles *in collaboration with team members from other disciplines.* Personnel preparation programs must provide specific training about collaborative roles (e.g., team planning and team teaching within activity-based instruction) and administrative supports (e.g., joint planning time, flexible block scheduling). When personnel do not know how to develop program structures and role definitions that support collaboration, individualistic roles will predominate.

Students will be more likely to put collaborative roles into practice in their careers when they have seen the strategies modeled and have participated in their use. One way to expose students to collaboration is through site visits and practica in various early childhood settings that demonstrate collaborative roles (Bailey et al., 1990; Effgen, 1988; Wolery et al., 1993).

Identifying programs that do, in fact, demonstrate collaboration can be challenging, however. Another way to introduce students to the concept is through collaboration among faculty members who serve as guest speakers and coteachers from varied disciplines (Hanson, Hanline, & Peterson, 1987; Mills, Vadasy, & Fewell, 1987). Building collaborative relationships in higher education is challenging and requires purposeful commitments from all participants, but it offers benefits for students, faculty, and administrators (Stayton & Miller, 1993). Fortunately, faculty have access to descriptions of personnel preparation program models that include the components outlined above (Bennett & Watson, 1993; Bruder, Lippman, & Bologna, 1994; Stayton & Miller, 1993) as well as to textbooks that delineate collaborative roles (Linder, 1993a, 1993b; Pugach & Johnson, 1995; Rainforth et al., 1992).

Communication

Communication is fundamental to sharing information, negotiating relationships, solving problems, and resolving conflicts. Early childhood special educators have indicated the need for training in communication with infants, young children, families, assistants, volunteers, and other professionals (McCollum, 1987), and some programs have included preparation in communicating with these partners (Mills et al., 1987). Some programs offer training in specified skills, such as active listening, problem solving, and conflict resolution, needed by teachers and their supervisors (Bennett & Watson, 1993; Johnson, Kilgo, & Cook, 1992). Within and across the eight disciplines that frequently participate in early intervention teams, the content of professional preparation varies widely, however, and few disciplines provide specific training in communication skills (Bailey et al., 1990). Even when team members have had preparation in interpersonal communication, teams undoubtedly will benefit from additional staff development and supervision in this area. Collaborative problem solving and conflict resolution, as discussed earlier in this chapter, are integral components of effective communication.

Cultural Competence

Because young children are best understood within the context of their families, societies, and cultures, it is imperative that practitioners are sensitive to children's natural environments and routines. Sensitivity to an individual's culture does not suggest that a profession knows everything about a specific culture or tries to become a member of that particular culture; rather, cultural sensitivity is demonstrated when a professional recognizes that cultural differences and similarities exist and that value judgments should not be assigned to these similarities or differences (Anderson & Fenichel, 1989).

To work effectively with young children, families, or professionals who have different cultural backgrounds, service providers must develop an awareness of their own beliefs and values and an understanding that language, culture, and ethnicity affect personal interactions (Lynch, 1992). Collaborative partnerships often require interactions among individuals whose styles, values, and techniques differ. Although honoring the diversity of families and children is a recommended practice (Bredekamp, 1991; Division for Early Childhood Task Force on Recommended Practices, 1993), competence and sensitivity must extend beyond culture and ethnicity to include respect for all individual similarities and differences. To instill young children with pride in their individuality and curiosity and respect for differences, professionals must consistently and naturally demonstrate these qualities themselves. Valuing the diversity of others plays an important role in collaboration among families or professionals, particularly when members of the team have varied training and experiences.

In summary, exemplary personnel preparation in early childhood education addresses the following four basic areas of collaborative teaming: competence in the discipline, collaborative roles, communication, and cultural competence. A strong background in collaborative teaming will have a significant influence on the quality of integrated services to young children and their families.

TOWARD EFFECTIVE COLLABORATION IN EARLY CARE AND EDUCATION

The implementation of PL 99-457 and PL 101-476 has resulted in increased attention to collaborative relationships in early childhood contexts. Young children, with or without disabilities, in community-based early childhood environments are likely to have contact with numerous professionals from various disciplines or specialties (e.g., early childhood educator; dance, music, or art specialist; social worker; therapists; nurse; early interventionist), therefore, teamwork is essential for integrated and coordinated service delivery. Professionals no longer are considered the entire team, however. Rather, parents and other family members are viewed as essential contributors and usually are considered to be the most important members of a team.

Understanding the Culture of Teams

To understand more fully the nature of collaboration and teaming, it is worthwhile to explore the culture of teams. *Culture*, as defined by anthropologists, sociologists, and, more recently, educators, generally is conceptualized as a framework for assigning meaning to actions, behavior, or beliefs of a group of individuals, environments, or events (Bogdan & Biklen, 1992). By thinking about teams within this context, one can begin to understand the complexities that exist when a group of individuals unites to achieve a common goal. Unfortunately, much of the literature on medical and educational teams focuses on the students or patients served by teams; as a result, a shortage of knowledge regarding the culture of teams themselves exists (Westby & Ford, 1993). According to Westby and Ford (1993), a team's culture is defined in the following four important ways:

1. Shared patterns of interpretations or perceptions so team members know how they are expected to act and think
2. Shared patterns of feelings and values so team members know what they are expected to value and how they are expected to feel

3. Definitions of members and nonmembers of the team
4. Team control system that prescribes and prohibits certain behavior (p. 323)

Understanding the culture of a particular team, therefore, provides insight into the expectations, beliefs, and values that guide team decisions and actions.

This framework for examining team culture implies that, like children and families, no two teams are alike. Teams are unique systems that can change as people, demands, or roles change. Because one or all of these factors can affect team dynamics, conflicts tend to be a natural part of the team process. When conflict resolution is an integral part of the school culture for adults, as well as for children, success is maximized (Willis, 1993). In early childhood education, peace education and its underlying values of cooperation and justice are promoted frequently (Judson, 1984; Reardon, 1988; Weichert, 1989). The concept of peace education offers an excellent foundation for building a team culture that includes productive ways to resolve conflict.

Factors Contributing to Effective Teaming

Numerous elements can influence the way a team operates, including the environment, time allowed for collaboration, resources, members, tasks, and team culture. When teams, and the administrators who support them, commit to learning about and improving the ways they collaborate, it is important that teams begin to analyze their cultures and practices. Several key elements that can promote effective teaming are summarized below, and corresponding questions to guide team self-assessment are listed in Table 9.2.

Mission Statement

A mission statement articulates the team's purpose and philosophy and usually includes the values that drive the team's decisions and actions. In addition, the mission statement for an early childhood team may include a list of beliefs or guiding principles about matters such as the chosen model of teamwork, family participation, and the importance of providing services in natural environments. A team's mission statement is one of the

Table 9.2.   Questions to facilitate effective team collaboration

1. What is the mission or philosophy of this team?
2. What are the goals of this team?
3. How does the social and political climate support team activities and outcomes?
4. What resources are available to and within this team?
5. How can internal and external resources be used to support team efforts?
6. How is leadership and participation shared among team members?
7. What is the structure for decision making and problem solving?
8. Does an environment of trust and respect exist? Why or why not?
9. What are some challenges and potential solutions facing this team? How are challenges addressed?
10. How can this team evaluate its processes and outcomes to improve team dynamics?

Adapted from Bailey (1987); Bailey & Wolery (1992); Briggs (1993); Friend & Cook (1992); and Kagan (1991).

most important aspects of the team process because it is the foundation on which all else is built.

Goals

A clearly articulated vision of the outcomes to be achieved enables team members to work toward mutually established goals. Goals are closely connected to and emanate from the mission statement.

Social and Political Climate

The social and political climate of a program has a vital impact on the nature of teaming. Practices and policies that do not support collaboration among team members undermine the outcomes of the team. An ideal environment is supportive, yet flexible, allowing a team to pursue its goals.

Resources

External resources are those resources that are outside the parameters of the team, but within the parameters of the school or other environment (e.g., clerical assistance, time, financial support). Resources within the team are considered internal (e.g., professional expertise, clinical skills, specializations) and should be identified and used to advance the goals of the team. One important resource that may be either external or internal to the team is administrative support, because administrators are in positions to enable team members to develop and gain access to other resources.

Shared Leadership and Participation

The sharing of authority and participation among team members is vital for effective collaboration. This sharing does not mean that every team member is given an exactly equal amount of time to speak, but rather that each team member has ample opportunity to share ideas, solve problems, and make decisions. Each team member also has *responsibility* for sharing, problem solving, and decision making, thereby, making a meaningful contribution to the team process.

Decision Making and Problem Solving

Establishing a solid structure for collaborating provides team members with clear expectations and guidelines. This structure serves as a functional tool when disagreements arise, enabling the team to remain on task and focused.

Trust and Respect

To achieve an atmosphere in which true collaboration exists, trust and respect among team members must be present. All members must believe that their contributions are valued and that they can discuss ideas or issues freely within the team context.

Challenges and Solutions

Most teams face issues regarding team dynamics, outcomes, or practices. What is important here is not how many challenges arise, but how these challenges are addressed. By identifying emerging issues and creating solutions, teams can stay on track and resolve differences in an efficient and expedient manner.

Formative Evaluation

Formative evaluation may be one of the most neglected aspects of team collaboration, but it is one of the most useful. Evaluating team processes and outcomes can encourage accountability among individual members as well as within the team as a whole. In addition, evaluation enables the team to examine its practices to determine whether changes should be made.

The questions outlined in Table 9.2 serve as a beginning point to assist teams in asking the questions and making the evaluations that facilitate improved collaboration. These are just some of the factors that play a part in defining the culture of a team. Although no one best model of early childhood collaboration exists (Kagan & Rivera, 1991), it is helpful to recognize that many factors affect collaboration within a team context.

FUTURE DIRECTIONS

Collaboration is an essential value and practice in early child care and education, and it benefits children with and without disabilities, their families, and the professionals who serve them. PL 101-476 encourages family–professional and interdisciplinary collaboration to improve services for children from birth through 8 years of age, as did the federal laws that preceded it. Professional organizations advocate collaboration in the early child care and education field, and numerous demonstrations and articulations have been made of the recommended practices related to collaboration. Personnel preparation and staff development practices that promote collaborative roles also have been identified. Despite widespread support for collaboration as a concept, the application of the concept is in its infancy, and considerable growth and development are needed to maximize the potential of collaboration. Some directions for future development are discussed in the section that follows.

Supports for Collaboration

Teams can use a collaborative model without external resources when sufficient internal support exists. The adoption and maintenance of collaborative models are greatly enhanced, however, when teams experience administrative support, which frequently optimizes external resources. Administrators can encourage staff to examine carefully the culture of teams by assisting them in articulating a philosophy of collaboration, identifying behaviors and procedures that have or have not been consistent with that philosophy, and facilitating the resolution of interfering problems or conflicts. Administrators also can assist teams in arranging a consistent time to plan together and in creating schedules that are flexible enough to support a variety of service options (Rainforth et al., 1992); administrators can do this primarily by recognizing team needs and encouraging members to explore strategies to address those needs. Rather than scheduling one in-service session on collaboration, administrators can provide for ongoing staff development that teaches collaboration. Administrator participation in activities of this sort suggests support far beyond mere approval.

Finally, administrators demonstrate the depth of their commitment to teamwork by ensuring that organizational procedures (e.g., staff evaluations) reward, rather than penalize, team members for efforts to collaborate, which, initially, may take more time and effort than would solitary performance (Hirschhorn, 1991). Ways to support and encourage teams to collaborate abound. As administrators learn more about collaboration and assume stronger roles in adopting collaborative models, early childhood teams will flourish.

Professional Development for Collaboration

Ongoing staff development programs, including both formal in-service training sessions and technical assistance, are needed to prepare practicing professionals for the collaborative roles they are expected to fulfill. Education is needed to improve family–professional partnerships, interpersonal communication (e.g., listening, supporting, negotiation, conflict resolution), and team activities (e.g., team assessment, joint planning and evaluation, team teaching). Reeducation only will be effective, however, if higher education becomes proactive and prepares professionals for collaborative roles in preservice programs. Although some models exist for collaboration in higher education, far more demonstrations are needed. Areas to address include models for faculty collaboration within and among departments, schools, and colleges; models for collaboration among varied combinations of education and related services fields; and models for collaboration among universities with varied missions and demographics.

Because university structures typically do not reward or even support collaboration, it is imperative to identify motivations and mechanisms to initiate and maintain interdisciplinary relationships. As long as collaboration within universities remains based primarily on the interest and initiative of individual faculty members and emanates primarily from university affiliated programs (Rainforth, 1985), the need to explore mechanisms for more systemic changes in higher education will exist. Future empirical investigations might address these and other questions: What does effective collaboration look like in higher education? What are some barriers that impede collaboration within a higher education system, and what are some solutions to these barriers? It is essential that such questions be asked so that emerging collaborative models can be evaluated systematically to determine the effectiveness of faculty teamwork, courses in collaboration and teaming strategies, and fieldwork in model sites to prepare professionals for collaborative roles.

Processes for Collaboration

Although professional collaboration seems to occur more often in early childhood programs than in higher education, few systematic studies have addressed the factors that contribute to or detract from collaboration in early child care and education. As a result, little is known about the relative impact of specific collaboration skills, approaches to teaching collaboration strategies, or personalities of participants. Expanding this body of information will assist program administrators in making informed decisions about the use of limited resources.

Unfortunately, few demonstrations or empirical studies of successful family–professional partnerships are available. Theoretical literature on, for example, family systems theory and family-centered practices (Beckman, Robinson, Rosenberg, & Filer, 1994; Brown et al., 1993; Turnbull & Turnbull, 1990) is very useful, but far more information is needed about actual family satisfaction with professional practices. In particular, practitioners need guidance for working effectively with families of varied backgrounds, structures, resources, and priorities. Broadening the empirical base on collaboration in early child care and education will result in the creation of stronger support systems for professionals and for families and their children. Some questions for future investigations include the following:

What types of administrative support lead to effective collaboration?
What skills do professionals need to effectively support and collaborate with families in ways that meet individual family styles, priorities, and preferences?
How can professionals collaborate with families or other team members when the parties have conflicting values?

As this information emerges, teams will become more complete, and collaboration will yield far more of the promised benefits. In addition, perhaps families like Ryan's will feel supported by and confident in early childhood systems and the individuals who work within those systems.

REFERENCES

American Occupational Therapy Association. (1987). *Guidelines for occupational therapy services in school systems.* Rockville, MD: Author.

American Physical Therapy Association. (1990). *Physical therapy practice in educational environments: Policy and guidelines.* Alexandria, VA: Author.

American Speech-Language-Hearing Association. (1991). A model for collaborative service delivery for students with language learning disorders in the public schools. *Asha, 33*(Suppl. 5), 44–50.

Anderson, P.A., & Fenichel, E.S. (1989). *Serving culturally diverse families of infants and toddlers with disabilities.* Washington, DC: National Center for Clinical Infants Programs.

Association for the Care of Children's Health. (1989, Spring). *Family support bulletin.* Washington, DC: Author.

Bagnato, S.J., Neisworth, J.T., Paget, K.D., & Kovaleski, J. (1987). The developmental school psychologist: Professional profile of an emerging early childhood specialist. *Topics in Early Childhood Special Education, 7*(3), 75–89.

Bailey, D.B., Jr. (1987). Collaborative goal setting with families: Resolving differences in values and priorities for services. *Topics in Early Childhood Special Education, 7*(2), 59–71.

Bailey, D.B., Jr., Simeonsson, R.J., Yoder, D.E., & Huntington, G.S. (1990). Preparing professionals to serve infants and toddlers with handicaps and their families: An integrative analysis across eight disciplines. *Exceptional Children, 57*(1), 26–35.

Bailey, D.B., Jr., & Wolery, M. (1992). *Teaching infants and preschoolers with disabilities* (2nd ed.). New York: Macmillan.

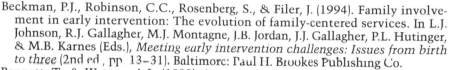

Beckman, P.J., Robinson, C.C., Rosenberg, S., & Filer, J. (1994). Family involvement in early intervention: The evolution of family-centered services. In L.J. Johnson, R.J. Gallagher, M.J. Montagne, J.B. Jordan, J.J. Gallagher, P.L. Hutinger, & M.B. Karnes (Eds.), *Meeting early intervention challenges: Issues from birth to three* (2nd ed., pp. 13–31). Baltimore: Paul H. Brookes Publishing Co.

Bennett, T., & Watson, A.L. (1993). A new perspective in training: Competence building. *Journal of Early Intervention, 17*(3), 309–321.

Biklen, D. (1992). *Schooling without labels: Parents, educators, and inclusive education.* Philadelphia: Temple University Press.

Bogdan, R.C., & Biklen, S.C. (1992). *Qualitative research for education.* Needham, MA: Allyn & Bacon.

Bredekamp, S. (1991). *Developmentally appropriate practice in early childhood programs serving children from birth to age 8.* Washington, DC: National Association for the Education of Young Children.

Bredekamp, S. (1992). The early childhood profession coming together. *Young Children, 47*(6), 36–39.

Bredekamp, S. (1993). The relationship between early childhood education and early childhood special education: Healthy marriage or family feud? *Topics in Early Childhood Special Education, 13*(3), 258–273.

Bredekamp, S., & Willer, B. (1992). Of ladders and lattices, cores and cones: Conceptualizing an early childhood professional development system. *Young Children, 47*(3), 47–50.

Bricker, D.D. (1976). Educational synthesizer. In M.A. Thomas (Ed.), *Hey, don't forget about me!* (pp. 84–97). Reston, VA: Council for Exceptional Children.

Bricker, D.D. (1978). A rationale for the integration of handicapped and nonhandicapped preschool children. In M.J. Guralnick (Ed.), *Early intervention and the integration of handicapped and nonhandicapped children* (pp. 3–26). Baltimore: University Park Press.

Bricker, D.D. (1989). *Early intervention for at-risk and handicapped infants, toddlers, and preschool children.* Palo Alto, CA: VORT Corp.

Bricker, W.A., & Campbell, P.H. (1980). Interdisciplinary assessment and programming for multihandicapped students. In W. Sailor, B. Wilcox, & L. Brown (Eds.), *Methods of instruction for severely handicapped students* (pp. 3–45). Baltimore: Paul H. Brookes Publishing Co.

Briggs, M.H. (1993). Team talk: Communication skills for early intervention teams. *Journal of Childhood Communication Disorders, 15*(1), 33–40.

Brown, W., Thurman, S.K., & Pearl, L.F. (Eds.). (1993). *Family-centered early intervention with infants and toddlers: Innovative cross-disciplinary approaches.* Baltimore: Paul H. Brookes Publishing Co.

Bruder, M.B. (1993). The provision of early intervention and early childhood special education within community early childhood programs: Characteristics of effective service delivery. *Topics in Early Childhood Special Education, 13*(1), 19–37.

Bruder, M.B., & Bologna, T.M. (1993). Collaboration and service coordination for effective early intervention. In W. Brown, S.K. Thurman, & L.F. Pearl (Eds.), *Family-centered early intervention with infants and toddlers: Innovative cross-disciplinary approaches* (pp. 103–127). Baltimore: Paul H. Brookes Publishing Co.

Bruder, M.B., Lippman, C., & Bologna, T. (1994). Personnel preparation in early intervention: Building capacity for program expansion within institutions of higher education. *Journal of Early Intervention, 18*(1), 103–110.

Burton, C.B., Haines, A.H., Hanline, M.F., McLean, M., & McCormick, K. (1992). Early childhood intervention and education: The urgency of professionals unification. *Topics in Early Childhood Special Education, 11*(4), 53–69.

Children's Defense Fund. (1992). *The status of America's children.* Washington, DC: Author.

Division for Early Childhood, National Association for the Education of Young Children, & Association of Teacher Educators. (1994). *Personnel standards for early education and early intervention: Guidelines for licensure in early childhood special education.* Washington, DC: Authors.

Division for Early Childhood Task Force on Recommended Practices. (1993). *DEC recommended practices: Indicators of quality in programs for infants and young children with special needs and their families.* Reston, VA: Council for Exceptional Children.

Dunst, C.J., Johanson, C., Trivette, C.M., & Hamby, D. (1991). Family-oriented early intervention policies and practices: Family-centered or not? *Exceptional Children, 58*(2), 115–126.

Education of the Handicapped Act Amendments of 1986, PL 99-457. (October 8, 1986). Title 20, U.S.C. 1400 et seq: *U.S. Statutes at Large, 100,* 1145–1177.

Effgen, S.K. (1988). Preparation of physical therapists and occupational therapists to work in early childhood special education settings. *Topics in Early Childhood Special Education, 7*(4), 10–19.

Effgen, S.K., & Klepper, S.E. (1994). Survey of physical therapy practice in educational settings. *Pediatric Physical Therapy, 6*(1), 15–21.

Elkind, D. (1987). *Miseducation: Preschoolers at risk.* New York: Alfred A. Knopf.

Erwin, E.J., & Soodak, L.S. (1995). "I never knew I could stand up to the system": Parents' perspectives on pursuing inclusive education. *Journal of The Association for Persons with Severe Handicaps, 20,* 136–146.

Feeg, V.D. (1987). Developmental disabilities services and the territorial imperative. *Pediatric Nursing, 13*(2), 78, 136.

File, N., & Kontos, S. (1992). Indirect service delivery through consultation: Review and implications for early intervention. *Journal of Early Intervention, 16*(3), 221–234.

Fine, M.J., & Gardner, A. (1994). Collaborative consultation with families of children with special needs: Why bother? *Journal of Educational and Psychological Consultation, 5*(4), 283–308.

Friend, M., & Cook, L. (1992). *Interactions: Collaboration skills for school professionals.* White Plains, NY: Longman.

Galinsky, E., Shubilla, L., Willer, S., Levine, J., & Daniel, J. (1994). State and community planning for early childhood systems. *Young Children, 49*(2), 54–57.

Galinsky, E., & Weissbound, B. (1992). Family-centered child care. In B. Spodek & O.N. Saracho (Eds.), *Issues in child care* (pp. 47–65). New York: Teachers College Press.

Garshelis, J.A., & McConnell, S.R. (1993). Comparison of family needs assessed by mothers, individual professionals, and interdisciplinary teams. *Journal of Early Intervention, 17*(1), 36–49.

Gelfer, J.I. (1991). Teacher–parent partnerships: Enhancing communication. *Childhood Education, 67*(3), 164–169.

Gilkerson, L., Gorski, P.A., & Panitz, P. (1990). Hospital-based intervention for preterm infants and their families. In S.J. Meisels & J.P. Shonkoff (Eds.), *Handbook of early childhood intervention* (pp. 445–468). New York: Cambridge University Press.

Graff, J.C., & Ault, M.M. (1993). Guidelines for working with students having special health care needs. *Journal of School Health, 63*(8), 335–338.

Hanline, M.F. (1990). Project profile: A consulting model for providing integration opportunities for preschool children with disabilities. *Journal of Early Intervention, 14*(4), 360–366.

Hansen, S., Holaday, B., & Miles, M.S. (1990). The role of pediatric nurses in a federal program for infants and children with handicaps. *Journal of Pediatric Nursing, 5*(4), 246–251.

Hanson, M.J., Hanline, M.F., & Peterson, S. (1987). Addressing state and local needs: A model for interdisciplinary training in early childhood special education. *Topics in Early Childhood Special Education, 7*(3), 36–47.

Hanson, M.J., & Lovett, D. (1992). Personnel preparation of early interventionists: A cross disciplinary study. *Journal of Early Intervention, 16*(2), 123–135.

Hanson, M.J., & Widerstrom, A.H. (1993). Consultation and collaboration: Essentials of integration efforts for young children. In C.A. Peck, S.L. Odom, & D.D.

Bricker (Eds.), *Integrating young children with disabilities into community programs: Ecological perspectives on research and implementation* (pp. 149–168). Baltimore: Paul H. Brookes Publishing Co.

Harbin, G.L., & McNulty, B.A. (1990). Policy implementation: Perspectives on service coordination and interagency cooperation. In S.J. Meisels & J.P. Shonkoff (Eds.), *Handbook of early childhood intervention* (pp. 700–722). New York: Cambridge University Press.

Hirschhorn, L. (1991). *Managing in the new team environment.* Reading, MA: Addison-Wesley.

Honig, A.S. (1975). *Parent involvement in early childhood education.* Washington, DC: National Association for the Education of Young Children.

Honig, A.S. (1990). Infant/toddler education issues: Practices, problems, and promises. In C. Seefeldt (Ed.), *Continuing issues in early childhood education* (pp. 61–106). Columbus, OH: Charles E. Merrill.

Hutchison, D.J. (1978). The transdisciplinary approach. In J.B. Curry & K.K. Peppe (Eds.), *Mental retardation: Nursing approaches to care* (pp. 65–74). St. Louis, MO: C.V. Mosby.

Idol, L., Nevin, A., & Paolucci-Whitcomb, P. (1994). *Collaborative consultation.* Austin, TX: PRO-ED.

Individuals with Disabilities Education Act (IDEA) of 1990, PL 101-476. (October 30, 1990). Title 20, U.S.C. 1400 et seq: *U.S. Statutes at Large, 104,* 1103–1151.

Individuals with Disabilities Education Act Amendments of 1991, PL 102-119. (October 7, 1991). Title 20, U.S.C. 1400 et seq: *U.S. Statutes at Large, 105,* 587–608.

Johnson, L.J., Kilgo, J., & Cook, M.J. (1992). The skills needed by early intervention administrators/supervisors. *Journal of Early Intervention, 16*(2), 136–145.

Judson, S. (1984). *A manual on non-violence and children.* Philadelphia: New Society Publishers.

Kagan, S.L. (1991). *United we stand: Collaboration for child care and early education services.* New York: Teachers College Press.

Kagan, S.L., & Rivera, A.M. (1991). Collaboration in early care and education: What can and should we expect? *Young Children, 47*(1), 51–56.

Katz, L.G. (1987). The nature of professions: Where is early childhood education? In L.G. Katz (Ed.), *Current topics in early childhood education* (Vol. VII, pp. 1–16). Norwood, NJ: Ablex.

Kontos, S. (1992). *Family day care: Out of the shadows and into the limelight.* Washington, DC: National Association for the Education of Young Children.

Koralek, D.G., Colker, L.J., & Dodge, D.T. (1993). *The what, why, and how of high quality early childhood education.* Washington, DC: National Association for the Education of Young Children.

Linder, T.W. (1993a). *Transdisciplinary play-based assessment: A functional approach to working with young children* (Rev. ed.). Baltimore: Paul H. Brookes Publishing Co.

Linder, T.W. (1993b). *Transdisciplinary play-based intervention: Guidelines for developing a meaningful curriculum for young children.* Baltimore: Paul H. Brookes Publishing Co.

Lipsky, D.K. (1989). The role of parents. In D.K. Lipsky & A. Gartner (Eds.), *Beyond separate education: Quality education for all* (pp. 159–179). Baltimore: Paul H. Brookes Publishing Co.

Lynch, E.W. (1992). From culture shock to cultural learning. In E.W. Lynch & M.J. Hanson (Eds.), *Developing cross-cultural competence: A guide for working with young children and their families* (pp. 19–34). Baltimore: Paul H. Brookes Publishing Co.

McCollum, J.A. (1987). Early interventionists in infant and early childhood programs: A comparison of preservice training needs. *Topics in Early Childhood Special Education, 7*(3), 24–35.

McLean, M., & Odom, S.L. (1993). Practices for young children with and without disabilities: A comparison of DEC and NAEYC identified practices. *Topics in Early Childhood Special Education, 13*(3), 274–292.

Miller, P. (1992). Segregated programs of teacher education in early childhood: Immoral and inefficient practice. *Topics in Early Childhood Special Education, 11*(4), 39–52.

Mills, P.E., Vadasy, P.F., & Fewell, R.R. (1987). Preparing early childhood special educators for rural settings: An urban university approach. *Topics in Early Childhood Special Education, 7*(3), 59–74.

Mitchell, A., Seligson, M., & Marx, F. (1989). *Early childhood programs and the public schools.* Dover, DE: Auburn House.

Morrison, G.S. (1991). *Early childhood education today* (5th ed.). New York: Macmillan.

National Association for the Education of Young Children. (1994). Position statement: A conceptual framework for early childhood professional development. *Young Children, 49*(3), 68–77.

Odom, S.L, & McEvoy, M.A. (1988). Integration of young children with handicaps and normally developing children. In S.L. Odom & M.B. Karnes (Eds.), *Early intervention for infants and children with handicaps: An empirical base* (pp. 241–268). Baltimore: Paul H. Brookes Publishing Co.

Odom, S.L., & McEvoy, M.A. (1990). Mainstreaming at the preschool level: Potential barriers and tasks for the field. *Topics in Early Childhood Special Education, 10*(2), 48–61.

Patterson, E.G., D'Wolf, N., Hutchison, D.J., Lowry, M., Schilling, M., & Siepp, J. (1976). *Staff development handbook: A resource for the transdisciplinary process.* Washington, DC: United Cerebral Palsy Associations.

Peck, C.A., Hayden, L., Wandschneider, M., Peterson, K., & Richarz, S.A. (1989). Development of integrated preschools: A qualitative inquiry into sources of concern by parents, teachers, and administrators. *Journal of Early Intervention, 13*, 353–364.

Perry, G. (1990). Alternate modes of teacher preparation. In C. Seefeldt (Ed.), *Continuing issues in early childhood education* (pp. 173–197). Columbus, OH: Charles E. Merrill.

Pizzo, P. (1993). Empowering parents with child care regulation. *Young Children, 48*(6), 9–12.

Powell, D.R. (1994). Parents, pluralism, and the NAEYC statement on developmentally appropriate practice. In B.L. Mallory & R.S. New (Eds.), *Diversity and developmentally appropriate practices* (pp. 166–182). New York: Teachers College Press.

Pugach, M., & Johnson, L. (1995). *Collaborative practitioners, collaborative schools.* Denver, CO: Love Publishing Co.

Putnam, M.L., & Habanek, D.V. (1993). A national survey of certification requirements for teachers of students with mild handicaps: States of confusion. *Teacher Education and Special Education, 16*(2), 155–160.

Rainforth, B. (1985). *Collaborative efforts in the preparation of physical therapists and teachers of students with severe handicaps.* Unpublished doctoral dissertation, University of Illinois at Urbana-Champaign.

Rainforth, B., & Salisbury, C. (1988). Functional home programs: A model for therapists. *Topics in Early Childhood Special Education, 7*(4), 33–45.

Rainforth, B., York, J., & Macdonald, C. (1992). *Collaborative teams for students with severe disabilities: Integrating therapy and educational services.* Baltimore: Paul H. Brookes Publishing Co.

Reardon, B.A. (1988). *Educating for global responsibility: Teacher designed curricula for peace education, K–12.* New York: Teachers College Press.

Safer, N.D., & Hamilton, J.L. (1993). Legislative context for early intervention services. In W. Brown, S.K. Thurman, & L.F. Pearl (Eds.), *Family-centered early intervention with infants and toddlers: Innovative cross-disciplinary approaches* (pp. 1–19). Baltimore: Paul H. Brookes Publishing Co.

Safford, P.L. (1989). *Integrated teaching in early childhood.* White Plains, NY: Longman.

Salisbury, C. (1992). Parents as team members: Inclusive teams, collaborative outcomes. In B. Rainforth, J. York, & C. Macdonald, *Collaborative teams for stu-*

dents with severe disabilities: Integrating therapy and educational services (pp. 43–66). Baltimore: Paul H. Brookes Publishing Co.

Shonkoff, J.P., & Meisels, S.J. (1990). Early childhood intervention: The evolution of a concept. In S.J. Meisels & J.P. Shonkoff (Eds.), Handbook of early childhood intervention (pp. 3-32). New York: Cambridge University Press.

Stayton, V.D., & Miller, P.S. (1993). Combining general and special early childhood education standards in personnel preparation programs: Experiences from two states. Topics in Early Childhood Special Education, 13(3), 372–387.

Sternat, J., Messina, R., Nietupski, J., Lyon, S., & Brown, L. (1977). Occupational and physical therapy services for severely handicapped students: Toward a naturalized public school service delivery model. In E. Sontag, J. Smith, & N. Certo (Eds.), Educational programming for the severely and profoundly handicapped (pp. 263–287). Reston, VA: Council for Exceptional Children.

Turnbull, A.P., & Turnbull, H.R., III. (1990). Families, professionals and exceptionality: A special partnership. Columbus, OH: Charles E. Merrill.

Weichert, S. (1989). Keeping the peace: Practicing cooperation and conflict resolution with preschoolers. Philadelphia: New Society Publishers.

West, J.F. (1990). Educational collaboration in the restructuring of the schools. Journal of Educational and Psychological Consultation, 1(1), 23–40.

Westby, C.E., & Ford, V. (1993). The role of team culture in assessment and intervention. Journal of Educational and Psychological Consultation, 4(4), 319–342.

Willis, S. (1993). Helping students resolve conflict. Association for Supervision and Curriculum Development Update, 35(1), 4–5, 8.

Wolery, M., Brookfield, J., Huffman, K., Schroeder, C., Martin, C.G., Venn, M.L., & Holcombe, A. (1993). Preparation in preschool mainstreaming as reported by general early education faculty. Journal of Early Intervention, 17(3), 298–308.

York, J., Rainforth, B., & Giangreco, M.F. (1990). Transdisciplinary teamwork and integrated therapy: Clarifying the misconceptions. Pediatric Physical Therapy, 2(2), 73–79.

VISIONS FOR THE NEW MILLENNIUM

FAMILIES, CHILD CARE, AND CARING

Nancy Balaban

As bleak as the present situation is for very young children and their families in the United States and throughout the world, the future does not seem to be much brighter (Lewin, 1995). Families everywhere contend with issues such as single parenthood, rising divorce rates, shortages of reliable child care, and the feminization of poverty.

Child care, the mainstay of working parents and a critical component of families' transitions from welfare to work, confronts a whole range of constraints. Foremost among these is the lack of sufficient funds for both teacher/caregiver salaries (further contributing to the feminization of poverty) and the creation of enough child care programs with enough vacancies for children to meet the need for reliable, high-quality child care. Several authorities bear this out: Children's advocates have urged increases in funding for child care subsidies for mothers with infants and toddlers who receive welfare (Blank, 1994). These mothers find the costs of child care to be prohibitive because the costs themselves are higher as a result of the smaller child-to-adult ratios mandated for children younger than 3 years of age and because the costs absorb a large portion of their limited incomes. It is questionable whether the proposed shift to block grants for states will in any way remedy this inadequate situation ("On Capitol Hill," 1995). An example makes the point: In Illinois in 1994, there were 118,000 children younger than 3 years of age receiving Aid to Families with Dependent Children, but there were only 25,000 child care slots for infants and toddlers. Bernice Weissbourd, writing on welfare reform, states that "welfare reform proposals...[are] meaningless if appropriate care does not exist" (1994, p. 28).

A serious issue for child care as a profession is the widespread lack of respect for the work itself and for those who do it. Although there are intensive efforts to create a climate of support, recognition, professionalism, and worthy wages, it is an uphill climb.

What would happen if there were sufficient funds for child care? If there were widespread, high-quality staff development and support for teachers and caregivers of our youngest children? If there were nurturing, affectionate, affordable child care providers and centers? Such a scenario would go a long way toward creating a supportive environment for young families in the new millennium, when 7 of 10 preschool-age children, including infants and toddlers, will have mothers who will work outside of the home (Carnegie Task Force on Meeting the Needs of Young Children, 1994).

If such professional support were made available for employees of child care centers, especially those that serve infants and toddlers, the majority of which have been shown to provide poor care (Helbrun et al., 1995), we could improve the quality of child care by helping providers

- Understand the critical importance and fundamental nature of the attachment relationships between young children and their families and the implications these relationships have for child care providers
- Study the nature of early development and individual differences in temperament; physical, intellectual, and emotional growth; and social adaptability
- Seek out, celebrate, and validate the ways in which all children bring their cultures into the group care setting

- Increase staff-to-child ratios and keep group sizes small
- Provide beautiful physical environments (no basements)

A solid base of financial support and professional development would enable the child care community to do what it wants to do—care. This desire to care springs from "an ethic of care," which, Nel Noddings writes, "starts with a study of relation. It is fundamentally concerned with how human beings meet and treat one another" (1993, p. 45).

In such an environment, we would see caregivers "strive continuously toward greater competence....Often critics of caring make the mistake of supposing that caring is inherently soft and sweet. In reality, caring requires heightened moral sensitivity" (Noddings, 1993, p. 49).

Although well-funded, adequate, and caring child care will not resolve all of the issues that families with young children will face in the new millennium, it will ameliorate some basic concerns. Could this dream become a reality?

REFERENCES

Blank, H. (1994, July/August). Washington watch. *Child Care Action News, 12*(4), 3.

Carnegie Task Force on Meeting the Needs of Young Children. (1994). *Starting points: Meeting the needs of our youngest children.* New York: Carnegie Corporation.

Helbrun, S., Culkin, M.L., Howes, C., Bryant, D., Clifford, R., Cryer, D., Peisner-Feinberg, D., & Kagan, S.L. (1995). *Cost, quality and child outcomes in child care centers.* [Available from Economics Department, Campus Box 159, P.O. Box 173364, University of Colorado at Denver, Denver, CO 80217-3364]

Lewin, T. (1995, May 30). Family decay global, study says: Troubled households are not just a U.S. phenomenon. *New York Times,* p. 28.

Noddings, N. (1993). Caring: A feminist perspective. In K.A. Stryker & P.L. Ternasky (Eds.), *Ethics for professionals in education: Perspective for preparation and practice* (pp. 43–53). New York: Teachers College Press.

On Capitol Hill move to block grant threatens children. (1995). *Children's Defense Fund Reports, 16*(3), 1–4.

Weissbourd, B. (1994). Welfare reform, child care, and families with infants and toddlers. *ZERO TO THREE, 14*(5), 28–29.

ALL CHILDREN MUST KNOW AND LEARN FROM ONE ANOTHER

Marilyn R. Wessels

"It's like a peanut butter and jelly sandwich. You can't separate the bread from the peanut butter any more than you can separate special ed kids from regular kids. They belong together." This statement was made by a general education student about her fellow classmates who happened to have disabilities.

More and more of our general education students, as they come to know their fellow students with disabilities through the practice of inclusion, are voicing similar statements. They are, when given the chance, learning the value of receiving their education with students of very diverse backgrounds, ethnicities, cultures, and abilities—an opportunity that should not be denied to any student if we are truly serious about providing the best possible education for all children.

For several years, I have acted in various capacities in my attempt to change the early childhood system that controlled the way we delivered services. The system of which I speak goes beyond preschool programs, such as prekindergarten, Head Start, private nursery school, and child care programs, and beyond public and private special education schools. It also includes social services agencies and county, state, and federal government, as well as the legislative and executive branches. All of these entities help decide how and where services are provided to young children. All too often, however, positive changes based on research and model programs fail to materialize because those involved in the system have their own agendas—agendas that protect and preserve the status quo.

In the late 1980s, when the New York State legislature passed legislation to mandate services for preschoolers with disabilities, I was the director of the New York State Senate Select Committee on the Disabled. Later, I headed a statewide coalition that was formed in an attempt to influence early care legislation for infants and toddlers. Fortunately, because of that coalition, some statewide changes were made; now, these changes are beginning to have an impact on where young children with disabilities receive services. For example, parents now have a choice about receiving services for their children in early childhood, community-based natural settings as opposed to segregated early intervention centers. However, as the mother of six children—the youngest of whom was born with Down syndrome in the 1960s—and as an educational advocate for students with disabilities, I continue to be amazed, frustrated, and distressed at many in the early childhood system who seem to be slow or unwilling to change the way they address the needs of children in light of what we know about how young children learn.

In 1967, when our son was born, no services were available in Schenectady County for young children with disabilities. It was unthinkable even to consider placing a child with a disability into a typical preschool setting. Looking back, I am glad no special programs existed, because I probably would have been convinced to place my son into such a program by some concerned and well-intentioned professional. Fortunately, despite the very negative and depressing information imparted to my husband and me, we still were able to look to the future, using the same common sense to raise our youngest son that we used to raise our other children. In so doing, we ensured that our young son was involved within his own community just like our other children were.

When Congress passed PL 94-142, the Education for All Handicapped Children Act of 1975 (subsequently reauthorized as PL 101-476, the Individuals with Disabilities Education Act [IDEA] of 1990), the spirit and intent of the legislation reflected the belief that, if children with disabilities were to live independent and productive lives in their communities, children with and without disabilities must know and learn from one another in the schools.

Despite the clear intention of Congress, we began to see early on the rapid growth of two distinct forms of education (special education and general education), reinforcing the message that children with disabilities, especially those with severe disabilities, belonged with their own kind. Now, many of us struggle to dismantle the empire that has evolved since the 1970s. We face an army of groups and individuals more concerned with maintaining the empire than with what is good for all children.

As the result of the passage of PL 99-457, the Education of the Handicapped Act Amendments of 1986 (Part H), the federal law that mandated services for infants and toddlers with disabilities and their families, parent choice has become the phrase of the 1990s. PL 99-457 was reauthorized in 1991 with the passage of PL 102-119, the Individuals with Disabilities Education Act Amendments. As a parent, I support parent choice entirely. It is, however, incumbent on we who work with parents to ensure that every scrap of information be made available and presented in an unbiased manner so that parents have the knowledge, as well as the freedom, to make well-informed choices.

Although it seems as though numerous unanswered questions exist regarding the provision of services to young children with diverse needs and backgrounds, all children do indeed belong together. Together, they will learn from and share with one another during their formative years, benefiting immensely from their diverse experiences. We are now faced with a moral and ethical choice: Either we ensure that children are provided with early experiences that will enable them to appreciate and honor diversity, or we will have contributed to the perpetuation of the terrible prejudicial and discriminatory practices that continue to be so destructive in the United States and around the world.

REFERENCES

Education for All Handicapped Children Act of 1975, PL 94-142. (August 23, 1977). Title 20, U.S.C. 1401 et seq: *U.S. Statutes at Large, 89,* 773–796.

Education of the Handicapped Act Amendments of 1986, PL 99-457. (October 8, 1986). Title 20, U.S.C. 1400 et seq: *U.S. Statutes at Large, 100,* 1145–1177.

Individuals with Disabilities Education Act (IDEA) of 1990, PL 101-476. (October 30, 1990). Title 20, U.S.C. 1400 et seq: *U.S. Statutes at Large, 104,* 1103–1151.

Individuals with Disabilities Education Act Amendments of 1991, PL 102-119. (October 7, 1991). Title 20, U.S.C. 1400 et seq: *U.S. Statutes at Large, 105,* 587–608.

III

A MODEL FOR THE 21st CENTURY

THE 21ST CENTURY FOR YOUNG CHILDREN WITH DISABILITIES AND THEIR FAMILIES

James J. Gallagher

Predicting the future is an interesting but risky business. Too many "wild cards," unexpected events or discoveries, can and do change the world as we know it (e.g., jet aircraft, DNA, the Internet). Unpredictable changes such as those often make invalid the easy projections of present trends into the future. It still is useful, however, to try to identify trends and to see how far into the near future those trends can be projected, because important planning decisions about the future allocation of resources depend, in part, on such projections.

Taking into consideration the policies in existence in 1996, the development of future policies affecting children with disabilities will depend on three major components that traditionally create specific policies. These components are 1) the knowledge base about the issue, 2) our concept of "best" practices, and 3) the values of key decision makers. Each new or amended policy can be a unique combination of these three elements.

FUTURE POLICIES

Future policies for young children with disabilities most likely will involve the following issues: inclusion, comprehensive services, personnel preparation, parent empowerment, and technology.

Inclusion of Children with Disabilities

Since the 1960s, responsibility has been accepted at federal, state, and local levels to provide a free and appropriate education for children with disabilities. One specific condition of this policy is that the child with disabilities should be educationally separated from other children only when necessary to provide special treatment or educational experiences. This policy is known as the *least restrictive environment* requirement.

This least restrictive environment provision was included in policies for infants, toddlers, and preschoolers with disabilities in PL 101-476, the Individuals with Disabilities Education Act (IDEA) of 1990. As a result, the inclusion of young children with disabilities with their peers without disabilities became a major goal. This inclusion was more difficult to achieve when there were few services for typically developing preschool children (e.g., child care) into which children with disabilities could be integrated. There is little reason to doubt that such a policy toward inclusion will continue to be supported in the future, although a need always will exist for special programs that provide comprehensive services as one option for children with rare and/or multiple disabilities. Many professionals serving children with sensory disabilities (vision and hearing impairments) and those serving children with severe behavior disturbances are among those who still reject *full* inclusion in the general education classroom or child care center.

Comprehensive Services

Another important trend is the emergence of multidisciplinary services and teams, which provide a variety of services to young children with special needs and their families. The diversity of issues affecting young children with disabilities calls for the attention of health, social services, and educational personnel, as well as other specialists, as needed in individual situations.

Exactly how this professional collaboration will be organized at the local level and monitored at the state level is not yet clear, but some type of community resource center that incorporates service personnel from many disciplines seems to be a likely organizational or structural addition to the service delivery system in the near future. From this center, services can flow out into the community; in addition, families can come to the center.

Personnel Preparation

It is likely that a major and continuing effort will be made to ensure that staff development is a major part of all programs that serve children with disabilities. Who will fill the large number of positions needed to staff the community resource centers of the future? In the 1990s, critical personnel shortages exist in fields such as occupational therapy, physical therapy, and speech-language pathology. Furthermore, the special education early interventionist specialty is relatively new in the 1990s, and few organized personnel preparation programs exist to train such specialists.

In the future, we may see the creation of a gradually changing pattern of service delivery to young children with disabilities, as it becomes increasingly apparent that training programs cannot prepare sufficient numbers of professionals from institutions of higher education to satisfy the growing need. Two future solutions to the chronic personnel shortages experienced in the 1990s may be the increased reliance on assistants and the removal of many professionals from direct service so that they can coordinate services and supervise assistants.

Parent Empowerment

Another trend that is likely to continue in the future is the increased participation of parents and families in the education and care of their children with disabilities. The trend toward family-focused programs has been supported strongly by professional leadership but not always implemented well at the local level. The individualized family service plan (IFSP) requirement and the presence of a service coordinator (formerly a case manager) to communicate directly and regularly with the family are two structural changes in service delivery that stress family participation, but we still have a long way to go before reaching this particular goal in actual practice.

The diversity of families involved in such programs, ranging from the two-parent, professional family to the single teenage mother, and the diverse needs of these families require the concept of family empowerment to be shaped to the particular characteristics and needs of individual families. There has been, however, a general acceptance of the role of the professional as a helper, who encourages the family to grow into its responsibilities, rather than pushing aside the family and taking charge as a director of treatment of the child. Such parental support roles have become increasingly accepted, and this acceptance is not likely to diminish in the near future. Instead, family empowerment is likely to be solidified as one preferred outcome of service delivery.

Technology

Programs that serve children with disabilities have pioneered various uses of technology. Meeting the special needs of children with disabilities often has required innovative approaches and technologically enhanced methods of communication, mobility, and learning. In the 1990s, technology also is used to help professionals in different disciplines communicate more effectively with one another, and devices such as distance learning (e.g., interactive television) are increasingly used in staff development. Such advances hold promise for the continued enhancement of the quality of service delivery.

Advanced technologies to aid in the mobility of, and our communication with, young children with disabilities are being developed, and professionals are learning to use available technologies to their advantage. It is impossible to even imagine the vast strides the service delivery system may make in the 21st century, given the continued rapid growth and increased potential of these new technologies.

FUTURE DIRECTIONS

The special educator of the future who works with young children with disabilities certainly will not lack problems to solve. Four recognizable problems in programs for young children with disabilities are financing, cultural differences, mainstream professionals, and public support; it is reasonable to expect that these problems will continue into the 21st century.

Financing

The resources for financing services for young children with disabilities remain unclear. The federal mandate for such services contains only enough funds for planning and development; the states are responsible for all other expenses. Medicaid has been proposed as one possible funding source; this solution would deem all children with disabilities eligible for support without requiring a means test. Medicaid, however, has been under attack, and likely reductions in funds, remove, for the moment, the possibility of full support from that quarter.

Given the extraordinary expenses that can be associated with the appropriate care and education of young children with disabilities (e.g., intensive care units, ventilators), most families will require some degree of public support from some source: local, state, or federal. It is likely that some version of the Medicaid approach will be offered in the 21st century, but its exact shape will have to emerge from continuing discussions about the provisions of health care for all U.S. citizens and be shaped by debates over balanced budgets.

Cultural Diversity

Although U.S. society is becoming increasingly multicultural, the programs that service young children with disabilities are staffed predominantly by Caucasian, middle-class, native-born women. The disparity between clients and service personnel can result in clashing cultural values and can weaken the important child–provider bond. In the future, attempts to recruit new personnel from various cultural and socioeconomic backgrounds should continue and intensify.

Mainstream Professionals

One of the lessons learned about the relationship of special education to general education in the public schools since the 1960s has been that there is a natural tension between the two groups that must be overcome. Special educators pay attention to the needs of the exceptional child sometimes to the exclusion of the needs of the general group. General educators often have problems with the exceptional child fitting into their routines and lessons and may also resent the presence of the specialist, believing it indicates some deficiency on their part.

We can expect a similar professional tension among professionals who work with young children. The child care worker may well be nervous about including a child with mental retardation or cerebral palsy in his or her group, and the specific treatments recommended by the special educator or physical therapist may be a mystery to and a bother for the mainstream professional. We must stress the importance of broader training and the uses of the multidisciplinary team, which harnesses the talents of all of the disciplines in programs for special children.

Public Support

Although it is relatively easy to devise a wish list of services needed in the near future, all of the changes detailed in this essay depend on a more complete acceptance of the responsibility of communities and of

U.S. society as a whole for the full development and education of all children in the future than is evident in the mid-1990s. The self-indulgence and cynicism that seem to pervade U.S. society in the 1990s must be replaced with compassion and commitment, because there is no escaping the fact that additional public resources will be needed to improve existing service delivery systems. Although the changes suggested by the author likely would reduce long-term future expenditures for children with special needs, such long-run savings through investment in expenditures in the child's early years must be stressed by responsible political leadership if the U.S. public is expected to support these expansions of services and their initial costs.

It is unlikely that the United States will, as a society, abandon its commitment to young children with disabilities in the 21st century. It is almost certain, however, that increased demands for proof of productivity will be required of programs for children with disabilities as well as other programs. In short, it is likely that the 21st century will bring a variety of innovative new methods and programs that will be reluctantly supported by a still caring, but skeptical, public.

REFERENCE

Individuals with Disabilities Education Act (IDEA) of 1990, PL 101-476. (October 30, 1990). Title 20, U.S.C. 1400 et seq: *U.S. Statutes at Large, 104,* 1103–1151.

SUGGESTED READINGS

Bryant, D., & Graham, M. (Eds.). (1993). *Implementing early intervention.* New York: Guilford Press.

Gallagher, J.J. (1992). The role of values and facts in policy development for infants and toddlers with disabilities and their families. *Journal of Early Intervention, 16*(1), 1–10.

Guralnick, M. (1991). The next decade of research on the effectiveness of early intervention. *Exceptional Children, 57*(4), 174–183.

Howe, K., & Miramontes, O. (1991). A framework for ethical deliberation in special education. *Journal of Special Education, 25*(1), 7–25.

Kauffman, J. (1993). How we might achieve radical reform of special education. *Exceptional Children, 60*(1), 6–16.

Skrtic, T. (1991). *Behind special education.* Denver, CO: Love Publishing Co.

A Quality Early Childhood Service Delivery System for the 21st Century

Ellen Galinsky, Dana Friedman, and Joan Lombardi

As the 20th century comes to a close, the early childhood service delivery system is barely a system at all. Despite the importance of such services to children and families, in 1996, we are faced with a largely uncoordinated array of programs and providers struggling to deliver services without the supports needed to ensure quality[1] and efficiency.

Across the United States, however, early childhood service providers, policy makers, business leaders, parents, and other concerned citizens are working at the community and state levels to make an improved system a reality. Efforts have been stimulated by various sources, including the following: a focus on the readiness goal, the first goal of PL 103-227, Goals 2000: Educate America Act of 1994, which specifies that, by the year 2000, all children should enter school ready to learn; research that identifies both the factors that affect quality and the repercussions for children who do not receive quality care; planning efforts needed for the Child Care Development Block Grant; and, finally, interest in linking child care services to educational reform efforts.

The authors attempt to set forth a vision for a quality early childhood service delivery system. This model is predicated on the notion that no single sector—business, government, or community—can make the changes necessary to foster quality. Successful change requires partnerships among all stakeholders and should address the following set of guiding principles:

- The early childhood service delivery system should include diverse programs that address various needs of families and children.
- Families should have affordable choices among quality options.
- The primary clients of the system are the children and their families.
- Support should be available to help programs achieve high quality standards.
- Consistency across the many forms of programs should exist in terms of quality standards and caregiver and teacher wages, training, and respect.
- New planning and development efforts should build on and strengthen existing services.
- All sectors of the community should take some responsibility for the adequacy of early childhood services.
- The exact structure of the community system should be determined locally.

KEY FEATURES IN A QUALITY EARLY CHILDHOOD SERVICE DELIVERY SYSTEM

At the community level, the three components of a community's early childhood service delivery system are as follows:

---

[1] Throughout the essay, "quality" is used adjectivally to connote a degree of excellence with regard to early childhood services.

- A network of child development programs
- Neighborhood child and family resource centers
- A communitywide leadership group

The following sections describe in greater detail the three key features at the community level.

A Network of Child Development Programs

The system we envision does not require the development of an entire set of new programs; rather, those that already exist must be woven together, strengthened, and expanded. Similar to the call for reinventing government, the authors call for the reinvention of early childhood services to create, from the fragmented array of programs that exist today, a more complete network that has a greater emphasis on improving quality.

Families Would Have Real Choices Among Quality Half-Day and Full-Day Child Development Programs in Homes, Centers, Head Start Programs, and Schools

To enable families to take advantage of their options would require a balance between institutional support that ensures an adequate supply of care and financial support that helps families pay for child care and other early childhood services. Services would be free to the lowest-income groups, and increases in cost would be gradual and based on family income. Public and private scholarships could help families pay the full cost of care.

Programs Would Meet Quality Performance Standards and Would Be Monitored to Ensure Compliance

Many businesses in the United States are run with the knowledge that, to become world-class organizations, all employees must emphasize quality; early childhood programs must be run with the same goal in mind.

Programs Would Provide Developmentally Appropriate Early Education Services

To meet the readiness goal of PL 103-227, programs and providers must help develop fundamental competencies in children, such as problem solving, continuous learning, critical thinking, and teamwork. Such abilities are critical to the future productivity and the well-being of the United States.

Programs Would Be Family Centered

Partnerships that strengthen the parent–child relationship would be built among families and providers. Programs also would involve parents as active participants and decision makers. Child care programs would include or be linked to family support services and parent education programs.

Programs Would Be Linked to One Another

Programs would cease to exist in isolation (e.g., a school would communicate with the Head Start program next door). Family child care homes could exist as satellites of neighborhood family and child resource centers or independently. Staff members from various programs would be encouraged to meet to share resources, in particular, training.

Programs Would Be Linked to Other Services

Programs would be made comprehensive, either by providing services directly on site or by creating links with community services. Parents who need help with housing, legal, or health services would be able to use the child development program as a point of entry to these services.

Programs Would Be Linked to the Schools

Whether they are housed in schools or operated independently, all child development programs would be in contact with neighborhood schools to ensure a smooth transition for children moving from preschool to school. Continuity of services is encouraged when schools are developmentally appropriate, comprehensive, and responsive to families.

Neighborhood Child and Family Resource Centers

The hub of the child development network would be neighborhood resource centers that provide support to families and providers. These neighborhood child and family resource centers may grow from existing programs, such as Head Start centers, school child care programs, family support programs, health facilities, libraries, resource and referral agencies, and community action agencies. In addition, communities would determine the most appropriate sites for such service centers as well as which services they would provide directly and which would be linked to the resource centers but offered elsewhere.

Resource Centers Would Put Families First and Would Be Based on Quality Principles

Services often are geared to the convenience of providers, not families. In the 21st century, services would be committed to quality and to meeting family needs, such as extended hours, one-stop shopping, and others.

Resource Centers Would Provide Parenting Support for Families

Parent education and ongoing support groups would be made available to families. Services would begin for all family members when women learn that they are pregnant and would continue to be available until children reach adulthood. Long-term programs that avoid breaks in services would provide a valuable source of support for parents and children.

Resource Centers Would Provide Families One-Stop Access
for Learning About the Early Childhood Development Programs

Parents seeking child care and early education for their children would be referred to appropriate child development programs in their communities and given information about selecting quality arrangements and monitoring their choices over time.

Resource Centers Would Provide Information
About and/or Assistance with Applying for Financial Aid

Funding streams would be merged (to create seamless funding) into a scholarship system to help families pay for child development programs. Resource centers would help families determine if they are eligible and/or provide information about how and where to apply for assistance.

Resource Centers Would Provide Information About Other Needed Services

Resource centers would serve as central locations at which families could learn about a range of community resources, such as health care, legal assistance, and family counseling; determine their eligibility; and submit applications. These services could be located in the resource centers, or they could be located off site and information about them could be available through an electronic network.

Resource Centers Would Be Tied into
Professional Development Systems for Early Childhood Professionals

Whether early childhood training is provided by colleges and universities, resource and referral agencies, other community-based organizations, or the resource center itself, such training would occur across program auspices, meet uniform quality standards, be affordable and convenient, be linked to credentialing systems, and be tied to increased compensation. Therefore, early childhood professionals could receive college credit for training and increases in pay for increases in education. Relatives and neighbors providing care who do not see themselves as, nor wish to become, professionals would have access to parenting education and support to help them do a better job.

Resource Centers Would Offer Support to Early Childhood Development Programs

Support to early childhood development programs could come in several forms. Resource centers could provide assistance in creating and following a budget, purchasing equipment and/or food in bulk for several programs, and maintaining networks of family child care providers and child care program directors.

Resource Centers Would Link the Business Community and the Child Development Network

Specialists working out of the resource center would be available to provide information and assistance to local companies in developing family-friendly business programs, such as flexible work hours, and/or in promoting local business involvement in the community, such as funds to increase the supply of quality dependent care.

A Communitywide Leadership Group

At the heart of the improved service delivery system rest local autonomy and community decision making. Community leaders must possess the flexibility and the authority to develop systems of services that fit their communities' needs. Each community would form a leadership group, composed of specific community leaders from early childhood programs; schools; family support and education services; social services; parent groups; and health, business, labor, religious, government, and philanthropic organizations. This leadership group would include an office staff and would be linked closely to practitioners in the field.

Leadership Groups Would Help Assess the Adequacy of Community Systems and Monitor Their Progress

Leadership groups would identify the needs of their communities and assist programs in addressing those needs that are not being met. Whether by sharing informally expertise gained over the years or by assessing community needs or conducting quality audits formally, leadership groups could examine the following aspects of service delivery systems:

- The supply–demand gap
- Professional development efforts
- Standards and their enforcement
- Consumer outreach, family involvement, and public awareness efforts
- Roles of business and government
- Coordination among early childhood agencies, other social services, and schools

Leadership Groups Would Identify Available Funding

Leadership groups would identify those sources for which programs and families may be eligible and could research the degrees to which such funding sources overlap and focus on remediation or prevention.

Leadership Groups Would Set Goals and Benchmarks

Leadership groups would use strategies developed by the business sector in its search for quality to set goals and benchmarks. These groups would determine their missions by identifying the systems they believe should evolve and by specifying changes that would be needed to create such systems.

Leadership Groups Would Help Effect Change by Setting Standards and Developing a System of Accountability

By raising funds; offering technical assistance; and providing ongoing monitoring, evaluation, and benchmarking progress, leadership groups would help to bring about the changes desired in community service delivery systems.

FUTURE DIRECTIONS

As violence, poverty, homelessness, and other problems have worsened or become increasingly more intractable, the early childhood services community has mobilized, reaching out to other decision makers in their states or communities, collecting baseline data, developing plans for systemic change, putting those plans into action, and collecting data to benchmark progress. A continuous problem-solving process has been put in place. This is the first step in achieving quality service delivery systems in communities throughout the United States. Although these systems will emerge differently depending on the needs of specific communities, the vision outlined above is becoming a reality.

REFERENCE

Goals 2000: Educate America Act of 1994, PL 103-227. (March 31, 1994). Title 20, U.S.C. 5801, *U.S. Statutes at Large, 108,* 125–280.

Index

Page references followed by *t*, *f*, and *n* indicate tables, figures, and notes, respectively.